Walking Away from the Third Reich

A Teenager in Hitler's Army

Claus Sellier

Hellgate Press
Central Point, OR

Walking Away from the Third Reich: *A Teenager in Hitler's Army*

Hellgate Press
a division of PSI Research
P.O. Box 3727
Central Point, OR 97502-0032

(541) 855-5566
info@psi-research.com *e-mail*

Managing editor and book designer: Constance C. Dickinson
Editors: Kathy Marshbank, Constance C. Dickinson, and Jan O. Olsson
Compositor: Jan O. Olsson
Map designers: Steven Burns and Constance C. Dickinson
Cover designer: Lynn Dragonette

Sellier, Claus W., 1925–
    Walking away from the Third Reich : a teenager in Hitler's army / Claus W. Sellier.
       p. cm. — (Hellgate memories World War II)
    ISBN 1-55571-513-3 (paper)
    1. Sellier, Claus W., 1925– 2. Soldiers—Germany—Biography. 3. World War,
1939–1945—Personal narratives, German. I. Title. II. Hellgate memories series.

D811 .S396 1999
940.54'1343—dc21
                                   99-052622

To my wife Dolores, my children and grandchildren,
and Mildred Klem

Contents

Foreword

In 1995 my daughter, Susan Lunas, sent me an article from the *Christian Science Monitor* she knew I would be interested in reading. The story was about two German soldiers, Claus and Fritz, who left their headquarters in the Bavarian Alps during those last few confusing days in Germany before the armistice. Their story brought back my own memories of the area they traveled through. It was in the general area where my division was located at the time. I also felt sure they were captured by my comrades and put with other German POWs. The cities they traveled through were so close to where we traveled and were posted just before and after Germany surrendered that I wanted to locate the article's author, Claus W. Sellier, and find out if my suppositions were correct.

I have always been interested in the perspective of World War II from the German people's point of view, because both my maternal and paternal grandparents were immigrants from Germany, and I had a cousin who served in Hitler's Youth Corps. But until recently, I was too ashamed to ask.

In 1997 my wife and I tried to locate Mr. Sellier on the German telephone directory Internet site, but with no success. When we looked in the U.S. directory, there was one Claus Sellier. I called and asked him if he was the same person who wrote the *Science Christian Monitor* article about the German soldiers who were captured and then released at the end of World War II. He said he was, and he was curious how I found him, so I told him the story.

We talked about various things including my division, the 20th Armored Division, which was spread throughout the area that he and Fritz walked through on their way home. I told him of some of my experiences, also.

After we landed at Le Havre, France, on February 18, 1945, the 412th AFA Battalion fought its way through Rouen, Amiens, Cambrai, and Anzin, France; Mons, Charleroi, Tirlemont, St. Truiden, and Tongeren, Belgium; then Maastricht, in the Netherlands; on into Aachen and Düsseldorf (the tail end of the Battle of the Bulge), and Cologne and Bonn, Germany.

With the southwest corner of the Ruhr pocket only about six miles behind us, we crossed the Rhine River at Bad Godesberg just south of Bonn over the General Hodges, a two-way pontoon bridge—the Germans were still trying to blow it up with floating demolitions. From there we went on to Hadamar (an extermination camp), Friedberg, Hanau, and Bad Orb, the site of a prison camp where thousands of soldiers, including Americans, had just been released. Here we found an abandoned trainload of Champagne and filled every container we could find with the bubbly. Next were Lohr am Main, Karlstadt, Werneck, Würzburg, Kitzingen, and Marktbreit, where we joined Patton's Third Army.

When the 20th Armored Division was under the Fifth Army we could do things like stay in houses or barns but that changed when we were put under General Patton's Third Army. Under his command we had many restrictions, which included having to sleep on the ground or in a foxhole.

We went through Mannheim and Donauwörth, then crossed the Danube on a pontoon bridge, and moved on to Haunsweis, Gunding, and Dachau, where we saw the horror of the crematory, the endless lines of gas chambers, and the dead and near dead prisoners left piled in box cars. We experienced our worst battle at Munich, where the headquarters and training center for SS troopers was located. We had the most fear and disdain for the SS, because they were Hitler's most fanatical—trained and ingrained in Nazi Party doctrine.

After Munich we continued on to Wasserburg, where we picked up the first U.S. POWs, and then to Rabenden (near Seeon) and along the north and east sides of Lake Chiemsee on our way to Salzburg, Austria.

In spite of the army's no fraternization policy—announced on a huge sign as we entered the country—we talked with the German people, and they were friendly. We would ask them to wash our clothes and would give them our GI soap. I don't know if they used the soap or not, but the clothes came back immaculately clean and always folded up the same way my Mom did. In return we would give them food, which seemed to be appreciated.

After the surrender on May 8, 1945, the 412th AFA Battalion returned to the area around Palling—east of Seeon and north of Traunstein—and my group of about twenty were billeted on the grounds of a Catholic Church across the street from a brewery with a generous brewmaster. Many of the neighborhood children came around. We gave them oranges and prune bars—some had never seen an orange. They would talk and play for hours. Some of the girls spoke English and translated for us. It gave us a good feeling to have them come around; we enjoyed their visits and were always happy to see them.

As a teenager in a war zone, you think about your training, your officers, and your comrades—you put your trust in them. You trust that each one will help each other regardless of the difficulty of the experience. At night while on guard duty you knew you were to protect your comrades and equipment above all else. Much of the time my thoughts were, "When is this thing ever going to end?"

My curiosity about what it was like to be a soldier—and in many ways, a civilian—on the other side has been appeased by Claus' fascinating story about his experiences as a German youth and soldier. I never realized how much he and many of the German soldiers had to get through. Also, his book vividly brought back many of my own memories of that time and the area around Palling, Traunstein, and Seeon, and the breathtaking landscape of Lake Chiemsee.

Claus' timeless and exciting story will provide enjoyment and enrichment for anyone, whether they were involved in this part of the war or not.

Fred C. Stueve, T-5
412th Armored Field Artillery Battalion
20th Armored Division

Acknowledgments

It was difficult to find a publisher who would consider a book relating to happenings in World War II as they were experienced from the German side. I thank Emmett Ramey, publisher, for his foresight to develop *Walking Away from the Third Reich* and his terrific staff, especially C. C. Dickinson, Jan Olsson, and Kathy Marshbank, for bringing my story to life.

A special thanks to Fred C. Stueve, an American soldier from Wamego, Kansas, who was part of the 20th Armored Division that took me prisoner in 1945. We were both twenty years old. All these years later, we have become friends, and the 20th Armored Division has invited me to their year 2000 reunion.

I wrote this book for my four children who did not know enough about World War II. I thank my daughter-in-law, Donna, for her editing and especially my dear eighty-six-year-old mother-in-law, Mildred Klem, for tenaciously correcting my spelling and punctuation.

Most of all I thank my wife, Dolores, for her faith and patience and for teaching me English. As a ten-year-old in Cleveland, Ohio, war movies and news about the war broadcast over short-wave radio impressed Dolores. "What shall I do if a German soldier parachutes down in our yard?" she remembers worrying. Her decision was, "I'll invite him for a cup of coffee." Eight years later I walked into Dolores' backyard and was offered a cup of coffee. We married shortly thereafter.

Chapter 1

Boarding School
Castle Bieberstein, near Fulda

In 1942 the war raged in its third year. I turned seventeen that year and thought I had a chance to become a war hero. All my friends wanted to be in the exciting Blitzkrieg. Our tanks rolled through Poland in three weeks, they swept over France in six months and finished what was not accomplished in four years during the First World War. I saw no danger signs on the German political horizon. In my opinion, Germany was in great shape. Newspapers printed the war successes in bold letters. The fact that they were edited by the government was not important. Nobody cared. Clandestine radio stations provided an equilibrium. After checking the headlines, I read the sports section and passed over the trashy love stories they always featured on page twelve. My friends read magazines which showed war pictures and Adolf Hitler smiling while pinning bravery medals on war heroes. We were proud of them. I wanted a medal too. A German victory was just a matter of time. But at seventeen we were stuck in school, afraid of being left out.

"I said the top of the Rhoen mountain is off limits for you boys!" The school administrator waved a new government document before our noses.

"Please, no more questions! Assembly is dismissed!" Four classmates discussed the announcement with me. Our school was near the mountain top, and everybody had seen the spindly structures gracefully gliding over the Rhoen mountains like giant birds. Why was the area suddenly off limits? Because the gliders had no engines? That was no secret. The off limits order presented a challenge. We had to investigate. A path led through dense forest to the top. We walked kicking rocks uphill, practicing soccer. We hit tree trunks with sticks to demonstrate our readiness for challenges. Halfway up a sign warned, "Achtung! Don't go further!" We stopped and read dutifully.

"What shall we do? Go back! No! Never!"

A second sign, further up and almost covered by foliage, was hard to read. It showed the same warning. I expected soldiers behind trees pointing rifles. There was nobody.

We discussed the second sign and walked on. At the top a heavy fence gate blocked the final way. Behind the gate stood two dome-shaped airplane hangers in an open field. They seemed deserted. There was nobody around. We saw only the blue sky and the horizon. Three hours of walking were useless. My best friend, nick-named Texas, danced around showing excitement. "I can't wait until I'll join the air force. Flying is fun," he yelled much too loud. He often demonstrated a bothersome lack of maturity.

"I will not join the air force," I said sternly intending to offend him. My mind was made up. "Can't you see, these gliders are useless? I'll join the mountain troops and hope it's not too late. Tanks and machine guns decide a war, not stupid gliders." I liked having the opportunity to show off my knowledge of weaponry which I had gathered from magazines.

Texas's parents lived in Argentina where they owned a huge cattle ranch. They had no schools close by and sent their son to Germany to be educated. When he arrived at Castle Bieberstein, our boarding school, he was assigned to a lower floor. His roommate named him Texas assuming that Texas was part of Argentina. "Call me Pampas, not Texas!" the new boy shouted. The roommate realized his mistake, but the name Texas stuck because the newcomer despised it. He got used to it. I arrived at the school at the same time, and for four years we had been friends.

"A pity the war won't last much longer," I sighed deeply. "We still have six months to the Finals. I hope they'll draft us before."

I saw the tower of Castle Bieberstein peaking through the forest's leafy canopy. The sight made me proud. We liked our school.

I was sent to Bieberstein after my grades in a Munich Real-Gymnasium Humanistic had severely deteriorated. My father attended Bieberstein long before me. He explained the values of a boarding school to my doubtful mother while they both pondered my horrible report card.

"Castle Bieberstein and the country atmosphere will do him good and help his development. He should get out of the city." My mother was still doubtful. I hid behind a thick curtain in the living room and listened. My concern was the report card.

"It's not this city that influences him. It's your father's palatial household which causes the problems." They passed my report card back and forth.

"He's lost here because he has no friends. The maids are his only friends. And I am lost, too," cried my mother. She very seldom cried, and my father showed his affection. "I remember how lonely I was in this complex household."

There was no further discussion. My things were packed, and I was sent by train halfway through Germany to the Middle Age city of Fulda, 20 kilometers from Castle Bieberstein. I knew castles, but I had never lived in one. It must be exciting. I took a little train which let me off at the castle's station. The building was behind a thick, stone wall on a steep hill hidden by oak-trees. The castle had a prominent gate. I liked everything. Later, I made friends, and my grades improved slightly. That made my parents happy. They thought they had made the right decision.

Most boys came to Bieberstein from aristocratic households. Some came from even larger homes than my grandfather's. They were also lost in the turbulence of social shuffle. Though my grandfather was not an aristocrat, he supported the school financially. So I was assigned to sit at the principal's table during meals. All boys sitting at the principal's table came from wealthy and influential families. They were sons of dukes, earls, and one was even the grandson of our former Kaiser. Nobody was arrogant, they couldn't care less. "We are a family," confirmed our principal, and his wife, a thin, tall lady, agreed. She always agreed. We saw them only at meal times. The principal made announcements after meals, then we boys would meet and adjust the new rules to our liking. We were taught we were a 'democracy.' But nobody knew exactly what that meant. Germany had been a democracy since the First World War. Hitler was elected by parliament and followed parliamentary rules for a while. But rumors floated, "Be careful! Don't be outspoken!" Hitler's government didn't appreciate opposition. But that didn't concern me.

Three years later as senior student, I was allowed to live in one of the castle's best rooms under the attic. Ten small rooms, connected by a narrow hallway, were called *D-Zug* (D-Train), because they looked like German train compartments. Each room had a magnificent view. Not satisfied with my view, I often climbed out my window onto the steep grey castle roof and disregarded the danger of slipping and falling from six stories high and certain death. Thoughts like that were frivolous. Challenges were the spice of life.

I could see the entire valley from the roof and spent hours there day-dreaming. I imagined how the fierce Germanic tribesmen once walked below into the forest. They were my heroes. They defeated heavily armed Roman legions with clubs and short swords and kept uncivilized Asian hordes from German soil. I was proud to be German. I agreed with Hitler's order to teach our Germanic heritage in school and about ancient Germanic Gods. Half-human Gods, they were strong and, in my opinion, fit the time. Why were they discarded? Christianity replaced them. Now we had one God and his son Jesus.

We could have at least kept some of them!

One day in class I asked the professor. "Why didn't our Germanic ancestors establish a strong and lasting European empire?" The old professor smirked. "Because the Germanic ancestors were busy quarreling." That sounded cynical. "They were selfish and undisciplined and actually accomplished very little." The statement was followed by silence. He noticed that nobody in the class liked the answer. "Remember, Germany was only united eighty years ago by Fuerst Otto von Bismarck. It took a genius to do it, because we Germans liked to quarrel. We prefer to fight each other." With that, he made his point.

We liked Professor Leopold. He was dismissed from a big Frankfurt school as principal because he stated his own views more emphatically than the government's.

"I don't know of any specific German Physics or German Chemistry, like they make us believe in Berlin. That is nonsense. It doesn't exist. There is no special German physics or German whatever. Schools should not teach nonsense! We humans have five senses, and we dabble with them in science. Scientists intend to find proof for everything. What we don't know is called religious faith. Though I am grateful for science and its constant introduction of new things, I don't care who invents what or where it came from. Science is international." He was dismissed for that statement. Nobody could hire him. By that time, though, most young teachers were in the army, and old Professor Leopold was given a second chance. He came to Bieberstein with the permission to teach history; but not science, and he could not become a principal.

Professor Leopold had a habit of hurrying into the classroom with several books tucked under his right arm. That made it impossible for him to raise his right arm and to give the required, proper Heil Hitler salute. He swung his right leg over the chair and mumbled barely audible, "Heil Hitler." We laughed and adopted his style. Gradually we eliminated the salute all together. Somebody asked if we weren't defiant? We didn't debate the issue.

Every night by 9:00 P.M., Texas and I had an additional duty as seniors. We patrolled the lower floors of younger students and turned their lights off.

"Why don't you turn your lights off in D-Zug?" they asked. We seniors never answered younger students. We were in charge, we didn't have to. They knew we had a secret light installation under the attic's roof which wired our ten rooms to a teacher's apartment. An alarm under a step warned when a teacher approached and gave me time to quickly turn off our secondary lights at the switch in my closet. Our windows were covered with blankets by government orders. That prevented Allied bombers from orientation. But more importantly, it prevented the teachers below from discovering our illegal light installation.

Most nights we turned in by 11:00 P.M. One night, still before 11:00 P.M. Volkmar, my next door neighbor, busted noisily into my room yelling, "Turn your radio on, quick! There is special news tonight."

Volkmar had his uncle's old WW I steel helmet on his head, which covered his face. WW I helmets were much larger than today's helmets. Volkmar was tall, but not athletic. Christian, from five rooms down the hall, was behind him. He always forgot that my door frame was only six foot high, and unfailingly banged his head. Christian had an even better short-wave radio. "Radio broke down," he explained. "And I can't get parts anymore!"

I reluctantly changed from soft dance music to the news station. They both fell onto my bed. Christian and Volkmar were tops in my class academically; but I was tops in sports. Their discussion often went over my head, but I would not admit it. We were best friends and enjoyed each other's company. The broadcast began to blare.

I turned the volume lower, "... 11:00 P.M., September 24, 1942. We have late reports from OKW (Army) Headquarters. Field Marshal Halder has resigned. The Führer Adolf Hitler appointed General Kurt Zeitzler in his place. He took command of all German forces in Russia ...." Volkmar frowned. "That doesn't sound good. The war must be turning. Halder was our best general. My father knows him well. Why did Hitler sack him? Rommel lost el Alamein in Africa. Why didn't they mention that. Why?"

"You are always pessimistic, Volkmar!" I tried to cheer him up, only mildly interested in the news. "The war is already won and over. Russia is finished. That was confirmed yesterday. England was finished months ago. The British will wave white flags. Our U-boats sank 700,000 tons last week. My only worry is that it is too late for us to get into the war. Five more months to the finals; and by then the war will be over. I need to get out of here. School is cruel mental torture—those unpredictable questions they come up with on final tests. My nerves are ruined."

Volkmar's helmet poked me.

"Why do you wear that awful helmet? You look silly, Volkmar."

"Because I want you to break my coffee cup on the steel helmet." Volkmar handed me his cup and bend over. I smashed the cup on his steel helmet without hesitation. Small porcelain fragments scattered over the floor. Obedience was a German virtue and nobody should dare question a senior, no matter how silly his wishes were. Volkmar von Richthofen was our elected student-body president. He deserved our respect. His wish was a command.

"I liked that," Volkmar grinned and took off his helmet. He was the nephew of the heroic Red Baron. "My uncle never wore that helmet. See, there isn't a scratch." We inspected the blue-black surface together. "The British shot him down. The helmet wouldn't have saved him, anyway. War is insane!"

Every time Volkmar said, "War is insane," it made me shudder. Hardly anybody in class opposed the war. Why was he in opposition? He came from a famous military family and had plenty of tradition. His father was field marshal in the air force and, most certainly, would not oppose the war. Nevertheless, we admired Volkmar, and not only because he was the nephew of the famous Red Baron. Somehow Volkmar reflected a mysterious presence which made many uncomfortable. When he spoke in the assembly, everybody shut up. Volkmar spoke with conviction and integrity. Our school was the last to tolerate free speech, a tradition adopted from British boarding schools.

Christian leaned back on my pillow and contemplated why war was insane. "Why do we have war, anyway?" he muttered. Christian usually agreed with Volkmar on most subjects, but he disliked his anti-war attitude. Christian had a habit of answering his own question before anyone else could. He turned to me. "I'll tell you why war is insane. Because whoever wins the war sets the conditions for the next war. The cycle repeats itself. Therefore, wars are unavoidable and insane! The loser has no choice. He complies with what is dictated to him in a peace treaty. From that day on revenge breeds and a new war stands on the horizon."

"Are you pessimistic, too?" I felt like confronting Christian. He upset me and I didn't quite understand what he meant. What was he talking about? The war was finished? Christian continued, "Germany is too small to effectively rule Europe. I agree with Volkmar. This war may turn out to be nonsense." He raised his arms and imitated his father, who was professor at the University of Ankara in Turkey. "The news is indeed bad. Check the military map in my room."

Christian had a European map spread over the entire wall in his room. And like a general marked every move of an army with black arrows or colored flags. He knew their locations, their numbers and size.

"German troops are already at the Volga River, close to Asia. That is much further than Napoleon went." He droned on. "The entire Mediterranean Sea from Spain to Turkey, from Tunisia to Cairo is occupied by German troops." That told me they had checked Christian's map before coming to my room.

"We are definitely over-extended," Christian determined. "Hitler told General Halder to split his Sixth Army, and Halder refused. Hitler fired him. See, the crucial points at the Volga are guarded by the Hungarian army, the Rumanian Third Army and the Italian Eighth Army, according to my father's observations. Hungarians and Rumanians don't trust each other. We know that. That is not the worst, however. Nobody trusts the Italians. These armies are not well armed. Dad says the Russians will attack at the Volga, at Stalingrad. One more thing, the entire Russian army from Asia is now heading toward the Volga. Please don't tell anybody. My father will be mad."

I jumped up. "How does he know all that?"

Christian blushed. "I talk too much. You know I get my information from the short-wave radio. But since my radio broke down I can't tell you anything more," he sighed. Christian had more information than usual. It didn't come from clandestine stations. I was often suspicious. Ankara was known for being the center of international espionage. Maybe his father spied for Germany? That had crossed my mind before.

I liked spy novels. Spies were important. They often changed a war's outcome. Christian sat up and assured us that his father was not a spy. Why was he in Turkey? And why did Christian spend so much time on his short-wave radio? Christian spoke Turkish. He had dual citizenship and was exempt from the draft. I began to wonder how a dual citizenship affects a person. Could Christian be loyal to two countries?

Every time Christian felt uncomfortable, he changed the subject. Philosophy was his second favorite subject. His first was mulling over war strategies. "I wonder if God created men to fight wars?" He went into philosophy.

"What do you think?" He suddenly addressed me. I decided to let Volkmar answer that. Volkmar didn't answer, and as usual, Christian answered his own question: "Adam and Eve stayed in paradise with little to do, and that was not satisfactory to God. Occasionally, Adam and Eve fussed with a snake which gave God the idea to lead them to the tree of wisdom. He told the snake to tempt them. After the snake tempted them, God had a reason to evict them. He ordered Adam and Eve to multiply. They bore many children and children's children, almost so that God worried about an overpopulation of his planet. That's when wars began." Christian looked at me. I didn't like Christian's interpretation of the book of Genesis. I found it strange. I also felt shy when they talked about religion. I did not believe in the traditional preaching in church. Religious affiliation was unimportant to me. I believed in God without a specific religion.

"I don't think you are correct, Christian," I challenged him. "God did not intend wars. God actually wanted human beings to become Supreme Beings. I agree, wars cannot be avoided. But a war gives a human being an opportunity to die as a hero, and to die a hero's death is honorable. Men do not fight like animals and eat each other. The hero's death makes us special! When we die, we know we fought for a noble cause. To believe in special, noble causes makes us special. I wouldn't mind dying the hero's death. I even look forward to it. I don't want to die in bed."

Volkmar sat up suddenly and almost pushed me from my bed. "You are nuts! No wonder you don't understand Nietzsche's work! Yes, humans are special, according to Nietzsche. But you should read him more thoroughly or you'll flunk the test! God didn't create the hero's death. You sound like Hitler. Nietzsche's ideology is, when he has Zarathustra say, 'God is dead,' it means that God is not like our religions interpretation of him or what our churches preach. When Nietzsche wrote 'God is dead,' he meant nobody knows God. A Supreme Man will eventually lead us to God on a spiritual path. Nietzsche wrote that 100 years ago. And your hero's death is nonsense. That is a fabrication of the Third Reich." Volkmar was sure he'd convinced me. But he didn't.

Christian smiled. He grabbed the rarely used volume of Nietzsche's work from my shelf and began turning pages. He looked for a passage. "Here it is, 'War breeds revenge!' says Zarathustra. 'Once humanity is delivered from the urge of revenge, it is the beginning of the bridge to high hopes and the rainbow after many long storms!'" Christian raised his finger. "That confirms my theory: 'War breeds revenge!' like I said earlier. Do you think Hitler understands Nietzsche? He thinks Germans are Supreme Beings. But that's not what Nietzsche meant. Hitler is older and wiser. He should know better."

Volkmar placed his helmet on my head and grinned. "You better use my helmet for protection so you don't die the hero's death. I don't want you to die for nothing. There isn't a noble cause in this world worth dying for. Believe me!"

The large, heavy helmet bothered me. I took it off. "How does Hitler intend to purify the German race when he himself isn't even blond and blue eyed?" I asked them. That still was a mystery to me. My friends didn't answer.

"Let's go to bed," they said and left. I was sure they would study and not go to bed, and that reminded me that I should read Hitler's *Mein Kampf* or I would flunk the finals.

Competitive sports was my major interest. After I broke two long-standing school track records, the administrator promoted me to part-time physical education instructor. Volkmar announced my promotion at a student meeting and warned everyone, "Seniors are to be respected, even when one becomes a part-time teacher."

Student meetings were held in our ancient castle chapel. The chapel had several functions. It was used for spiritual services, lectures, piano recitals or poetry readings after supper and before "free time." Customarily, teachers did not attend student meetings, but as a part-time teacher and a student, I attended both. Students considered me a spy.

I talked to the older teachers and noticed that they worried about the war. In math class the teacher strayed from the subject and discussed the entry into the war by the United States.

"I researched the American industrial capacity. When the United States entered the war in December, they began converting their entire industry to war weapons production. Their capacity is ten times our industrial output, including Japan's. Accordingly, they soon outnumber us ten to one. One can only hope that the United States industries are slow in converting. I calculated that they will need ten months to catch up. Therefore, we must win the war in ten months. Our production is in high gear and we have superior weapons. But if they catch up they will undoubtedly win the war. Remember, Germany lost the First World War when the Americans joined in against us. I hope history won't repeat itself."

We were all stunned by his calculation. Not winning the war never entered my mind. My first reaction was, "He shouldn't talk that way!" I noticed my friends looked concerned and Volkmar's look expressed, "See, I told you so!"

When we left the room a new fellow by the name of Igor whispered, "That man is crazy! Hitler is a genius and Germany is lucky. There will never be a Führer like him. We'll win the war this year! Look what Hitler already accomplished! He kept his promises and corrected the shameful dictates of Versailles."

Igor came from Yugoslavia. He claimed to be a close friend of Yugoslavia's King Peter and told us the story of how they escaped a Bolshevik demonstration in Belgrade. They slid down a royal palace rain pipe and hid in the bushes.

Igor had dual citizenship and that made me suspicious. "Are you German or a Yugoslav?"

"I am both, but I can't serve in the German army. They won't allow it because my father is a Serb. Serbs are not admitted. My mother, though, is

German." I felt sorry for him. He couldn't join us when we went before the draft board. The poor fellow had to suffer through finals.

The next day there was a fire drill, and I was in charge. Yesterday's math lecture was forgotten and the uneasy feeling evaporated, but Allied airplanes cruised nightly near the castle and could mistakenly drop a bomb. The danger of fire was real.

I lined the students up in one row. Water buckets were hoisted from the water well and handed, man to man, to a person standing on the castle's stone wall. This last person poured water over the ancient crumbling stones. It didn't make much sense; but it had to be done. It was the century old method. The nearest fire station was kilometers away, and the road to the castle was too steep for any fire engine to climb. We relied on ourselves.

I felt like an officer commanding an honorable but hopeless task.

The Hitler Youth Sports Festival in Fulda

Fulda was a dormant medieval city twenty kilometers from Castle Bieberstein. The city didn't interest us. Occasionally we had to go to Fulda to see a doctor or go to the hospital. Once a year, we attended a Hitler Youth State's Sports Festival and looked forward to it. We had to be members of the Hitler Youth, and our *Gefolgschaft* number was eleven. The winner in the track and field competition would advance to the national competition held in Breslau later. Twenty of us went to the competition in Fulda. I knew this year was my last.

The little Rhoen mountain train serpentined slowly down the endless curves to the city. There was an unusual abundance of flowers at the railroad station. Swastika flags girded the streets, signifying that it was a special day. A band of brown-shirted Hitler Youth played and marched from the rail station to the sports stadium. But we did not. I cussed myself for the mistake. We looked like idiots. That morning before breakfast somebody casually suggested, "Let's not wear the Hitler Youth uniform today! We'll show them our blue and white school outfit, which looks just as good or better." Without thinking we all agreed.

As the team's captain I should have known better. I was responsible. We rarely wore our Hitler Youth uniform at home because our teachers didn't insist. Now, realizing the mistake, I was angry with myself. It was a stupid idea. We were good athletes. We trained hard and they should respect us anyway. I tried to rationalize. Our identity does not matter. Our goal was winning. We'll win most of the events. Most of us will qualify for the national competition. I swore to myself, "In Breslau we'll wear the Hitler Youth uniform."

We walked down the steps to the stadium's cellar locker room and were greeted with animosity. Brown-shirted youths stared at us, made faces and wondered who we were.

A corpulent brown shirted official at the basement entrance bellowed, "Who the hell are you? Why aren't you in uniform? Who is in charge here? Where is the list of your names?" I handed him my list of categories in which each of us would participate.

"I'll determine who competes in what, not you! Your bunch is not even in uniform. You may not be eligible at all. We already have too many in the 100 meter race. None of your outfit, Gefolgschaft 11, competes in the 100 meter," he determined and crossed the 100 meter category from my list. Then he crossed all aristocratic titles from my list. A duke, a baron, or an earl was made a commoner. He overlooked the S.K.H. which stood before the Kaiser's grandson's name. He didn't know that S.K.H stood for *Seine Kaiserliche Hoheit*, His Royal Highness. He gave me the list, and now the name S.K.H. Welf von Hannover was just Hannover.

"Don't you know that Hannover is a city, and not a name?" I protested.

"I don't care. This guy's name is Hannover. And nobody runs the 100 meter!" That upset me because we had a sure winner in the 100 meter race. Georg Müller ran the 100 meter in 10.4 seconds, an Olympic time.

"Georg Müller is not an aristocrat, and he should run!" I protested correctly assuming that he disliked aristocrats. Georg Müller pushed me aside. He wanted to battle for himself. "I'll ... I'll run 400 ... 400 and ... the 800 meter instead," Georg stuttered.

The official blinked and felt sorry for Georg. "If he stutters, he won't win, anyway," he thought. "Is your name Müller? And you are not an aristocrat. All right, I will let you run the 400 and 800 meter race." I was concerned that Georg would run two strenuous middle distance races, one after the other, and might lose both. The official was aware of that. My comrades were disappointed, too. "Let's get out of here! It stinks."

We left the locker room and trotted to the field opposite the stadium. In full view of the spectators in the stadium we changed our clothes and dressed into our blue and white outfits. Harold set up his gramophone and played a Louis Armstrong jazz record, his hoarse voice belting loudly across the field toward the stadium.

"Isn't that guy American? Be careful! They'll arrest us." Harold didn't care. "I also have a Duke Ellington record, he is another American. You want to hear him?" Harold showed us his American Jazz record collection.

Max was the smallest among us. He was half-Italian and often felt the need to prove himself because of his small size. But he was a tenacious long-distance runner. His mother was the daughter of Italy's King Victor Emmanuel, who married a German *Füerst*. Max walked away in the direction of the stadium and to the governor's booth in the center. He climbed the three rows until he stood before the governor. There, he aggressively placed his blue Basque-style school cap on his curly black hair. A bodyguard ripped the cap off. Max grabbed the cap back and waved it victoriously in our direction. The burly bodyguard hassled Max. But Max ran off. The bodyguard followed him, and I had just enough time to stop the Louis Armstrong record. The bodyguard caught up to Max and cornered him.

"Who are you?" He yelled.

"Who are you?" countered Max. "I am an Italian and you can't touch me. Go away! Victor Emmanuel is my grandfather." The official hesitated. He knew the Italian king's name.

"Spell your name!" he ordered and took a pencil and paper from his pocket. Max spelled his German aristocratic name.

"That's not an Italian name. That's a German name," yelled the guard.

"It doesn't matter. Victor Emanuel is my grandfather, and if you don't believe me, call Mussolini! He knows my grandfather." The guard stared. He believed Max. He walked away shaking his head. I wondered what would happen next?

The competition started. The loudspeaker announced the 800 meter race in which Georg Müller participated. He walked casually to the starting line, then turned and waved unconcerned. Seconds later, the starting pistol rang. Nine runners in swastikas shirts sprinted off. Georg, in our blue and white school shirt, stayed behind. He ran in last position. The sprinters positioned themselves strategically for the long 800 meter race. Georg stayed in last place and lost ground but I began to wonder if Georg was actually suited for this race. He was a superb sprinter. The group ran by, and Georg, in last place, waved unconcerned. The stadium loudspeaker announced positions, "First place is held by Gefolgschaft 8, second place by Gefolgschaft 3, ... and in last place is Gefolgschaft 11." Georg ran by a second time and waved unconcerned. He was hopelessly in last place. We cheered him on, and I wished he would run faster.

Suddenly Georg sprinted like in the 100 meter race passing everybody. I sighed with relief. The loudspeaker dutifully reported the changes and even mentioned the ease with which Georg took the lead. He was now in first place and deliberately slowed the pace. The runners became impatient and passed him. Georg fell back to last place again. Again he ran by and waved unconcerned.

What was the matter with him? The loudspeaker announced the change. Now there were only 150 meters to the finish line. Three runners accelerated frequently changing positions. The rest fell further back. Georg, still in last place, suddenly sprinted like before and passed everybody. The front runners kept up with him, but Georg could still accelerate and crossed the finish line ten meters ahead of them.

We jumped and screamed hilariously and showed utter excitement. Georg joined us with a big grin. He wasn't exhausted. Minutes later, they announced the 400 meter race. Georg trotted calmly, without a rest, to the starting line. They sprinted off. Georg ran the 400 meter effortlessly. This time he ran in first place from start to finish. Georg did not stutter before or after a race. Too bad the Olympic Games were cancelled. Georg Müller would have easily won a medal for Germany.

The competition finished, I counted that we won most of the first and second places. There was still a parade to come with a presentation of the prizes.

Gefolgschaft 11 marched in civilian clothes in a sea of brown shirts and swastika flags. A band marched in front. Thousands of young athletes made a large shape in the center of the sports field. No doubt we stood out.

The announcer tested the microphone. "This bunch of vagabonds in the formation's center, clad in gypsy clothes, will be disqualified," he said.

"How can he make that decision?" I asked the others, while the spectators mildly applauded.

It had dawned on my friends that there would be repercussions. We knew of severe actions which were taken against people who had opposed the government. Some were even sent to concentration camps. Could that happen to us? But we didn't oppose the government or anybody. We just made a big mistake. Isolated from the German mainstream, none of us thought there would be consequences when we appeared in civilian clothes. We had heard of concentration camps, but didn't know what happened inside. There were rumors, but rumors were exaggerated most of the time. There was nothing we could do about it at this point. I had to admit that our behavior was out of place and was surprised that some of my friends still grinned defiantly. They thought what we did was fun. The silence after the announcement seemed too long. That worried me. All eyes were on us.

The governor stepped to the podium and took the microphone. He began by first expressing in general terms his pleasure with the event. Relieved, I relaxed. Three minutes into his speech, he suddenly raised his hand and pointed in our direction.

"The bunch of gypsies, there standing in civilian clothes, is disqualified." he yelled. The announcement followed a litany of accusations, most of them untrue. He said twice, "You showed no discipline and no respect. You wouldn't even be allowed if you were wearing brown uniforms. Your arrogance will no longer be tolerated in Germany. You will be punished. Disqualified, you will not receive trophies and will not be eligible to compete in the national competition in Breslau! Let that be a warning to all of you! Gefolgschaft 11 is a disgraceful bunch. You disgraced yourself and all of us. You will hear further from me."

The governor stepped down and then approached the trophy table. He was ready to award the prizes. The loudspeaker crackled and called a first and a second prize winner. Two brown-shirted youths stepped forward and sprinted to the trophy table. The governor shook hands and handed them a trophy. They ran back. The loudspeaker crackled again, and after a pause announced fifteen times, "The winners of the following events are "Gefolgschaft 11 . . . ."

Nobody stepped forward. There was an embarrassing silence. Tension mounted. The stadium was too quiet. Why didn't they tell the announcer that we were disqualified? That was not my fault! I almost felt sorry for the governor who stood helplessly waiting. He held a trophy in his hand and expected a youngster to come forward who he could congratulate. The stadium remained silent. The crowd was ready to burst into applause, but couldn't. We spoiled the festival. That was now clear.

I didn't want that to happen, I told myself, and didn't know what to do.

Finally, the dreadful ceremony ended. We escaped to the railroad station with nothing in mind but to get away from the embarrassment. We boarded the waiting train, and this time nobody made the usual jokes. The athletic successes were forgotten and left behind. Nobody talked. We sat quietly on the hard wooden benches in the train. We knew that this would not be the end. Our behavior caused trouble and severe consequences would follow. When we came to the castle entrance gate, a student waited. It was already dark. I wanted to disappear, get to my room and crawl into my bed. But bad news travels fast. "The principal wants to see you in his office at once," the student told us.

Dr. A., the principal, was in his office waiting with only Volkmar von Richthofen. They talked quietly. I expected Dr. A. to holler, scream, and perhaps expel us from school. But he said nothing. He ignored us. He didn't get up. I noticed his face was pale. He looked worried and tired.

"Our school will be closed," he announced in a surprisingly calm way, "which was caused by your indefensible behavior in Fulda," he paused. "Someone from the governor's office called and notified me that a contingent of SS inspectors will be coming tomorrow and stay for the week. That usually means the end of a private school. It already happened to Salem and two other private schools. The state took them over. We were the last private school. I wondered how long we may last. I don't have the desire or the nerve to scold you. You are seniors and smart enough to realize that your behavior caused this turmoil. I urge you to show your best behavior tomorrow when the SS inspectors come." His voice faded.

He went on. "Everybody must wear his Hitler Youth uniform and salute properly. We are in a desperate situation. I hope I can count on you."

Deeply embarrassed, I stepped forward to apologize on behalf of the group. "Tomorrow we'll be the sharpest Hitler Youth these inspectors have ever seen," I said. "We seniors will make sure that all students are properly dressed and behave like Hitler Youths should." The principal waved me to shut up. He asked us all to leave. "Go to your rooms and get your uniforms ready!"

Volkmar signaled me to come to his room. We sat down and talked.

I telephoned my dad that evening at air force headquarters and explained the situation. I rarely called him before, but Dad listened carefully. Of course, he was furious at first. He calmed down after a while and promised to talk the Führer directly. He would urge him to leave our school alone. He also said he didn't have the time to worry about me or my school matters, and neither did the other gentlemen who worked with Hitler and had kids here.

Volkmar grinned. "I hope he can convince Hitler. That will be our only chance. By the way, I congratulate you for behaving like stupid asses in Fulda and showing off. I know you didn't mean to demonstrate. But these Nazi folks don't understand that. You behaved like stupid spoiled brats."

The next morning at 6:00 A.M., fully dressed in Hitler Youth uniform, a smell of must swayed from my body. My uniform had lay untouched for months in my closet. Volkmar was in uniform, and so were all D-Zug dwellers. Wearing our immaculate brown uniforms, we decided to split into groups to inspect all the students on the lower floors. Guards were assigned to inform us when the SS inspectors arrived.

At noon, as expected, two black limousines entered the gate. They drove into the courtyard and six SS officers in black uniforms stepped out ignoring our sharp salute. They hurried to the principal's office. Fifteen minutes later they were in our classroom with our principal behind them.

Dr. A. wore his finest dark suit and a swastika emblem was attached to his lapel demonstrating that he, too, belonged to the Party. I had never seen him wearing the swastika emblem before. We stood behind our chairs, raised our right arms, and shouted, "Heil Hitler!" Our crisp salute surprised them.

Everybody sat down and listened to professor Leopold's lecture. His face glowed, when he enthusiastically spoke about the disciplined, brave, ancient Germanic tribesmen and their glorious victories. He was in his best form and allowed us to jump up and answer many questions. I was often called on because he knew I desperately wanted to make up for yesterday's mistake, and because I had a good memory for dates and names.

After lunch the principal introduced me to the SS group as the school's assistant physical education instructor. We left for the sports field. On the way, I explained that everything on the track and field was built by us. Afternoon practices had just begun. I made sure they saw Georg Müller running the 100 meter in near-record time. That impressed them.

"Is his name Georg Müller? We thought, everybody here is an aristocrat!"

"I am not an aristocrat, either," I told them proudly, "and neither is half of the group." They relaxed. They must have known that Hitler surrounded himself with aristocrats and liked them. Most SS men came from the poor class. Liking aristocrats was not their style.

"Are you still a student? A student who does teacher's duties?"

"Yes, I am both," I answered proudly. "Our teachers are in the war. Therefore, I am proud to help out. The Fatherland needs everybody to fight the 'Total War.'" I cringed at my own words, wondering if it sounded phony. "I can't wait until I join the army." That was more convincing. They looked at me and saw my genuine enthusiasm. I spoke from my heart. Satisfied, they left the sports field. I clapped my heels and saluted correctly. They nodded showing their approval of me. My classmates stopped and saluted from the field, and raised their right arms to shoulder height shouting, "Heil Hitler."

The six inspectors sat at the principal's table and tried to make pleasant conversation. They even claimed to like our simple food. Most of the time they spent in the classrooms taking notes. Three days later they had relaxed and weren't taking notes. They even went to our evening chapel to listen to a piano recital or a lecture. We stretched on the floor while they sat in our large King Arthur chairs around the massive center table. By the end of the week they laughed and greeted us with a casual, "Hi!" and not, "Heil Hitler!" But I warned everybody, "Salute smartly! Never relax! Always raise your right arm shoulder high! And show discipline, no matter what!"

At the end of the week they climbed into the black limousines and left. Everyone smiled. The principal called a meeting in the chapel and smiled broadly as he entered. "We were informed by the State Ministry of Education that our school can remain a private school. That was a direct order from Adolf Hitler." A roar of applause drowned his last words. He smiled and said no more.

Volkmar, Christian and I went to my room. "Do you suppose the inspectors knew about Hitler's orders?" I asked them. Volkmar shrugged his shoulders. "Hitler always has the last word in everything. He is unpredictable."

After we passed the SS inspection, we went back to the daily routines. I began reading the required book, *Mein Kampf* and prepared for the finals. On the following Wednesday the long expected draft notices arrived in the form of a simple postcard. We celebrated by screaming and hollering. Our future looked bright. "We won't make the finals!" I announced running through the D-Zug hallway.

"We'll be in the army in three months!" counted a guy four doors down the hall. "And we'll get our graduation certificate without an examination!" That was the most important issue. Seventeen classmates, besides me, received draft notices and the order to appear the next Thursday in Kassel.

We boarded the whistling country train, hollering and hanging from the windows expressing our utter excitement. The engine laboriously steamed downhill, bypassing Fulda on the way to Kassel, our State capitol. Busses waited at the train station. Hundreds of other future recruits streamed from trains. We all boarded busses which took us to the city's outskirts. We passed the barrack gate and were left off at a sports auditorium which served as the recruiting office.

"They'll draft us to the infantry. You'll see! We'll have no choice!" observed one classmate.

"Not me!" objected Ernst Suhren. "I'll join the navy! My two brothers are U-boat commanders. I'll insist they send me to the U-boats. My two brothers have the highest medal, the Knight's Cross, and I want that too, as soon as possible!" That sounded reasonable. But would the draft board comply?

We Bieberstein boys stuck together. We undressed and went to the physical examination in a hall that looked like an emergency room. We passed the physical easily and received a stamped paper classifying us A+ material. Half-naked, undignified, in shorts only, we were herded into a sports arena where the draft began. Five long tables in the center created a line separating us from the draft officials. A metallic voice echoed from the high wall.

"All men, classified A, line up at right! All classified B and C line up on the left at table five!" We stepped up. Somebody explained, B and C were lower categories and wouldn't have to go into combat. My friends and I qualified for combat. We were proud.

"Classes B and C will be assigned to police and military administration," the announcer confirmed. "In spite of your shortcomings, you should be proud to serve the Third Reich."

We A-material men lined up and faced table one, staffed by SS officers.

"They'll draft us to the SS. You'll see! SS always has first choice, as usual," Texas grumbled. "Not me! I'll join the navy!" said Ernst Suhren, determined as ever. "Not me either!" answered a chorus of my classmates behind me.

"I don't want to salute their way! I'll ask my father to liberate me from their claws! My dad is an army general and has influence. He will do it."

"What's wrong with the SS?" asked Volkmar turning around. He wasn't joking. We were surprised. "Do you want to join the SS?"

"Why not? They get the best weapons and that's good enough for me."

We were speechless. "I don't like this crazy war anyway," he explained, "But since I don't have a choice and want to survive, I might as well join the outfit that gets the best weapons." Volkmar's sophisticated thoughts were often difficult to follow.

"It's time Germany takes over in Europe and picks up where Napoleon left off," voiced Harold. "Perhaps you will be an SS guard in a concentration camp," grinned Suhren as he poked Volkmar.

"That won't happen! They'll assign group C to the police and make them prison guards. They stand at table five." Volkmar was annoyed. "Table one recruits are only for the SS fighting forces. There is a big difference between them and the guards."

The recruiters settled at their tables with friendly smiles. Ernst Suhren, always the most aggressive, walked to the first table without being asked.

"I want to join the navy," I heard him telling the SS officer. "Where is the navy table? Two of my brothers are U-boat commanders and I want to join them." He sounded much too demanding. "You should have volunteered for the navy and not waited for the draft," answered the SS officer, but kept smiling. "Yes, we do respect tradition. Go to the navy table, at number three! Good luck."

"Next!" Volkmar stepped forward and, without hesitation, signed up. We shook our heads in disbelief. Even the friendly SS recruiter was surprised. "Are you von Richthofen, related to Baron von Richthofen?"

"Yes Sir. He was my uncle, and my father is a field marshall in the air force." The SS officer's face glowed. He lifted himself up and shook Volkmar's hand. He thought he had a big fish on the line and SS Headquarters would approve of him. "I am delighted to meet you. You can still enlist to the air force if you wish, because you are a von Richthofen. That is at table four."

"No! I don't want to join the air force," Volkmar was determined, but never explained why. "Welcome to the SS." The officer pushed papers in front of Volkmar. "Next!" He bellowed and looked at me. I stepped forward.

"Sir, I would like to join the First Mountain Division, Artillery Regiment 79." The recruiting SS officer kept smiling. However, he found my request unusually specific.

"Don't you want to become an SS soldier like your friend here?" he pointed at Volkmar, who was signing papers next to me.

"With due respect, Sir, I would like to join Artillery Regiment 79. My three older brothers are officers there, and my father is a major in the staff of the First Mountain Division." The SS officer was not pleased. Though he had said before that he respected tradition.

"Go to the next table! You should have volunteered to get into a specific unit! Good luck!"

An army officer at the next table heard the conversation and had already pulled documents from his drawer. "These forms are for volunteers. Fill them out! The State of Hessen does not have a mountain division. Therefore, you must send your application to Garmisch, in Bavaria, to the First Mountain Division. You must also have your father's approval and signature! This form is a release from the draft in Hessen. Good luck!"

The assignments finished late in the afternoon. We gathered and compared our draft results. The draft board officers were generally considered nice and accommodating. Everybody joined the unit they wanted. Some teased Volkmar guardedly and congratulated him on being our lone SS soldier. No one liked the SS, and Volkmar knew it. We respected him, not because he was the famous Rote Kampflieger's nephew but he was our leader and friend. We wondered why he joined the SS? But he had always been different.

"I know why you wonder," he said and grinned. "My dad will be much more upset than you. Consider, that some SS combat units are good. I am not going into this war with the intention of getting medals like you guys. My reason is simple. The SS gets the better weapons, and I can defend myself. I intend to survive. When the war is over, I'll become a pastor and preach peace. In my opinion, there should be no more war, and diplomats should be trained better. We must work harder to avoid war. War is insane."

When he said, "war is insane," I wondered when they would arrest him. We linked our arms and walked to the bus. Somehow, we sensed our time together would not last. I felt a strange lingering sadness.

The next day I sat in my attic room and wrote my father a letter: "Yesterday I was called before the draft board in Kassel where I volunteered for the First Mountain Division. I shall soon join you and my brothers. You must sign the enclosed approval forms. Please send the papers back to me as soon as possible!"

My father returned the letter with the forms unsigned. He explained, "You're seventeen, and I want you to finish school first! Our family has four men in combat. That's enough. The government allows only four men of one family in combat." That was all he wrote.

Stunned, I laid the letter aside. I was sure he would sign my application.

I thought I knew my father well. His principal interest had been the military since he was infantry officer in World War I, and he often told us how miserable the four years were in muddy trenches in France. He was bitter. He claimed Germany had not lost that miserable war. He and his soldiers did not lose the war. My father's military career ended.

After the war the Versailles treaty demanded that Germany reduce its army to 100,000 men. My father became a civilian and managed my grandfather's printery in Freising. He didn't like it and left early many afternoons to go hunting. On weekends, he was joined by his war buddies, and we heard them endlessly discussing First World War military strategies and what could have been done to change the unfortunate outcome.

"I don't approve of Corporal Hitler nor his running Germany's affairs," said my father. They all agreed. "Hitler doesn't have the experience, neither does he have the stature for the job; though I do support his fighting communists and his intention to eliminate that shameful Versailles treaty."

My father had told us, "When I returned in 1918, there was a mob of communists waiting in the streets. They spat on our uniforms and threatened to rip them off. They took our medals away." My father never got over that. "I hate communists!" My father said. "The Allies ordered Germany to pay reparations we couldn't afford. Our government printed money to pay debts without having the financial foundation. That caused the worst inflation anybody had ever experienced. A loaf of bread cost one million marks one day, and a billion by the end of the week. That should never happen again. It suffocated us. The so-called peace treaty of Versailles kept Germany in a blockade for years after the war. As long as Germany tolerated the shameful Versailles dictate we had no chance to survive. The Versailles dictate must be revoked!"

After fifteen years of complaining, my father and his First World War buddies gladly put their uniforms back on and joined in 1939. The victory was in sight, but my father would not let me go. Why wouldn't he allow me to volunteer? I wanted to be there.

I sat down and wrote a second letter, this time mindful of my father's disposition and dislikes "Dear dad, If you don't allow me to volunteer to the mountain troops, then the SS will draft me."

I knew he disliked the SS. He believed they had no business fighting alongside of our regular German army. They were police, but not soldiers. I continued my letter, "I don't mind joining the SS, because I like danger and I want to become a hero. I heard SS combat troops are excellent, they have better weapons which is the reason for their success. They are more exposed. Of course, you know that the SS is no longer a political police force. They have become fighting troops and always seem to be in the worst battles. I know you don't like the SS, but they will draft me because you didn't allow me to volunteer. I'll be in Kassel in an SS uniform in three months."

The last sentence was pure speculation, meant to carry special weight. It worked. My father returned my volunteer application signed and added, "I talked to General Kübler, the commander of the First Mountain Division. He approved your application. You may join Regiment 79 of the mountain artillery, anytime." I forwarded my application to Garmisch, in Bavaria. Three weeks later I received their favorable reply. I could join within fourteen days.

Two weeks later, my senior class packed and we were ready to leave school. There was excitement mingled with sadness. We hugged each other, which we had never done before. Home addresses were eagerly exchanged. Some had tears and didn't mind showing them.

Dr. A. had arranged for a dignified farewell ceremony in the castle's chapel. He handed us our *Abitur* graduation papers. I had passed with low grades, but passing was the important part. Nobody would ever look at my grades. Why still worry about it?

A famous scientist and former student came to bid us farewell. His speech stuck long in my mind.

"In 1939, I was on a tour with three British scientists in Greenland when the war started," he began. "We had an exciting experimental project in the arctic. During the summer we lived in tents, but in September we moved into an ice cave. Our work progressed slowly. Absorbed with what we were doing, we didn't pay much attention to the threat of war. One evening early in September, we listened to the short-wave broadcast from England. It said, 'England has declared war on Germany.' Perplexed, we stared at each other, hoping the news wasn't true.

"What shall we do? We were best friends and our work intertwined. We weren't finished and couldn't just leave the Arctic. We lit a candle and stared at each other. We tried joking and opened a bottle of champagne. 'What the hell! Let's be good enemies!' We toasted. But the jokes sounded hollow. None of us wanted to believe the news.

"We didn't know what to do. 'Let's fight the war among ourselves,' one Brit suggested. 'Let's fight between the icebergs and throw ice balls. But to make it fair, one of us Brits must cross the line and fight with a German. The two winners decide what should be done, whether we shall stay or leave.'

"The three British tossed coins and one became my comrade. We shook hands. We went outside and hid behind huge ice blocks, rolled icy snowballs and threw them. Nobody got hurt. We fought tirelessly and chased each other for hours, laughed, and had fun. To be honest, I hadn't had that much fun in years. We mature scientists played war games in far-away Greenland and acted like little boys. But there was sadness. We didn't want to stop. Nobody wanted to make the decision whether we stayed or left. Tired to the end, we gathered and jointly declared, 'There is no winner!'

"We returned into our ice cave with tears in our eyes. We sat staring.

"War seldom has a winner but will always exist. 'Why can't war be like the one we just fought?' somebody asked. The battle between the icebergs bonded us more than our work had done before. We opened our last bottle of Champagne. 'Let's stay and finish our project,' we decided together. 'That is more important.' We continued to work and listened to the news every night. What we heard was not good. It made us sad. We knew one day we would have to leave.

"The time finally came. We crossed our hands and swore never to shoot real live bullets at each other. Scientists are predestined to help mankind and not to destroy it. I returned to Germany, and became draft exempt.

"What can I tell you? What advice can I give you? I am fortunate to work at home as a scientist. I don't have to take risks like you will have to. You soldiers are not as fortunate. You must risk your lives. I wish, the war could be fought like we did between icebergs in Greenland. I remember my friends and deeply regret that we are enemies.

"My advice to you is treasure your friendships, make them last! Every friendship is a precious gift from God. Nourish the friendships you made in school. And respect the soldiers on the other side as well. Remember, without war, we would be all friends.

"God bless you!"

Chapter 2

Military Training

Garmisch, Bavaria

I read my draft notice, "New recruits will be met at Garmisch's railroad station. Busses will take them to the barrack grounds." It gave no details on which bus to take or where.

The train pulled into Garmisch's station. There was a sergeant at the ramp wearing the red mountain artillery stripes. He grabbed me without hesitation. "Meet Hugo Geiger, he's new and comes from Berchtesgaden. You look alike." We were both still in civilian clothes. How did he know where we planned to go? But he seemed friendly. I didn't know he would be the last friendly sergeant I would see for months. I shook hands with Hugo Geiger, who was a good looking fellow about my height. I wondered why Hugo came wearing awful custom-made black Bavarian leather pants and an embroidered Tyrolean jacket. Did he want to start his life that way as a recruit? I wouldn't have wanted to be caught in that showy outfit. Hugo arranged his blond hair neatly in long waves, probably to attract the curiosity of young ladies. That was a good reason to stick with him. We were told to board a military bus, but Hugo's loud voice was annoying and caught the attention of older soldiers.

"I am from Berchtesgaden which is much prettier. How do you like this town?" he yelled, causing me to check the other soldiers. I had to assume they all lived in Garmisch or in Partenkirchen, the next town. Hugo was insulting. Should I talk to him?

"If you don't believe me, then tell me, why did Hitler build his summer home in Berchtesgaden and not in Garmisch!" I didn't know Berchtesgaden. That annoyed him. That I knew Garmisch fairly well made it worse. My parents took me to various events of the 1936 Winter Olympic games held in Garmisch and my brothers served in the artillery barracks. We visited them frequently.

"Hitler knows," Hugo insisted, "why he likes Berchtesgaden. Garmisch is flashy and is over-run by tourists. Have you heard of Hotel Geiger in Berchtesgaden? That's my parent's hotel. We've owned it for generations." I had heard of Hotel Geiger, but I wouldn't tell Hugo. My grandfather stayed there and claimed it was the finest hotel in Bavaria, and my grandfather knew every good hotel in Bavaria. I looked around and worried about the veterans on the bus. Garmisch was their home base. The faces were stoic and turned toward the windows. They seemed to ignore us. We were civilians and what we said wasn't important. They knew we would learn manners soon, but we didn't.

The bus passed through Garmisch's fashionable main street. Many show windows had even gaudier Bavarian outfits on display than Hugo's. Cafe chairs were outside of the hotels for tourists to enjoy the fresh air and fancy pastry. The ride to the barrack buildings took twenty minutes. There were new modern buildings side by side and stables stretched along the foothills of Germany's highest mountain, the Zugspitze. At the barracks gate a top-sergeant pulled us civilians from the bus. He yelled, "This is the most disgusting sight I have ever seen. You are nothing!" I thought he must have been referring to Hugo's garish outfit, but he didn't like any of us. He sent us to a nearby building. My life as recruit had begun.

Inside we heard yelling, "Take your stinky civilian clothes off! When you are in uniform, at least you'll look alike, which is absolutely Nothing. That is exactly what you are. Nothing!" The sergeant who fitted us into uniforms kept insulting us. To my surprise, Hugo took the insults in stride. He even thanked the sergeant for the "fine" trousers which were the worst in the inventory. Hugo handed him his new gaudy Bavarian outfit, the sergeant held the leather pants up and away as if they stank. Hugo didn't mind. He adjusted much better than I did.

The first assembly was called and held in the barrack courtyard. We were now in uniform. A grim looking sergeant walked up and down the long rows and inspected us. "Who has an *Abitur* certificate? Step forward!" Hugo and I stepped forward. I was sure our *Abitur* certificate would help us for the first time. At least they acknowledged higher education. I was wrong. "I want everybody who wears eyeglasses to also step forward! You can read and, therefore, you all must be intelligent. I want the intelligent people to start in the mule stable. Cleaning mule shit takes intelligence. I want these stables to look like paradise on earth. Do you understand me?" We yelled, "Yes!" but apparently not loud enough. We yelled six more times. "Yes, Sir!"

They downgraded higher education! That didn't make sense. They taught us in school we were equal. Socrates and Aristotle taught that analyzing and critique was a virtue and appropriate. I figured since uniforms made us all look alike, we were even more equal and explained my thoughts to the stable sergeant. He was not impressed.

"You are not equal, and don't dare question orders! I want you to run five rounds around the building!" I ran the five rounds, came back, coughed and raised the same question again, adding, "What they teach in my school is right." I was insistent. "Five more rounds!" yelled the sergeant. I didn't mind. I liked running. I was good at it. I only wanted to be helpful. Why didn't he understand my suggestions?

From that first day on, whenever I opened my mouth I was ordered to do special drills, sometimes they lasted way past midnight. I sat in the kitchen and peeled potatoes, or I had to clean toilets until they were spotless. After finishing, the sergeant inspected the toilets and always declared my work useless. He claimed the toilets were dirtier than before. He made me use my toothbrush. "A smaller brush is better and takes care of details. You have trouble with large brushes." My frustration mounted. I thought making me use my toothbrush to clean toilets bordered on sadism. My enthusiasm for the military slowly evaporated, but I kept my desire to earn a bravery medal alive. The Alpine Edelweiss flower embroidered on my right arm sleeve was the emblem of the famous elite First Mountain Division. I was proud of that.

Between punishment drills, I learned a few useful things, like how to dismantle a 7.5 cm cannon in minutes and carry cannon parts over rocky slopes to the top of the Zugspitze mountain where we put them back together under hazardous circumstances. Since physical education was my hobby in school, I was competitive, and my cannon team became the fastest. I also liked sharp shooting and took a third prize. After that, they assigned me the oldest rifle, numbered 1309, to cause me severe anguish. Number 1309 was the rustiest rifle in the arsenal. She was especially rusty inside the barrel. There was no way to remove its rust. Every rifle inspection ended with me being sent to the stable and to clean mule dung. The stable sergeant would be waiting for me. He was glad to see me because he didn't like me. He didn't like anybody.

"Wash the stable!" he yelled. "One learns the mule's mentality by washing his home." The mules paid no attention, but were capable of kicking with deadly accuracy. They didn't like me there and often attempted to kick me in the head. I decided to outsmart them and climbed around them. Most horses in the stable were friendlier and much more mellow, but most of the animals were sure-footed mules, because they were better suited for the mountain artillery. They could carry incredible loads and managed the narrow mountain path without ever slipping. After I had cleaned stable a hundred times, I began to wonder why Hugo never did stable duty. It occurred to me that he kept his mouth shut and that was smart. But I just couldn't keep my mouth shut.

Hugo explained, "I want to be a reserve officer, and I'll do anything to become one." He had a custom-made, light grey officer's cap in his bag, which he would often put on and stand before a mirror turning his head and admiring himself. We called him Dandy, but even that didn't bother him.

Once, in the barbershop, Hugo argued with the soldier-barber not to cut his blond locks too short. He argued as if his life depended on it. The man said, "Your hair will be cut according to regulations." When he finished, Hugo's hair was still longer than ours. Hugo told me later that he bribed the barber. He was smart. I still had to learn some tricks. Applying simple logic in military training was almost useless

We were in our fourth month of training. I hated every sergeant and their disgusting cynicism. The extra drills made me totally disgusted, so I visited the administration office and requested a transfer to combat. I didn't disclose that I hated training. "Most rules and regulations we have here in training are out-dated," I explained to the concerned master sergeant, "I cannot comply. It does-n't make sense, and I want to go to combat"

The master sergeant listened and showed concern with a stern face. I continued, "I came here to fight a war and not to do senseless training forever. Please send me out!" I used my best logic, citing instances like toilet cleaning and stable washing. The master sergeant shook his head. He did not understand and threw me out.

"Request denied!" he yelled furiously.

Surprisingly, Hugo and I were called to the office a month later. They may have changed their minds, I thought.

"You both will be transferred," announced the master sergeant. "You will receive training in a preliminary reserve officers course," he said. I was horrified. Please, don't give me additional training! "You'll leave tomorrow for Albertville, in France," he ordered.

"Why me?" I responded spontaneously. The master sergeant's face froze. He thought for an eternity. Thinking appeared difficult. He tried to refresh his memory. Wasn't that the incorrigible recruit who questions every-thing? How many times did this recruit make him correct the punishment schedule? The master sergeant hated office work and now the scheduling routine would become easier.

"Did you ask, 'Why me?'" He poked a finger into my chest. "I'll give you an explanation. Unfortunately, you have a lousy learning certificate, called the *Abitur*. That stinky piece of shit-paper supposedly certifies intelligence, which you don't have, or I fail to notice. That depresses me. That paper makes you eligible for the reserve officers training course. It is outrageous! Army regulations, yes, need corrections! Neither of you is material to become an officer. Anybody can see that. Come back tomorrow morning and get the travel papers!"

Hugo and I clicked heels and simultaneously shouted: "Yes, Sir!" and left the office. Outside Hugo scolded me. "Why do you question him? Let's get out of here. Forget him! Keep your mouth shut, at least this once, until we are gone. It's OK to become officers."

Chapter 3

Officer's Training School
France

The next morning back in the office we were surprised that the master sergeant smiled broadly. He promoted us to corporals and handed us the travel documents. We received two silver stripes and had to fasten them on our shoulder lapels. They signified reserve officer candidates. The master sergeant kept smiling. I assumed he was glad to see us leave.

Without wasting time we rushed to Garmisch's railway station. A cattle train sat on a sidetrack and was destined to go to France. We climbed in and found nothing, no furniture, beds or benches, only a wooden floor which had long splinters made by real cattle. I spread my blanket, but the splinters pinched through. "Where, you suppose, is Albertville?" I asked the sergeant who took our names. He didn't know either. "Southern France, maybe, near the Alps," he ventured.

We were now corporals and cadets. Fifteen other cadets gradually came into our wagon. We waited, for what seemed forever, until our train rocked and began to rumble from Garmisch. I wondered if I would ever return. It was my first time out of the country. The train stopped frequently and had to be pushed onto a side track for a faster train to pass. Sometime, we heard air-alarm sirens. Delays didn't bother me. Who cared where Albertville was, or how long it would take to get there.

Two older guys lay next to me. They kept away from everybody. We talked after a while, and I found out they were Nazi Party members. They had had comfortable city administration jobs but were now unhappy, since they had thought they were draft-exempt.

"They seem to need everybody, even us old guys."

"How come they're sending you to the mountain artillery?"

"We had one choice, the SS. But they didn't want us. The infantry didn't want us either, we were too old." I wondered about the elite status of our mountain division.

"Look, there is the Rhine River!" shouted somebody from the open door. We pushed our way to the door and watched the disappointing sight, a slowly flowing dirty brown river.

"I thought France would look different," said a fellow with an Austrian accent. He looked disappointed. "France is different," I assured him. But how would I know? I had never been in France. I always enjoyed an opportunity to show off. It was a temptation left over from school. I just gambled and said it, hoping that France's countryside would change. But it didn't. I had bet against myself. A guy from Ulm didn't help my dilemma,

"France is no good anyway, not worth fighting for," he said in a heavy Swabian accent. Nothing looked different outside. I stretched to rest on the floor and hoped for a change of landscape by morning. Hugo rested at my feet. Before we left, we heard rumors that most recruits would be transferred to Russia.

"I wonder if they were transferred to Russia?" I asked Hugo.

"They will be in combat sooner than we are. That's for sure."

"France is nothing!" repeated the guy from Swabia. "We won't get a chance to fight for a long time." The real war was in Russia. I hadn't seen a newspaper in months and had no time to read one. We had amplifiers in our barrack dormitory that brought news and told about a troop build-up in England. Nobody paid attention.

A guy spread a blanket next to mine. He was also older and had a bravery medal. There was one cadet with combat experiences. "My name is Fritz," he introduced himself politely. I wondered where he came from. I guessed him to be about seven years older, and I started a conversation. He seemed mature without showing superiority. "I overheard your conversation," he stated, "I am also from Munich." In spite of the age difference, I knew we would become friends. We talked about our hometown.

I focused on Fritz's gold-framed, Hitler Youth emblem. I was curious. He wore the emblem below his iron cross. He explained, "I joined the Hitler Youth before 1933, the gold frame indicates that, and we old-timers can wear the Hitler Youth medal on our uniform. Hitler Youth was fun at that time. We left the city and as we rode bicycles we played war games in the forest. I found comraderie that I hadn't known before. Those were the good old days," he sighed. "Later, I became a Hitler Youth regional leader and in 1936 was transferred to Berlin where I worked directly with Baldur von Schirach in his administration." I wondered why he came here. It seemed strange, coming from a high government position to being a cadet. Fritz noticed that I was puzzled.

"I volunteered to become a soldier. I thought I owed that to my fatherland." His explanation sounded simple but didn't satisfy me. Maybe he would tell me later. I didn't press for the rest of the story. Instead I told him about my boot camp experiences.

"You'll find the reserve officer training course to be fun! Our training is on a higher level." Fritz leaned back and tried to brush my skepticism away.

"Why do they use sadists for training recruits? I can't understand that."

"Trainers become a special breed. Unfortunately they are like a club." Fritz frowned, "That makes it worse. Trainers stick together. How they manage to stay away from combat bothers me."

France still looked the same. We were in our third day, and nothing had changed, not even the buildings. But they showed French writings. We enjoyed the frequent stops. France was more peaceful. It was not bombed and war-torn like Germany. That was different.

Albertville, France

The city of Albertville was larger than expected. She nestled into the valleys of Savoy in the high mountains. We left the train and made five rows, three in a row. A master sergeant led the small group from the station to the city barracks bellowing German Alpine songs which echoed through the narrow streets of Albertville. The French people rightfully shook their heads. Our singing was embarrassing. While I sang, I admired the ornate medieval trade signs dangling from the sides of shops. Our future trainer, Lieutenant Baumgartner waited at the barrack gate.

I disliked him at once. The color of his face was too pale. Was he healthy? He was athletic, though, and tall. He greeted us with a strained smile. He had no medals. How can an officer, obviously without combat experience, be in charge of training future officers effectively? That made no sense. He must be a coward to be here.

An hour after we settled in the barracks, Hugo brought more first-hand information. A clerk in the office confided in him, "Lieutenant Baumgartner is cynical. He hates every officer cadet. He is tough and becomes a sadist."

"Why is he training?" Hugo asked his source.

"He is effective and can stay forever. He is considered an indispensable trainer." The following day, in our first lesson, I asked questions using my best analytical logic. During our instruction on artillery science, I told the lieutenant, that his last statement made no sense and calmly stated my reasons.

He looked at me long and hard. Without answering, he lifted a slim notebook from his left upper pocket. While his eyes penetrated mine he asked in a barely audible voice, "What is your name?"

"I beg your pardon, lieutenant. I didn't hear you." I stayed seated.

In my boarding school when I interrupted the lecture to the delight of my classmates, I always repeated the question until I received an answer. But in the military, that didn't work. I believed future reserve officers had the right to ask questions. I was wrong. My fourteen colleagues shook their heads. The lieutenant asked for my name again.

I stated my name and rank and kept smiling pleasantly. The lieutenant wrote the name on top of page one in his notebook and stared. He walked back to his desk, grabbed a heavy book and dropped it on my table with a bang.

"That is the army book of rules and regulations. Everything you'll find there is carved in stone and will outlast the Ten Commandments. Spell me your name again! Ah, that sounds like a French name?" I detected cynicism. France was an enemy. Perhaps he blames me for that. Could he trust someone with a French name?

"Lieutenant Baumgartner," I began to reason, "I asked you if you believe that today's army regulations are still up to date. Don't you think that at least a few revisions should be made? A regulation kept too long becomes inflexible and distorts the desired standard. Therefore, vigilance must be applied and compromises should be made. The mistakes in this book, which you kindly handed to me, certainly contain many innocent oversights. But used frequently, these oversights become methods, that cannot be accepted. That must be changed. I am sure . . . ." The lieutenant waved his arm before me. He made me shut up. Without saying a word, he scribbled under my name, wrote until page one was full, and continued to the bottom of page two without ever looking up.

Annoyed, I continued, "Frankly, too many rules in this book make no sense." I tried to sound sincere, but sounded angry. The lieutenant remained calm. He stepped back and pointed at the book before me.

"I want you to read this book tonight, and we'll discuss the content tomorrow, intelligently." A red glow of anger showed behind his face. He shouted using the force of his full voice, "Tomorrow, I want you to explain all 'mistakes' you found in this book! We'll go through the entire book, every rule from the beginning to the end."

"The entire book?" I asked perplexed, "I can't read the entire book in one night."

"Yes, I want you to memorize the entire book! And, from now on, this book will be your only reading material. You seem to be very smart, so it won't be hard for you."

"I beg your pardon, Sir, reading a book of this size in one night is not possible." I hoped my comrades would support me and lifted the heavy book and showed them. But they pretended not to notice. That made me angrier.

"Lieutenant, I volunteered to the army for one reason only." Now I stood up. "I volunteered to be in combat to prove myself." My face was red. I continued, "Your request to memorize an outdated book will never earn me a medal. The order to read a book of this size in one night borders on sadism. Why are you allowed to teach when you don't even have combat experience?" I pointed my finger at his empty uniform jacket. That was the end of the lieutenant's patience. All hell broke loose.

"I am in charge here and not you!" he cursed non-stop. He yelled so loud that an alarmed top sergeant rushed into the room to investigate. The lieutenant turned to him and ordered him to take me out for some boot-camp style punishment which was to last three hours. The top sergeant marched me to an exercise field. I was used to three hours of punishment exercise from boot camp. It was normal.

The next day in class I wasn't allowed to open my mouth. We did not discuss the book. I opened my mouth once, the lieutenant interrupted the lecture, ordered the top sergeant in and made him march me to the exercise field. Punishment drills consisted of running, frequent knee bends, then push-ups, and were longer and more severe on the second day.

Fritz's positive prediction about the high level officer-cadet training went out the window. Toilet cleaning and potato peeling were not yet on my schedule. I was angry and disgusted and, increasingly, I found my comrades very impatient with me. Fritz finally took me aside.

"You punish yourself. Why do you keep questioning your superiors? They'll expel you from the course. Realize a superior must teach discipline. The German army won't win the war without discipline. You are a bonehead and your behavior makes you look stupid. I don't agree with every military rule either but it doesn't make sense to swim against the flow. The lieutenant told us he'll punish all of us if you continue with your insubordination. He asked me to tell you that." That made me furious.

"The bastard wants you to turn against me," I shouted. "He wants to break my back. But he won't succeed, I guarantee you! You can tell him that!"

"You are a stubborn ox." Fritz shook his head. He didn't know what to do. Recently elected as our spokesperson, he first felt honored, but now, he didn't want the responsibility. Totally exhausted, I cursed him and threw myself on my straw mattress and sobbed desperately.

"I won't change. Even if all of you turn against me! It's none of your business. I am doing it my way. That jerk can't get away with treating people like idiots. He doesn't show respect!" I lay on my stomach and felt a hand resting on my shoulder. It was Hugo.

"I don't agree with you but I'll stick with you," he simply said. I grabbed his hand in desperation. At least there was one friend. The others ignored me. Hopelessly depressed, I was near a nervous breakdown. I heard them talking. They cussed the lieutenant and that consoled me. The next day the lieutenant became even harder. But that made me harder, too.

A month later, I was assigned to help with the training of new recruits. They had live hand grenade lessons. I was glad to get away from the lieutenant for an entire day. The lecture began. A top-sergeant showed the recruits a live hand grenade and how to pull the grenade's cord. He repeated the simple method countless times, and always repeated how dangerous a grenade was. He made them count to three, and then act like they would throw the grenade toward a target. After an hour of theory lesson we marched to an open field. The top-sergeant marked a line. I was to stand behind him. The recruits lined up forty meters away. Every recruit, one by one, had to run to the firing line. Now my job began. I showed them, once again, where the cord was and told them how to pull the cord, count to three, and quickly throw the now ignited grenade. Everything went fine until recruit number fifty-two ran to the firing line. He looked very nervous and never lifted his eyes. I wasn't sure if he even listened to my instructions. I handed him the hand grenade. He held it as far from his body as he could.

The sergeant stepped before him, "Pull the cord!" he ordered, and the recruit pulled the cord, but did nothing. He kept staring. His face went blank. Two seconds elapsed, and he still didn't count. The sergeant grabbed the now ignited grenade and attempted to throw it. But it was too late. The grenade exploded in his hand while he clutched it to his chest. He turned sideways, away from the recruit, fell forward on his stomach and wiggled desperately.

His back seemed unharmed. I was paralyzed and hoped he was not hurt. There was no visible wound on his back. I jumped and turned him half over, now I saw his chest was ripped wide open. He still clutched the wooden part of the hand grenade to his chest with a bloody hand. I had never been close to a dead person before. But the bloody open chest left no doubt. He had taken the brunt of the explosion. For the first time I saw a dead, mangled body. The sight was awful. Soldiers ran to me while I was holding the sergeant's lifeless body. The recruit who caused the dreadful accident sobbed and knelt next to me, unhurt.

"Are you all right?" An officer grabbed my shoulder.

I felt pain in my left leg. "Yes Sir, I guess so," I said in spite of the pain and continued to hold the dead sergeant. Two soldiers pushed me over and attended to the sergeant. I fell sideways and clutched my left leg. The two soldiers now attended me. "The grenade hit him, too," one said and pulled my torn trousers up. I heard the ambulance arrive. They moved the dead sergeant carefully inside, and then laid me next to him. I was in shock and felt no pain anymore. The recruit who caused it walked away still sobbing.

We sped to the army hospital. The horns blared their up and down sound. As soon as we got there, somebody ripped my trousers and examined my wounds. "They are minor," I heard him say.

It took a doctor more than an hour to pull the small splinters from below my skin. He worked and talked constantly. He wanted to know how the accident happened. He wasn't satisfied with my explanation. I was trembling from shock. His talking brought me back. I was surprised how little there was to explain. He asked for my civilian profession.

"Student of medicine," I told him proudly. That surprised him and he became curious. A thought came to my mind. Could I become an army doctor and get away from Lieutenant Baumgartner and his damned reserve officers' course? I asked the young, seemingly intelligent doctor bluntly. "Do you think I can still transfer to the military medical corps? Yes, I want to become a medical doctor." He didn't answer, he just said that the small wounds would heal quickly.

The next morning while he removed my bandages he asked innocently, "Do you really want to be a colleague of mine?" I felt somehow I could trust him. Slowly, I began confiding my problems. I told him about my miserable experiences during training and described fully the evil character of Lieutenant Baumgartner.

"I am not sure if I can recommend the life of a military doctor. It's not easy, either. You must always conform, so, judging from what you tell me, the military life is not for you, not even the life of a military doctor. I strongly suggest you wait until the war is over and become a civilian doctor. You cannot transfer to the medical corps, anyway. I checked that last night. You spent too much time in artillery officer training. You should have enlisted to the medical corps before you volunteered to the artillery."

I was disappointed and hurt that he had rejected me. The night before I dreamt I was wearing a white coat and worked in this hospital. But it was just a dream, and now I enjoyed my comfortable hospital bed. The doctor seemed happy with the healing progress of my leg. He would soon dismiss me.

I hated to return to the reserve officer's course. I wanted to stay and complained once more about the nonsense in training. "Even my shooting is poor," I explained, "because they won't exchange my rusty, ancient rifle. I have to aim a meter to the left and a meter down to hit the black center. It is disgusting." The doctor listened patiently.

"I may be able to help. You have diminished eyesight and need shooting glasses. You should go and see an eye specialist. But there is only one in the area, and he is in Lyon." I became offended. There was nothing wrong with my eyesight. I had won third prize in a contest with a good rifle. I wanted to tell him that but something told me not to. Use your brains, for heaven's sake. Swallow your stupid pride! Take his advice! And go to Lyon! A tingle went down my spine. For me a tingle always confirmed an important inner thought. I began pondering the suggestion. If I go to Lyon, I'll miss several days with Lieutenant Baumgartner and his course.

I swallowed hard. "If you think, my eye sight is bad, doctor, maybe I should go to Lyon," I said pretending to be grateful. The doctor left the room and came back with a notepad showing his name printed on top. He wrote an order to see the eye doctor in Lyon, and then released me. Still pale and wobbling I reported to Lieutenant Baumgartner. "I am very glad to be back, Sir," I lied and showed him my bandaged leg.

"Did you enjoy your vacation in the hospital with these minor scratches?"

The lieutenant showed no mercy, nor sympathy. I didn't expect either, but I was mad. If the hand grenade had killed me, he wouldn't have given a damn. Steaming inside, I wanted to ask him exactly that, but I decided to use a different strategy. I said, "The hospital doctor gave me an order for an eye examination," and handed him the papers the doctor had given me. Lieutenant Baumgartner looked suspicious. I had to admit he was smart. He immediately suspected a scheme behind this request.

"Do you want more vacation? Is that what it is? Travel to Lyon, hey?"

"No Sir. The doctor was sure, I have diminished eyesight based on my poor shooting record." I clicked my heels to enforce the point. The lieutenant looked straight into my face.

"By the way, you did a decent job at the hand grenade drill," he sounded serious. "But, no, you can't go. You missed an important part of my lecture." He stayed firm. "We started a new chapter while you were gone. We began learning adjustments to artillery fire and how to calculate wind velocity. You can't miss that." He turned, "Perhaps I'll let you go in a few weeks." That surprised me. Maybe he wasn't that bad. It turned out better than I had hoped. "Does your leg still hurt?" Now he sounded almost concerned. I was going to say, "Yes, my leg still hurts," but the lieutenant didn't wait for my answer. "I want you to attend tonight's night maneuver," he said abruptly and motioned for me to leave. Was he sick? He looked awfully pale, more than before. According to schedule we had cannon exercises. Afterwards my leg felt numb, but I could rest until ten that night.

At ten o'clock, the entire regiment lined up in the darkness of the barrack courtyard, turned right, and marched singing into the streets of Albertville to keep the tired French population from their well deserved sleep. I had to carry a steel ammunition box on my shoulder that carved a deep line into my skin. After five kilometers, the assignment changed. I became a messenger, thank God, and got rid of the heavy ammunition box. I ran from place to place delivering messages and felt my leg hurting. It became swollen, and I was tired. The long hospital stay had taken its toll. After running messages until three o'clock in the morning, I received my last order to reach a platoon four kilometers away and wait for their return message. Everybody at the central command post looked tired.

"To hell with that!" I mumbled to myself and hobbled 200 meters until I was out of sight from the central command post. I sat down with a large boulder against my back and rubbed my sore left leg. Leaning further back and rubbing my leg, I slowly drifted into a deep sleep. I remembered my last thoughts, why do I need to become a reserve officer? It's not worth the trouble.

Something startled me, I woke up and checked the darkness. How long did I sleep? Perhaps an hour, maybe more. My watch had no illumination. I began thinking. Delivering the message and returning would have taken at least an hour. My leg was stiff, but it didn't hurt. I got up, stretched, and jogged back to the maneuver command post, not far away. On the way, I frantically figured what to say. Much popped into my mind, but nothing was satisfying. I got there and saw they were in the process of leaving. An officer listened to my confused message, which didn't make much sense even to me. He didn't respond. Maybe he was satisfied.

The horizon already showed the morning lights. We marched silently back. The rhythmical click of boots tapping on asphalt sounded eerie.

The last order at the barracks was, "The first class begins at 2:00 P.M.!" shouted the master sergeant. Where was Lieutenant Baumgartner? It dawned on me that I hadn't seen him all night. Why didn't he attend the night maneuver? Nobody seemed to miss him.

The next day we waited in class for an hour. The board still showed a sentence explaining wind velocity. Where was Lieutenant Baumgartner? We waited.

A nice young lieutenant came. "I am Lieutenant Berger. I shall conduct today's lecture. Lieutenant Baumgartner became ill and is in a hospital in Lyon." We grinned. Thank God! Hopefully the bastard is so sick that he will never come back! The new lieutenant was of medium size, not very athletic and not as sharp as Lieutenant Baumgartner. I was too sleepy to pay attention to him or the lecture.

The next morning, when we assembled in the barrack court, Lieutenant Berger immediately called my name.

"Step forward, cadet!" I stepped forward and planted myself before him. "Weren't you ordered to take a special message to platoon IV when the night maneuver took place? They told me you never arrived and the platoon officer had to wait an additional hour. Where were you, I ask?"

"Yes, Sir," I replied. "I talked to a sergeant who relayed the message to an officer at the central maneuver's post." I lied and wondered how long that lie would stand.

"What was the sergeant's name, and who was the officer?"

"They didn't tell me. I was in a hurry and forgot to ask."

"You forgot? I shall find out! In the meantime, you and I will do special exercises. I'll conduct the punishment drill myself, and I promise you, I'll break your stubborn neck."

"Turn right!"

The master sergeant took the class, and they turned left. Lieutenant Berger and I marched side by side past the gate. We marched, lockstep, to the exercise field. There, he ordered me to run four rounds circling the field. I trotted and remembered that, according to army rules and regulations, "A drill commander must perform every exercise as well in a drill." For the first time I appreciated the fact that Lieutenant Baumgartner had made me read the entire book. It might finally pay off.

Far back I heard the lieutenant screaming, "Lie down!" I did so slowly, observing that he himself did not lie down.

He walked toward me. "Fifty push-ups!" he yelled, but he did not do a single push up. He stood next to me.

I'll fix you, you little bastard, I thought; aren't you supposed to do the same exercises? "Fifty knee bends!" he ordered. I first knelt on my knees and rested ten seconds.

"Lie down!" the lieutenant screamed, utterly disgusted. I moved forward, laid down, and didn't move. He ordered me to run. I trotted and almost walked. There was nothing the new lieutenant could do. He was furious. I understood why the rules and regulations demanded the trainer must do the same exercises, because he determines the speed and rhythm. But this lieutenant didn't do that. He allowed me to set my own pace. I was in charge, and I set a very slow speed.

It was different with Lieutenant Baumgartner. He enjoyed drill exercises. He started fast, did everything with us, and tried to wear us out. Baumgartner was strong like an ox. Some of us collapsed, but when he saw that, he would accelerate the pace, pretending not to notice the exhaustion.

I felt my left leg began to hurt after two hours of this soft drill. The hospital stay made me weak. I decided to go one more hour; that was enough. I trotted away thinking, I hope that embarrasses you, my little lieutenant. You should have read the book of rules and regulations just like I had to.

When we were in the third hour, I began to drag my left foot and ran even slower. The lieutenant screamed, furiously, "Lie down!" I collapsed and didn't move. "Run! I want you to run faster!" Finally, he began running, his face purple from the yelling. He ran fast. But it was too late! I allowed him to set his speed and run away. Then I began to walk.

The lieutenant made a curve and returned. "You are the laziest SOB I have ever seen. One hundred knee-bends!" he ordered and counted fast, indicating the speed he wanted. He did not do a single knee bend. That was fine with me. I ignored him and exercised slowly. Serves you right, I thought, while his count became faster. At knee-bend fifty-three, I fell to my right, clutched my left knee, and pretended to be in pain while I moved from side to side.

"What's the matter?" the lieutenant sounded concerned.

"I am sorry, Lieutenant, but I can't do anymore." He knelt next to me.

"Why? What is it?" I grimaced and enjoyed seeing his worried face.

"Just let me lay, Lieutenant. I must stretch. I have cramps in my left leg."

"Do you have cramps often? You didn't look tired, the way you spared yourself."

I didn't answer, I just kept groaning and pretended to be in agony.

When it seemed the right time, I showed some recovery. "Don't forget, Lieutenant, I was recently wounded. A hundred little pieces of shrapnel are still stuck in my left leg. I was released from the hospital only a couple of days ago. Maybe you didn't know." That hit home.

The lieutenant's face turned pale. He began thinking about how he could explain the drill? He remembered that according to the rules and regulations he would be questioned. Why did he order a wounded soldier, just released from a hospital, three hours of excessive drill? Rules and regulations stated it was not permitted. I was glad to have read that paragraph two months ago. I grimaced, pretending my pain increased, and watched his face. He looked concerned. I decided to rub it in even more and made my leg jerk feverishly. The lieutenant sat down and massaged my leg. The massage felt good. I told him so.

"Lieutenant, did you see a report about the fatal hand grenade exercise?" I knew every officer had to read the report. "I happen to be the soldier who was hit by the shrapnel. I assisted the lesson."

I let that sink in. "Can you help me, please, I need to get up?" He squeezed his shoulder under my arm. "I'll walk you home." He was determined to help. I hobbled next to him and put my weight on his shoulder. Then an idea popped up.

"Lieutenant, you have a paper on your desk directed to Lieutenant Baumgartner. It's an order for me to see a specialist in Lyon." I groaned, but neglected to add that the specialist was an eye doctor.

"No, I didn't see the order, but it seems obvious that you need to see a specialist. I'll look for the order when we get back." When we came closer to the barracks, I began walking. The lieutenant was pleased because it spared him embarrassment. I hoped he appreciated the gesture and would let me go to Lyon.

"You should take the afternoon off and rest your leg. I'll look for your doctor's order." He left me at the entrance to my barrack building.

"Are you sure you can travel tomorrow?" It sounded like a done deal.

I sensed the little guy would give me the travel pass to get me out of his hair. I shook his hand gratefully, "Thank you, Lieutenant, for bringing me to the door. I am sure I'll be able to travel. Thank you very much, Lieutenant."

Alone in my barrack room, I fell on my bed and began to worry. Would he sign my travel pass? Surely he will see the doctor's order was to get shooting glasses and not to see a specialist. Lieutenant Baumgartner even made a notation, "Denied!" on top of the paper. What will this lieutenant do? I considered my chances.

Lieutenant Berger was a replacement officer. He didn't want me around to make trouble. He'll let me go to Lyon. That would make sense for both of us. My left leg was indeed swollen. He noticed that. He knew I wasn't supposed to go into a night maneuver or do three hour punishment drill. The book of rules and regulations did not permit either. The book wasn't so bad after all. I quit worrying and fell back on my bed.

Somebody knocked on my door. An orderly came and brought the signed travel papers. I relaxed. You guessed right, this time!

The door bounced open. My comrades stormed in and stared at me lying comfortably on my bed. I grinned and stayed in a restful position.

"Look at him! He was to do punishment drills, and now he rests, while we obedient soldiers serve the fatherland like slaves." They joked and fussed around. I pulled my tobacco pouch and rolled myself a tobacco cone full of awful, strong, black French tobacco. I lit the cigarette, exhaled leisurely, my lungs burned, and I coughed heavily.

"Tomorrow I'll travel to Lyon for medical reasons," I announced still coughing. The news hit them like the explosion of a bomb. They grouped around me.

"Are you serious?" At times I captivated them with audacity and gained their temporary admiration. "Yes. I am serious. I'll be on my way to Lyon tomorrow, and shall imagine how you sweat in the morning drill while I sit in a comfortable train compartment." A thought popped up, "I shall visit our beloved Lieutenant Baumgartner in his hospital in Lyon." That caused roaring laughter.

"Do you know where he is, which hospital he is in?" I didn't.

"Tell him, Hugo!" They grinned and Hugo whispered, face up close.

"Baumgartner is in the hospital for venereal diseases. He must stay in quarantine. The guy in the office told me. Yes! And you must visit him and bring him the very best wishes from us and our regards and hopes for his complete recovery which may never take place. We wish him a never-ending restful stay!" They danced and roared laughing. I was surprised. I didn't know. I really had no intention of seeing Lieutenant Baumgartner. I was just joking. But now I was committed, and to embarrass the bastard was tempting.

"Will they let me go inside a quarantine hospital and visit?"

"Who knows? You must try, promise, please!" They stood around excited. Hugo sat on my bed and composed the get-well letter. When he finished, everybody signed it.

Lyon, France

The next morning, I went to the railroad station before anybody got up, still afraid somebody might call my travel orders off. The ramp was already crowded, it seemed everybody wanted to board the train to Lyon. When it steamed in, I pushed through the crowd and landed in a compartment smelling of strong French tobacco. A bunch of farmers sat down behind me. Women held baskets full of food on their knees. One even had a live chicken. These people could have been German farmers, all hard working simple people. Men wearing Basque-style black caps ripped square pieces from a newspaper, poured tobacco on the paper squares and twisted them into a cone. The open end was lit while the crumpled end stuck in their mouth. The smoke smelled awful.

The women wore *babushkas* like our farmer-women at home. They looked anxious, like they didn't trust the situation, especially with a German soldier sitting next to them. After a while, they got used to me, and must have decided I was too young to be mean. The worried stares changed into smiles. They opened their baskets, pulled bread, cheese, and sausages from them. Slices of cheese and sausages were stuck on pocket knifes and passed around to everyone, including me. I blushed and hesitated, but they insisted that I share their breakfast.

I strained to understand them. I wished I had paid more attention to my French lessons in school. The more I listened, the more I understood. The subject was terrorists, and whether they would blow up the tracks. They also seemed to worry about Allied airplanes, and if they would bomb the train. We shared the danger, which I hadn't thought about. I relaxed and joined the conversation. They were intensely interested in what I tried to say and answered me politely. I figured each sentence, translated the words from German into French and talked without paying attention to the grammar. They answered slowly. The women enjoyed it the most. They laughed and kept talking. I told them my family name was French which they didn't believe at first but then, was rewarded with another slice of sausage. We laughed and became friends.

I felt good about my first meeting with French people. We weren't really enemies. They trusted me, and I could never betray anyone who trusted me.

The train ride took five hours. We rolled into Lyon's railroad station which seemed as big as Munich's. I wanted to look for the German 'Soldatenheim' which every major city had. A Soldatenheim was an oasis for German soldiers. There would be German beer and familiar food. They would also have a bed to stay overnight and somebody to help find my eye-doctor and Lieutenant Baumgartner's hospital.

Lyon's street traffic crawled, like Munich's. Painted blue streetcars rolled in the streets between tall, dark apartment buildings on slowly curved, narrow streets. The cars were mostly taxis. Lyon didn't have the war destruction like Munich. Soldiers walked with civilians in the crowd, not just German soldiers but also French soldiers who wore yellow-brown uniforms.

I had forgotten that the French Vichy was our Ally. Old French General Petain was President. My father said he was a tough general and fought the German army fiercely in the First World War. He signed the peace accord in 1940, and we became allies.

The Soldatenheim was like a YMCA. The clerk had a bed, but only for a limited time. "You must be out by Friday." That would be no problem. He even found the eye-doctor's office.

"But medical offices close at 5:00 P.M. You better hurry!"

"And if I don't get there in time, what happens?" I asked innocently.

"You must get your papers stamped and have a confirmation of when to return. If you forget and the military police catch you without the proper stamps, they don't fool around, they haul you to jail. Too many come to Lyon and overstay." That was very useful information.

I went to the eye-doctor's office shortly before 5:00 P.M. The nurse was sorry, but I was too late. Other soldiers waited, too. I wasn't upset when she stamped my document. I would get to stay an extra day and an extra night. That seemed like a gift from heaven. "The stamp doesn't tell the specific time?"

"Because everybody must come early in the morning. It's the only stamp I have."

I had all evening to check out Lyon's bars. As inexperienced as I was, they looked glamorous and unusual. They were filled with exotic women flirting not only with German soldiers, but with Moroccans, Algerians, Muslims, and French civilians. Long after curfew, I ducked passed the dark Soldatenheim desk. Nobody saw me.

The night's adventure caused me to oversleep the next morning. It was difficult to get up. It was fifteen minutes before noon when I arrived at the eye-doctor's office. "The traffic was terrible." I explained to the nurse, breathing heavily and pretending to have run up the many steps to the office. The nurse was not concerned.

"I am sorry, but the doctor has left for the day." She took my paper and without scolding me stamped it for the next day.

"Come at eight in the morning!" she reminded me with a stern face.

I was delighted to have one more day off. The whole afternoon was mine. I could tour the city, go sightseeing or visit one of the famous brothels which soldiers had described admiringly in a bar last night. I also had to visit Lieutenant Baumgartner. Now I was sorry I had promised to. My time in Lyon was too precious. I didn't want to waste time visiting the bastard in the hospital, but my friends' get-well letter stuck in my pocket. They would never forgive me if I didn't go.

"Why do you want to visit this hospital?" asked a friendly sergeant. He frowned when I named the hospital.

"Is there something wrong with you? You can't stay here!"

"No! Nothing! I just want to visit a friend, my dear lieutenant from Albertville."

"There are only bad guys in that hospital. And when they are released, they do an additional three days in jail." I was grateful for that information, and imagined how delighted my friends would be to know that our lieutenant would do additional time in jail. A bus took me to Lyon's outskirts and left me off at a modern hospital building where a German military flag swayed above the entrance. I walked past a sign: "For Officers Only," and walked passed into a spotlessly clean lobby.

"We don't allow visitors here," remarked a stout medical employee in a white coat. He must be a doctor.

"Did you say you were a friend of Lieutenant Baumgartner? And you came all the way from Albertville?" He grinned. "No visitor ever came that far. Let me see what I can do! Wait in the quarantine room." He pointed to a glass-enclosed waiting room with comfortable, modern furniture.

I waited forty minutes. I wondered if Lieutenant Baumgartner behaved as obnoxiously here as he did with us. I decided to wait fifteen more minutes and then leave. I saw him coming slowly down the hallway. He wore slippers and a heavy blue bathrobe and appeared paler than usual. He was really sick. I almost felt sorry for him. He broke into a pained smile when he saw me. He didn't shake hands. I beamed the biggest smile I could muster.

"Very glad to see you, Lieutenant," I lied, enjoying myself immensely.

I wondered how embarrassed he was. It didn't take him an hour to put his robe on. When they told him he had a visitor, he delayed as much as he could, but there was no way out.

"Nice of you to come, Corporal," he lied too, inspecting the floor and pushing a crumb away. I looked into his eyes and sensed that he wanted me to leave. But here I was. We settled down, and I produced my buddys' get-well letter. I relished the time it took for him to slowly open the envelope. Now he knew that everybody knew where he was. I felt devious satisfaction. The lieutenant only glanced at the letter and read superficially. He tried to make the best of the situation and started a long tale about how he was suddenly attacked by an intestinal virus. No hospital beds were available anywhere else. But he would be transferred to another hospital, which is equipped with everything he needed to treat his unusual ailment. My eyes hung on his lips. I didn't miss a word. I listened much more attentively than I ever did to his lectures. He noticed that.

I frequently nodded to confirm his lies, and again after each sentence. My face expressed the utmost sympathy. When there wasn't anything else to explain, he seemed drained. He could have asked about my comrades. But he didn't. I had nothing else to tell him either. He got up abruptly and smirked. I wondered if he knew why I came.

"It was very nice of you to think of me, Corporal." He lied for a last time.

"Please say 'hi' to the boys for me." With that he pushed the letter into his coat pocket and left. He wasn't allowed to shake hands.

The next day was Thursday. I slept in contentedly and had a late break-fast. I went sightseeing and went to the eye-doctor's office shortly before 4:30 P.M. The nurse recognized me. I used my best manners on her. She blushed and seemed flattered and unused to it.

"Why are you late again? The doctor leaves in a few minutes." She scolded me softly, her face was still red. I sensed a motherly touch in her voice. "Now you must promise to come early tomorrow morning. Friday is our busiest day." She took my document and had to look for a remaining space for her stamp. She turned the document sideways and found space in the right upper corner. She certainly had never read the book of rules and regulations.

It was to be my last night in Lyon. I already knew the best bars and stayed out until well after curfew. I used the dark path around the desk. But nobody was there. The next morning, I managed to get up and arrive at the doctor's office not much after 9:00 A.M. The nurse smiled and was pleased. She had hoped to experience more of my exquisite manners. I was tempted to kiss her hand.

"The doctor will see you at ten o'clock," she explained graciously.

I waited, but worried. What will happen if the doctor finds nothing wrong with my eyesight? I can't come back without shooting glasses. I spent an entire week in Lyon. I shuddered imagining the consequences.

At 10:00 she guided me into the doctor's office. The doctor, a thin man in his fifties, looked worn out and disinterested in his profession. He paid no attention to me or my story and asked me identify color charts.

"You are not color blind," he came to his first conclusion. I would have to do better than that. He inspected my eyes and said nothing. He made me sit on a dentist chair and rolled a machine up next to me holding unknown attachments.

"I want you to read all the letters on the poster on the wall, but wait until I get my lenses ready." That gave me time to memorize the letters. I focused feverishly to learn the smallest letters. He made me read through a window glass. "Read as far down as you can," the doctor ordered. I could read all letters easily, but I read to row four. "I can't see the other letters," I said.

"That's interesting," remarked the doctor. He tried different lenses. "Now, read again." My vision was slightly blurred, but I read past row four quickly and stopped at row six. The doctor exchanged lenses without commenting. The next set of lenses blurred my vision even more. I barely saw the letters. I recited from memory and quickly past row six. The doctor didn't care. He changed lenses. With the next set of lenses I couldn't even identify the letters in the first row. But I pretended relief and recited from memory all the letters down to the bottom row. The examination ended with doctor's conclusion, "You sure need shooting glasses!" I was relieved, and he was satisfied.

He went into an adjoining room and rummaged around. He came back holding a pair of shooting glasses with rubber straps attached and tied them behind my ears.

"Yes, your eyes are very bad," he said seriously." I wonder how you managed shooting without glasses. You also need glasses for everyday use. I'll write you a prescription. You can buy the regular glasses in a store. But your shooting glasses are courtesy of the German army."

I left the doctor's office after noon and hurried directly to the railroad station. Something inside of me warned me to go to Albertville quickly. The only train to Albertville had just left. A station soldier stamped my papers and complained how unreliable trains were these days.

"Terrorists attack them every day. They don't arrive on time anymore."

I was lucky. The Soldatenheim had my bed, but only for one more night. The eerie feeling that something was wrong in Albertville haunted me. I stayed in my room, went to bed early, and got up at 8:30 A.M. It was Saturday morning.

I went back to the railroad station and heard the train to Albertville was two hours late. With nothing else to do, I went to the station office and had my documents stamped to confirm the train's delay. I strongly sensed that things were not well in Albertville. Chills went down my spine. I had stayed in Lyon too long. The train finally came. I sank into a seat and hoped my nerves would recover by the time I got to Albertville. It was dark when I arrived.

I hurried to the barracks. The guard at the gate examined my papers with unusual thoroughness. He even knew my name. "I have a message for you, Corporal," he said. "You're to report to the office." Instead of reporting to the office, I went to my room. I wanted my friends to tell me if there was something wrong. They looked bewildered when they saw me, as if I had come from outer space.

"Where were you? They've been looking all over for you, even the military police came. Southern France is under alert and is searching for you. They say you are a deserter and should be shot on the spot."

"What?" I couldn't believe it. At least I was warned before I went to the office to report my return. "I got new shooting glasses." I pretended happiness showing the sergeant my new glasses. He looked worried.

"Didn't you have a pass for just three days? But you stayed a week? I have to call the master sergeant." He took the phone. I smiled when the master sergeant came.

"I must call the lieutenant," he said. "Wait here!" He shook his head and pushed me in a side room. I wondered if I would be arrested. Twenty minutes later the lieutenant arrived in full uniform regalia. He walked to the desk and sat down. "Where have you been corporal?" he asked calmly. "You left Monday with a three-day pass, and now it is Saturday evening. You overstayed three days!"

I tried to smile. "I needed the six days, Lieutenant. I have the shooting glasses." As calmly as I could, I unpacked my new glasses to show him.

"You didn't need an entire week to get glasses," he screamed. "That is impossible and you know it!" The short lieutenant planted himself before me. "You tried to run away. Then you thought about the mistake. Isn't that the truth?" He kept his voice low to sound threatening. "We will have you court martialed. The major will see you tomorrow morning in this office at 8:00 A.M. sharp. Dismissed!"

I searched my pockets for the documents as proof that I was innocent. I couldn't find them. He hadn't even asked for them. I had the stamps and could easily prove my weeks stay was justified. Where were my papers? I was horrified. That bothered me more than the screaming lieutenant. The book of rules and regulations stated that a lieutenant could not order a court martial, but a major could.

Back in my room, I searched my pockets and found my papers. I told my comrades what happened. Without much enthusiasm I related the visit with Lieutenant Baumgartner. I was too nervous to enjoy the story, and they were genuinely more concerned about what would happen to me than about Lieutenant Baumgartner. Hugo polished my belt to prepare me for the meeting with the major. I put an extra shine on my boots and dreaded the meeting. I passed the night sleepless.

At 8:00 A.M. sharp I stepped into the major's office, checking, one more time that my papers were in my side pocket. The lieutenant stood behind the major's chair. The major didn't look as grim as I had expected. It was Sunday morning and he seemed rather sleepy. He noted my papers and waved for me to hand them over. He examined them without saying anything, checked the stamps one by one, turned the document to its side, examined it again and shook his head. "Explain these stamps to me," he ordered calmly. I stepped next to him.

"The stamps are not in sequence," I explained and pointed out the significance of every stamp. The major listened, nodded, until he understood. He asked a few more question. He seemed satisfied.

When there were no more questions, he turned to the lieutenant. "These stamps seem to be in order. They explain why he stayed that long." The major didn't know what else to say. Neither did the nervous lieutenant. The commander got up and frowned. He had to say something more.

"Corporal, I have seen your training record. It is a disgrace. I don't want to hear one more complaint about you, you milk-face cadet. This time I'll give you a warning. But if I hear any more complaints about you, you'll be expelled, and I'll make sure, you'll never become an officer." The lieutenant and I left together. He was not satisfied.

"You have stable duty starting today at 8:00 P.M., and you continue watch for six nights, until next Saturday," he ordered, "You will also attend all daily lectures and the daily exercises. You had a week off on a self-induced furlough. You are rested and can do double-duty. I don't understand why it took you from Monday to Saturday to get shooting glasses. Dismissed!" The hallway walls echoed the lieutenant's shouted order. Soldiers passing us saluted sharply in fear of being yelled at as well. I clapped my heels sharply. Somebody up there likes me, I thought. My friends didn't expect me to come back. They thought I would be in the barrack jail.

The Sunday afternoon schedule included rifle shooting practice, which would be the first test of my shooting glasses. I worried. My new lenses were very thick and useless. What could I do?

We marched singing past the gate to the rifle range. While marching, I fingered my shooting glasses in my pocket and secretly pressed the right lens from the flexible steel frame. When we arrived at the rifle range I made sure the master sergeant stood to my left and would not be able to see my right eye. I strapped the shooting glasses over my ears. I aimed my cursed rifle a meter low of center and a meter to the left, then prayed before pulling the trigger. Please hit the black center, please!

The first shot hit the center. "Must be your lucky day," remarked the master sergeant as he inspected the result. The second and third shot also hit right on target. Everybody applauded, even the master sergeant. Nobody noticed that my right lens was not there. I smiled after taking the shooting glasses off.

I still had three hours until the 8:00 P.M. night stable watch. Stable watch consisted of four hours of walking up and down aisles, watching mules, cleaning stables and of four hours of sleep in an empty stall compartment. At 4:00 A.M. the real work of cleaning and feeding the animals began. If lucky, I would get a short rest before beginning the day schedule.

In full uniform and regalia I reported to the office at 8:00 P.M., my steel helmet on my head, the rifle and gas mask slung over my shoulder. The sergeant on duty wrote my name in the watch log. That done, I saluted and marched across the courtyard into the dark stable. The mules munched peacefully, ignoring me. First, I checked the stall compartment where I would sleep later. The hay was still reasonably fresh. Then I walked the dimly lit aisle and found a light at the far end. The light was unusual. Anything unusual, I had to report. I was glad that something unusual happened today during the boring watch. The mysterious light shined from below a door frame. Somebody must have forgotten to turn a light off. The door wasn't even locked. I pushed it open and walked into a room.

A middle aged soldier sat comfortably on a dingy bed in his underwear. He grinned and reached for a tin cup to offer me wine. The room had only the bed, an old stool, and a cast-iron stove with a blazing fire that produced enormous heat.

"Hey, what are you doing here?" I asked the man. He looked like an old farmer who had escaped civilian life. His bald head was pale from wearing a farmer's cap.

"I take care of sick animals," he reported in a familiar heavy Bavarian accent as he leaned back. He seemed glad to see me. "I have one sick horse. She's in bad shape. Take some wine." He pointed at the stove. Red wine boiled in an iron kettle.

I lifted the lid and observed how the wine bubbled. "The wine is too hot."

"I like hot wine," said the farmer and handed me his tin cup. I was tempted, but I was on guard duty and wasn't allowed to drink. "Have some," he kept encouraging me. "A little sip won't hurt. It'll warm you up."

"Where are you from?" I asked because his dialect sounded like mine. To be friendly I took his cup and poured boiling red wine into it until it burned my hand.

"I am from a place near Freising, if you know Freising," he answered.

"I was born in Freising," I told him. He was surprised. We clicked our metal cups.

"We'll toast to that." The rim of the cup burned my lips. I took my helmet off, hung it over his bedpost, and leaned the rifle against the wall.

It was too hot near the stove. Before I sat down, I took my heavy overcoat off and folded it neatly on his bed. The farmer watched me unconcerned.

"Don't worry. Nobody checks the stable. At least not in the first fifteen minutes of a watch." I figured he was right, I sat on his only wobbly stool.

"Do you live here full time?" I asked my new friend. "You don't do drills, or attend maneuvers, or anything?" He nodded affirmatively. I unbuttoned my jacket.

"They work me full-time with the animals. Because they know me, I am good." He grinned with pride in his skills. "I am not good for anything else, though. I can cure any animal. I look once and know what's wrong with them. But I can't shoot, I can't handle a rifle or throw a hand grenade. I would shoot myself before I hit a target or the enemy." He replenished my wine. It wasn't bad. "Sometimes, it gets lonely in here. They are lucky they have me and don't need a veterinarian. Nobody checks me. I haven't seen a sergeant in four weeks."

As soon as he said the word *sergeant*, goose bumps went down my spine. I emptied my cup quickly, got up, buttoned my jacket, and put on my overcoat. I didn't know what made me do it. I crammed my steel helmet over my head and went for my rifle leaning against the wall. At that moment, the door swung open. The master sergeant stood in the door frame and spread both legs in a threatening manner. He pointed at me, "What the hell are you doing here?"

I clicked my heels, shouted my name, rank, and my watch assignment and was glad that I was fully dressed. My cursed rifle still leaned against the wall, though. Did he notice?

He didn't. His face was red with anger. "Aren't you the freshest SOB I have ever seen? How dare you report to me. You are a deserter, you left your watch. I searched the entire stable for you for the last hour. You are not getting away with it this time! You are relieved! And report tomorrow at 8:00 A.M. to the captain's office. Dismissed! Get the hell out of my sight!"

"I beg your pardon, Sir." I tried to rectify the situation, "I saw this mysterious light and thought I should investigate like I am supposed to. That's why I am here in this room." My explanation didn't work.

"Shut up! You are dismissed. And not one more word. Save your explanation for 8:00 A.M. tomorrow!" He pointed at the shivering farmer still standing at attention in his underwear, holding his tin cup of hot wine. "I want you in the captain's office, too! You will be my witness." The farmer shivered, probably more from the excitement than from the cold that came from the open door.

The master sergeant walked away. I stayed behind him and thought about my chances in this new and dangerous situation. I had spent only ten minutes in the quarantine room. He claimed he searched an hour. I was lucky, he found me fully dressed. He didn't see me drinking wine and didn't notice the rifle still leaned against the wall. Perhaps there was a chance to get out of this situation.

Two hours before the meeting with the captain, I shined my belt for the fourth time and furiously polished my boots. I wanted to appear to be the cleanest soldier the German army had ever seen. I needed to be sharp or my case was hopeless. I had seen the captain only once before and assumed he was an administration officer with nothing to do. He didn't seem to care about the reserve officer-cadets.

Two seconds before 8:00 A.M. I entered the captain's office, clicked my heels immediately and saluted, stating name and rank before shutting the door. The captain ignored all of that. He sat behind a desk and studied my records. The lieutenant handed him papers. The master sergeant and the quarantine soldier stood at attention alongside the wall and watched. Nobody reacted to my salute.

I tried to analyze the situation. The captain looked unconcerned while he read. That was a good sign. He ignored me; that was not good. After he finished, he got up and held a sheet of paper in his hand as he confronted me.

"Do you know that two of your older brothers are my good friends?" he asked. I didn't answer. That had nothing to do with my case. He wore the iron cross on his uniform and an artillery combat medal, but most important, he smiled.

"I spent the coldest winter in Russia with your brother, Peter, halfway up the Elbrus Mountain in the Caucasus. We lived in an ice cave 12,000 feet above sea level." Why is he telling me that? I asked myself, becoming optimistic.

"We froze our butts. Actually, living in an ice cave is warmer than anybody thinks." He turned to the nervous lieutenant. "A punishment battalion was stationed next to us. Which I shall never forget." He fixed his eyes on the lieutenant's face. "Most of them were condemned soldiers and demoted officers. There was an entire U-boat crew, the commander and all his men who had disobeyed orders. Nobody wore insignias. It was hard to tell who once was an officer and who was not.

"These men were wild! They condemned them to death and were to be shot. But instead, they created a punishment unit and send them to the worst places in the war for them to die. None of them showed mercy or remorse, they fought fearlessly with brutality I had never seen before." The captain talked to the lieutenant, not to me.

"They made posts from dead frozen Russian soldiers and set them up inside their camp as direction signs. After they were shot but while they were still warm, they twisted their arms and hung signs from their necks, Stay Away, in both languages, Russian and German." The captain waved his arm in disgust. "The camp was a scary ghost town," he continued, "with hundreds of dead Russians standing as crude direction posts. They selected the most distorted bodies with bloody faces to make it even more scary; then stood around and laughed. Too scared, no Russian soldiers attacked them. A Russian patrol almost ran into our trenches, screaming, after they saw their dead comrades and believed they were ghosts. They held their arms up, giving up without protecting themselves. They could have been easy targets, but we didn't shoot. I wanted them to know there were differences in war. We were real soldiers; and not like these human animals in German uniforms." The captain backed off, turning to me.

"Why do I tell you this? Because I was asked to use the option of sending you to a punishment battalion like that. I decided against it. I have learned that men become sadists given the opportunity and the inspiration from like-minded characters. Men can become more cruel than animals.

"Officers in this camp were the worst. They were survivors who enjoyed their new kind of life. They drove each other by excelling at cruel acts. Brutality fascinated them. Torture was taught. They learned how to kill slowly and enjoy it. They stuck together. 'How could they get away with these things?' I asked at army headquarters. Everybody knew about them, but did nothing. 'They fend for themselves.' They said, 'It's war,' and left them alone.

" 'These men are terrific soldiers,' was the excuse. 'So far, they have turned back every Russian attack.' And that was true, they had. It was required from them. They saved our lives by repelling Russian attacks."

Now the captain stood in front of me. "I will not send you or any other human being to become one of these animals." He turned to the lieutenant.

"That is my decision as an officer of the German army. You may disagree with me. And I'm not favoring him because he is a brother of my friends. Is that clear?" The lieutenant didn't answer, but it dawned on me that the lieutenant wanted me to go to a punishment battalion. The captain was not finished.

"Life in a punishment unit is not better than jail. Jail is better." He paused. "I wonder sometimes how guards in prison camps behave and what they are doing in concentration camps? Guards can become cruel like these men and claim to be just doing their job. Nobody orders torture. Cruelty feeds on itself."

He faced me. "I'd like to know why you left your watch?"

"I am sorry, Sir, but I did not leave my stable watch. I investigated a light at the far end of the stable which came from the quarantine room." My farmer friend nodded agreement, emphatically. The captain noticed and addressed him.

"How much time did the corporal spend in your room?" The farmer shook his head. He couldn't answer. He looked like a scarecrow in uniform. His sleeves were too short and his trousers too long.

"I don't know, Sir." he mumbled. I hoped he wouldn't spoil my story.

"I don't have a watch, Sir, I never owned one." The captain realized the soldier would protect me, but he didn't know how. He turned to the master sergeant and asked for more details. The master sergeant clicked his heels several times before answering.

"I made a routine check, Captain, arriving at the stable at ten minutes after 8:00 P.M. and could not find the guard. I looked in the aisles, which took twenty minutes, before I found the corporal in the quarantine room."

The captain went back to check the report and found what he was looking for. "You stated in your report that you searched for more than one hour. Now, it is only twenty minutes. How did you find him? Was he drinking, sitting on a chair? You didn't mention that." The master sergeant clicked heels. "No Sir."

The inquisition was over.

"In view of your mediocre performance during training, I expel you from the reserve officers course, as of today." The captain stood before me.

"And as of today, you are demoted to private and will lose your cadet stripes. You may think disobedience is a virtue. I read the report and see that you are very undisciplined. Nobody trusts an officer who doesn't obey his superiors. The German army wins battles with disciplined soldiers."

He paused. "I will have you transferred to our combat troops with a request to assign you to a suicide squad. I wonder if you know what a suicide squad is? I'll tell you what it is. An officer must sometimes send a soldier on a dangerous mission. That is called a suicide mission. He hates to send his friends. But unfortunately these deadly missions must be performed. You stated to an officer that you wanted to earn a bravery medal. You can earn a bravery medal in a suicide mission if you survive."

My face lit up. It was exactly what I hoped for. Danger! The captain noticed my joyful expression and shook his head.

"We tried to make you a good soldier. In combat you may still learn what war is all about. It may not be what you think. But once you have a taste of reality, you may change and become useful." He paused indicating that he was not yet finished, "In addition to being demoted, you will spend three days in the barracks jail."

He checked the report once more. "You will never become an officer. Your demotion takes place at noon before the entire battalion. It will be a warning for everybody." Without saluting, he left the office. The lieutenant clicked his heels with an expression of satisfaction. I did not click my heels.

End of the Officer's Course

"Cadet Officer Sellier step forward!" shouted the master sergeant. I stepped forward and turned around. The entire battalion stood at attention. Eleven officer cadets stood on the side of the recruits. The master sergeant posted himself before me and fished for his pocket knife in his trousers. The captain was on the other side and began reading the list of my wrongdoings. Much of it was exaggerated. Some of it I had never heard.

The monotonous recital took at least five minutes. At the end he emphatically proclaimed that I was the worst soldier in the German army. He demanded everybody watch the following demotion proceeding carefully.

The master sergeant produced his pocketknife. He cut off the silver cadet-officer stripes and worked on my corporal's triangle. When he finished, the captain asked the lieutenant to take over. The lieutenant ordered the jail sergeant to step forward and take my belt and the suspenders. "Gunner, remove your shoelaces!" ordered the sergeant. I was now ranked lower than the recruits before me. I loosened my shoelaces and handed them over. The sergeant gave me a loaf of bread and a blanket. The disgraceful ceremony ended.

I attempted to salute but failed. The loaf of bread was under my left arm, the blanket under my right arm, and because my left hand had to hold my trousers, it was impossible. Nobody asked me to repeat the failing salute.

I glanced in the direction of my comrades. They stood at attention and looked uncommitted. The jail sergeant yelled a command. I turned and followed him with difficulty. Without shoe laces my boots made me waddle and threatened to slip from my feet. We arrived at the nearby jail.

"Why did you take my suspenders and shoe laces?" I asked.

"Because you might hang yourself in jail." He stuck the huge key into the lock. "Did anybody ever hang himself in jail?" I asked.

"Not that I know of. But as far as you are concerned, you should! You are the worst soldier in German history." He recited some of the captain's speech.

I went inside the cell which was dark and narrow. Two bunk beds were on each side and had no mattresses. Between the beds stood a filthy open toilet bowl without a seat. I began inspecting the paintings on the faded blue walls. Graffiti, scribbled in French with graphic illustrations of male and female sex organs, adorned most of the space.

"Hang myself? For what? I won't do you that favor," I shouted back at the closing cell door and heard the turning key. I was mad and felt like shouting at somebody. "I'll let you know what some of that smut on the wall says, if you are interested." I was mad at the whole world, I hoped the mean jail sergeant was listening.

The dreariness of the cell depressed me. Everything since the day before began to bother me. I was in jail, and the reality finally hit me. What would my father say if he knew where I was? I tried to gather my wits and, mockingly saluted the dirty wall. Cheer up, I ordered myself.

"I salute all you French comrades who spent time in this lousy cell," I shouted at the wall. "If you served time for insubordination, I commend you. I especially salute soldiers who refused to shoot at German soldiers. We are comrades. Good for you!"

I began deciphering some of the writing. Graffiti in German public toilets wasn't much different, but I was shocked. No wonder they don't let women into the army. Women should not be exposed to this stuff! Women deserve more respect. A woman wouldn't even understand most of it, I thought innocently. Why should women enlist in the military anyway? Women should stay home, rear children, and embroider linen. War is a man's job. I am glad the German army doesn't allow women in combat. They don't need to see dead frozen Russian soldiers posted as direction signs on ice banks with bloody mutilated faces. What would happen to a woman if she was caught by brutal fighting men? There is nothing nice about war. My sense of decency made me turn away from the graffiti.

War is for men only. God is masculine. I contemplated. Men kill and God looks from behind those cold glittering stars and doesn't care. He produces the hurricanes and the fury on earth. God lets volcanoes erupt and watches the destruction emotionless. He must be masculine. All men enjoy killing and eating animals and plant life. That regenerates vegetation. I felt hopelessly depressed.

Why do people pray to an emotionless God? I hated the world, cried, and threw myself on the hard wooden bench. The sergeant was right. One might be tempted to hang himself.

I noticed that the small square window above the toilet had thick iron bars. The bars could be removed. There's an opportunity to hang myself. The light faded. The small window intrigued me. Was it large enough to squeeze through? I would have to remove the iron bars, I thought. But where would I go? My French is terrible. I leaned back and listened to the voice inside me.

Don't you dare, my voice said. Isn't your situation bad enough? What should I do, hang myself? I leaned back and listened.

You are much too belligerent. You don't want to die, said my voice. Besides, three days in jail won't kill you. I don't know where the voice comes from, but it was always there when emotions run high. I continued listening.

I am here for you. I closed my eyes and sat dreamlike.

I can hear you, said my voice, but you must talk louder. My body began to vibrate. That had happened before. I hadn't doubted the advice since. I always felt better when I followed the advice.

I guess you are right, I answered my voice.

I wished you would thank me sometimes. My voice always demanded excellent manners.

Thank you, I said firmly and was glad I had this voice inside of me.

Do you think there is a reason for me being in jail? I asked. There was no answer. What do you think my father would say if he knew I was in a French jail?

Again, there was no answer.

I knew the answer myself. He would be horrified, of course. What do you think my mother would do? She would be horrified, and all hell would break loose. I could see my mother's deep blue eyes, and how she would turn away in disgust. She would tell me about my grandfather, who once was an honorable judge on Germany's Supreme Court in Leipzig. She always used him as the disciplinary weapon. She would say that he would turn around in his grave and, in this case, possibly several times.

I am deeply ashamed of you, she would say. During the thousand years of our family's proud history, no one has been in jail. You are the first. You are the black sheep.

My father would nod in agreement. He always nodded when she lectured. She had top grades in school, much higher than my father's, so he let her lecture.

My three older brothers won't say anything. You deserve it, they would tell me later in private. They didn't think much of me anyway. I was the youngest and spoiled and a nuisance to them. They were too busy with their own problems.

The pale blue graffiti wall became dark. I leaned back on my blanket.

My mother was too strict. But I missed her. I often hated her for never compromising. I knew she cared about me. She took me to the mountains, taught me rock-climbing and skiing. She was better than most men in sports and tougher. I also knew how she dearly loved my father. She would compromise with him. He accepted her advice. My father made notes of what she counseled. She was alone at home and worried about her five men in the war. Luckily, she didn't know I was in a French army jail. Soon I would have to tell her. Why did I always refuse when she tried to comfort me. I needed her. I was emotionally drained, worn out, and fell asleep.

Noises woke me up. They came from below my window. It was past midnight. There were several voices. I stepped up on the toilet bowl and could see the dark outside.

"Hey, Claus, are you there?" I heard. There was a dark shadow, I recognized Hugo's officer's cap, and three more shadows under the chestnut tree.

"Hey guys, what's up?" I whispered lifting myself up on my toes.

"We brought you food." I recognized Fritz's deep voice. "You must be starving. We went to the city and bought food in small packages for you to hide."

"Gee thanks, guys!" My voice cracked, but I didn't want them to notice. Emotions burst inside. Fritz held the packages up, and I squeezed them through between the bars.

"The first package is French pastry, which I know you love. The others are cheeses and sausages. The plastic pouch is Savoy wine from a barrel."

Tears dropped from my cheeks. It was dark, though so they couldn't see.

"I won't forget." I choked. "I mean, I won't forget that you came." My voice cracked again. But I didn't care anymore. I let the tears drop openly.

"Fritz, you were right. I am a stupid ass. I am sorry I got you in trouble. I promise, I'll change" I extended my hand through the iron bars.

One by one they came and shook my hand. Fritz came last and whispered, "Never mind! We talked about you all night. We wanted to help and at least get some food to go with the loaf of bread. The lieutenant said he wanted you sent to a punishment battalion, but the captain blocked the request. The jerk was upset. I agree, you are a blockhead! I'll see you in Yugoslavia. You may be in combat before we go. Lots of luck!"

"Lots of luck to you!" they whispered from below. I choked and couldn't answer.

My chin rested on the window ledge long after they'd left. My depression miraculously disappeared. I had friends! What else does a guy need?

I thought about friendship and how precious it was.

Claus was born in Freising and went to school at Freising's Gymnasium Humanistic—the building in front of the towers—before the family moved to Munich where he attended a Real-Gymnasium Humanistic. Freising celebrated its 1250th anniversary in 1988 A.D.

Aerial view from above the Wasserkuppe mountains of the Castle Bieberstein and farmlands to the west, near the medieval city of Fulda. It was built as the seat of the Bishop of Fulda

Claus (in the picture) and his friend Dieter were sent to Austria for a month to study skiing under the guidance of former Olympic champions. Upon their return to Bieberstein, they became the school's ski instructors. Dieter was sent to fight in Russia where he was run over and killed by a tank

Claus and Igor clown around during a time out while building the sports field for the Bieberstein school

Bieberstein graduate-recruits, including Claus and Volkmar von Richthofen (far right), manage a smile for the camera before getting on the train and going their separate ways to the war

View from above Garmisch of Lake Eibsee and Bavaria's highest mountain, Zugspitze. During basic training, both mules and recruits carried the cannons up and down and around the mountains of this area

First Sunday off after joining 79th Mountain Artillery Regiment in Garmisch, Germany

Claus (left) and a buddy enjoying some off-duty time during basic training at Garmisch

Political map of Europe identifies where Claus grew up, was in boot camp, went to officer's training school, and was sent on an odyssey that took him back home at war's end

Political map of the Balkans at the turn of the 21st century identifies, in light of current disputes in the area, some of the places where Claus fought. During the war, the area was united as Yugoslavia

Division recruits loading 1916
Skoda cannons onto mules at the
base near Garmisch. Mules carried
the cannons up as far as possible
into the mountains, then the men
had to carry them up further when
necessary

Claus and three others
loading the base of a
cannon onto a mule.
This was the heaviest
part of the cannon and
lifting or carrying it
required four men

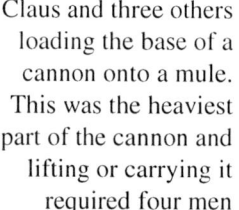

Artillery training continued in the Savoie region of France around Albertville in the summer
heat (Claus is sitting on the cannon)

Burial of Sergeant Müller who was killed during hand grenade training in Albertville

Claus with a French nurse while recovering from the injury he received in the hand grenade training incident

Albertville, France, 1943. Training exercises were conducted in the surrounding mountains

In Val-d'Isère, France—near Mont Cenis—on a training
exercise shortly before shipping out to the front
(Claus is on the right)

The Alpine flower Eidelweise was the insignia of the
First Mountain Division (Artillery and Armored
Regiments). It was chosen by Rommel during World
War I. The patch was worn on the right sleeve

Off to the War

Yugoslavia

There were no seats in the overcrowded passenger train to Vienna. I plunked my stuff into the passageway and sat on my knapsack, holding my unloaded rifle between my knees. People climbed over me on the way to the bathroom. Most were German soldiers returning to their units. A dirty gray curtain of a first class compartment made me wish I could be inside and sit on one of the nice wide upholstered seats.

My travel document read, "Dispatched to: The First Mountain Division, Artillery Regiment 79 in Yugoslavia." It said nothing else, no location, no train or anything.

The office clerk had given me the papers the day before with the usual air of superiority. The swastika emblems on his documents made him feel important. "When you get to Vienna, check the railroad station office. They have schedules to Yugoslavia," he was not concerned with me in the least. Yugoslavia is big. How could I find them? A soldier shouldn't ask too many questions.

I had just turned nineteen, but hadn't celebrated. I had nobody to celebrate with. On my birthday I looked forward to combat and to becoming a hero.

Next to me was a bunch of civilians also crowded in the isle. They must have been displaced people, evacuated from a destroyed northern city. Huddled together were four women with four children and an old man between them. Younger Germans were in uniforms. Since Secretary of Propaganda, Dr. Joseph Goebbels, declared Total War, all Northern Germans were evacuated to farms in southern Germany. Objections were not tolerated. Total War was the slogan that explained everything. The stout woman sitting next to me spoke with a northern accent.

"Why should a brown-shirt officer occupy a first class compartment all by himself?" she asked, then turned to me, "the curtains are drawn, so we can't see his face and his fancy uniform. I hope he is ashamed of himself. We 'evacuated' must squeeze ourselves into a train's passageway. Haven't we suffered enough? And this brown-shirt travels first class with five empty seats in the compartment."

"Why?" said the old man, "I'll tell you why: Because our party big shots fight the Total War in luxury. They never heard a bomb falling, not like we did in Aachen."

He waved a knotty finger at the drawn curtain in disgust. What could I say? I nodded agreement. The soldier on the other side nodded, too. People had a right to speak up. They had lost their homes and all their possessions. They must have been bitter. In my hometown of Munich, civilians had started to complain. Five years of war was enough for anybody. People grew impatient. The celebration of victories and the excitement of a successful war was gone. Today's discussion was of the nightly raids and the damages caused by fire bombs which were dropped relentlessly. They would burn an attic while women and children took shelter in their basement unaware of the fire upstairs. The house would burn, and when it collapsed, it would bury them in their basement.

In the meantime, Dr. Goebbel's propaganda machine blared victories in all the headlines of Europe. The U-boats sank tons of Allied ships in the Atlantic. General Rommel built the "unbreakable" defense line in Northern France along the coast of Normandy. People at home sat on rubble in the street and clung to their furniture. They were angry. Soldiers on furlough were glad to get back to the war on the front line. "Let's win the war fast." They mumbled to each other, "Civilians are worse off."

Those were the circumstances in 1944.

The woman next to me complained a second time. "Why does a government official get the privilege of having a reserved seat in a first class compartment on an overcrowded train?"

The soldier on the other side got up and pulled the first class compartment door open and said, "Excuse me, Sir." He shoved the civilian's suitcases inside. The children pushed in and sat down. The brown-shirt official turned his face away and looked out the window pretending not to notice. He buried his face in the official newspaper, *Der Voelkische Beobachter*. I spread my stuff further out in the hallway.

The train arrived two hours late in Vienna. The customary punctuality of German trains had become history. The glass domed roof in the gigantic railroad station showed damages from the previous night's bombing. Usually, railroad stations and tracks were the first things to be repaired.

I followed a stream of soldiers to the information office and stood at the end of the line. An hour later I was finally inside.

"Your train to Yugoslavia is on track twenty-three tonight. You are going to Osijek," said a fat soldier in his sixties whose talk was barely audible. He leaned back behind a large desk, bored with his work. He wore a spotless gray uniform but didn't look like a soldier. "Next!" he shouted. An older soldier without any insignias stepped forward.

"Stamp my papers, please Tony! One more time, I missed my train!" He made his request without worrying whether any of us heard him. The flabby soldier leaned further back, still resting from the stress of his afternoon.

"This is the fourth time, Georg, that you missed your train," he pondered in the heavy Viennese dialect. "How many more stamps do you want?"

"I know. I know. I helped my sister in the butcher shop. I'll give you my meat ration stamps, and I'll have more tomorrow." A sheet of meat ration stamps, clumsily hidden under George's travel document, changed hands. The soldier covered the stamps with his big hand and let them fall into his half-open desk drawer. He routinely applied the stamp to the man's document. We watched, and nobody complained. He was the boss. He determined who would go to combat and who wouldn't.

I went to sidetrack twenty-three, which by now, was in darkness. The alarm sirens sounded. I was used to them. I had heard them many times before. Allied bombers came but were often diverted to drop bombs on other cities. I hoped that was the case tonight. Two aged corporals guarded sidetrack twenty-three. They began debating if I could board the train during an alarm, or if I should go to a shelter.

"Stay here," one decided. "They aren't bombing Vienna tonight."

"What time does the train leave?"

Because each air raid changed the schedule, they didn't know. My train consisted of joined cattle wagons, all neatly furnished with bunk beds and new straw mattresses covered by new blue-checkered sheets. I was first and selected a bed with the fullest mattress on the lower level.

The nearby flak cannons began thundering. Their ignition looked spectacular. I watched from the open door. Light beams circled the dark sky in search of bombers. I heard the deep monotonous sound of airplane engines but I couldn't see them. They flew invisibly into the vast expanse of a city of millions, and minutes later their bombs exploded in rapid succession. I watched and felt safe. I went to bed, stretching myself on the comfortable mattress and enjoying the smell of fresh straw. The possibility of becoming a hero drifted through my mind, and I fell into a deep sleep. The air attack didn't concern me. I'll be in Yugoslavia, in combat soon.

The rumbling of train wheels across tracks woke me. Next to our railroad tracks a dirty, green river flowed in the same direction. It was the Danube. The sky was gray. All the beds in my car were now occupied. Soldiers sat on mattresses and talked. They were considerably older and had probably come from a furlough, or were released from a hospital. Most had bravery medals. I smiled. So far nobody teased me.

"Are we in Yugoslavia?" I asked a gray-bearded husky fellow next to me. He poured tobacco into a white paper square and twisted it into a cigarette. The train stopped and somebody called, "Coffee! Coffee!"

"We crossed the Hungarian border a while ago." He stared. I suspected that it bothered him that I had no apparent rank. But he couldn't be sure because my uniform jacket was folded on my mattress. He had an impressive array of bravery medals. "You missed two meals already," he told me. "I wondered why you didn't get up. The next stop is Osijek. That's Yugoslavia and our last stop."

"Why don't we go further south?"

"Because Tito partisans ambush trains. They don't like Germans, but they sure like German supplies. We would be dead ducks on a train in the mountains. They would blow up the tracks and then have us for target shooting practice. This train unloads in Osijek, and Osijek is a good size city. You'll see mule carts waiting across the railroad station. They'll take everybody inland to their unit. The guys in the station information office will tell you where your regiment hangs out. If you have not been there before, just follow me."

I thanked him and wondered why old timers were so much nicer than the trainers in France. In Osijek, I walked with him to the office. But a tall husky top sergeant leaning against the information office door grabbed me. He acted like he knew me. "Are you going to mountain Artillery Regiment 79?" He asked in the typical guttural accent of Tyrolians.

"Yes. How did you know?"

"I saw your embroidered Edelweiss flower on your arm sleeve, and the red artillery stripe. Where else would you want to go?" Behind me were other soldiers also wearing the red stripes and the embroidered flower, the symbol of the First Mountain Division.

"I need one more guy to help me with the supplies. We'll head to the Sava River. The regiment and 6th Battery are there." That was my exact destination! How did he know?

"You don't need to wait in line. We are loading across the street. Get yourself two boxes of live ammunition in room seventy-three. My name is Joseph. Call me Sepp. I don't like to be called Joseph." We shook hands. Sepp wrote the requisition for the ammunition. He opened his raincoat, and I saw that he had both a first and second class Iron Cross. "We want to leave soon. Hurry!"

I got the live bullets and found Sepp across the street working with a mule column of at least fifty carts. Each wagon had two mules hitched to it. Sepp's huge figure stood out. He waved a heavy '42 machine gun. He was strong! The new model 1942 machine gun was just released and shown to us by an infantry sergeant during my last stretch of training. He explained, "This machine gun is by far the fastest in the world. It spits 1,000 bullets per minute. There is no competition."

Sepp's soldiers were covered by canvasses to protect themselves from the rain. They had just finished loading the wagons and threw ropes across them to tie them down. The thought of meeting them made me nervous. After all, they were all real combat soldiers, even though they were not much older than I. Joseph didn't introduce me. The rain canvass covered their ranks.

"I am glad you came," said Joseph without interrupting his work. "Help Roland with the fourth wagon." Everybody nodded as I passed Roland a rope across the wagon.

"Tie that!" he shouted from the other side. I tied the rope and felt accepted. Sepp came over to me and explained what could happen.

"The trip takes six hours. You can sit on the wagon. But remember, we'll travel in hostile country. You'll be an easy target on top of the wagon. Always keep your rifle ready and the safety off."

"Partisans like rainy weather," added Roland. "They will lay an ambush today. I can feel it." He opened his coat. He was a corporal and had an Iron Cross. Sepp walked away. "Watch Sarge Joseph," said Roland, respectfully.

"He never sits down. He always walks next to the wagon and carries his machine gun. He smells partisans! Watch him, and keep an eye on the forest. When you see movement, blast away! Don't wait to find out what it is. I'll never know why Joseph volunteers to do the supply run. It's the worst and most dangerous job." Roland sounded disgusted, "I don't like this job, but I'll go with Joseph. He likes danger. He is used to it, and he needs me. I carry his ammunition. Nothing will ever happen to him."

"What do you mean, he *smells* partisans?"

"You'll see!" Roland's sounded mysterious.

Our five wagons rolled noisily over the uneven cobblestones. We came to the outskirts of Osijek where the road turned to mud. In the distance, hills lined the horizon covered by drifting fog.

"That's where the partisans hide," explained Roland. The mules struggled to pull the wagons through the mud and were often stuck in deep holes. They never seemed to mind the challenge and pulled even harder. "They are going home," explained Roland. We helped by pushing and pulling on the wheels. The drizzle bothered me. I almost forgot about the partisans.

"Did you know that half of Yugoslavia is full of Turkish Muslims?" Roland asked.

"You mean like the Muslims living in Turkey or in Persia?"

"Yes. They wear white silk pants down to their ankles, made from British parachute material they find in the woods. It's an insult, but they don't care. I don't like them wearing that British stuff. They know darn well we know where that stuff came from."

After two hours of pushing wagons, we were near the fog covered hills and a dense, wet forest. Joseph stopped suddenly and crouched behind his wagon. He focused on the forest. "Something is bothering him!" whispered Roland. He pulled hard on the mule's leather straps. Joseph laid his machine gun carefully on the wagon's edge, and for no apparent reason blasted two quick volleys into the forest.

"Down into the trench!" yelled Roland pushing me. Bullets whistled over my head. I stuck my face deep into the wet dirt. The bullets were aimed too high. They came from the forest. The mules reeled and strained to take off.

"Hope they didn't hit my mules," whispered Roland and crawled to them.

"Stay down!" shouted the guy in front. Another round of bullets whistled overhead. This time they were much closer. It lasted just minutes. We stayed in the trench. Joseph came calmly back, grabbed the rein of our lead mule, and calmed him down.

"The bastards are gone." He told Roland, "I want you to check the forest, and take the new guy along. In the meantime we'll calm the mules down and feed them."

Roland took an assault rifle from the wagon, and without saying a word ran zigzag up the hill. I followed close behind in the wet field. Sarge Joseph blasted a few more short bursts from his machine gun to cover us. He hit the edge of the forest precisely.

So that was my first combat experience, I thought. I found it disappointing. That was nothing. It was like training where nothing happened. I kept up with Roland and noticed I wasn't scared.

"Let's see where these guys are." Roland stopped where the forest brush began and walked carefully to a place where the snipers had hidden. The wood coals still smoldered. From here we could see our wagons well, presenting themselves as beautiful targets.

"They are gone." Roland pushed the coals apart. "Smart, how they keep the fire going in the rain!" he said admiringly. "Did you hear the rifles? They were all German rifles stolen from a supply wagon; they had six. These bandits really thought they could take a machine gun and steal our wagons. They must be nuts." Roland scratched his head. "Besides, the ambush was laid too far inside the forest. They must be stupid. What do you think?" Everything Roland said was new to me.

But I wouldn't admit it and gravely nodded my head.

"Joseph shot before they did. How did he know there were partisans?" I asked the second time.

"Beats me." Roland beamed a grin. "You aren't the first to ask that question. He just does. I learn from him. He says nobody can teach the sixth sense. That's why I go with him. He has that instinct, a sixth sense."

It stopped raining. We walked back. Drops from the wet foliage hit my face. There is lots more to learn. Why didn't they teach instinct in training? It dawned on me: Instinct cannot be taught, yet, survival depends on instinct. There may be a few more unexpected bumps for me in the future. I felt ready.

Roland seemed to like my interest in his lectures. "You know what? Nobody ever dares to touch Joseph's machine gun." We walked back to the open field and saw the wagons close by. "Joseph is very superstitious. His machine gun is sacred. He carries the gun with him all the time and thinks without her he would die. He even sleeps with his gun as a pillow, treating her like a bride. Don't tell him! It's an obsession with him, like the violin was for Paganini." How could he compare the violin with a machine gun?

"Don't laugh! We from South Tyrolia like music. The machine gun has a rhythm. It's a musical instrument. Joseph shoots her with a special rhythm. Machine gunners recognize Joseph. It's true. One day he yelled, 'Listen! I know that machine gun on the Russian side. The man was in Charkov.' Charkov was the bloodiest battle we fought in Russia. Joseph shot a volley to greet him. First there was silence. Then the Russian answered. He shot a short volley. 'Did you hear him? That's him!' Joseph was excited and shot again. And the Russian answered. Joseph acted like a kid. 'Yeah, that's him.' They practiced a song, shooting alternately. It was crazy.

'Machine gunners are the same,' Joseph told me, 'no matter where and which side they are on. I'll meet this Russian when the war is over, I swear to God!'"

"Where did Joseph come from?"

"From Innsbruck, Tyrol. I am from Girlan, further south, but we speak the same dialect."

"Did the Italians allow you to speak German? They governed South Tyrol?"

"They sure did. Mussolini is our friend."

"How did the Italians treat you? Did you like them?"

"They never bothered us. We are grape farmers in the mountains near Bozen. My mother likes Italians because she likes the Pope and listens to their music. She goes to church every day and doesn't understand a word."

"Do they preach Latin in your church?" I quickly added, "I am not a Catholic."

"I don't go to church, I wouldn't know." Roland's remark sounded harsh, "I don't want to listen to something I don't understand. Aren't you Catholic in Bavaria? Your Bishop Corbinian came from Freising, your hometown. He started our wine industry."

"No. My mother is Prussian and raised us as Protestants. Freising has only a few Protestants, and we don't have a church."

"You don't have a church? I can't believe that. Every village at home has a church. What do Protestants believe in, besides in Hitler and his Great Germany and all that?"

"We believe in Jesus being a messenger from God. In a Protestant service they preach in German and not in Latin. A Lutheran minister can get married. Martin Luther was a Catholic monk who made the rules simpler and reformed the church." Roland didn't understand. We got back to the wagons, the conversation ended and Joseph wanted to know what we had seen. Roland told him about the coal fire.

"They were amateurs, just bandits. Probably farmers from the neighborhood who wanted to steal our supplies. They are nuts. Next time I'll hit them harder! Let's go!" The episode was over for Joseph.

My heart still beat hard from the excitement. I touched the lead mule, and he raised his forelegs aggressively. Roland talked to him and he became calm in seconds and allowed us to climb on the wet wagon. Roland whistled sharply, the mules pointed their ears and pulled the cart.

"You said there were six bandits in the forest. How did you know?"

"Easy! You count shots. That tells you the number of rifles. I learned that from Joseph." He whistled once more, the mules pricked their ears and fell into a soft trot.

"I wished I could handle mules like you."

"You can, but they must like you first. It comes with time. Animals always listen. Their brain isn't different from ours. They can't reason, but they are not dumb. They use their instincts. I believe they are better off than we are. They sense danger before we do and let you know. If you respect them, they tell you and will work for you." I let that sink in.

Roland changed the subject. "Tell me, do Protestants believe in God and the Holy Spirit?" Roland had never talked to a Protestant and was enjoying the talk.

"Protestants are Christians, too. We do believe in God and in a spiritual life. Martin Luther posted the new Christian rules on the door of his church in Wittenberg in 1517. He denounced the Pope and his all-powerful role. The bishops condemned him and put him in jail.

In jail, he translated the bible from Latin into German, now everybody can understand God's word."

"That makes sense," Roland nodded. "What did he think about Jesus?"

"Jesus is God's son and his messenger."

"Did Luther know that Jews killed Jesus?" Roland made an angry face. "We are lucky we have no Jews in Girlan. I don't like Jews. They hate Christians."

"Did you know Jesus was a Jew? Our religion teacher told me."

"Don't tell my mother. She'll kill you," he laughed. "I don't believe that."

"In my home town, Freising, the largest stores were owned by Jews. Everybody shopped in these stores because they had better merchandise and lower prices. But Jews were in the minority, just like we Protestants were. We Protestant kids had to walk home together to protect ourselves. Orphan kids called us pagans, and Catholic priests told them to throw rocks at us."

"That's bad! What did they call the Jewish kids?" I hadn't thought about that.

"*Stingy* is what they called them in South Tyrol."

"Jews were called names, but not a particular name. People shopped in Jewish stores, but didn't like them. Every Catholic church preached against the Jews. They said Martin Luther also preached against Jews. His word was like the gospel up north. When I was about nine, Nazi storm troopers blocked the Jewish store entrances. It doesn't surprise me that Jews aren't liked when everybody preaches it."

Roland shook his head. "We don't have a Jew or a Protestant in my town." He counted fingers, "maybe three Protestants in the next village. I think the Pope and his priests are corrupt. They collect money to stay in power. I agree with Hitler, Jews and gypsies are bad. Every gypsy steals and every Jew cheats."

"What do you think is worse, the Catholic priest who makes orphan kids throw stones at me or a Jew who never hurt me. We should be more tolerant. Roman soldiers ordered Jesus killed when they occupied Palestine. They put Jesus to death."

"How long did the blockade of Jewish stores last?"

"About a week. My father didn't like it. He went to Neuhauser's store, and I went along. Neuhauser was his friend. He was a Jew, but he served in the First World War in the German army and had an Iron Cross. The brown-shirt guards at Neuhauser's store greeted my father respectfully. They knew my father."

"What are you doing here?" my father asked them. They shrugged their shoulders. We went inside the store. My father seldom shopped. He didn't know what to buy. Herr Neuhauser was alone in the store. He remembered my mother reserved a special material. He handed me a candy and made a package of the material. I liked Herr Neuhauser. His store was closed and never opened again. We heard the Neuhauser family left without telling anybody where they went."

Roland was not impressed. "Jews should go back to Jerusalem where they came from. I have no use for them."

"I'll take the Neuhausers anytime before the Catholic priest who would have me stoned. They didn't even allow me in their church."

"I can understand how you feel."

Roland thought silently. We had come to the end of the forest. A steep valley opened and a dozen stone houses appeared at the bottom, where soldiers sat. The familiar sight of four 7.5 cm mountain cannons sat in a near-by field. We had arrived at the 6th Battery position. The soldiers swarmed up the hill to greet us.

"The supply wagons are here," shouted somebody.

"They want their mail," explained Roland calmly. "They are not running to see you or me." Nobody wore a proper uniform. Sweaters were tied around their necks. Some had dark green military shirts on, but nobody wore a jacket or the military cap. The sight was very unusual to me, coming from my rigid training. An oval aluminum identification tag dangled from everybody's neck. Sepp handed them a burlap sack with mail. Somebody asked, "Joseph, how many partisans did you shoot today?"

"None," Joseph said annoyed. He tucked his machine gun under his arm and walked into one of the stone buildings. "We shot at a bunch of farmers, who were amateurs. They shot badly." Roland trailed behind. Nobody was really interested in Joseph's tale. A sergeant grabbed the mailbag and called names.

A hand rested on my shoulder. I turned and saw the master sergeant who was the only one in full uniform. The sight made me shudder. I remembered the master sergeants from training. "The Battery chief wants to see you right away!" he said calmly and smiled.

My trainers never smiled. I liked this man. I sensed an amazing energy in this man when his deep brown eyes focused mine. I felt right away I could trust him. I hoped he hadn't heard of my bad reputation. My documents were still in my bag. There was no way he could know what was written in them.

"Do you care to see my papers, Sir?" I attempted to click my heels. His smile broadened. He wore both Iron Cross medals, first and second class Artillery Combat Medal. He was an experienced combat soldier.

"Save your papers and show them to the captain. You should leave now. The captain is in the next village, in a stone house like those we have here, but he is six kilometer from here. Follow the road until you come to our infantry defense line. Our Advance Observer is there. Hurry! You might make it by daylight. And watch the forest! Not everybody around here is friendly." I acknowledged the order, clicked my heels again. The master sergeant looked surprised. Apparently that was not done out here. I swung my gun over my shoulder and walked toward the road. A sharp whistle stopped me.

"For Christ's sake, hold the rifle in your hand, and keep the safety off. Be careful! Don't forget, the password is *Nibelungen.*" The master sergeant walked away.

"Yes Sir!" I shuddered when I walked into the forest. I began to feel my frazzled nerves. Even though they were amateurs and had shot far over my head, these bandits scared me. There could have been more of them in this forest. I checked each tree and thought I felt eyes on me. I wished Joseph and Roland were here to protect me. And I wished I could *smell* partisans like Joseph. This road wasn't safe. My body ached from drudging in mud all day. Too much had happened. I stopped and searched the trees, as far and as many as possible. Bullets would soon fly. I thought I saw movement. I threw myself on the ground. There was nothing! My imagination was in high gear. I got up and stared bewildered into the semidark forest. Now I was really scared for the first time. I wasn't ashamed. What would a suicide mission be like? It can't be any worse than this. The captain must be mean, he is ordering me to walk at night in a dark forest. He must have read my report. He received the report over the wire. That's why he doesn't care. I felt the thick yellow envelope in my pocket.

I remembered every word in the report. I had read it on the train. The envelope had slipped from my knapsack's side pocket with the flap almost open. It was easy to open and I began reading. It was worse than I expected. Everything on the four long pages was embarrassing. Most wasn't even true. There was only one good remark at the end, "The soldier is in excellent physical condition." That was true. I read the report three times then licked the remaining glue, pressing it hard between my thumb and fingers. But the glue would not hold. I sat on the envelope for hours, shuddering at what would happen if the captain found the envelope already opened?

I looked at the trees. They appeared even more menacing. Why do trees look taller at night? Why did I ever want to be a hero? That was ages ago. I had never walked alone in a dark forest with the enemy swarming all over the place. Heroism was easy in a nice comfortable warm room. Cold sweat formed on my skin. The sweat felt like wax. I imagined faces lurking behind trees. There must be partisans or even Russian soldiers here ready to attack. My life is important, too. I will not throw my life away. I shouted aloud while walking. The forest echoed my voice. I had never imagined how scary a dark forest could be. If I had known I would not have volunteered for the army. Will anybody find me when I am dead? Will they look for me? Probably not. Nobody cares. The captain sure doesn't. You are nothing said the first sergeant I met in boot camp. He and the captain must have the same opinion.

The black sky turned gray, I walked into an open field and saw the shadows of houses. Suddenly somebody yelled, "Password!" The voice penetrated my body. It felt like a knife had carved into me. Two soldiers appeared from behind trees. They stood before me with pointed rifles. A third soldier joined them. I was paralyzed and shuddered.

Password? My mind went blank. They were Germans, thank God. Frantically, I searched my memory. I can't remember? Password! They'll shoot me! I didn't pay attention. I forgot. The password never anchored in my memory. Like magic, the word *Nibelungen* burst from my lips. The three soldiers burst into laughter and held their sides. The laughter relaxed, and I reluctantly joined in.

"Were you scared? Are you new? Look at the milk faced greenhorn, how he shudders." One bent forward coughing from too much laughter. "I forgot the password, didn't I?" I said meekly. "The walk was boring. You almost scared me. My nerves are a little frazzled from an ambush we experienced this morning. Bandits attacked us as we were transporting our supplies." My excuses did not impress them.

"So, you are artillery! No wonder you are scared. Artillery guys are always scared." They laughed again. I was mad and didn't say anything anymore. "Our watch was boring, too," the one who coughed explained, "until you came along. Your artillery is in the second house in this God forsaken place." At least I had directions. I walked off and heard them laughing for a while. I should have told them off. Did I become a coward during training? I straightened myself and gathered what was left of my courage. I walked toward the artillery house.

A wobbly wooden door squeaked and almost fell off when I pushed it open. A corporal sat behind a kitchen table talking on the telephone. He hung up and lifted his feet from the table when he saw me. "Are you the new gunner we are waiting for?" he stared. "Where were you? I just called to find out. The captain is waiting for you." It was now eight o'clock.

He shouted at a closed door, "The new gunner is here, Captain," and put his feet back on the table. I heard nothing. Five minutes later the door opened and the captain appeared in full uniform and regalia. I had expected a front-line casual outfit. He looked like the German officers they portray in magazines, quite handsome with dark brown, short wavy hair, the kind that never needs combing. I judged him to be in his late twenties, old by my standards. He didn't greet me, he just waved for me to follow him into his room. He wore thin stylish leather officer's riding boots. I wasn't impressed. I was still mad.

Medals and ribbons adorned his spotless uniform jacket. After I closed the shaky door, I turned, clicked my heels and shouted my name, rank, and serial number as loud as I could. This captain expected that. He stared without responding. There was no smile and, of course, no welcoming handshake. I grabbed the yellow wrinkled envelope from my pocket and handed it to him. A shudder drifted down my spine. Would he notice the envelope was opened before? Thank God, he didn't. With one hand he reached into the envelope and pulled the crumpled pages out and immediately began to read. I watched his face. I knew exactly where he was reading. Silently, I recited every word on each page following his eyes. I tried hypnosis to make them sound better. It didn't work. He read slowly and showed no change in his demeanor. I stayed at attention. After he finished the dreadful report, he tossed it carelessly on the table.

"Gunner, you are a marked man!" He walked calmly around the table posting himself a half-meter in front of me. "The report tells me that you are the worst soldier in the German army. What shall I do with you?" Did I hear some concern in his voice? No I didn't. I was mistaken.

"I have no choice but to accept you or whatever they send me these days," his voice was now razor sharp. "You are a shit replacement for the fine soldiers who already sacrificed their lives for Great Germany." He turned and picked the papers up from the table and searched for page two. He recited a paragraph in the center, "... no discipline, no respect, this milk face SOB, (he added that!) never showed obedience ...." I knew which cuss words were in the report, and some he used were not. A long silence followed.

"What news do you have from your brother, Peter?" he asked almost casually. "You may know that Peter and I attended the artillery officers school together. We were room mates. I went to your home with him once before we transferred to

Russia. I believe you were still in a boarding school." He grinned, reflecting back, "We had a lot of fun."

"Yes Sir," I was relieved. "Peter, as far as I know, is stationed in a cloister, which is called Monte Casino in Italy, near Naples. He is commander of an independent mobile artillery unit. We haven't heard from him for months." The captain nodded showing no emotion.

"How is your older brother Kurt? We were all friends," his voice was now soft.

"As far as I know, Kurt fights against the Allied invasion in France. We haven't heard from him either, Sir."

"And your oldest brother, Alfred? How is he? He was my training officer in Garmisch five years ago. We went into Poland together."

"Alfred, as far as we know, is recovering in a hospital in Sweden, Sir. He was severely wounded defending a bridge in Finland. A dozen of his men were killed by advancing Russians. Alfred was hit by nine bullets which shattered his arm. The Russians brought him back to their camp and decided to let him die. But a Finnish doctor friend took him away secretly at night and took him by rail car across the Swedish border. He saved his life. We received the customary letter from army headquarters declaring Alfred missing in action and presumed dead. But, by coincidence, the same day we received a postcard from Sweden, from a nurse who said that Alfred was in a Swedish hospital, and he is safe. Her writing was hard to understand. She wrote that the doctors had removed nine bullets and had begun repairing Alfred's arm."

"I am glad." The captain sounded genuinely relieved. "I admire the Finns. They are the toughest soldiers in the world. They can win even when they are outnumbered ten to one. They proved that when they fought the Russians in World War I." He showed more emotion than before. But his voice turned sharp again. "You will not get away with the behavior you showed in training. Combat is serious business. We depend on each other. I shall watch you, and if I hear one complaint, you'll be on a suicide squad. Is that clear?"

"Yes Sir!"

"I assign you to the first cannon as their first gunner. That is not a promotion, mind you. I want to make that clear! I need a first gunner. You had extensive training and can fill that slot. Perhaps, I should have started you with tending mules; but I can't afford to waste your training. I may also use you as an observer some time. I only have a few skilled observers left." He checked his watch. "It's now nine o'clock! I want you to go back and take your position at cannon one. And call me, when you get there. Dismissed!" I saluted, clicked my heels and left.

Back in the darkness, I realized I wasn't scared anymore. I was relieved. The anticipation of this meeting had bothered me. With it in the past, I felt as if a weight had fallen off my shoulders. The captain was tough, but he seemed fair.

He assigned me as first gunner. That was unexpected. It was the highest position on a cannon. I promised myself I wouldn't disappoint him. I was glad he hadn't assigned me to the mules. He gave me an opportunity. I would not disappoint him. Not this time.

"Password!" The same three soldiers were still on duty. I answered calmly, "Nibelungen."

"Are you crazy? You are going back into the forest alone? My advice to you is to transfer to the infantry! The artillery captain has lost his marbles. He let you go by yourself?" They discussed the artillery captain's qualities. One had another idea. "Maybe he is smarter than you think. He knows the partisans are asleep. Partisans must sleep, and they don't expect a single dumb soldier to be walking this road at night. He may be right."

They debated the issue, as I walked on. They were right. There wasn't anybody on the road, and I wasn't scared anymore. Shortly after midnight I saw the lights of the stone houses. One hundred and eighty men slept inside. Everything was quiet. Except for a sentry who stepped from the shadows of a house.

"Password?"

"Nibelungen," I answered.

"Did you walk the forest by yourself?" he shook his head. "That is nuts!"

"Why not?" I pretended walking alone in enemy territory was my specialty. "I have to report to the master sergeant. Where is he?"

The sentry pointed to the third house and shook his head. "If I were you, I wouldn't wake him up. Go to sleep and report to him in the morning. He'll be very grouchy if you steal even a few minutes of his sleep."

I went to the third house, the door squeaked as I walked in the dark room. The unpleasant smell of warm used air was overwhelming. Carefully, sliding one foot at a time forward to avoid bodies curled up on the floor, I searched. They snored. One man raised himself and I whispered in his direction. "Where is the master sergeant?" The man next to him sat up. "What do you want?" The voice sounded grouchy like the sentry predicted.

"I must report to you, I am the first gunner, first cannon, Sir!"

I whispered and applied the correct military words. A yell was the answer. "Get to hell out of here! Go to the first house and lie down! Leave me alone!" The dark figure turned displaying his backside.

"I am sorry, Sir, but the captain ordered specifically to call him as soon as I take position." The body turned halfway back. I couldn't see him, but sensed his impatience.

"For Christ's sake, it's 2:00 A.M.! The captain is in bed. Everybody is sleeping! Get out! Go to the first house! Lay down and sleep! We'll call him in the morning!"

Stunned, I left the house. What a lousy start. What could I do? I have the worst luck in the world! I wasn't tired and didn't want to go to sleep. Where were the telephones? I must call the captain! His order was explicit: "I want you to call me as soon as you get back and take position." I didn't know how to operate the telephones, even if I had found one.

By the time I found the first house I had tears in my eyes. It wasn't my fault. The captain won't believe me. There was nothing I could do. Bad air hit me in this house too. Curled bodies lay on the floor, and steady snoring greeted me from the darkness. I felt an empty bench next to the door and sat down. Slowly, I slipped off my boots and folded my jacket into a pillow. The hard, eight-inch wide board was too narrow, but it was too late to change. I stretched on the board in despair and clamped my rifle in my armpit to keep balance. I fell asleep at once.

A draft woke me. It was daylight, and the door was open. "What time is it?" Discouraged from last night, I got up. The unshaven face of a large man appeared from the floor. He wore long, gray underwear and smelled badly.

"It's seven o'clock!" he answered smiling. I didn't remember having asked him. He was about forty and offered me his hand.

"Heard you coming in last night," he said. "Are you the new gunner? My name is Rudy! Glad to meet you! We need you." His handshake was powerful. Twenty bodies were still on the floor curled in their underwear; some got dressed and folded blankets.

"No bed bugs tonight. Not one bit me," a voice broke the silence. Bed bugs became the topic of conversation for the next five minutes. "Yeah, I saw bugs walking around. They were scared of your smelly body." They noticed me. One by one they came and shook hands. Then they mumbled a name I didn't understand. I paid little attention and was sure they didn't understand my name either.

Why wasn't one of these guys first gunner? I felt inadequate. They all had a rank. I was the youngest and had no rank. They talked and joked among themselves and didn't care about me anymore. Nobody was in a hurry.

I dressed quickly.

"Taking the bench last night was smart," said Rudy. "Bed bugs don't like climbing furniture. Keep the bench tonight, and you'll be safe. The bed bugs drop from these cracks in the ceiling when it gets dark. They march in a column, like soldiers, and search for the warmest body. I swear they can smell. That's for sure. Do you have lice? If not, you'll have them in three or maybe four days. It doesn't take longer than that. We all have lice. No way you can get rid of them here in the Balkans. Lice are worse than bed bugs. Next door, they have no bed bugs. I wonder why." Rudy continued chatting and didn't care if I listened. While we dressed he described the varieties of insects in the Balkans, especially the ones in this room.

"Some of these guys have fleas. I don't. Balkan fleas don't like humans. See the fellow over there? He is Rolf. He catches fleas and keeps them. He wants to open a flea circus after the war and trains his fleas at night. They jump and do what he tells them." Rudy's major concern, though, was lice. "Lice live in the seams of the clothes. At night, before we lay down, we take off our shirts and squash as many as we can with our fingernails. You'll never get rid of them. Lice are everywhere."

I had other concerns. "Where is the master sergeant?" Rudy was surprised at my lack of interest in the local bugs. I left the house and went outside. The road was still muddy from yesterday's rain; but the sky was blue.

How should I address the master sergeant? Why didn't he call the captain last night? That bordered on insubordination. I hesitated in front of his house, but like the day before, I felt his hand on my shoulder. "Don't worry! Calm down! I already talked to the captain," the master sergeant stood behind me in the mud and smiled. "The captain is informed. You took your position. He is fine. You'll get used to our style. We are little more casual." He read my mind. He knew I was worried.

"Artillery practice starts in fifteen minutes. I want you there on the first cannon! The captain told me you had training on the old 1916 Skoda cannons. That may come in handy. The old buggers are reliable. We still use them. But now we have the '36 model." Everything felt good about this man. He was the real boss. I wondered how much the captain told him about my bad report. Did he really expect me to call him last night?

Within three days, I had lice, just like Rudy predicted, and I couldn't get rid of them. The bed bugs didn't bother me since I stayed on the narrow bench at night. It was hard to get used to the Balkan environment. The daily chores were the same, artillery drill in the morning, cannon cleaning in the afternoon, eating and squashing lice at the end of the day. That became the routine.

Almost four weeks later Hugo came. He arrived on the same donkey supply trek with Joseph, and I recognized him from a distance by his officer's cap. I wondered why he insisted on wearing that cap when he wasn't an officer. He had been promoted to sergeant and had the two silver cadet stripes we received at the special training in France. It made me realize how close I had been to becoming an officer.

Hugo smiled broadly when he saw me. With measured cordial steps he came to greet me. Displaying too much joy was not the custom of nineteen-year-olds. We rarely showed emotions, but we were both delighted inside. He told me our eleven comrades had to join different units in other areas. Only Fritz had come to the First Mountain Division, but he joined the heavy artillery. I was happy Hugo was assigned here.

"What's this place called?" Hugo pointed at the twelve stone houses.

"I can't pronounce the name. This village is between Bosnia and Croatia and the people here believe in Allah and are Muslims."

"I thought it was all Yugoslavia. I've never heard of Bosnia. How come Muslims live this far north? I thought Muslims lived in Persia and flew on carpets." Hugo was just as surprised as I had been. But he carefully avoided showing his lack of knowledge. He now had a superior rank and was ambitious. Hugo would never accept that I knew more about anything. His officer's cap dangled dangerously on the right side of his head, threatening to fall off. "Since when do they allow you to wear the officer's cap?" I showed I didn't like it.

"Nothing in the rules and regulations that says an officer cadet can't wear the officer's cap," Hugo bragged. I worried about it. The veterans here didn't like anybody bragging. They were willing to help anybody, especially if you were new, but they turned away from somebody who bragged. Hugo would have to learn the hard way.

"When did you get here," asked Hugo without showing much interest. He inspected our four model 1936 mountain cannons, lined up not far from us in the practice field.

"I came four weeks ago. The captain assigned me to be first gunner."

"He did? You are first gunner? With your lousy record? Congratulations! I can't believe that! I thought you would be driving mules!" His crude reaction annoyed me. But Hugo was my best friend. He sensed that I was angry.

"Congratulations!" he said, and this time he reached for my hand. I accepted his handshake.

"Why do they keep the First Mountain Division in Yugoslavia? Seems an awful waste not using the unmatched battle experience. Have them sitting around idly in Yugoslavia isn't smart. Nobody can get a medal in Yugoslavia."

"Do you still want a bravery medal? Are you that ambitious?" I knew that Hugo would not change in that regard.

"The First Mountain Division is recuperating from battles in Russia. They deserve the rest. They didn't get a furlough for three years. Did you know that?"

"Hitler is nice, keeping his best division resting. He doesn't take a day off. Why should his elite division rest?" I detected sarcasm in Hugo's voice. That was new. Hugo had been a very enthusiastic supporter of Hitler's plans to expand and have Germany become Gross Deutschland.

"Do these old timers like the partisans and their ambushes?" I felt Hugo needed more information whether he liked it or not.

"They don't like a sneaky war like we have here in Yugoslavia, and they don't like partisans. But they don't complain. Partisans are a nuisance to them. The ambushes are serious, though. To them, partisans are bandits who don't wear uniforms. That makes them dangerous. They work the fields during the day and attack at night. That's not a normal war. They don't consider them soldiers. Nobody respects terrorists." Hugo listened and seemed to want to hear more. We sat down on a cannon.

"Veterans don't brag." I was blunt in warning him because he was my friend. I didn't want him to be misjudged because of his stupid officer cap. "They don't talk much about heroism and battles. They've been through a lot. When they talk, you'll be surprised. They talk about unusual stuff, death, and even fear. Everybody is the same, regardless of rank. I am too shy to think like that. They discuss death. It fascinates them. I don't know why. Did you talk about death and fear in school? We never did. They talk a lot about instinct, and admire anybody who has the sixth sense. I'd like to learn more about that. Anybody with the sixth sense is special and they follow everyone who has it. Nothing else counts around here very much. Don't be surprised if they check you out to see if you have the sixth sense. You'll gain respect with them if you show instinct, an old timer once told me. We depend on intuition. That's a natural defense.

"The sixth sense is more important than our rifles and tanks. Why didn't they teach us that in training?" Hugo shook his head. I wasn't sure if he was listening or if he wanted to understand.

"How do they treat you? Are they nice? I hope they realize that we are not recruits anymore!" When Hugo didn't understand a subject, he usually became defensive, "I don't know anything about an instinct."

I was fascinated when Joseph shot before the bandits did. That was the first time I saw someone use the sixth sense. I didn't know it existed, and it has intrigued me ever since. I told Hugo the story of my first ambush.

"I am sure everybody has the sixth sense. I guarantee everybody has it. They never told us about instinct in training. That was a mistake. I can see how important that is. They taught us the stupid cannons, but not how to stay alive. The old timer advises, 'Practice using your instinct every day, every minute, as often as you can,

Chapter 5

The Russian Army Closes In

Bosnian Mountains

A week later, we left the Muslim village. The artillery column stretched back around the next bend of a narrow mountain road. "We crossed the Drina River," said somebody. I couldn't care less. I had no idea where we were and hadn't seen a map.

Hugo walked next to me. Twice a day we stuffed ourselves with fresh mutton meat until we gradually became sick of the penetrating odor and decided to buy pork in the next Muslim village.

On a farm, we saw pigs were for sale. I didn't know that even though Muslim didn't eat pork, they sold pigs. We pooled our money and I went to the farm to buy a pig. The farm lady negotiated the price using sign language. When the price seemed right, I concluded the deal and asked her to lend us a pot to cook the meat in. She gave me a new black kettle and grinned happily, probably thinking she had made a good deal. None of us cared about money. It came and went fast.

We built a fire. An experienced gunner slaughtered the pig. Soon the meat began to boil. We added potatoes and carrots to make a thick stew. After we ate, I returned the kettle and saw the Muslim woman was very angry. She smelled the inside of the kettle and began yelling. She threw the pot on the kitchen floor, kicked it into a corner, and began to cry. I tried to calm her but it didn't work. She pushed me aside, grabbed the kettle and holding it far from her, ran into the forest.

We heard her lamenting in a distance. She came back empty handed. She had buried the pot in the woods.

The gunner who had butchered the pig said, "'Don't lead me to temptation,' said Jesus Christ. That woman doesn't believe in Jesus, but she sells us her pig, takes our money and gets mad after we ate her pig. She keeps our money, though. Something is not right in the Muslim religion." We agreed. But since most Muslims were friendly, we decided to switch back to mutton in spite of the offensive smell.

Hugo came back to my cannon to walk with us. He always had the latest. "The whole Regiment is on the move. The Mountain Division will take a position near Belgrade to defend the city, all 15,000 of us are marching."

Joseph and Roland also heard the news behind our cannon. Something went wrong with the brakes on the supply wagon. We helped hold the wagon until they fixed the brakes. "We should take the cannon apart," Tony said when he checked the problem. "The road is too steep."

Hugo was very happy today. The captain had given Hugo his blessing, he could officially wear his custom-made gray officer's cap. He poked me, "Fritz is nearby. The heavy artillery is not far; only a few kilometers behind us."

"I am hungry, it's noon. Why didn't they announce a lunch break?" The captain and two lieutenants galloped by to check something further back. "I hope they check the kitchen. I am hungry. The road is steep, the mules need a break," confirmed Rudy. Rolf, who walked next to Rudy, was in deep thought, "I don't mind fighting the Russians," he referred to the news Hugo brought, "we'll drive them back like we did before, and we'll be in Moscow in no time. It's about time this war ends so we can go home."

"We should have finished them off two years ago. We had them by the throat," said a guy behind him. "I'd rather fight a regular war anytime, than these partisans. They bother me. They are like the lice and bed bugs here in Yugoslavia. You never catch them. I still don't understand how the Russians rebuilt their army. Where did they get that stuff? When we left they had nothing. Now they come and chase us with new tanks."

"It's about time we finish them off," agreed Rolf. I wondered where Rolf kept his flea circus if he still had them. Rudy and I became friends. He often asked me about history and geography. His questions were intelligent. He heard I had an Abitur diploma and now he wanted to know everything.

"What did they teach in your school about Yugoslavia? What are we supposed to do here?" Since everybody was listening, I had to think about the answer.

A superficial answer would diminish the new confidence they had in my nineteen-year-old wisdom. Everybody waited. I took my time.

"'The purpose is to maintain order here,' said my professor. Yugoslavia is rather new, just created by a consortium headed by President Wilson of the United States. They renamed the fragmented country in 1929. Wilson stayed in Paris after the First World War, and became sick while he was still President of the United States. Wilson spread a huge European map over the floor in his office. The diplomats who recreated Europe crawled on the floor to make a border change. That's how Yugoslavia was created. The British needed an additional monarchy to replace the German and Austrian."

"You are kidding," Hugo interrupted, "I didn't know that." Hugo had an Abitur certificate as well and was my competition. We both liked to show off. He explained the Versailles treaty in 1919, his specialty. I let him take over.

"You remember how the First World War started, when a drunk Serb student assassinated Arch Duke Ferdinand of Austria in Sarajevo? Sarajevo was an insignificant provincial capital created by the Ottoman Turks who ruled Bosnia since 1463." None of the gunners knew that, nor did they care. But listened attentively. They were intelligent men who liked to learn. Most only had elementary school education.

"I learned quite a bit about Yugoslavia from a friend in school who came from Belgrade," I took over again. "His name was Igor, and he was a friend of young Prince Peter of Yugoslavia. In 1941 there was a communist demonstration in the center of Belgrade. Igor told me he and Peter were sixteen and had to escape the royal palace by sliding down a palace drainpipe. They hid in the bushes. The communists found the young prince and crowned him the next day making him their king and firing the prince regent.

Igor went to Germany where his mother lived. King Peter did not rule long and also fled. It was funny. The hard work done in Paris by diplomats after the First World War, went, literally, down the drain pipe." The gunners laughed.

Hugo took over. "The British sent their cousin, the German Kaiser Wilhelm, into exile in 1918. The stinky Versailles peace treaty got rid of two monarchies, Russia lost the czar, and now, it seemed the end of monarchies came. I wonder why anybody still fights for a monarchy?" Hugo turned to me. "Did your friend Igor know this guy Tito, the leader of the partisans? Did he meet him? Does anybody know him?"

"Tito is a communist who was trained in Moscow, he is not a Serb, he is a Croat." That didn't make sense to Rudy. "He leads the Serbs and is a Croat. While they made Croatia our Ally. He should fight with us and not against us! Why are we maintaining order among all these characters who fight each other?"

"Nobody knows. They don't have the foggiest idea in Berlin either, or they forgot to tell us," remarked Rolf. He asked how many religions exist in Yugoslavia. Nobody knew that for sure, not even Hugo. They didn't teach that in school either.

Tony, our master sergeant, joined us. He heard the intelligent talk. "They have six religions here, as far as anybody knows, there could be more. There are the Muslims, Roman Catholics, Orthodox Christians, gypsies, Jews and bandits. Every faction, though, has different beliefs. One thing is for sure, they hate each other." Hugo said that Tony studied history at the University of Innsbruck, a corporal had told him.

"What religion do the Chetniks believe in?" asked Rolf.

"They don't follow a religion. As the traditional Serb bandits, they show patriotism by wearing long beards, they let them grow and won't cut their hair until their last enemy has left their soil. Their problem is they don't know who their enemies are and where the border runs. They scared the pants off me when I first saw them with the draped ammunition belts around their filthy clothes and smelling like they did in the Middle Ages. I pointed my assault rifle at them and yelled, "Get lost! Two kilometers off and away and not one step closer!" They talked broken German and laughed. "We are friends!"

"But don't believe them! They are nobody's friend, not the Russian's or ours. They steal from everybody and hate Tito and his partisans." Rolf confirmed the story.

"Don't ever trust a Chetnik. They hate Tito because he is a Croat, and they are the traditional Serbs. They all need a hot bath and a haircut after the war," added Rudy.

"Everybody takes advice from gypsies who think stealing is virtue," continued Tony. "They all steal! Some steal more than others. We know Tito is our enemy. He fights us officially as a dedicated communist. I am not sure about the Croats. They are our Allies because Hitler made Croatia into an independent state. I don't trust them either. The Croatian Ustasha military kill Muslims and Serbs. Muslims hate the Serbs. Serbs hate the Muslims and the Croats. Slovaks hate Serbs. The Macedonians don't like anybody. There are Albanians, too. Would you expect these folks to like us Germans who came here to keep order and protect them?" Tony fell silent.

I had a private talk with Tony a couple of days earlier. First, he told me to call him Tony because everybody else did. I felt uneasy having only been there for six weeks. He wanted me to tell him what had happened in my reserve officers training. He had seen my report.

"Why were you fired?" I explained the reason from my perspective.

"That's a damn shame. We need advance observers, and you have the training." He hesitated and told me, "Your brother Kurt and I are friends. Kurt saved my life in Russia, which I will not forget." Now I knew why Tony had looked out for me from the first day on. I was anxious to hear more, but he didn't continue. I didn't want to press further.

He told me he enjoyed being the master sergeant. "I won't become an officer. After the war, I'll go back to Innsbruck and teach history at the university." I was proud that Tony walked next to me.

In the meantime, the road had become smoother. The cannons rolled unencumbered downhill. A valley below expanded to the horizon. We must have been at the end of the mountains. A steep rock bank was the last sign of them. It was carved from a mountainous bank high on our right side. To the left, a field covered by large boulders sloped gently down to a fast running stream, dividing it. Behind the stream on the other side, ascended a hill covered by dark trees. It looked like a green wall.

"Did we cross the border?" asked Rolf.

"What border? There are no borders in Yugoslavia," replied Rudy.

"We crossed the Drina River. That's a border between Bosnia and Herzegovina."

"I didn't see no border signs," said the guy next to Rudy, shaking his head.

Tony smiled. He liked his men. Their geography and knowledge of history wasn't always correct, but he didn't bother them with academics. "What do they teach in Munich about the Balkans?" Tony asked me.

"I had a few semesters at your university. They gave us texts from Berlin, a poor selection." I didn't want to tell him that I didn't attend school in Munich but at a fancy boarding school. Tony didn't wait for the answer anyway.

"The German professors don't realize the importance of the Balkans. It's important for Austria. The Turks occupied this land for centuries, and we can see the influence, even up to Bavaria. Churches in Bavaria are topped in Turkish-Byzantine style, onion shaped domes. We would have become Muslims, if it weren't for an Austrian army that defeated the Ottomans in the 14th century. They still call the Muslims 'Turks' in Yugoslavia. German history doesn't explain the Balkans." Tony sounded more like a professor of history, than a master sergeant.

"Most of the Balkans were part of the Hapsburg Empire," he continued. "We can still see the influence." He grinned suddenly, "Austria had a clever idea. At the beginning of this century, Austrians sent a poor architect student, named Adolf Hitler, to Germany, had him enlist as a corporal into the German army, and twenty-five years later he unified Austria with Germany, which was the dream of kings and queens." All around us laughed.

Hugo needed to demonstrate his history knowledge. "The Prussian Hohenzollern wanted unification also. Frederick the Great defeated Austria's Maria Theresa, but they did not unite. Instead, they annexed Poland and split the land into three parts. Austria and Prussia took two thirds, and Russia one third, just like in 1939. That time Poland lasted thirty years after it was re-established in 1919. Hitler and Stalin conquered and divided Poland. They had a deal made before that."

"I am glad Hitler united us and we finally became Gross Deutschland," Hugo added thoughtfully.

"I agree," Tony confirmed, "Hitler should get credit for that."

The gunners listened attentively. A sergeant, twenty-six years old and a long-time friend of Tony, asked, "Tony, why are there still borders between Bavaria and Austria? You and I live twenty kilometers apart. I don't understand why we still show a border between us.

"If the Drina River is the border between two states which we've never heard of, but they don't post border signs, maybe they are smarter in Yugoslavia. Bosnia cannot be that important." After pausing a while, he added, "The only border I'll fight for in the future is the fence around my house. What do you think?"

Tony didn't answer. His question made sense to me. Why do we keep border signs and wear the same uniform? Tony kept thinking.

"A border gives an individual freedom," he said after a while. "The space between fences tells you own something. That makes you special. That space is yours. The old border signs are traditional signs. Those who live between those borders are special." Max nodded, without understanding. "Doesn't war always begin because of a border dispute?"

I saw in the distance, in the valley, a road joining our mountain path. An endless column of soldiers approached the joining point, I thought they must have been the infantry of the First Mountain Division—15,000 men, enough to stop any Russian advance. Soon we would go into battle together. I wondered what my first real battle would be like.

Tony left and walked to the front of the column. Something bothered him. I sensed nervousness and everybody became uneasy. The talking stopped. Did they see something I didn't?

A motor bike behind us stirred incredible amounts of dust. He drove like a lunatic and yelled. The shouts were muffled by the roar of his engine. He waved his arm. "Save yourselves as best you can!" I heard as he passed and sped away.

"Save yourselves! Why?" The command lingered. Our column grounded to a halt. "He was crazy."

The order to disband usually came when the last bullet was spent, most soldiers were killed and there was no hope for escape. That could never happen. That order was only reluctantly mentioned in training. Why did this guy shout an order like that? We didn't hear a shot? Yet, nervous, I wanted to ask somebody. Silence lingered in the air and felt eerie.

Rudy broke the silence. "The guy was crazy."

"No! He was not joking if you ask me," said Max. "Something is wrong."

Where were the officers? They know what's going on. Suddenly we heard an ominous sound, a deep rumbling of many cannons firing in the distance. Artillery men knew that sound. It came from heavy artillery cannons. And the danger was now clearly imminent. We had no time to discuss it.

In seconds, hundreds of grenade shells exploded in the field on the left. I fell instinctively on the hard ground. So did the others, spreading out on the road. The road wasn't hit. But my eardrums threatened to split from the explosions in the field. We had no cover on the road. No one was hurt, but dirt flew up in clumps and rained back on us—much fell on my back. The road must be the target. They misfired their first shots. The field became saturated with explosions down to the stream. The rock wall to our right bounced with whistling shrapnel, and worse, the wall blocked any escape. We were trapped. Grenades exploded in rapid succession leaving deep holes in the field. Everybody lay on the open road.

We can't stay here, I thought. Off this road, ordered something inside of me. Why didn't they hit the road? Maybe the road is safer and better?

I crawled to the edge of the dangerous field, hesitating to get closer to the explosions, but then I saw a large boulder. It would be good protection. The road is the target, my head told me. Get away from the road!

I slid down the field in spite of exploding grenades and landed in a new crater. Smoke from the explosion still lingered. New grenades exploded coming closer. Stupid of me to be on an open field between exploding grenades, I cussed and rolled further. Even if it kills me, I must get away from the road. Some grenades exploded on the road. That convinced me the field was the right direction. My knapsack was caught on something but the knapsack was good protection. Rocks hit us hard. The grenades will be my death! I was now really scared.

Go further down! The road will be their next target, repeated my brain. I obeyed and rolled, but missed the boulder that was to be my protection. Grenades began to explode on the road and hit by air pressure, I stuck my body to the ground. My knapsack snapped a second time. I adjusted the straps and crawled to my right. I thought there were fewer explosions. But I was wrong.

I heard a new sound. Infantry bullets whistled over my head and hit the road. They came from the forest at eye level, from straight in front of me. I even saw the rifles igniting. It looked like stars against the black background. The bullets were aimed higher. They hit everything on the road with precision. They wheezed off the rock wall, from boulders, and from metal. They made awful noises as they ricocheted, before hitting the ground. I was scared. Men and animals were hit one by one. I was glad I had left the road and pressed my head into the soil. Lying still, I felt paralyzed and numb.

A grenade exploded nearby, leaving a huge crater. I hardly heard the explosion, it was so close! The valley became an inferno. One grenade after another fell into the field and exploded. I listened hard and clearly heard an additional sound. The 'tack tack' of Russian machine guns filtered through the noise, I saw their ignitions between the line of rifle fire. Bullets whistled in an endless barrage. My crater was too shallow. Where could I go? Definitely not back to the road! But where? I weighed my options. The bullets wheezed over my head, hit the road and kept me down. Can I go to the stream?

But instead of getting up, I laid still, scared to go anywhere. The stream down below seemed too far. I should go there, I thought, and rolled further down. Now I was even closer to the enemy. That's the wrong direction.

I had no choice. I pushed and rolled despite my fear. A larger boulder was to my right. It'll protect me! I'll go there. I crawled through a barrage of infantry fire. Stupid! Can't you see the forest is close? I looked back and saw the road. That became a scene of execution. Bullets hit them by the thousand and mowed men and animals down pinning the rest against the rock wall. They tumbled over each other. The situation seemed hopeless.

Why am I still alive? I wondered, pressing against my boulder.

An urge to run away anywhere took hold. I stood up, now highly visible between shots and ran unprotected with grenades exploding right and left. Bullets whistled, but miraculously, I wasn't hit. I stumbled over a rock and landed exhausted in a crater. My knapsack kept me from sliding. Rocks and dirt rained on me. This is the end, I thought. Where am I? My chest hurt. Am I wounded? I checked and found nothing. I had fallen on my rifle's steel lock, and it hurt. Angry, I wanted to toss my rifle away. Something told me not to. The rifle is your protection. I obeyed and laid still.

I had no time to shoot, and the enemy was so close that shooting would attract their attention. I wished I was wounded and couldn't go further. I checked my body. Everything seemed fine. Only I felt numb. A grenade exploded only three meters away; the air pressure pushed me into the dirt and rocks hit. Get away from here, said my voice. Where to? Without thinking, I obeyed and crawled from my hole. Something was guarding me. I was convinced. But why me?

A large piece of iron fell where I had lain seconds ago. It was a dud, sticking in the ground. A dud doesn't explode, but is deadly if it hits you. It stuck two meters away in my previous hole. Safe, I thanked somebody up there.

No time to think. The Russian machine guns blasted from only 120 meters away. Bullets whistled over my head. Can they see me? It was obvious they could not since I was an easy target. I felt trapped. An uncontrollable shudder ran over me. I give up! I don't want to go anywhere anymore. The dud should have killed me! I mumbled. Suddenly self-preservation took over. No, they didn't kill me. I will live. I am alive.

"Yes, I want to live! " I heard myself yelling. I purposely shouted at the forest, now defiant and relieved. I even stood up and yelled. "I want to live." I yelled loud without caring who heard me. Nobody did. That made my survival urge even stronger. I stood recklessly between bullets, and foolishly defiant, I shouted, knowing I was a target. They still didn't see me. I stood and walked a few steps away from my boulder, ever more convinced that nothing could hit me. Maybe, they don't try hard enough. Why are they missing me? I noticed the stream; I was close. Shoot, you bastards! I repeated and breathed heavily.

Shots whistled, but they hit the road, a much broader target. Suddenly it became eerily quiet. My ribcage still hurt. That damn rifle lock!

They must be taking a break? A boulder attracted my attention. I could take advantage of the momentary lull and began crawling frog-style toward it. They are reorganizing, I thought, who knows what they will do. They are in control. A few rifles still fired, but into a different direction. What is happening? What are they up to? They have new targets. I now remembered the infantry column marching into the valley. They must have seen them.

Poor guys, you've walked into the trap, too. The lull brought no relief. It was temporary—I was smart enough to figure that out and ran to another boulder. This time they saw me. A barrage of bullets hit the rocks and soil before me and on my sides. I made it to the boulder and looking back, I saw Hugo's light grey officer's cap. He stood between men and animals struggling with a raving mule. Both disappeared as Hugo hung on the mule. The mule dragged him along. Only the heads of the mules were visible. They trampled relentlessly over boxes, across humans and even tried to climb the wagons. A cannon rolled off the road with a dead mule tangled in its straps. I didn't recognize anybody. But I was glad I saw Hugo and knew he was alive. The others must be dead by now. I turned away and felt a splitting headache. The explosions, shots, the entire inferno came back, full force.

I covered my ears and felt my knapsack snap. Bullets hit everywhere. They wanted to prove they hadn't forgotten me. I embraced the rock and gave thanks for its protection. That they kept missing was almost annoying. Shooting from that close and missing was an embarrassment.

"When are you going to hit me? How long will it take you?" I yelled from behind my rock. Back on the road bodies piled on top of each other, men and animals. Scared, I glued myself to the stone.

Loud and clear I heard from inside, you can't stay here! Go to the stream! I remembered to listen to my sixth sense. There was a rock wall, a flood barrier, twenty meters down the stream. The stone wall was inviting. That's high enough to keep me out of sight. I crawled there and found a wagon upside down in the water at the end of the wall. Should be good cover. I ran the last few meters. Again, the Russians didn't see me. No shots!

The wagon was not good cover. I heaped rotting boards on top of each other to make the best of it. While I worked, I thought I heard the rapid bursts of a German machine gun not far away. "Hurrah! I am not alone," I screamed from behind my boards. The German machine gun inspired me. Could it be Sarge Joseph? Yes, that was him. I was sure. Only he can shoot like that. I searched until I found them. I could see Joseph, his massive body crouched behind a boulder, and Roland knelt next to him, handing him ammunition. The rhythmic 'tack tack' of Russian machine guns sounded slow compared to Joseph's gun and its rapid bursts. Thank God, the guys are alive! My heart pumped, and I wanted to go and join them. Don't go, flashed my mind. But why not? I want to go.

I was suddenly entangled by boards and couldn't get out. Four boards were in my way. At the same time, a grenade exploded just a meter away. The explosion threw me back. Boards fell and covered me. They had taken the brunt of the iron. Another grenade exploded, and another. A fourth and fifth in rapid succession fell into the field where I was on my way to join Joseph and Roland. Now, the falling boards didn't seem so bad. I leaned back and was glad I hadn't run.

The smoke lifted. I couldn't see Joseph or Roland or the boulder. They must be in the stream. The field was full of new craters. Dazed, I climbed out to rearrange the boards. I was disoriented. I remembered Roland telling me, "Nothing can ever happen to Joseph!" If that was true, they are alive.

I strongly believed that. They are alive, I shouted into the sporadic infantry fire that suddenly stopped. I took advantage and ran downhill toward the valley. Run! Run! I told myself. I ran full speed, upright without looking back. Faster! I ordered myself and ran until my legs wobbled. Joseph's machine gun will keep them down.

Exhausted, I stumbled and hoped that it was Joseph who kept shooting. That would be just like him! I fell on soft sand. Don't black out now, I ordered myself and breathed heavily. A Russian machine gun shot, but was out of my range. I stretched to recover and heard voices in the smoke. That was Lieutenant Stoll. "Stop! Do you hear me? Let's take the cannon apart."

I crawled toward the voice while smoke bit my eyes. When I heard the word cannon, I immediately thought of my equipment. They had carved it into my brain during training, "Always stay with your equipment!" Where was my cannon? Why did I leave her? Frantically I searched. My cannon was with Lieutenant Stoll in the smog. I knew it was my cannon and crawled under the barrel. There were legs on the right side of it. A body was covered by the barrel. I yelled into the noise, but received no answer. A body crumpled and fell next to me. I saw a bloody face trying to say something. It turned toward me. The face was distorted, struggling with death. Behind me a man wrestled a mule. I saw earth lifting from explosions; but I could no longer hear the sound. It was muffled. My hearing was gone! The mule stood trembling while the dirt settled. Slowly, the mule folded its legs and slumped to the ground. The loss of hearing frightened me. I need my senses, I shouted in panic. A grenade exploded about six meters away, but only the muffled sound rang in my ears.

Men rushed to the cannon and began taking her apart. I went to help them. Usually, we could take a cannon apart in less than two minutes. I worked feverishly on my end without looking up. I saw three twisted bodies hit the ground. They had been hit by a grenade that I hadn't heard. Desperate, I shouted, "Lieutenant Stoll!" There was thick smog. As loud as I could, I repeated, but my voice sounded muffled. "Are you there?" No answer.

Somebody came to my side. A familiar voice sounded dull but clear, "Let's load the wounded on the mule. Forget the cannon. Give me a hand!" Rudy stood next to me.

Delighted, I grabbed his shoulder. At least he was alive. Rudy's beard glowed red from the reflection of an explosion as we pulled a body toward the mule. Rudy spoke, but I couldn't understand him. Suddenly he began to stagger sideways. Then he sat down. Blood spurted from his arm. Soon the blood soaked his torn trousers. I held the mule's straps and pulled the frightened animal toward Rudy in an attempt to load him. I couldn't manage.

"You'll have to help me," I ordered Rudy. His voice was fading, "I am losing blood." Rudy slumped to the side. "I'll get you on that mule, Rudy. Please help! Don't give up!" I desperately pushed him on the mule. I used all my strength, lifted and pushed Rudy halfway on the mule. Yes, he was still alive. I was sure of that. His eyes were half-open.

A grenade exploded nearby. This time I heard it loud and clear. The mule rocked, and Rudy fell off. The animal was hit and slumped forward, slowly folding its legs. The mule's body dropped onto my feet. It rocked, fighting death, and allowed me to move my legs from under its weight. Rudy lay not far from me. His stomach was opened by the grenade. There was no doubt he was dead. His right arm still pointed up as if asking for help.

I choked and cuddled my dead mule. Tears streamed down my cheeks.

"This is insane," I hollered into the inferno. The mule's huge body felt warm and strangely comfortable. I laid still and thanked him for protecting me. I felt weightless and numb. Am I dead? I couldn't understand why I was numb and I couldn't do anything. I needed time. Behind the mule's warm body, I told myself, take your time! With my left hand, I checked my body. I needed to know if my legs were all right. I needed to get away. A tingling sensation vibrated my body. Nothing is wrong, I calmed myself. There are no wounds. I should be dead like the others.

Then a single bullet ricocheted off the barrel of my cannon. That convinced me I wasn't dead! I told myself, I am scared, but I am not dead. I laid still and soon felt better.

My cannon stood majestically in the smoke. Unattended, she looked like a monument. I could hear metal ricocheting off it with a wheezing sound. Gradually, I collected my thoughts. Where is Hugo? Where is everybody? The whole thing is a mirage. Why did nothing happen to me. The urge to survive took over once again. I saw moving shadows coming. Are they Russians? Smoke still covered them.

"Go! Run! We are trapped." I heard, "Russians are behind us." A man plunked down next to me. He rudely squeezed me over. "That mule was my cover," I mumbled.

"Hi!" he greeted me unconcerned. I pushed back and noticed he was an infantry sergeant. He laid his rifle across the mule's back and shot five times, reminding me that I also had a rifle. I fired five shots without aiming.

"The bastards caught our General," he cussed and reloaded. "They caught the whole Division staff and hit us from the back. We are trapped. There is no way out. We are dead here in the middle!" There was an unfamiliar sound; a missile soared by. "Damn! They got our Ratsch-bum," he shouted. Ratsch-bum was a new German missile that fired from launchers in rapid succession. The sound, Ratsch——bum, became its name. These missiles were scary. "The Russians don't have a Ratsch-bum, not that I know of. They took ours and are shooting them at us. They'll kill us with our best weapon."

A mule bounced into my cannon and stopped, dazed. I grabbed the leather straps. The mule resisted, jerked, reeled and wanted to shake me off. I held on as he ran. I fastened the straps around my body. My legs bumped bodies and equipment. We seemingly ran forever. My arms lost strength and gradually I had to let go. The mule stopped and began trembling. I had experienced that many times and knew what it meant. The mule was hit.

My feet planted firmly on the ground, I pressed against the mule trying to keep him upright. He collapsed with a groan. This time I was careful not to get caught under his weight. The legs stretched up one more time before the life faded away. I held the mule's hind leg up for protection. Soldiers crawled by. I wondered if I should go with them. They disappeared momentarily in the smoke. When the smoke lifted, I saw the last two men tumbling, felled by a Russian machine gun. Afraid, I held onto my big mule's hind leg. I clutched him firmly, thanking him for letting me stay. The knapsack rocked, again hit by a bullet only inches from my neck. I reached back to check. There was no blood on my fingers. I was lucky again.

Not far in the distance on a hill, I saw T-34 Russian tanks appearing, covered on and off by sways of smoke. I hoped my eyes were playing tricks. It must be my imagination. If it were true, we were trapped. Russian tanks coming from the north, and the infantry from behind. There was no more doubt. About fifty tanks rolled downhill. The steel bodies waved as if mowing through turbulent water. I looked feverishly for an escape. They won't go into exploding grenades. I reasoned, they have to stop! And they did, 300 meters away. They turned and fanned out, turned again and waited in a frontal position.

What could I do? They may drive by and miss me behind my dead mule. Grenade explosions lessened. I heard faint German march music in the distance. Unbelievable! German march music came from the center tank. Are they crazy? Playing the enemy's march music before an attack? The music came in waves from an amplifier mounted on the side of the lead tank. The tank rolled about 150 meters and stopped again. The music droned louder. I recognized Hitler's favorite, the *Badenweiler March*, which they played when he walked into a stadium as masses of brown-shirts roared. They knew Hitler well.

The center tank rolled twenty more meters, stopped, and the lid opened. A wooden skeleton, from which a German general's uniform hung, was hoisted from the opening and was slowly swung in a circle. The march music continued. Grenade explosions had completely stopped. The march music also stopped. A deep amplified voice droned from the loudspeaker, "I present to you your General, Edelweiss Pirates. Do you recognize your General? Salute him!" The voice sounded cynical in German with a Slavic accent.

An eerie silence followed the announcement that ended in a roar of laughter. "This is revenge for Charkow! You bastards! Do you remember Charkow? Think! You killed thousands of Russians. We waited for this day." A Russian soldier's head appeared attempting to fasten the uniformed skeleton to the side of the amplifier.

One shot rang out, and the Russian soldier's body slumped forward, hit in the head. A barrage of infantry shots followed and rocked the lifeless body.

Invisible hands grabbed the dead Russian and pulled him inside. The wood skeleton and the German general's uniform was stuck and now leaned sideways. Once more, German march music began to play. This time, the music was drowned by small arms fire from our side. Mostly single shots, but between them blasted the rapid bursts of German machine guns. The shooting made no sense. But hearing German bullets was a relief. It showed them we weren't dead, yet. I emptied my magazine and felt exhilarated, though it was useless. The shooting rhythm of a machine gun convinced me that Joseph was alive and with us. I grinned defiantly, feeling like a veteran.

I will not die, I promised. As long as Joseph and Roland were alive!

"Get going, you bastards!" I yelled toward the tanks. "Come and kill us!"

The shooting from the few remaining Germans gradually ended. There was no escape. The German march music played from the lead-gray steel monster. Death was just a matter of time.

Behind, from out of the smoke suddenly appeared a ghostly figure of a man on a white horse. The man sat high, his horse smartly circled the many craters. There was no better target than a white horse. Everybody could see him, including the Russians. He rode toward me. I could tell by his uniform, he was a high-ranking officer.

"Follow me, soldiers," he shouted waving an arm. Soldiers crouched behind him and the horse. I jumped up without hesitating and ran to him. Forty soldiers had gathered.

"Follow him!" I heard. The rider turned and pointed to the forest. The Russian tanks stood still. No shots were fired, and none came from the forest. It was eerily quiet.

Why is he going toward the forest? They'll kill us, I thought, exasperated. I stumbled, but managed to stay close. The white horse walked fast.

Committed, I ran with them. He rides into hell. Doesn't he know the Russian infantry is there? I was angry, but I ran along like the others.

"Follow me, soldiers!" I heard the officer's voice fading. The Russian tanks began to roll. That made me run faster. "This way soldiers!" We were near the forest, and there was still not a shot. The Russians must have left.

"He is a miracle," groaned a limping soldier. Now fifty soldiers ran and crouched behind me. "Why is he going into the forest?" I hoped to draw somebody's attention. Nobody cared. I had no desire to reason, and ran to catch up. Horse and rider disappeared in the trees. The forest remained silent.

"Just follow him! He knows what he is doing. He is a miracle," somebody behind me heard my concern. Obviously, there were no Russians in this forest. I made one last effort, then tumbled and sank into a thorny brush at the edge of the forest.

Thank God, I made it. I am safe. I let my head rest but my instinct would not allow it. Catch up or you won't be safe, it said. Annoyed, I got up and followed the last three soldiers, who had just disappeared into the trees. The forest was dark and dense. The battle field noise became muffled by the foliage.

I remembered when my mother explained, "Every human being has a guardian angel." I didn't believe her at the time. But now I was convinced. She was right. The officer on the white horse was like a guardian angel. Or was he a ghost, or perhaps Jesus Christ himself? Whoever he was, he saved my life. How could that horse manage the brush? He must be a special horse. He'll manage.

We came to a small green patch. The first of my group yelled joyfully, "Here they are!" Eight exhausted German soldiers laid on the ground. Some leaning back on their elbows made little effort to welcome us. Their eyes were half-closed as if in a trance.

"Come here," I heard from behind me. It was Tony, my friend and protector. I was stunned to find him here. He sounded hoarse. I couldn't believe he was here. To make absolutely sure, I grabbed his arm and collapsed by his side. "I am so glad to see you. How did you get out of that mess?" I yelled from excitement.

"Don't yell," Tony scolded. "We are by no means safe." He squeezed my hand. "I am glad to see you, too," he whispered and leaned back closing his eyes. Nine infantry soldiers made a semicircle, including the three I had come with. They all seemed to know each other and shook hands. An artillery top sergeant was between them. He kept his eyes closed and groaned in pain.

"Where is Major Eisele?" asked the burly infantry sergeant who led my group. For the first time I heard the mysterious officer's name. Major Eisele was their commander. They marveled at how he rode his horse and dared the bullets.

"He is my hero," said the burly sergeant. "How did he know that the Russians had left here. That will remain a mystery for as long as I live."

"He knew because God told him," answered the soldier next to him.

"Where is he? We should look for him! He'll lead us the rest of the way."

"Eisele was God's messenger! God did not want us to die. He risked his life to save us. God didn't want him to die either. That is obvious. Not a single bullet hit him." The man prayed silently. I had forgotten how religious some soldiers were. The one next to him ripped a surgical dressing apart and bandaged the praying man's bleeding hand. The artillery sergeant didn't move. I wondered if he was still alive. He was bandaged with a shirt wrapped around his left arm, which was soaked with blood. Tony noticed me staring.

He sat up and pointed in the man's direction. "That is Ernst, a good friend of mine, of the 4th Battery. He is bad off, I am afraid," Tony laid back and mumbled, "They sure got revenge for the battle of Charkow today." He stared into the air.

"Ernst and I were there. We were machine gunners. Our Division closed the gap. No Russian could escape. We shot all day and mowed them down. Our machine gun barrels were hot. We had to wrap wet towels over them. God knows how many Russians we shot and killed. They outnumbered us five to two. They came drunk. The commissars gave them all the vodka they wanted, then sent them in our direction. Row after row of drunken Russians staggered before us, had their arms linked to keep in balance and came fighting barehanded, stone drunk. They lost their rifles on the way, were helpless and couldn't fight. We had no choice; we shot them down. And they kept coming by the thousands, drunk and wanting to fight bare handed." Tony sighed.

"They had their revenge today." With that he stopped the terrible confession.

"I can't blame them. I wonder why we keep killing each other? Anybody who declares war is nuts. Stalin and Hitler are insane. War is insane!"

Chapter 6

Escape

A Swamp near the Drina River

Utterly exhausted, we rested for an hour sitting in a circle and discussing who might lead us. Tony was elected. He was high ranked, and the infantry soldiers knew of him. Reluctantly, he accepted the responsibility.

"Let's not assume we are safe yet." Tony's voice sounded hoarse. "Those who want to leave and find Major Eisele, go ahead! I don't recommend it. We are, figuratively speaking, in the eye of a hurricane. The center of a hurricane feels nice and cozy. But wait until the storm circles, it's only a trap, and that's the case here. A huge Russian army is out there. The storm may break loose at any time. It never fails. Did you see the Russian tanks? They closed the trap while the Russian infantry was behind them. Russians are everywhere, and Tito partisans are in the hills. We were lucky to get this far." He waved for us to move closer. "We can't stay here. You and I know that much," he whispered. "I'll leave in ten minutes. Anybody who wants to come with me, get ready." A few infantry men hesitated. The burly sergeant who led my group waved an arm. "We've got to stick together," he warned. "I'll go with you." The others agreed, but Tony hesitated. He still wasn't sure if he wanted the burden.

"I didn't ask to lead you. You elected me," he motioned. "I agree, we must stick together. Twenty-four eyes see more than two eyes, besides, we can split the watch and everybody gets a rest. But I will set the rules. Better listen before you decide. My rules are tough and made to help us survive. First, you must throw all non-essentials away, socks, shirts, underwear. Keep your gun and ammunition. Also keep your food and iron ration. Does anybody still have water?" Two men showed water bottles.

"Good! We have two water bottles. We'll share them."

"Second, and this is the tough rule. Anybody who can't walk anymore must be left; and that is for any reason. Anybody who can't walk, is hit by a bullet, falls asleep, or won't get up, must be left." Tony's face was hard. "We can't carry anybody. We may have to walk for days, maybe for weeks, without food and water. I intend to walk at night. Nobody objected.

The burly infantry sergeant raised his hand. "Why don't we find Major Eisele? He isn't far; and he has thirty soldiers, which gives him a solid defense."

Tony looked annoyed. "I repeat, anybody who wants to leave, can go. That's final." He stuck his forefinger in the burly sergeant's chest. "I don't know where we are. Neither do you. Your guess is as good as mine. If you think you can find Major Eisele in this damn forest full of crawling Russians, then you should lead. I don't have a map. I'll use my instinct. I want to survive just like you do. Major Eisele has a horse. He won't wait for us. He is gone." Tony paused. "Be thankful Eisele got us this far. He saved our lives. We owe him. I'll thank him, and you should too." Nobody answered.

We emptied our knapsacks and began discarding unnecessary things.

"Damn! If I can't smoke these Greek cigarettes, then the Russians can't smoke them either." A lance corporal tore a dozen Greek cigarette packages apart and stamped on them. He threw them into the brush.

"Look at this fine leather from Macedonia. This leather was to become the finest leather purses displayed in any leather store." He fingered the velvety soft leather before throwing each sheet, one by one, into the brush. He looked dirtier than the others. His clothing was more torn. But everybody's face was caked with mud. For the first time, I looked down at myself and saw how torn my clothes were. The guys looked older than they were, and now, they were acting like kids who didn't want to give up their toys. I got rid of my stuff, but I kept a pair of fine leather gloves I had bought in Grenoble, France.

The sky faded to dark blue. Tony lifted himself up, sniffed like a bird dog and checked the trees. They all looked the same to me. Then he shouldered his bag, kept his assault rifle in his right hand and walked briskly into the densest part of the forest. I followed him. We stopped. When Tony listened and dropped to the ground, I dropped as well without asking why. So did the others behind me. We repeated that motion a hundred times. I focused on Tony, able to see only his outline. I never heard his steps. Gradually, I felt my body beginning to ache and fatigue crept in. Concentrate! I can't lose him! I repeated the phrase a hundred times to stay awake.

Tony walked slowly in a low crouched position. He fell forward and stayed much longer than before. He crawled away slowly. It was completely dark. I moved closer, almost touching his heels. He lay still for several minutes, got up and gestured like nothing happened. Without looking back, he walked away and didn't stop. We walked non-stop for what seemed like ten kilometers. Nobody talked.

I found it harder and harder to concentrate. In order to stay awake, I checked every noise, a breaking stick, something in the brush or rustling of foliage. I struggled and wondered about every movement between the trees. Imagination generated plenty. Fear kept me awake, even when I realized there was nothing. We kept moving. My fear was matched by my exhaustion. The treetops gradually showed the first color of morning.

Tony stopped. We moved up and formed a semi-circle. Tony counted, using all his fingers. "We are nine," he concluded, "we lost three. We will wait ten minutes."

I collapsed and fell on the cold moist ground and immediately closed my eyes. Scary scenes from the prior day's battle raced through my brain. I couldn't watch. I opened my eyes and the gruesome pictures left; but a shudder lingered. I felt like I had been submerged in freezing water.

I'd rather walk, I told myself. I hope Tony calls us, and we start walking again. I can't close my eyes. I don't want to see those terrible scenes. Resting makes no sense. I checked the others. Nobody slept. They leaned on their elbows and kept their eyes closed. They were more experienced and smarter. Most likely they didn't see battle scenes. I strained to keep my eyes open.

Ten minutes passed. Tony got up and shouldered his assault rifle. That was the first time he shouldered the gun instead of keeping it in his hand. He walked away and didn't care whether we followed. An hour later, he turned around and waited until we caught up.

"We lost three." The count was final and sad. "I hope they'll make it on their own." The burly infantry sergeant called, "Sarge, why don't we rest for a couple of hours? We have walked for twenty kilometers and must be far behind Russian lines."

Tony didn't answer. He just stared and became angry. "Twenty kilometers is nothing. We are still in the middle of a large Russian army. Don't you realize it's not safe? If you want to sleep, I am not going to wake you up. You know the rules. I'm going to walk for three more hours."

Ernst, Tony's friend from the 4th Battery, walked at the end of the column. But Tony wanted him to walk in second position behind him. He looked awful, like a ghost. Ernst was a big man, but I wondered how long he would last? His shirt-bandaged arm was heavy from fresh blood, and his face looked gray. To encourage myself, I thought about how strong and experienced he was. He had bravery medals and was wounded twice. He should be able to make it. He is used to it.

I walked behind Ernst. Walking was hard, physically and mentally. I used both arms to brush thick foliage off my face, convincing myself that Ernst was fine. Tony's behavior became a barometer for me. He had his gun over his shoulder, therefore we must be safe. Or was he tiring? A guy called from far back for a bandage. His knee was wounded and bled. Tony stopped. "Does anybody have a bandage?" Somebody had one. "Let's rest," said Tony. "It's almost noon. You can eat your iron ration now. I suggest that you save some for later!" At boot camp I was taught that the iron ration was holy. The iron ration was the only food we had and packages could only be consumed with an officer's approval.

I'll eat mine, I decided. I was very hungry. I munched the dry stuff, but could not swallow. There was no saliva in my mouth. It was frightening. I choked and spit the precious food on the ground. The trees began spinning; I leaned back and the treetops turned in a large circle. The water bottle came by. I grabbed it and just swallowed twice, the allotted amount. The water in my mouth made the food melt and go down. I closed my eyes. But again, the mangled bodies of the battle, piles of dead mules, and horror crossed my vision path. The pictures went by rapidly. Frightened, I strained to open my eyes. I must sleep! Desperate, I forced my eyes to close and instantly fell into a deep coma-like sleep.

Hours later, Tony shook my shoulder. He stood over me, his face was in a haze, the treetops swayed calmly, and the sky was deep blue.

"Get up, it's time." He turned without waiting and walked into the brush. I scrambled to my feet and followed in fourth position. But my feet hurt. The new mountain boots had fifty heavy nails along the edges had become too heavy.

Why didn't I take my shoes off before I fell asleep? Drowsy and angry with myself, I dragged my feet close to the ground to save strength. Did I actually sleep? For how long? Four hours? The sleep didn't refresh me at all. I felt worse and more tired. My mind wasn't working anymore. I stumbled over roots and embraced a tree. Concentrate, I commanded myself. I fished the rest of my iron ration from my pocket and munched. Slowly, before swallowing, I counted to thirty. The dry stuff was finally gone, and there was no more food.

To hell with it. I may be dead by tomorrow. The stuff is better off in my stomach. The walking rhythm gradually returned. I began to walk normally and didn't feel tired anymore. I heard my soles squeaking. The heavy boots pushed spongy moss. We were in a swamp. Lifting my feet was hard work. The moss sucked my shoes and made them even heavier. Tony stopped.

"It's late afternoon. We can't rest. We got into a swamp." For the first time I noticed how exhausted Tony looked. "It makes no sense to turn around," he said. "At least, the swamp is safer than an open field. I warn you, don't drink that water! It will make you sick. Brush moisture from the leaves and keep your skin moisten, as tempting as it may be, don't swallow that water."

Ernst stood swaying beside me. He clutched his bloody left arm firmly. His eyes stayed half-closed, his face twisted in excruciating pain. Everybody looked at Ernst, not at Tony. Pretending not to notice, Tony kept talking.

"Unfortunately, we can't sit on wet ground. We have no choice; we must walk. As soon as I find dry ground, I guarantee we'll take a rest. Most important, don't drink that swamp water! Lick moisture from the leaves! That'll keep you busy." Tony searched the ground, he turned and walked further into the swamp. I took fourth position. The water reached beyond my shoes. I hoped, it would not go higher. As Tony had said, I licked moisture from the leaves. Everybody did the same, except for Ernst. He couldn't.

How can I help Ernst? The question nagged me. Tony's second rule was: Those who can't walk for any reason will be left. Ernst could barely walk. He was that far gone. He swayed with every step. None of us had the strength to carry him, not even on a stretcher. The mud water became higher. Every step was an enormous effort. I changed places and walked behind Ernst in third position. Tony first, Ernst second, and I was third. Ironically, we were all artillery. Usually, the infantry walks first, but the five infantry men dragged behind us. The customary animosity between infantry and artillery was long gone. We shared the same predicament, trying to save ourselves. We walked from one miserable defeat to another in a miserable swamp. Depressed and exhausted, I concentrated on walking and lifting one foot at a time. It was necessary to avoid one foot sinking deeper than the other. Nothing else mattered.

I heard somebody shouting behind me. "That's much better!" They had stopped and everybody had taken off their boots, even Tony. My voice reasoned, Don't! The boots are your protection, you must keep them on! I hesitated. But everybody had done it, so I pulled mine off, too, and set them next to me in the swamp.

Ernst didn't. He staggered to a rotten tree stump and crouched down. Too exhausted, his body slumped forward. His right arm dangled off his side and desperately tried to reach his shoelaces. He tried several times and groaned when he was unsuccessful. He leaned further forward, resting his weight on his good arm, until his big body finally slumped over. The fingers still fumbled with the shoelaces. He had given up. "I can't anymore," he groaned almost inaudible.

Life sprang into Tony. He threw his shoes in the mud and briskly walked to his friend. He firmly grabbed Ernst's shoulders and wildly shook him with both hands. He kept shaking and wouldn't stop. None of us wanted to stop Tony. It was useless. Ernst was unconscious, but he kept shaking him. A thick lump grew in my throat. I choked but couldn't cry, it hurt. No moisture came to my eyes. Meanwhile Tony kept shaking relentlessly. It made no sense. He finally gave up, breathed hard and walked into the swamp with his head raised high. He disappeared. We stood helplessly and lost sight of Tony. Nobody could help Ernst. We knew that. We could hear Tony, howling from deep inside the swamp. I am sorry, my comrade. Farewell, my friend. It sounded like a wolf was howling. He repeated the farewell over and over.

I started to faint and was almost thrown off balance. I swayed and desperately battled against it. My mind worked strenuously. It seemed useless. Trees and men were hazy and began to turn, first slowly; even Ernst's body, then the circling became faster. I was losing my will to fight. Something, though, made me labor fiercely to stay in control. For unknown reasons, I lifted my right leg as high as possible in the air. That had a surprising effect. I kept my balance on one leg and the effort broke the spell. Trees stopped spinning and my vision became clear again. Tony had returned.

We formed a circle around Ernst and joined hands. Nobody spoke, not even Tony. Nobody had the strength to speak. I was convinced Ernst had just died. I became angry and adrenaline pushed into my veins. Without wanting to, I broke from the circle and walked into the swamp. I was mad. In first position, I led the group without asking. Without looking I knew Tony walked behind me. I walked for a long time. Like a robot I paid no attention where I walked or where I was. My mind was a black screen. The desire to become a hero was now dead. I abhorred the thought and felt like a coward walking away from Ernst. I was ashamed, but I didn't want to go back.

"Every man for himself!" is the last order a soldier receives when everything is lost. The order repeated in my brain. But survival limits your choices. The world is cruel. Why do men kill? War is insane! These thoughts floated through my mind: Tony's rules were valid. We had to leave Ernst to keep ourselves alive. I didn't think it was selfish.

My foot imprints formed large impressions to help the guys behind me. I was glad I could help them, especially Tony. How exhausted he was. He had walked the first two days and nights and never complained. I made my imprints larger to make walking easier for him and the group.

A cold breeze tormented me. My feet were frozen. The icy swamp water spilled over my naked ankles and sent freezing chills through my body. I shuddered violently. I wished I had warm socks. Why did I take my boots off? I was angry with myself. But it was too late to be sorry about that.

Like a vision, I saw my boots sitting neatly next to Ernst's slumped body. The picture was clear; not like a dream. I shuddered. And suddenly I saw Ernst walking from the swamp toward me. He was still a distance away and walked effortlessly. At about eighty meters away, he found a tree stump and sat down. Ernst waved his arm as he sat. It was Ernst, I was absolutely sure, and his wounded arm was healthy. He smiled and waved his left arm. And nothing about the vision frightened me.

As I moved closer, Ernst's smile fascinated me. An uncontrollable shudder went down my spine. I had to stop walking. The seven behind me closed up and formed a semi-circle around me and stood silently. I shuddered violently and could not stop. Nobody spoke. They appeared like ghosts in a haze. None of them had facial expressions. The mysterious haze lingered. I felt their eyes were on me, but I couldn't see them distinctly. I only knew, they worried about me.

The burly infantry sergeant stepped forward and put his finger on my chest. "From now on you walk last in line!" he ordered quietly, full of sympathy. Strangely, there was warmth flowing from his finger straight into my chest. I stopped shuddering. I noticed a pale reflection from the dim moonlight bounced off his Iron Cross. It fascinated me. My eyes moved gradually from the reflection to the face. But the face was not the sergeant's. It was Ernst's face! That didn't surprise me. Ernst stood clearly before me. And like before, he smiled. I vaguely remembered that Ernst had the Iron Cross. The flow of warmth increased. I felt strength returning. Inexplicably, the warmth came from the pale reflection of the medal. I stood silently, trying not to disturb the comfortable feeling. It was Ernst that stood before me. Couldn't it be true? I knew we had left Ernst's body behind hours ago. New strength filled my body. And my spirit awoke. I was proud to be part of this group. They were fine men. They relied on me. I felt they respected me even though I was just a private. I was now a veteran like them, even without a bravery medal. It made no difference to them. We were the same.

I'll walk as long as I can, I promised silently. They seemed to understand. "You don't need to worry about me. We may not find a dry spot, but even if we can't rest I'll still make it." I was proud to know they worried about me. That feeling made me stronger. The burly sergeant turned away and took the lead without saying a word.

Tony stayed behind with me. He was in seventh position, one place before me. My body felt warmer, but not my legs. They were like ice blocks. I repeatedly pulled one foot up and warmed my toes with one hand when I fell behind. Tony waited and watched me.

"The footprints you made were nice and large." He tried to encourage me. "We are lucky to be last. But don't fall behind!" he sounded like a brother. He didn't want to offend me. I focused only on walking. The burly sergeant changed positions and now he walked behind me. They changed the lead. He grinned. Since Ernst's image appeared I felt very good. Nothing bothered me anymore. My mind was clear again. I wondered why I wasn't exhausted. What was the difference? Yesterday, after I had slept, I was even more tired and bumped into trees. When was that? I counted the hours several times, but the result was always different. I recounted and gave up. Walk, urged my brain. Conserve strength! Keep your feet low and concentrate.

During a school sports event, I remembered, I urged myself to concentrate and propelled myself to jump farther than ever before. I broke a long existing school broad jump record. There was always a mysterious energy left in a body. I concentrated intensely on what I had learned there—to use my body energy in various physical stages. When a level was exhausted, another level replaced the previous one, with less intensity however. We had walked three days without food or water or sleep. A time had to come when all energy was gone. How long could we last? I figured I was on my sixth energy level. How many energy levels are there?

Concentrate! interrupted my brain. Don't stop, and don't sit down or you won't get up. These were Tony's rules. I must obey. When was the terrible battle? I counted and figured for a long time, but slowly drifted to sleep while still walking. I woke up feeling drowsy. How long did I sleep? Did I sleepwalk?

The ground under my feet was firm and the sky had turned blue. I noticed the colors were brighter to my right. We walked in a northerly direction. A new day had just begun. Three men were ahead of me. I was in fifth position. Soft grass was on both sides of us. Tony walked one place ahead of me. Tony's stride hadn't changed. He turned and grinned. "Good morning," he whispered.

Why did he whisper? Were the Russians near? Tony's voice was hoarse. My bare feet had open sores, and they hurt. But the pain was tolerable. Puzzled, I watched my feet walking by themselves. I didn't order them. Perhaps, my brain ordered them. They were part of my body. Right, left, right, left, right, left. Nobody told them to walk like that. I moved into fourth position. Soon it would be Tony's turn, and then, I would be leading. Tony stopped and motioned to catch up. It was light. On both sides of us were green fields. A mountain range appeared on the horizon in sway of the swamp's moisture.

"Where is the swamp?" I asked Tony, still not believing we made it out.

"We are on firm ground. I guess we deserve a rest," Tony's voice was completely hoarse. "Yes, we made it," he added and grimaced, "That miserable swamp is behind us. Let's be grateful. The swamp may have even saved our lives." The burly infantry sergeant touched him. "Thanks! That's all I can say."

Rescue

"A cabbage field," I yelled. Forty meters in front of us were heads of cabbage. Rows of cabbages stretched for kilometers. Everybody ran and sank between them. They looked irresistible; they were moist! Nothing could hold me back. I stumbled forward into the first row. My comrades disappeared in the next row.

Moisture! Food! Nourishment! Moisture! God blessed cabbages! The need for moisture dominated. Food was secondary. I lay between two cabbages too exhausted to do anything. Only inches away, one cabbage head glanced at me lovingly. Slowly, I ripped wilted blue green outer leaves off to get to the juicier yellow leaves. Suck the juice; don't eat the leaves, I ordered myself. I peeled off a yellow leaf, folded it twice and stuck the bundle in my mouth. Chewing was awkward. My mouth was like parchment paper. Chewing without saliva hurt.

That cabbage isn't moist. I dug deeper into the leaves near the core and forced the raw piece down and began folding another. I stuck that into my mouth too. My stomach revolted. Then my whole body convulsed and the convulsions didn't stop. Everything went black. I spit everything out, but my body still convulsed. Nothing was in my stomach, but I couldn't stop. I was scared. Concentrate, I ordered myself. Don't black out! Don't let go! It became dark, but my mind worked. Don't let go, I told myself in desperation. Slowly everything came back to normal. Eat! You must eat! I need moisture. Eat cabbage moisture!

I ripped a yellow leaf into tiny pieces and stuck them into my mouth. I chewed counting to thirty-three; and then swallowed. The saliva came at count twenty and gradually joined the cabbage juices. The mixture tasted good, honey-sweet, and the swallowing became easier. I ate another piece and another, one after the other. Don't eat too much of that stuff, I cautioned myself. The stomach can't take it. I ignored the message and kept munching. I saw my friends in the other rows munching like rabbits.

A thought popped into my mind, if there are cabbages, there must be a farm. Thinking was hard. The ground was too cold. Another thought popped up. Are we safe here? Russians may be waiting in a farm. We are not safe. After all we went through, I won't defend myself anymore. It's not worth it, I decided and peeled a dozen yellow cabbage leaves off. Instead of eating them, I stuck them into my pocket to build a new supply of food.

I was not refreshed but I crawled away. My body scraped the ground as I crawled and made strange noises. In my imagination, it sounded like exploding grenades. I stopped crawling. The sensation was gone. The silence was soothing. The battle is over. Stop imagining. I won't allow my memory to play tricks. I stuck my face into the ground and found relief in the smell of fresh earth.

I saw Tony was already at the edge of the field and chatted with the burly sergeant. Tony called him Jakob. For the first time in four days, I heard his name. We never paid attention to each others name. Both of them were eating small pieces of Jakob's cabbage, which he had cut with a pocketknife.

"Your cabbage is much sweeter than mine," Tony told Jakob.

"That's just your imagination. Cabbage tastes the same. By the way, I am sorry that I almost collapsed and caused you trouble." That was news to me. "I couldn't have gone 100 meters more." He had probably collapsed while I walked asleep. The other fellows came one-by-one from different rows. We sat together and munched yellow cabbage leaves.

For the first time I noticed how haggard and spent they all looked. Their faces looked aged. Lumps of dirt still glued to their beard stubble. They were fresh from the battle. Everybody's feet were swollen and red, like mine. Their skin was chafed and their faces were the unhealthy color of gray. Jakob observed me staring at them. He grinned. "We made it! Didn't we? We made it against all odds! That's all that counts." He passed me a yellow cabbage leaf. His leaf did taste sweeter.

"Tony, I would like to know how you figured that goddamn swamp? How did you know we would make it through?" Instead of answering, Tony lifted himself painfully and, like he had done so many times before, he shouldered his assault rifle and walked off. But this time he turned around.

"When I am stuck, I allow my instinct to do the thinking. That wasn't me who guided you." Three days and nights in the swamp had seemed endless.

We walked slowly uphill along the cabbage field. I dragged my bare feet close to the ground until I got my walking rhythm. I ignored the pain from my feet. There has to be a farm somewhere close by. From the top of the hill we finally saw what I had expected. Four buildings spread peacefully into a valley around a huge willow tree. A windmill in the center turned peacefully. Six military motorbikes were parked in front of the main building. A shudder of anxiety took hold.

Russians. My God, I mumbled. My frazzled nerves sapped the last bit of my strength. But Tony kept walking and as usual, I followed. I completely trusted him and so did the others. As we got closer I could tell that the motorbikes were distinctly German. They had the typical passenger boxes on their sides. We were safe! In a last burst of energy, my feet began to fly. We all accelerated and ran side-by-side to the main building. Exhausted, I collapsed against the rough white wall.

"It's a miracle!" yelled one guy and kissed the ground as he fell.

Tony walked up to the heavy wooden door and stumbled over the threshold into a hallway. I followed him into a warm kitchen. The hot air threw us back. The air was very uncomfortable. Still dazed, I saw six German soldiers jump from a corner bench and point their guns.

What's the matter with them? Don't they recognize us? Obviously they did not. They saw filthy, dirty, clay covered uniforms and bare swollen feet. We looked worse than a band of Chetnik bandits! One-by-one, the young German soldiers dropped the guns. "Are you Germans?" They smiled. A young lieutenant, about nineteen, still hesitated, stepped forward and confronted Tony.

"Who are you?" He had a high pitched voice and a sharp Prussian accent. The voice penetrated my dulled senses. "Give me the password? And your identification, please," he demanded.

Tony straightened up. Even without shoes he was a foot taller than the soldier. Tony pushed his forefinger disrespectfully into the young officer's chest. "Look, kid soldier, you sit here nicely drinking warm milk, but you left your motorbikes unattended. We could have stolen them easily,"

Tony's deep guttural accent left no doubt that he was born in the steep mountains of Tyrol. We were proud of him and formed a threatening semicircle. Six battle hardened dirty men stood behind Tony and were ready to slug it out. Adrenaline pumped through my blood.

The lieutenant's already pale face turned even whiter and then became red. "Are you, by any chance, from the First Mountain Division?" He still had a dubious look. "We searched for survivors. We came as far as we prudently could," he said, apologetically. "Nobody escaped. That we knew. You must be the only survivors."

His voice changed and his hand reached out for Tony's. His five soldiers hustled from the table to greet us and shake our hands. The sticky warm air sickened me. The room's furniture turned, and for the fourth time, I fought against a black out. Everything was hazy. Tony's large body swayed and he collapsed. The lieutenant rushed to help him to a chair. He said something, but by then the furniture was spinning, and I tumbled to the floor. I could still hear the Prussian officer's voice close to me.

"Get water! Quick! They are dehydrated. See if they have blankets!" The voice sounded urgent. Everything happened like in a dream. I wasn't completely blacked out, only in a fog. My disabled brain made it impossible to react. But I could observe. The warm air and the discomfort it caused was real. I tried to complain about the air, but I couldn't talk. Please open the window, I wanted to tell them. And then black closed my mind.

I felt water dribble down the left side of my mouth. Somebody spoon fed me. I felt two people lifting me onto a bench. Somebody inspected my feet, and one cut the end of my trousers. Somebody touched my feet with a sponge. They felt numb. The voices sounded concerned. Her German sounded strange. A woman's voice was among them. She spoke with a Swabian accent that was difficult to understand.

"They need a good soup," she told somebody. "The kettle is on the fire, Hans. Bring more wood." My body convulsed and shuddered. Fear of seeing the dreadful battle scenes again overwhelmed me. I closed my eyes and saw only black.

When I opened my eyes I was surprised to see the wrinkled face of an old woman. She hovered over me and patiently washed my mouth with a warm wet cloth. "You threw up a lot of cabbage," she said when she noticed my eyes were open. She patted my left cheek softly. Using a large spoon she fed me water. I checked the furniture. Everything stood firm on the rough wooden floor. There were six chairs, a table, and a carved chest.

An old man's face appeared. He stared down at me. "Please, let me do the cleaning, Martha," he ordered using a different German accent that was also hard to understand. "You go and cook the soup. Scramble some eggs, and keep them soft. Good hot food won't hurt them."

"You are safe," he continued turning to me as he sat down. "We'll get you to safety. Yesterday, a Serb partisan group came by and after them, a band of Chetniks. They don't like each other. They only wanted to steal. Close your eyes and sleep. The food will be ready soon." He tore a strip from a sheet and laid it on my feet. I dozed and was asleep seconds later.

The smell of food woke me. The old lady's face appeared. I was now wide awake. She lifted my head and lowered a soup bowl to my mouth, but she wouldn't allow me to take the spoon myself. When I tried to lift my aching body, I fell back immediately.

"Are you German?" I had to ask her. The hoarseness of my voice surprised me. My throat was raw from the lack of saliva. But the soup was delicious. Tiny chicken pieces floated in a mixture of vegetables. I could squash everything with my tongue, even the large pieces of onions and vegetables.

"I am not sure, but I was born here," she answered. "My folks came from Germany a long time ago," she said and kept spoon-feeding me. "About a hundred years ago they came from a place they called the Black Forest. Many came from the same area. They speak German here. We belonged to Austria. We had our own church. We spoke German in school and we had a good life then. But when the First World War ended, everything changed. It's different now." She paused. "Eat scrambled eggs, and be careful with the bread. Your stomach isn't used to heavy food." She looked around. "The lieutenant sent for a truck. They said, when it comes, they'll take you to Bijeljina to a hospital."

She wiped her eyes with the ends of her babushka. "I am afraid of the Russians. What will they do to us? Hans, my husband, served in the Austrian army from 1917 to 1918. Will they take our farm? I wish they would go home, back to Russia. They don't belong here," she cried, and some of her tears dropped on my face. Why does she insist on spoon-feeding me like a baby? I felt better. She still didn't allow me to hold the spoon. Maybe she never had children.

"Serbs don't like us," she continued. "We got along with everybody, until that Tito came from Russia and started his army. We sell only to Muslims. They are our friends and don't like the Serbs either. Why can't we all live in peace together? I hope the war ends and our life will be like before, a long time ago."

We were now the only ones in the room. I noticed my friends were outside. From the window, I saw a truck and German soldiers arriving. "Blankets!" somebody shouted. "Bandages, medical supplies!" Spontaneously, I hugged the old lady. I sensed she wasn't used to hugging. I wasn't either, but I needed to thank her.

"I am not used to hugging," she said. Embarrassed, she patted my cheek again. She went from her kitchen into the storage room. A few minutes later she came back with a large piece of bread, she cut the loaf into small pieces. Secretly, she pushed the bread into my uniform pockets. I got up to join my comrades outside.

"You are still so young," she said, while I struggled to get up. "You don't even have to shave." Jakob leaned against the door frame. He had just finished putting a bandage around his upper arm. I never knew that he was wounded. I kept staring at his arm.

"You look good," he said, "much better than most of us. Must be because you are the youngest," he poked me. "Look at my arm!" He pointed at his right upper-arm. "That arm was bleeding badly and I was afraid I would end up sitting next to Ernst in that damn swamp. Tony told us we walked 100 kilometers. I hope Ernst makes it."

The thought that Ernst could still make it had never occurred to me. "Do you think Ernst is alive?"

"Could be. He was alive when we left him. He is about forty kilometers behind. Some guys are tougher than you think. Maybe he needed some sleep." Jakob became pensive. "Though, I doubt it. He lost too much blood. There was no way we could help him, not after he lost that much blood. The lieutenant said Russians cleaned the battle field." He poked his forefinger in my chest like he did that night in the swamp. He didn't know about my vision of Ernst. The thought caused my body to vibrate again.

"I am not complaining about you artillery guys anymore. If it wasn't for you and Tony, we would not be here. I, for sure, would have drowned in that God forsaken swamp. I could use some of Tony's instinct. How he found the way around the deep parts of that swamp, I will never know. He's got plenty of angels watching. I am not a religious man, but when I get home, I'll get myself a bible. I could never have gone through that swamp by myself."

We climbed in the back of the truck with the soldiers' help. I sat uncomfortably on a narrow bench and shouted, "Damn, we made it!" The others repeated it, and everybody smiled.

"Thanks, Sarge," said Jakob for the second time. He sat across from Tony. Everybody joined him, "Thanks, Tony," and one added, "Thanks a lot."

Tony's face was red. There were six outstretched hands that he covered with both of his. "Tell you the truth, I couldn't have made it without you either. Let's thank each other."

Jakob grinned, "We did outsmart that mean swamp, didn't we?"

Chapter 7

Reunion

Bijeljina, Bosnia

Cold air hit the open truck hard. We drove along a bumpy dirt road, and I was glad I had a blanket. The first houses of Bijeljina appeared. I had no idea how long we had driven. The soldier next to me said we had passed the Drina River while I slept. I didn't remember anything. The town's first houses stood on stilts and looked like cottages of no more than two rooms. I saw skinny spindly minaret towers extending above the red roofs of Bijeljina. The town was once a farm town, but now it was a German garrison. Military vehicles and motorbikes were parked in rows in the square marketplace. Groups of soldiers swarmed in the streets; most wore the SS skull. Some had purple fezzes with black tassels dangling from the tops.

"These are Muslim soldiers trained by the SS," explained a soldier. We stopped in the marketplace. An excited SS officer rushed to the truck to greet us. He waved to a few soldiers to help us from the truck. "Welcome home," he shook our hands excitedly. "The hospital is prepared." He noticed we were in bad shape. "We expect more doctors shortly."

"Are there others from the First Mountain Division?" asked Tony.

"Yes! We expect more, a lot more, perhaps. And some have already come. Bijeljina is the meeting place for your division. Every survivor will be brought here. Congratulations! We are glad you made it. I am sorry your general and his staff cannot be among the survivors. We heard they were captured and killed by the Russians. Major Eisele is now in charge here. So far, there is no higher officer here in town."

"Hurrah, Eisele!" shouted my friends. We were glad that Eisele made it.

"Major Eisele saved our lives," Tony explained. The officer was surprised. He wondered why we weren't more concerned with the fate of our general and his staff. He didn't know that our overconfident general had led us into that Russian trap or that we had seen his uniform flying from a Russian tank. None of us had a desire to share the story with the SS. We kept our mouths shut. Animosity between the SS and the traditional army existed ever since the SS leader, Himmler, had Hitler approve the change from the traditional army salute to the Nazi salute. All the army soldiers were offended. It was sad that tradition was not valued in Berlin any longer.

"We want you to feel welcome," said the exceptionally friendly SS officer.

"We got rid of all the partisans who blocked the railroad tracks. Trains from Vienna can now run safely. Supplies will arrive tomorrow, and we have adequate housing for you. We evacuated the civilians and had our Muslim soldiers move into a tent camp. Bijeljina is a training center for Muslim volunteers. We'll have them ready in a couple of weeks."

He would have continued his litany about the SS efficiency, but noticed we were too exhausted. Four soldiers accompanied us to the hospital.

A jovial doctor in an ill-fitting white coat greeted us in the hallway. The building that served as a hospital was formerly a school. The corpulent doctor liked to joke and laugh often. Only two buttons held his coat together.

"Let me see what we have here," he began inspecting our feet in the hallway. "You'll need a good rest. That is most important. I'll take care of your feet while you sleep. Don't worry about the sores, and whatever else I find." He inspected Jakob's arm. "Your arm will heal before your feet. I won't amputate the arm, I promise." He laughed heartily and clapped his large belly. "To be honest, I like cutting off arms. Have you ever met a field doctor who doesn't like to amputate? Amputation works fast and is less frustrating. I hate watching nasty skin wounds and infections. You may have infections, if you know what I mean." He pulled us aside, away from the SS soldiers.

"I was once an army medical staff doctor but now I work for the SS," he whispered. "I don't mind because the SS gets more supplies. I get everything I order. Before, I never got my requisitions filled. The SS leader, Himmler, gets everything. He is smart. He established an empire for himself and, at the same time, stays away from Hitler. I am afraid our Führer isn't aware of Himmler's power. Maybe he should look into the matter." The SS soldiers stood away from us and didn't listen. The doctor continued louder, to be less conspicuous, "Your schedule will be, number one, sleep for three days. I'll order you a special diet. Then I will fix your feet while you sleep. In one week, you should be able to take a delightful Turkish bath. The Turkish bath here is by far the best in the area, much better than a Finnish Sauna."

Four days later, while taking my first steaming hot Turkish bath, I overheard prophetic voices in the steam. "I'll change religion for a Turkish bath and won't even mind becoming a Muslim." Naked bodies lay in steam on hot marble tables enjoying a long wet massage, which was soothing and relaxing. Older corpulent women worked on us and weren't in the least bashful about attending to naked soldiers. For them, it was a matter of course. None of the women was pretty, which made it easier for a young man to get used to.

Our doctor was very busy. Trucks arrived every day and unloaded limping and wounded soldiers. On the fifth day he said he needed our beds. German patrols had found more soldiers and brought them from a long ways away to Bijeljina. Most were worse off than we were. "There are still more out there," he told us.

We parted from our infantry comrades. Tony and I shook hands, but we didn't show how sad we were. They went to the infantry part of town, and we looked for the houses assigned to the artillery. A clerk explained where the various sections of our Division were.

Tony and I walked, still heavily bandaged and without shoes. One street corner had a crude handmade sign, Artillery Row. Chickens pecked around the signpost. We limped along the street and found a house with another hand lettered sign, 6th Battery. We stood before the house for a while and hesitated. Neither of us wanted to be the first to go in. Who would be there? Tony was thinking. I had now learned to read his mind.

Our Battery originally had 200 hundred soldiers. The two room cottage in front of us was the smallest house on the street. How many would be in that cottage? Tony had known everybody for years. They were all his friends. It was easier for me to go first. I walked up the porch and opened the door. There were about fifteen men in the dark room gathered around an open fireplace. They sat with their backs toward the door. I didn't recognize anybody. One turned and got up.

"Look who is coming," yelled Captain Kroener. Then the rest jumped up. My eyes had now adjusted to the darkness. Lieutenant Stoll stood beside Kroener. I saw the huge frame of Sarge Joseph and Roland. They gave me a bear hug and my heart leaped. But where were the others? Where was Hugo? I remembered last seeing him racing down the road, hanging onto a mule. The captain hugged Tony, then me, like a brother. This time his greeting was different from the first time I met him. Officially welcoming us, he roared joyfully.

I was sad that Hugo wasn't here. I checked every new arrival at the hospital. But none of my crew came, and neither did Hugo. Hardly any artillery men came after Tony and I arrived. They were mostly infantry soldiers. They had less equipment to worry about.

Captain Kroener held Tony at arms length. He inspected him from top to bottom and checked his bandaged feet. "What happened? How did you make it?" The others pressed the captain aside and hugged Tony again.

"Our Sarge made it," they clapped their hands and danced. It was always amazing to see how well Tony was liked. A lump formed in my throat I couldn't talk, anyway. I was still hoarse. Captain Kroener made us sit next to him at the fireplace. "Warm yourselves and tell us what happened," he ordered Tony.

Tony shrugged his shoulder. "It's a long story. I'll tell you sometime, Captain. How did you make it?"

Captain Kroener was ready to tell his story, which he had told the others several times. His story was short and he told it as though nothing unusual had happened.

"We brought one cannon out," Lieutenant Stoll said proudly. I remembered hearing his voice during the battle, but I never saw him. There was too much smog with all the explosions. "We hitched a couple of mules to the cannon and pulled her out." That sounded very simple. But I was there, and I knew it wasn't. A shudder drifted down my spine as I thought back. I saw Rudy's face and when he and the four gunners died.

"We have the only cannon in the Regiment," said Stoll proudly "The SS gave us three old 1916 Skoda cannons as replacements. They were surplus. They got our new Model 1936 cannons. With our three Skodas, and one Model '36, we have a full battery, but we don't have the gunners. We have 19 men and we need 150." The captain looked worried.

"I don't understand why the Muslims got the new Model '36 cannons. That pisses me off. As if we hadn't done our job," Lieutenant Stoll was angry. "These foreigners aren't even trained yet and don't speak our language."

"Something is shifty in Berlin," Tony remarked, "don't you think Captain? Why does the SS have so much pull in Berlin? They get first choice, even in the draft. It's ludicrous! Every new tank rolling from the assembly lines— guess who gets them—the SS, because Himmler has his office next door to the

Distribution Center. Hitler favors the SS. Though he spends all day with his army generals, they don't dare to speak up. Doesn't anybody see what's going on? What are they afraid of?" Tony became visibly upset.

"I wondered about that myself," said the captain. He leaned back before answering. "The generals with Hitler don't have the guts. Hitler fired all his good generals. Are we supposed to win the war with leftovers and World War I cannons? It doesn't make sense. They give the new stuff to the Muslims, and that makes less sense." The mood turned sour. Everybody stared into the fire.

The next day Tony and I went to get new uniforms. We received two blankets, two sets of underwear, two shirts, socks, and dreadful, new, long-shafted infantry boots. "I won't wear those long shafted infantry boots." Tony yelled at the surprised SS clerk. "Give me the mountain boots you wear. We are the mountain troops, not you."

"These mountain boots are assigned for the Muslim volunteers," the man said firmly. "Let's go!" Tony pushed me to the door. "I'll ask the captain to straighten this out." Very upset, he turned back to the SS soldier. "For your information, mountain boots were designed for mountain troops and not for Muslim soldiers or anybody else."

"My feet won't fit into these. I can't wear shafts." I told the soldier and showed him my oversized calves. "Do I have to walk bare foot for the rest of this war?"

Tony pulled me away. "Don't worry, we'll get mountain boots; one way or another."

When we got back, Tony talked to the captain. And the same afternoon our captain went to see Major Eisele. They talked, and Major Eisele went with two officers to see the highest ranked SS officers. Eisele complained in plain old fashion language that he wasn't satisfied with the second hand stuff we had been receiving. The SS officer was furious.

"Don't you understand that our Führer is furious with you. He still mourns the loss of the First Mountain Division. I received a cable this morning." He showed Eisele a paper. "Adolf Hitler wants the commanding officer of the remaining First Mountain Division to report to him," he ordered Major Eisele.

"Who the hell are you, to order me to report to Hitler?" Eisele's face became red. He was too upset and Captain Poessinger took over and spoke for him.

"If Hitler wants somebody punished, then he may as well punish all of us and throw us in jail. I'll go with Major Eisele and find out why the damn SS gets all the first-class merchandise, and we get the leftovers." The SS officer was equally ranked with Major Eisele and couldn't order him.

Major Eisele and Captain Poessinger left and immediately prepared to report to Hitler in his northern headquarters. We talked about nothing else in our cottage. But we doubted that our officers would even get close to Hitler. Before Eisele and Poessinger left, hundreds of soldiers assembled and blocked the way. They formed a tight circle and urged them not to go. They feared Hitler would arrest them and throw them in jail. Major Eisele had become a god for many. "We won't let you go," they shouted until Eisele waved them off. "We'll be back, don't worry!"

They left and were back within a week. They had even been promoted. Eisele was now a full colonel and decorated with the Knights Cross, the highest German bravery medal. The promotion made him the highest ranked officer in Bijeljina and he immediately informed the SS officers. Colonel Eisele called a meeting. He reported the Führer had received them well. He had been friendly and listened to them attentively when they voiced their complaints about the lack of supplies, Hitler promised to look into the matter and called on an assistant to take notes.

Outside, infantry soldiers were jubilant and insisted on seeing Colonel Eisele. They hoisted him on their shoulders and, after they lowered him, he addressed them and the SS officers.

"The Führer salutes you and your spirit of survival. He is proud of you," he spoke. "Our Commander in Chief promised to rebuild the First Mountain Division to its full strength. He ordered, in my presence, to get new supplies to us. We will shortly receive new weapons. The First Mountain Division is assigned to be the cornerstone of the German defense in the southeast campaign of Europe. We will have a new general, who has already been appointed." The soldiers cheered and fired shots, against rules and regulations. A worried SS officer stepped forward and congratulated the new colonel. Now Eisele had direct contact to Hitler, and that must have worried him.

We had time to recuperate. Our exercises consisted of three hours cleaning cannons. We were bored polishing the old Skoda cannons. Every day I tried on my long-shafted infantry boots but they didn't fit and I wore sandals instead. Hitler's new supplies didn't come. Everyday a few more survivors came either by foot or by truck.

One day, a miracle happened. I saw Hugo standing on our street corner reading the Artillery Row sign. He was still wearing his light gray officer's cap. Excited, I yelled, "Hugo!" He saw me and ran toward me. We hugged each other. Hugo looked fine and well nourished. I couldn't wait to hear what had happened to him. We sat down on the street and he began his story. "This mule ran by. I tried to avoid bullets while grabbing the mule's reins and holding on. I almost fell off a couple of times. When I couldn't hold on anymore, I slid off and somehow, miraculously, landed in a deep hole carved into the side of the road. The cavern was a perfect hiding place, for a while. Four guys were already inside. We were protected from the grenades and laid on top of each other. We stayed until dark.

"The grenades gradually stopped exploding and the infantry ceased fire. We waited until it was completely dark and crawled onto the field. Russian soldiers were there and searched the bodies. They yelled and motioned to each other. We could tell that they were not all Russians. There were also Serbs.

We often had to play dead, slowly working our way toward the forest. I hid behind bodies while soldiers came and took watches and jewelry off the dead. A few groaned. I noticed that they left the wounded alone. So I groaned when they came close. We stayed together. At about midnight, we reached the forest and almost crawled into the Russian camp. Soldiers lay around an open fire. We avoided the sentries and it wasn't easy. We crawled all night without a sense of direction.

"In the morning, we found a farm and a tool barn. The barn was close. We hid inside between rakes and shovels and stayed until midnight. Serbs seemed to be in the house, but nobody checked the tool barn. We didn't dare move. When it was very dark and everybody was asleep, we crawled back into the forest. We crossed from one patch of wood to another, always staying at the edge. When we heard soldiers, we hid in the brush. Nobody saw us.

By noon we discovered another isolated farm between patches of trees. Dehydrated, we crawled to the well. I lifted the water bucket from the well. At that moment, a young woman came out of the house. I dropped the water bucket and we ran to the barn and hid in the deep straw. The young woman, unafraid, followed us into the barn. She left the door open for light. I could see her from my hiding place.

"She was tall, blond, and very pretty, about twenty years old. She said in German that we should come out and show our faces. We didn't answer because we didn't know who was in the house. She left the barn and left the door open. We went to the darkest corner to hide and covered ourselves completely with straw. A while later, she came back with an older man. Since we couldn't hide forever and she spoke some German, I showed myself and called, 'Wasser!' in German, motioning to my mouth.

"She smiled and showed she understood.

"'Guten Morgen,' said the old man beside her. He sounded friendly, so we crawled from our hiding place. The girl had a basket and took out a piece of bread. She sprinkled salt on the bread and produced water and cups. We gladly accepted the bread and water. 'Willkommen,' she said in clumsy German."

Hugo leaned back, stopped his story and stared dreamily in the sky. I suspected there was interesting news to come. He probably fell in love with that girl. I wanted to know everything.

"Of course, you fell in love with her instantly," I said to challenge him. Hugo took the bait and became defensive. I didn't mean to tease him, but I could tell I was on the right track. "She was a very unusual girl," he answered still staring at the sky. I was near the truth and had to figure out how to get it out. "Naturally, your high-class Bavarian charm made her fall in love with you." That did it. It was exactly what a smart interrogator would ask. Now he was anxious to tell.

"She was really pretty. You could never find a beauty like that in Bavaria. After the bread and water, the father questioned us. He wanted to know about the Russians and the battle. He asked his daughter to go to the house and get more food. I sensed that he really wanted us to leave as soon as possible, but he didn't have the heart to tell us directly.

"The girl came back with food and milk. He told her we would leave after we ate. She looked sad and frowned and kept looking at me while she talked to her father in Slavic. Obviously, she wanted us to stay. The man shook his head. He left and went back to the house, but she stayed. Her German was not good. She tried to say that her father wanted us to leave. But we pretended not to understand. We worked clumsily on the food.

"She waved and showed us an underground turnip holding place. It was a perfect hiding place. She whispered that we had her permission to hide there. She explained that she had used it to hide from her father when she was little." Hugo paused again. The story was too long. I was anxious to find out what happened with him and the girl.

"I have no idea what she told her father," Hugo continued. "We just moved into the turnip storage place. She brought us food and milk twice a day, and we all fell in love with her. She knew that very well. Like a woman she played us, one against the other. But I knew that she liked me best," Hugo was full of self-confidence, in spite of his dreamy look.

"Of course," I said without a hint of sarcasm, "she liked you best."

"She would come early before her father got up. Sometimes we sat behind the barn and talked. I helped her with her German. The danger of Russians being near was real. That didn't seem to bother her. She took her babushka off and let her long blond hair fall over her shoulders. She was really pretty." Hugo paused.

It wasn't very long ago that I'd listened to Hugo's detailed description about flirting with an upper-class girl from Berchtesgaden, who he claimed found him irresistible. This time he was in love with a Yugoslav farm girl. How did that happen? "What happened next," I urged him impatiently. The story dragged too much.

"What do you think? A pretty girl, like Magda, living on an isolated farm, of course, is lonely. She doesn't have the opportunity to meet guys. I felt sorry for her."

"Sounds like schmaltz," I told him. "Tell me, were you in love with her or not? What really happened?" Hugo acted annoyed, but his dreamy look showed he was ready to reveal everything.

"Yes, I made love to her. That's what you wanted to know, isn't it? But we only did it once," he blushed, which was unusual, too.

"When and where?" I insisted.

"We made love in her house, in her room. She showed me her room when her father left. And the others didn't know either." Now I was satisfied. I had heard what I had suspected, and let the story end. I still couldn't believe that Hugo was really in love.

In Hugo's previous stories, he had described himself as the superior, irresistible playboy. It wasn't love that had charmed the Berchtesgaden girls. That was for sure. I was familiar with every detail of Hugo's incessant flirtations. Bavarian girls were fortunate to cross his path, Hugo insisted and were not taken serious. But this time it was different. Hugo was in love.

I changed subjects. "What did it mean when they sprinkled salt on bread?"

"That's their custom to welcome visitors. Hospitality is important to them. We don't remember how precious salt and water once were to all of us."

"Did you intend to stay with her?" I wanted to test how serious he was.

"I should have stayed." Hugo answered spontaneously. "Her father knew we were in the turnip barn. He even knew that his daughter had a crush on me. He asked if I wanted to stay and told me that his wife had died and that he had no sons. He only had Magda. He said he didn't mind if the others stayed, too. He offered to let us work for clothes and food. But my friends declined. I didn't say anything, and seriously considered his offer. Magda was a beautiful girl. I had a long talk with her. I asked her to consider that I was a German soldier and not a farmer. Then I made a decision, which was the hardest thing I ever did. I told Magda I couldn't stay. She pushed me off and cried. The next day she came and gave me directions to a farm owned by a Croat. 'He is friendly to Germans,' she said. She wanted to help and wanted me to be safe."

Hugo choked. "You are right. I almost changed my mind. But the guys scolded me. We left quickly to find the Croat and his farm. I can't forget Magda. She acted calm when we left, but I saw how hard it was for her to hold the tears back."

"Now tell me how you got here. Quickly, I am getting hungry," I knew the following story would not be as interesting. Hugo wasn't anxious to tell the rest of his story. He still had to see the captain and report. "We walked through open fields, saw nobody, and there were plenty of hiding places. We came to the Croat's farm when it was dark. He was outside, but acted very unfriendly. He pushed us away, cussed, showed us to the barn and closed the door. At that point I was ready to go back to Magda. My comrades insisted, 'You don't belong in Yugoslavia!' But I couldn't sleep.

"The next morning, the Croat farmer had a new attitude. He apologized and spoke in almost perfect German, 'I was rude last night because a band of Chetnik militia was in my house. I didn't want them to see you. They were planning to ambush a German patrol not far from us.' His wife brought milk and bread from the house.

"'I'll take you to that road. German patrols drive by all over the place.' He readied a carriage and hitched a horse to it. We hid in the back covered by blankets.

"Ten kilometers from the farm, we saw two German trucks. It was almost dark, so we had to jump in their lights to stop them. They drove us to Bijeljina to the hospital. I still have mixed feelings about Magda. Tell me what's wrong with just being a farmer?"

"Nothing! What's wrong is that Magda's place is too isolated for you."

That was the end of his story. "I am glad to be back, anyway," he sighed. "Believe me, I have changed." I could easily see that. I had changed, too.

The captain greeted Hugo like a lost friend and so did the others. We were now twenty-seven men, including Hugo. It was all that was left of our 6th Battery. One hundred seventy-three men were dead or missing. Hugo was ordered to relax for two days.

Two days later, Tony cornered Hugo and me, "The captain wants you two to help with the training of Muslim recruits." Tony turned quickly so as not to hear our objections. "Why do we have to train foreigners, and why should we help the SS?" I muttered.

"These SS guys don't know the '36 model cannons. Give them a hand," Tony talked sharply. It was final. I felt insulted.

"Give them our old Skodas, and we'll keep the new cannons," I suggested. Tony didn't argue; he just walked away.

We helped train the Muslim fellows. Once we got to know them better, they were fun. We teased them about their maroon fez and black tassels, and told them their outfits were impractical. "Your tassels will get stuck in the branches."

They called themselves Turks. Turkey was our Ally during the First World War, perhaps that was the reason they wanted to wear German uniforms. They obviously didn't know the difference between the German army and the SS. The SS trainers treated them well, much better than our trainers treated us in France. The Muslims acted respectfully toward us. They wanted to know everything about the battle at Belgrade. We talked during breaks. They were curious but they spoke German poorly and many times didn't understand.

Since it was their homeland, I figured they should know but checked it out with Hugo. "I wonder why they want to know so much about Tito and his partisans."

"I think they are afraid of Tito, and that is the reason they volunteered. I always thought everybody here was a Yugoslav." One young Muslim overheard my comment. He spoke German fluently and was their spokesman.

"Serbs are our arch-enemies," he explained. "Tito provides them with guns sent from Russia. Serbs hate Muslims and that has gone on for centuries. We follow the Islamic religion. Our ancestors came here from Turkey. Turkey is neutral in this war. But every Turk roots for the Germans. The Serbs want us to leave. But Yugoslavia is our country, too. We want the Austrian-German armies to win and live in peace. Years ago the Austrian administration was good. They built hospitals and schools and treated us well."

He made sense. Impressed with how well this Muslim spoke German, I asked, "Where did you learn your German? You speak without a trace of an accent." He was flattered.

"Muslims who can afford it attend private schools in Vienna. We don't go to the schools in Belgrade. We would like you to stay in Yugoslavia. But don't let the Italians take over as administrators. Nobody trusts Italians. They stole Albania, and since then the Albanians are worse off. I would not fight for the Italians," he said boldly.

His SS trainer listened. I wondered what he thought about the Islamic religion and the fact that Muslims would not fight for the Italians. I directed my next question to a SS trainer.

"What do you think? Should they trust the Italians?" He showed only mild interest and laughed. "Why should they?" he said and shrugged his shoulders. "I wouldn't trust the Italians either. They switch sides in a war when it seems convenient. Who can trust them?" Everybody laughed. The Muslims laughed the hardest.

"How about the Russians?" I asked the Muslim. "Why do you fight the Russians?" Questioning foreigners was fun. I felt like a statesman.

"That's easy," said the intelligent Muslim. His face was red. He didn't often get the chance to explain his side. "We must fight the Russians for two reasons, they don't belong here, and they support the Serbs. If the Russians succeed, the Serbs will exterminate us. Can't you see we are the minority and fight for our lives."

The SS trainer intervened, "Muslims fight to defend their wealth," he pointed at the Muslim spokesperson. "Isn't your family wealthy? You guys live in cities, but you don't share the wealth. Your Muslim farmers don't like fighting the Russians." I thought SS ideology was based on socialism and always supported the poor. They taught people to distrust Jewish bankers and wealthy Jews! Anybody wealthy was regarded with suspicion and considered a parasite sponging on society.

The young Muslim sat up. "Muslims are both, rich and poor. What matters is our common religion," he declared proudly. "Many Muslims are farmers and will fight for our land. We have gradually become a minority. The Turks cannot help us anymore, we must defend ourselves." His comrades clapped to show their support. It was a history lesson directly from the source.

Hugo and I discussed what we heard. Our ancestors were crusaders who rode through the Balkans and drove the Turks from Jerusalem. But now the Turks were our friends. We supported the Muslims. How did this happen?

I asked the SS trainer, "What do you think? Why are we in Yugoslavia?"

He looked surprised. "We fight communism! Don't you know?"

We trained Muslims for one week. One afternoon, we joined a Battery meeting already in progress. The thirty-three men of 6th Battery sat in a field next to the four cannons. Captain Kroener explained, "The 6th Battery is an independent unit," he sounded disappointed and didn't hide his feelings.

"What is an independent unit?" I asked.

"An independent light artillery unit goes anywhere army headquarters orders them to go on a moment's notice. We are no longer part of a division and must fend for ourselves to get supplies. Colonel Eisele told me, he will keep in touch and will order our return as soon as possible. I don't like that kind of independence.

We'll get 120 soldiers from the heavy artillery who will join us tomorrow. Our Battery is back at combat strength. We'll move out in two days. You guys are the backbone of my former battery. We have one day to show the new guys how to handle our various cannons."

Tony grouped the new soldiers for the one day training. Hugo and I were delighted because we saw Fritz again. He came with the 120. We talked about Albertville and made plans to celebrate our unexpected reunion in a Turkish bath. They had unlimited quantities of apple wine after a massage.

Tony did not want us to go. He took us aside. "A couple of things will happen tonight before we leave," he smiled like a devil. "I'll let you go, but you must be back by eight. Before we leave in the morning, we'll take three Model '36 cannons and sixteen mules from the SS and leave them all except one of the old Skoda cannons. We are forced to do it because we didn't get our promised supplies. We are forced to help ourselves."

Hugo whistled. "Wouldn't you call that stealing, Sarge? When are we going to do this?"

"At midnight. We'll go to their camp while they all sleep. We'll silence the sentries, pull the tent poles down, take their mountain boots and run." We laughed. "Shall we leave them our long-shafted infantry boots?"

Sarge Joseph asked, "How about taking a couple of their '42 machine guns?" Tony said simply: "Why not?" He outlined more details. Six groups of twenty were assigned various tasks.

"Everybody should take a short nap. At midnight, we'll move. Silence is the element of surprise. Messengers will circle between the groups. A hundred meters before the Muslim camp, we'll have two men from each group jump the sentries. They must be bound and gagged. Make sure they are well tied up, and leave them."

There was no moon when we started. My assignment was to pull tent poles. I saw twelve shadows moving slowly and deliberately before me in the darkness. They jumped the six guards and tied them up. I didn't hear a sound and crawled to the tents. The poles were quickly pulled, tents folded slowly and dropped on the sleeping Muslims.

A wild scramble followed. Before anybody realized, we were inside and each of us grabbed four pair of mountain boots, hoping at least one pair would fit. My long-shafted infantry boots were outside in the field. I quickly crawled away from the downed tent. Muslim soldiers fighting the heavy tent canvas yelled and tried to put their clothes on. But they couldn't find their shoes. I ran quickly from the turmoil. I sat in the field near Artillery Row to try on the boots and found one pair that fit. Guys who came by on the run took the other three pair. I had socks in my pocket and was exhilarated to have mountain boots again.

We had planned ahead. Our stuff was packed. All I had to do was go into the house, grab my knapsack, and join everybody at the designated meeting place. The meeting place was on a dark street at the edge of town close to Artillery Row. Nobody knew where we were going. But neither did the SS.

The captain waited. One old Model '16 and the three new Model '36 cannons rumbled in the dark street pulled by sixteen fresh mules. Ten minutes had been allowed to assemble them. Silently, we walked between the wagons and our four Skoda cannons. We left the town of Bijeljina sleeping.

SS military police were probably aware, by now, and would give chase.

Chapter 8

A Step Ahead of the Russians

Osijek by the Drava

The long artillery column slowed. Four cannons rumbled over rocks, but the mules stopped them. The sickle moon hung in the east. The night gave way to the first morning rays. We were four hours from Bijeljina walking fast. The SS military police gave chase behind us. The air indicated rain. Not a soul was on the steep mountain road. We were 155 men; 50 short of the required artillery battery. One hundred twenty recently replaced the 165 who died at Belgrade. Only 35 of the original 6th Battery survived. I was one of them and considered it a miracle.

Our captain climbed on a supply wagon. "We'll take a break," he announced. "Next stop will be Brcko. We'll defend a bridge across the Sava River. Units of the Greek army must still cross the river."

Why didn't he mention the raid on the Muslim SS camp? He pretended not to know, but wore new mountain boots, just like we did. We talked all night about the raid on the Muslim camp and how we had taken their stuff.

Somebody voiced the opinion, "The SS military police won't catch up."

"No kidding. You wouldn't want to get into their claws. I wonder if Colonel Eisele knew about the raid. If he did, he'll send the SS on a wild goose chase. They would have been here by now." Everybody agreed.

Raiding the SS Muslim camp was fun. It was worth the risk. They forced us to take the stuff. Why didn't they give us the new cannons and new boots? The SS police are probably waiting at the next supply place.

I walked between Hugo and Fritz. Fritz joined the heavy artillery men with us, and we became inseparable, just like we were in France. Fritz didn't say much. His views differed from ours. "What we did was stupid and irresponsible," he said.

Hugo and I disagreed. "You don't know Captain Kroener. He is smart." I wanted to change Fritz's mind. "Trust him! Kroener plans in details. He won't jeopardize his career as an officer. He is a friend of Colonel Eisele, and they'll protect each other."

Fritz snapped back. "Looks like the time you spent in jail didn't make much of an impression on you. Did you forget the jail? They'll convict all of us and send us to a punishment unit." Fritz showed his old age, I thought. He was close to thirty. He acts too cautious. He couldn't keep up with us younger guys during training. The army exercises were too tough. He confessed, "I guess I spent too much time in the office in Berlin."

"Why did you join so early?" We all had become Hitler Youth on our tenth birthday.

"The reason was my father," laughed Fritz. "He was a traditional communist. But that didn't matter to me at the time. The fact that he abused my mother mattered. He beat her every time he came home drunk from a meeting with his rowdy friends. He neglected us. He went to the beer garden every weekend. Most of the time they carried him home. One morning he came back so badly beaten that we didn't recognize him. He fought the Nazi Party rowdies. My mother felt sorry for him and wanted to wash his face. He spat on her. That made me boiling mad. "I'll join the Nazi Party," I screamed.

"He became furious and beat me. I was stronger and could have defended myself, but I didn't, because he was drunk. That made things worse. He didn't hurt me. We screamed at each other. My mother went upstairs, packed his stuff and threw everything he owned onto the street from the upstairs window. "Get out!" she yelled. My father left the house without saying a word. He never came back. I was afraid he would.

I kept my promise and went to the nearest Nazi Party office and applied for membership. I thought that if my father saw me in a Nazi uniform, he would never stay in the house with me. They wouldn't accept me, though, and told me to join the Hitler Youth."

"What did your father do?"

"Somebody said they saw him in Hamburg boarding a ship to the United States. But we never heard from him. The Hitler Youth was fine. We were boy scouts. We trekked in the woods, built campfires, and learned war songs from the middle ages. Not many wore the Hitler Youth uniform before 1933. But when Hitler became chancellor, suddenly everybody wanted to join. Since I was already a member, they appointed me to be a regional leader. I planned weekend activities and sports events. In 1936, they transferred me to Berlin to become an assistant to Baldur von Schirach."

I still thought it was strange that Fritz had left his high government position. Something must have gone wrong. But he would only say that serving our country on the front line was more important than doing office work. That still didn't satisfy me, but I didn't push for more.

"Hot coffee!" yelled somebody. I got up to get coffee, and when I returned they were still talking about Captain Kroener. Fritz thought Kroener was not a good leader.

"We needed cannons," I told him. "We needed supplies. They promised us but they never came. What do you expect him to do in that situation? We depend on ourselves."

"Are you suggesting that we should steal now? That is wrong. It shows a defeatist attitude. We have not lost the war." Fritz was bitter.

Our oath was based on 'Führer, Reich, and Fatherland.' They were the most important words in German. But those words had sunk to the bottom of my list since I escaped from the swamp. Everything had changed. I began looking out for myself and only wanted to get the best for us. I didn't care how or where it came from. My oath was to my friends, my comrades. The thought of jail didn't bother me.

"Maybe we can still win the war," I answered Fritz in order to pacify him and myself. But I wasn't convinced. Maybe the new Tiger tanks they have now will help win the war. They had announced over the radio that it was our secret weapon. The once proud First Mountain Division certainly couldn't win the war. They had crushed us.

The captain sipped his coffee at the cook wagon. He pulled me aside. "I want you to join the observer group," he told me without explanations. My friends were glad. Even though we had different ranks we stayed together. Had the captain forgotten my bad training report? The simple answer was that we had only two officers left. Cadets had to do officer's duties. The captain forgot my demotion and what was said in the report, "... he can never become an officer." Perhaps I still can become an officer. Advance artillery observer was usually an officer's job.

The bridge across the Sava River was a disappointment. I imagined a massive stone bridge built centuries ago. This bridge was old, but it was built of thin wood and barely good enough to drive cows or sheep across, certainly not heavy army equipment.

Tents of an infantry battalion bivouacking on the other side of the river looked grey in the rain. The observers crossed the bridge. The cannons took positions a few kilometers from the bridge. Captain Kroener remained with the cannons while Lieutenant Stoll led the observer staff to an abandoned farm house which became our headquarters. Rainwater leaked in every room. Broken walls laid on the ground. Only parts of the house provided shelter. We walked through puddles coming from leaks in the roof but we had no choice, there was nothing better.

Sarge Joseph was first inside. As usual, he clutched his '42 model machine gun. Roland following him, checking every room, every nook and corner. He smells partisans, went through my mind. The forest behind the building was full of them. Even I could feel that they were watching.

"They won't attack," said Lieutenant Stoll, casually reading my mind. "They are waiting for bigger fish, the army from Greece." Two infantry patrols walked up the hill, and sporadic rifle fire greeted them. Now there was no doubt that partisans were up there. Roland said. "Nothing serious. They are just playing around. Don't worry!" He enjoyed teaching, and I didn't mind.

"That's part of the Tito militia," reported Sarge Joseph. But I didn't see anybody. The lieutenant selected a dry corner and began to work. I helped him by grabbing an old table where he spread his map. As he marked positions, I watched how he identified possible targets. They were entered in his book. He went outside checking wind and air density and explained patiently what he was doing. He appreciated my interest. I had a chance to really learn from an experienced officer, and I found that quite different from training.

A small van crossed the bridge and turned into our driveway. It was not a military vehicle.

"What the hell is that? Not the SS military police, I hope," mumbled Lieutenant Stoll. He ripped his pistol from the holster and brusquely walked to the vehicle. Joseph stayed at the door and readied his machine gun. Would they shoot at German military police? If they do, I will, too. The decision came surprisingly easy. An elderly officer, not from the military police, stepped from the van and waved joyfully. He was upset that his new boots were splashed with dirt.

"For God's sake, mud is all over the place, even on my new boots."

He introduced himself, "I am Captain Schmidt, military public relations from Berlin," and reached for Lieutenant Stoll's hand, wondering why Stoll held a pistol. The spotless uniform neatly fitted his corpulent body. His laughter became insecure when he discovered we all had our weapons drawn. He stepped back, but his men climbed from the van.

"Our Propaganda Minister Goebbels ordered us to show you a new film which has not even been released in Berlin." Shots rang from the forest. The public relations people flinched and ducked. "I hope it's safe here," the captain's face turned pale. Lieutenant Stoll put his gun away and pumped the man's hand.

"Of course, you are safe. We have fashionable accommodation in this house for you. Our barn-theater will do well for showing movies. Everybody will help. The roof leaks a bit, but that can be fixed. Don't worry about shooting. A German patrol is in the forest chasing a few Tito partisans. They need practice. It's not serious. The barn is ample and large. I am glad you came. It's hard to believe that you came all the way from Berlin. May I see your identification, please?"

Stoll's request was abrupt, and Captain Schmidt frowned. He wasn't used to showing his identification. "We must ask for identification in the front line," explained Lieutenant Stoll as he read the captain's papers superficially. He led him to the barn. The barn was not what Schmidt expected. His three men complained and refused to unload.

"We will provide the canvasses to protect the film equipment," assured Lieutenant Stoll cheering them. "We'll cover the holes in the roof." No way would he allow this film crew to leave without seeing this film from Berlin. That was an unheard of opportunity.

We showed our eagerness and helped with the unloading. In no time the equipment was in the barn. Shots rang from the hill. We ignored them but the older men were shocked. "It's nothing! Don't worry! You'll get used to that." It was no consolation. Rain poured into the barn, and the stubborn film crew wanted to leave.

Lieutenant Stoll took action. "Captain, I need to check a discrepancy in your travel papers." He became sharp. "I am the Artillery Advance Observer and the last officer on the front line. I must be sure your papers are in order." Stoll was stern and demanded respect. Captain Schmidt shuddered. Stoll inspected the documents a second time, but this time line by line. Captain Schmidt was quite concerned.

"Ah, here, I see!" Lieutenant Stoll seemed relieved. "Congratulations, Sir! You have arrived at your destination. It states on line 8: Destination is Brcko, or nearby. You did, indeed, arrive near Brcko. I can report to headquarters that you arrived safely."

The film crew didn't complain anymore.

"Help with setting the movie screen! Quickly!" Stoll ordered. The corpulent captain was glad. He had passed the unusual scrutiny. Infantry soldiers helped eagerly. The news about a film from Berlin spread magically through the infantry camp. Soldiers climbed rafters and pulled on the screen which, unfortunately, had gray streaks from the rain. The film crew protested claiming the picture would be distorted. The complaints were ignored. A hundred infantry soldiers arrived with tent canvasses. The projector was now covered. Shouts and whistles urged them to begin showing the film. "No more excuses," sounded between repeated shouts. Wet hay became seats. We covered our heads with a tent canvass. The first flickers appeared and were greeted with applause. Captain Schmidt stopped the film and climbed onto a wobbly chair. He had to make an announcement first.

"Dr. Goebbels and the Führer send you their greetings." There was silence. "Our Führer saw this film at a premiere performance in Berlin. He was so excited that he ordered the film to be shown to the combat troops. Any public showings were canceled. I risked my neck to get here," he smiled and expected applause. Only a few shouted, "Bravo."

"You will see the star, Marika Roeck, dance and sing. I guarantee, this film is the best she ever made." Mild applause followed. The captain concluded, stepped down, and was greeted by tumultuous noise and shouts, "Let's go!" The movie could now start.

Marika Roeck appeared on the wet grey screen, and the picture was indeed distorted, but her dancing and singing was exactly what Captain Schmidt promised. The wet barn rocked. The loud singing and whistling attracted all the German soldiers in the vicinity. Patrols were canceled, and sentries left their posts. Like a miracle, not one shot was heard during the performance. "The partisans are listening," explained Roland.

The film ended with ear-splitting applause. Yells and whistles gradually subsided to shouts of "Repeat!" They became more frequent. The captain climbed on the chair scratching his pale, bald head. "We anticipated your approval, and therefore brought two older films as well. Their titles are . . . ." He was drowned out by shouts, "We want to see Marika Roeck again! Show her once more!" The yells became a rocking rhythm. Unable to continue, he stepped from the chair and Marika Roeck returned to tumultuous applause.

"Louder! To keep the partisans quiet. They want to listen, too," was shouted.

I started memorizing catchy songs and sang loud along with the showing. Everybody did, and the singing became louder as we all became more familiar with the songs. The showing ended under enormous applause. The barn vibrated. But strangely, the forest stayed quiet. Partisans seemed, indeed, to be listening. Even the rain had stopped. Marika Roeck, a Hungarian singing German with an accent, was understood by everybody.

Unexpectedly, the performance was interrupted. A tank unit sergeant barged into the barn frantically yelling, "The bridge broke. Our tank sits in the river. We need help!"

Lieutenant Stoll jumped up and the film stopped. We all went to the river bank. A huge German Tiger tank sat half-submerged in the rapidly flowing Sava River with wood debris circling around it. Only parts of the bridge still stood. The tank tried unsuccessfully to climb the slippery wet surface of the steep river bank. The crew sat forlorn on top waiting.

"Tell them to wade over, I'll call for help," ordered Lieutenant Stoll. He telephoned the tank's commanding headquarters and arranged for engineers to come to rebuild the bridge. To build a ramp to get the tank out of the river bank was the first thing needed. Nothing else could be done.

We all returned to the barn to see the third showing of Marika Roeck's film. The tank's crew came along and saw the film for the first time. After this showing, the applause became even more deafening. Nobody wanted to see the old movies. And the film crew began silently to dismantle, but they were stopped. "You can't leave. The bridge is broken. Kaput! You can't cross over." Soldiers circled the projector. "That's right! You can't get across the bridge. Don't you see?" Yells and whistles started again, accompanied by louder shouts.

"Show the Marika Roeck film!"

"I am sorry," said Captain Schmidt from atop his chair. "We don't have enough fuel to operate the projector."

"No problem," said one of the tank crew as he got up. "We have fuel in the tank. I'll get what is needed;" which was followed by "Yes!" Everybody went to the river bank and watched him wade to the tank. He returned with a large container on his back. We helped him climb back up the steep river bank. The fuel tank was taken to the reluctant film crew.

"There is enough to last you for a month. No more excuses!"

Soon, the Marika Roeck film played again, and she danced and sang. The fourth showing ended noisier than ever. By now, I knew all melodies but couldn't remember the words. We all sang "la, la, la" as loud as we could. Because we were too emotional, we forgot to concentrate on the words.

Not a single shot rang outside. Partisans might have occupied the bridge, but we would not have noticed. "These goddamn partisans must enjoy Marika Roeck, too," somebody remarked. Before the fifth showing, a few sentries left reluctantly and were posted outside. The projector operator was now ordered to only show Marika's dance routines.

Lieutenant Stoll had a call. "Captain Kroener wants to talk to you." Stoll went to the house. "Stoll, aren't you the luckiest son of a gun in the world? You can watch Marika Roeck?" From five kilometers away, they had heard about Marika Roeck's musical. "You get every word and every song and sing me the entire movie. I don't care if it takes two days. You are not a musical genius, but at least you can memorize the songs with the help of others. That's the least you can do. Try to be accurate!"

Lieutenant Stoll's musical memory was not good. He needed help. Each of us memorized one song. Lieutenant Stoll told the projector operator to stop the film each time he gave a signal. "Those are my orders from headquarters. When I tell you to stop, you turn the film back and play the same section again."

By midnight we had most of the songs down. We rehearsed two more times before Stoll called the captain. He sang the songs with only a few variations. It sounded tolerable. The performance took an hour. When the captain was finally satisfied, we fell asleep where we sat. It was 2:00 in the morning.

By daybreak, a battalion of engineers came and worked quickly. Within an hour they had a ramp for the tank. The huge tank crawled back onto land slipping and sliding. While taking a deserved break, the engineers heard about the fabulous Marika Roeck film. Their commanding officer confronted Captain Schmidt. "We are entitled to see the film, too."

Captain Schmidt couldn't leave as long as the bridge wasn't built. He made a deal. Considering the time, he suggested showing the Marika Roeck film twice. He had heard the Greek army was only three days away, and thought the engineers would work faster if they knew they would get to see the movie. Everybody helped in order to see the film. I counted. I saw Marika Roeck dancing and singing a total of seventeen times.

The bridge was finished before the third day. The captain of the movie crew volunteered to cross the bridge first. After they crossed, they disappeared quickly. The first vehicles of the Greek army arrived by late afternoon. Officers walked gingerly across the new planks inspecting the construction and declared the bridge passable. The tank which broke the bridge was a blessing in disguise. The Greek army's heavy vehicles could never have crossed the old wooden bridge. They would have been stuck for three days.

"Pack up! Get ready!" ordered the captain from his place five kilometers north. "We'll leave this God forsaken place and move to Hungary to join the First Mountain Division." Lieutenant Stoll was glad.

"They have a new general, by the name of Kuebler. He has a thousand new soldiers and supplies. The trouble is, the soldiers are fifty or sixty years old; and other, younger ones are maybe sixteen or less. The First Mountain Division had become a kindergarten and an old folks retreat." The lieutenant was disturbed. "Hitler has no idea what combat is. He doesn't get around. We can't last much longer with those kind of replacements."

Stoll leaned over his map. "If the Russians go to Budapest, we may be safe. Stalin wants Budapest. His generals obey against their better judgment. They could easily cut us off by going further west rather than east to Budapest. They are too damn smart. The captain thinks the Russians will move along the Sava River and then go toward Budapest due to Stalin's orders. We won't get cut off if we stay in Croatia, close to the Hungarian border. We don't have to worry about SS patrols. SS will defend Budapest. In order to get around the Russian army, we must move fast. Our captain is smart. He'll outsmart them. I spent three years with him. He has an uncanny instinct which gets better all the time. He'll lead us in the mountains south of the Sava River. If we reach Osijek before the Russians, we'll be safe. I can read Kroener's mind like a book."

Osijek, late November 1944

"The Russians are at the Danube, east of Osijek," announced the captain in our first meeting. "We'll go through the mountains to Osijek. The roads are bad. We may have to dismantle the cannons. The mules will carry them. Timing is important. We'll walk six hours, rest four hours, and walk six hours again, day and night. We must outflank the Russians." That was exactly what Lieutenant Stoll predicted.

"The cook wagon will be open and there will always be coffee. Food will be ready during the rest periods. We'll assign guard duty before breaks. Whoever is on duty can sit on a wagon. Those are the rules. Remember, the animals need food and rest, too."

"Why do we walk day and night with only four-hour breaks?" Somebody asked.

"Dumb question. The SS is chasing us."

"What will the captain do when they catch up?"

"He'll arrest them," said a new sergeant with a short blond beard who had come with the heavy artillery. "I'll be glad to help. They can't fight 175 men. The captain can do what he wants. We are an independent unit, remember!"

"Are you kidding? He can't arrest military police. He'll be court marshaled."

"I am sure he's thought about that. Didn't he allow an ambush on the Muslim SS?"

Fritz joined in, "That was wrong. We can not fight each other. Discipline is falling apart. It's over. They'll court marshal all of us."

"They have to catch us first," countered the sergeant. "How can they drag us to a court? That is impossible. There is no court nearby. Trust Kroener! I've known him for a long time. If he orders, 'shoot!' I'll shoot the SS. I never liked them."

Not a soul was on the road, not even the donkeys that often grazed on the roadsides. At the next break I informed a sergeant, "I want to volunteer for guard duty." Observers were not required to do guard duty. But I discovered my feet hurt and figured I could sit six hours on a wagon if I did four hours of sentry duty. The new mountain boots didn't fit. They were too new and the old sores from the swamp were still red. Blisters developed. I cleaned my feet at every break, especially between the toes, and changed socks.

One night, I hung by a mule's tail—mules don't kick during the night—and he dragged me without complaining. I learned that during stable watch. I also learned to respect a mule's accuracy. Mules hit at the face, while horses hit anywhere.

To preserve energy nobody talked. The monotonous rumble of wagons was the only noise. My mule patiently dragged me. By the fourth day the road gradually evened and we were at the end of a forest. The immense valley of the Drava spread before us. Morning mist swayed over fields, and the outline of the city of Osijek appeared far on the horizon.

I had seen Osijek for the first time when I arrived by train from Vienna. That seemed ages ago. Joseph was at the railroad station, Roland and I had spent a day on a supply wagon. We were ambushed by local thieves who had been nearby. Thinking back I shuddered at how inexperienced I was. Now, only five months later, I am a veteran.

The column stopped. The captain called an assembly. He confirmed that it was Osijek in the distance. "Lieutenant Stoll and I will ride to the city for supplies. In the meantime, you take a rest. I'll contact our Division and hope they'll order us to join them."

The two officers galloped away. We settled on frozen ground. I took my boots and socks off and checked my feet. Freezing air drifted from the river. The rest period was miserably cold, but I kept my boots off hoping that it would help my blisters. Both feet were blue and red. After the hot coffee, we sat shuddering and waited.

The officers returned three hours later, but the captain looked disappointed. They brought bad news. Maybe they didn't get supplies?! Anyway, walking was better than sitting on frozen soil.

"We'll defend Osijek," he announced. "The Russian are across the river and Osijek is defenseless without artillery. Our four cannons may give them some hope. But you and I know they won't help much either." He sounded disgusted. "Frankly, I don't know how our four short-range cannons can prevent the Russians from taking Osijek? These are new orders. At least by staying here we'll get supplies. We'll go into position here, in range of the river." The captain was more outspoken when he joined us.

"What I saw in Osijek was terrible. The city commander promised me the moon. I had no choice. Supplies are issued only to those who defend the city. He promised to let us leave when the heavy artillery arrives." We made a circle. "I always told you guys the truth. This time, frankly, I am worried. The city is a pitiful mess. They caught fragmented troops from the general retreat. Most soldiers are either too old or too young. I hope the Russians aren't any better off. Luckily, the Russians have no artillery either, and they don't have an air force. Which means they are also in bad shape. They can't take Osijek without artillery, because they can't just walk across the bridges.

"The good news is, the city commander has artillery shells and supplies that will last us two weeks. The best news is, there is no SS in Osijek. The SS stayed in Budapest. They defended that city. I telephoned our Division near Lake Balaton in Hungary. I was told to join them as soon as the city commander allows us to leave. Let's make the best of a bad situation! Tony, you will be VB (advance observer) in the city. Get yourself an assistant and two radio men and report to the city commander in Osijek. He'll take care of you and set you up."

"Yes Sir." Tony pointed at me. "You! And Roland and Alfons are my radio men. We leave in thirty minutes." Why didn't he take Hugo or Fritz?

"The officer cadets will stay with me and the cannons," ordered the captain.

"If the Russians take the city, how are we getting back?" I asked Tony on our way to the city. "Our Battery is so far from the city."

"On foot, of course! You showed me how you can walk a swamp. I selected you because I know you. But this time we have communication."

We loaded the communication equipment and took small knapsacks along. It took an hour to get to the center of Osijek and twenty more minutes to find the German headquarters. It was in an abandoned school building. The commander was a refined elderly colonel. His lack of combat experience was obvious. He greeted us and looked disapproving. He had expected an officer, of course. That made me mad. Tony overlooked the cool welcome. I felt like yelling, do you have an idea how much experience our man has? He is the best!

The commander's assistant, a major, had no medals either. Recently, most officers were transferred from administration jobs and in charge of defending large cities. They had no idea what to do. It was obvious the invincible German Army was now a shadow of its former self.

Tony seemed unconcerned. We climbed the stairs to the second floor where we would stay overnight. The entire second floor was once classrooms. They were empty and had no heaters. Freezing, moist air blew in from shattered windows. I spread my blanket on the cement floor and had nothing left to cover myself." Go look for paper to spread on the stone floor; and then lay the blanket on top," ordered Tony. We found nothing, no paper or anything useful to protect us from freezing. I sat on the stone floor and stuck my feet in my knapsack. My uniform jacket covered my face. The breath from my lungs warmed me, but that was not enough. That was the coldest night I ever experienced.

The next morning an infantry captain came and brought us steaming hot coffee. The coffee contained fennel, but tasted good because it was hot.

"Good morning," the captain shouted and laughed at us shivering. "I am glad we have artillery and can defend this city." He didn't know how much the 7.5 cm shells could do. At least he looked like a real soldier. He was young and energetic. We finished the coffee, and he led us into the empty streets of Osijek, which he seemed to know well. We passed massive three-story brick buildings. The air became colder as we walked toward the river. All buildings were empty. Small arms fire interrupted our sparse conversation. The civilians had left. In a city park, a cluster of Russian mortar shells exploded in the trees. We covered ourselves. But the fragmented shells fell harmlessly into the foliage.

"Mortar launchers are all the Russians have," explained the captain still laying on the ground. "Only every second mortar shell explodes. They have trouble with their factories. The mortar shells are probably made by German prisoners of war," he joked. "They are not worth a damn." He pointed at the empty city hall and its badly damaged roof.

"I wonder where these administrators went? They left the city in one day."

The smell of the river became noticeable. Next to the river was an eight-foot stone wall, built to protect a cluster of buildings.

"This is a monastery," explained the captain, "quite ancient and probably built during the middle ages. The pointed top of the church tells us these parishioners were Christians. You can see the entire Russian line and the other side of the river from the church tower."

We crouched to pass inside into the monastery courtyard. There was the dirty Drava River flowing slowly to join the Danube. Posts of German infantry stood along a thick two-foot wall that gave them excellent protection. This wall, built centuries ago, extended 200 meters along the river. The wall was meant to protect the city from the Turks and marauders. Occasional rifle shots whistled from the Russian side to tell us they were there, but weren't serious. I could tell when shots were to be taken seriously. The infantry men were old and looked worried. Their casual smiles were not convincing.

They were probably thinking, we'll show you young punks we can still do a job, but their eyes lacked the veterans' confidence. And their uniforms didn't fit. They were more like grandfathers who played war games against their will. Tony noticed my puzzled look.

"Well, that's all there is left to fight the war," he said. "I hope these old geezers are a match for the Russians." He shook his head walking away and joined the captain. The captain seemed competent. "We sure needed your artillery," he told us for the third time. "I am happy you came." Our artillery's range was about five kilometers, but our shells didn't make deep holes. Obviously, he didn't know that.

"You have the tower for yourselves. I don't allow infantry to go on top. The Russians know how valuable the tower is. Every day they shoot what they have against the tower trying to get rid of it. But with only mortars, they don't have a chance."

I counted seventy-eight worn steps in the narrow circular stairway until we came to a drop door. It was the bell floor, the captain explained. Alfons and Roland stayed below and set their equipment up next to the entrance. From there they could hear Tony's orders from upstairs. When we opened the drop door, we were rocked by an enormous explosion. I was afraid the explosion had burst my ear drums.

"You'll get used to it," explained the captain. "There are two bells, and when bullets hit them the sound is terrifying." He climbed through the drop door. We followed and crawled to the left, to a corner. The thick stone wall had arches without windows. Once we settled in the corner, Tony used his stereotelescope.

"Holy smokes! From here I can see the Russian line as clearly as Mount Zillertal in a good morning's sunshine. They have mortar holes, trenches, and houses. This place is an observer's dream." Tony let me look. I was amazed. I could clearly recognize features on the Russians' faces. With the river between us, they were 300 meters away. Our telescope made them look so close.

"Check the bunkers in the river bank," the captain pointed at important areas. He already had names for them. "The Austrian army built bunkers during the First World War. The Russian mortar crews live in the bunkers and take practice shots every three hours."

"I see a big tall fellow, just now, in a yellow raincoat. He is going to a mortar hole." I told them.

"He is the officer." The captain whispered. I wondered why he whispered. The tall Russian walked to the mortar hole. "He goes first, then the others come and start mortar practice. Watch for soldiers, they should be running from the bunkers."

"Yes, here they come. They just jumped into the holes."

"The mortar where the big guy stands shoots first. Four grenades, nothing serious!" The captain's description was amazingly accurate. He knew the Russian routine.

"They ducked their heads. Here come the shells." Mortar shells ascended as high as the church tower, and then looped turning in our direction. Thirty meters from us, they exploded on the courtyard cobble stones. They made no damage. A second round ascended, looped, and fell on our church roof, but three did not explode and rolled harmlessly down into the courtyard. Tony took the telescope.

"I am glad they have so many duds," said Tony. "The dumb asses want to destroy the tower. They have a one-in-a-million chance to hit the top, the angle is too steep."

"They really would like to see the tower go," confirmed the captain. "They concentrate on it. They know, that observers would be here if we had artillery.

"We know they have mortars, and they have machine guns and rifles, but they do not have artillery." Tony checked the river bank, starting on one end and gradually moving to the other. "What is in those farmhouses on the hill?"

"One house is the headquarters, and the other is a hospital," said the captain. I could see both houses with my bare eyes. I pulled my notebook from the observer's leather case and started to make sketches of the Russian positions. Russian soldiers walked the path above the bunkers. They chatted and felt safe, assuming the high embankment would cover them. I found snipers in strategic holes and penciled them into my developing map. The Russian line and their positions began to take shape.

"The snipers are dangerous. I'll give you a copy," I told the captain. "I hope your infantry knows their places." Snipers were set up to focus where the embankment was the lowest. Whenever a German head appeared, every shot was deadly.

I used my field glasses and drew my map. The captain considered my job important and made room for me next to Tony. There was only enough room for two in the corner, so he knelt behind us. It was fun to watch the Russians. They joked and laughed and were casual. When guards were replaced, they didn't leave immediately. They stayed and talked and clapped each other on their shoulders. They bent over laughing; I thought the joke must have been very good. For the first time, I saw a Russian woman soldier. First, I couldn't tell because she wore the same brown uniform as the men. But her hair was neatly tucked under her cap.

"There is a woman soldier. She is with a man, and I think they are going to make love," I told them casually.

"Where?" Tony yelled and became excited.

"Look at the line of bushes east of the hospital." Tony adjusted his telescope and found them.

"I saw them a while ago," he remembered, "they had left the hospital and yes, they were holding hands. I didn't pay attention. I thought they were homosexuals. You are right. They wear the same uniform, and they look alike and wear the same caps."

Tony kept them in sight. I watched with my field glasses. She took her cap off and sat down. He tenderly touched her hair. We had them clearly in sight. The bushes were sparse and couldn't hide the lovers. With considerable hesitation they kissed. The action became gradually dramatic. Observing them from our high angle, the view was magnificently magnified.

"I'll be damned! She sure is a woman. Look at her long hair. She is letting it down. He is opening her shirt." Tony became more fascinated. The captain behind us complained. He could not see details. After all, he was the superior. I had to hand him my field glasses. That was a mistake. Since I was the observer and had to do a job, I grabbed them back. If the Russians had crossed the river, we would not have noticed. The scene in the bushes was too fascinating. They undressed, slowly helping each other. He kissed her neck and let his mouth wander to her breasts.

"She is definitely a woman, look at her big bust," Tony observed and reluctantly made room for the captain and gave him the telescope.

"They are taking their time," observed the captain. Tony grabbed my field glasses. Fortunately, the captain recited the details splendidly. I watched with bare eyes. The two were almost naked, but suddenly disappeared. Tony fingered my field glasses as if something went wrong with the sight. I could see better with my bare eyes. The lovers embraced firmly and suddenly slid into a hole behind the bushes. The bush seemed to sway, but from our angle we could not see the action. Their hole was too steep and large.

"I can't see them," Tony said accusingly, as if it was my fault. He gave me the glasses.

"She was a nurse, not a soldier," insisted the captain. "The Russians don't have women soldiers." He kept searching with the telescope.

"If Hitler ever sends women as replacements into combat," said Tony, "I'll be horrified. Imagine Mongolian soldiers taking blond German girls prisoner? They'll rape them and pass them on until they are dead. And they wouldn't use bushes and hide."

"The other day I saw a woman soldier on the road without a brown cap. I am not sure, but they may have women soldiers." The captain admitted, "You can't tell until they take the caps off."

"That tells me the Russians are hard up. If they need women soldiers, they must be scraping the bottom of the barrel." Tony adjusted his telescope. "Nothing," he said, "they are out of sight. But that raises my hopes. We may yet win the damn war if they use women."

"We most certainly will win the war," answered the captain, annoyed. "There is no doubt. We shall shortly have an incredible weapon, probably a missile, that is capable of carrying a bomb anywhere in the world. The bomb is so powerful that it can destroy an army. This weapon will end the war, I guarantee. It's only a matter of time. We just have to hang on a little longer." His face flushed and he continued to explain the prospect of the final Germany victory. But he had to leave. "I suggest you take up quarters in the monastery? A few nuns live in the basement. The rest of the nuns left and went to seek refuge in Croatia." He pointed to a large building across the courtyard and left hurriedly.

I worked on my map and prominently named the most exciting spots. 'Love nest,' east of the Russian headquarters became target NR-1. The bunkers were target NR-2; mortar positions NR-3; and the storage areas NR-4. Tony corrected my numbers. He assigned a spot near the river to be target NR-1.

"That is the place where they will attack," he predicted. I changed numbers and dropped 'love nest' to the bottom of my list. It became target NR-9.

We hurried down the spiral stairway. Tony told Alfons and Roland to leave the equipment on the bottom floor. There was no need to bring the heavy stuff to the monastery. We had our VB station. The next most important thing to do was to find our quarters.

A few mortars fell into the courtyard. We ran to a broad stairway leading to the basement. We heard muffled voices behind a heavy oak door. I knocked politely. The voices immediately faded. Nobody answered. I pushed the brass handle and went inside. Three worn stone steps lead into the convent's kitchen.

Four elderly nuns, immaculately dressed in black robes, sat at a massive oak kitchen table cleaning vegetables. Nobody looked up. They weren't even surprised, just annoyed. Plenty of German soldiers had passed through the convent. The nuns worked.

I went to them and asked politely in German if they had a room. Nobody responded. They kept working. We waited patiently. Finally, the oldest nun waved negatively, "Leave!" which didn't sound nice, even in Slavic. Tony became impatient. He spoke German as he pointed at her.

"Then we'll just stay in your kitchen. Guys, spread your stuff out. It's nice and warm here." Suddenly, they all understood and chattered in Slavic. The oldest nun got up and, without addressing us, waddled to the door and waved for us to follow her. She led us to a large empty room, her eyes said, "That's all there is, an empty room."

She expected us to protest and leave angrily. She added in a decent German, "No furniture, no beds. I am sorry," and thought we wouldn't stay in an empty room. Tony walked into the room, turned and smiled.

"No problem," he said, "across the street are empty apartments. I saw plenty of beds and furniture. We'll borrow four cozy beds." The nun was stunned. She covered her mouth with one hand and said nothing.

"Don't worry! We'll take only what is necessary. When we leave, you'll return the stuff to the people. Their beds are better off in a convent where they are protected."

We went across the street and selected four cozy beds from the first apartment. We brought them back along with four chairs. Two tables were taken from another apartment. Within thirty minutes, the large monastery room was sparsely furnished.

The four nuns watched in silence and began inspecting the furniture. Amazed, they began making suggestions in broken German about how one or another thing would make the room look nicer. We went back across the street and got a desk and three mirrors, several pictures, four chairs, and a table for the kitchen. Everything was placed neatly according to the nun's suggestions. When we sat down to relax, the nuns found that a miracle had happened. They made coffee and invited us to the kitchen. All four nuns spoke passable German. Alfons was best at communicating with them. He spoke patiently and frequently repeated sentences in his deep melodious voice. He spoke with a Bavarian dialect which the nuns understood well.

"You don't think borrowing from an abandoned apartment is a sin, do you?" he asked. "The people fled in a hurry. They knew their beds were lost. Now their furniture is safe. They will be thankful to you for watching their things." The nuns understood and nodded eagerly, convinced that they had actually done a good deed.

An infantry soldier came into the kitchen. He had food for us.

"Oh no! You don't need food," the nuns protested. "You eat with us." They pushed the man away. He didn't understand.

"The captain ordered us to bring you food," he said in amazement. "They were never friendly to me." We thanked him and looked at what he brought. The nuns were also curious and inspected the lousy military hash. We jointly decided to keep it, and the nuns said they would add fresh vegetables to make the hash passable. We shared the meal.

After we ate, Tony and I returned to the tower. He began making calculation. He figured where the first shot should land. The target was NR-1 at the river. Alfons, downstairs, tried to establish contact with the battery but had difficulties. "He'll make it, don't worry. Alfons is our best communications man," said Tony. Not only did the bells ring loud and deep when a bullet hit, but the bullets ricocheted in the small room.

"We'll have to get used to that," remarked Tony casually. He checked the Russian side. Using my field glasses, I found the Russian who had just shot at the church tower. A group of Russians calculated the damages. I was mad, marked them with an asterisk and assigned them target NR-10. They were a target for eventual revenge. I felt safe in my corner.

Tony measured and penciled all nine targets in his book. "Target NR-1, mark it down! That's where we shoot first. Look, they are changing guards." Tony scanned the left side while I watched the changing of the guards and found another woman among the Russian soldiers. She lived with them in the same bunker. I told Tony about my discovery.

"If they are smart, they maintain discipline in these bunkers," Tony remarked. "Women become a distraction in war. But never underestimate the Russians. We made that mistake before." He checked all the entrances to the bunkers and told me to mark them down and assign each a number. Alfons called from downstairs. "I have the battery. Do you want to shoot?" Tony finalized his measurement.

"Let me talk to the captain." Tony went downstairs. I heard him describing the Russian side. He gave estimates of how many soldiers and mortars and how much equipment they had. "They don't have artillery or tanks, you were right," he told the captain, "they can't take this city. It seems they are setting up a defense and are waiting for more stuff to arrive from Budapest."

"I don't care," declared Kroener, "start shooting! And appoint five targets. I'll give you thirty shells per target."

"It's unheard of to use thirty shells per target," said Tony later.

"We targeted two areas on the river, named Assault I and II. They'll attack from there with boats. But I don't see boats. Give me six shots each!"

Tony scanned the area with his telescope. "The next target is 'cross road' between the bunkers, and the fourth target is their headquarters." Tony lectured, "You make the adjustment when the first grenade hits! I want you to refigure, but I'll check the numbers, then we'll call in the correction. I want you to learn this stuff. You will never have a better opportunity. Our friends back there depend on an observer's skill."

Tony turned and looked at me. "I might as well tell you who taught me shooting. It was your brother, Kurt, in Greece. He was the best observer. It's strange that I am now teaching you. I was once a reserve officer cadet like you, and they assigned me to him. Our targets were the fortresses in the Greek Metaxas line. He hit every bunker with amazing accuracy. We had only a few shells. Later, they dropped us off by parachute on the island of Crete. Sarge Joseph was there, and another radio man. None of us had parachuted before. And, luckily, none of us broke a leg. We had a perfect view from the high mountains. The British searched for us but didn't find us.

"It didn't take Kurt much time to measure. We blitzed the British positions with the might of all sorts of German cannons. The grenades exploded awfully close. The high-caliber cannons could excavate a basement for an apartment building. Your brother never wasted a shot. The Greek and British troops ran up the hill, but at the same time our infantry landed in boats. The invasion was fiercely fought, but soon Crete was ours. All of us were awarded the Iron Cross. We were the first artillery men with that medal."

I was flabbergasted. Kurt never said a word about Greece. But he never talked about his war experiences. And that Tony was once a cadet officer surprised me.

"How long were you together?" I asked. Tony laughed.

"A long time. We were always assigned the VB spots, it seemed. Kurt did the measurements, and I assisted. Our division general in Greece was

Joseph Kuebler. You heard the name of the new general. He is also a Kuebler. Joseph Kuebler's younger brother. Joseph Kuebler became army commander for the south of Russia. One time he refused an order from Hitler and was sent home. Nobody ever contradicted the Führer." Tony grinned. "We were also demoted together in Russia, your brother and I. Since then, I have no desire to become an officer. Kurt saved my life." I asked him to tell me about it.

"You heard about the Russian winter, in 1941, that was the coldest winter of the century. Kurt and I were assigned as VB in the Ukrainian plains. We froze our butts for three weeks without relief. At least we had a small bunker. Kurt radioed every day asking for relief. They promised. And one day, unannounced a very young lieutenant came with three radio men. The temperature was in double digit below freezing. Not a Russian or German soldier was to be seen.

"We left at noon. But, an hour later, completely unexpected, the Russians launched an attack. We were walking in an open field when we saw the new Russian tanks. Heavy artillery bombardment came first, but suddenly stopped. Not far behind the exploding grenades came dozens of new T-34 tanks crossing a creek. Covered by frost, they looked like ghostly, white steel monsters rolling slowly toward us in the icy misty air. There were only a few bare bushes to cover us. Scared, I kept running, but stumbled. A tree stump was in my way. I couldn't get up. My knee felt broken and sprained in the freezing weather. Kurt laid beside me. He checked the approaching tanks.

"They look awesome!" He never checked my leg. I had no idea what we could do. We laid in an open field as perfect targets. The tanks were only 200 meters away and slowly came closer. "Why don't we have tanks like that?" Kurt sounded like he admired them. I had seen a picture of a T-34 in a magazine and remembered their sight shutters were too small. The crew had only a very small range of vision. I told Kurt about it.

"Let's find out. That may be our chance." He grabbed two hand grenades and jumped toward the first tank, only twenty meters away. The tank's high chains became his protection. He jumped the tank and crawled toward the gun barrel. Kurt ducked in front of the shutters. I lay frozen. I couldn't move. Kurt pulled a hand grenade, got up, and stuffed the damn thing into the barrel. He ducked and waited until the grenade ripped the barrel. But the tank kept rolling until it was almost on top of me. I couldn't move. I saw the tank lid open. Kurt dropped his second hand grenade inside. The explosion sounded muffled. The tank stopped only five meters from me. Dark smoke drifted from the shutters. Kurt was stuck on top of the tank with his trousers caught on something. I was horrified. Russians would be crawling from the tank. Kurt pulled his leg, ripping his trousers, and jumped off, leaving frozen skin stuck on the metal.

Nobody opened the lid. The tank stayed quiet. A second tank rolled up and stopped behind the first one. Kurt pushed me under the smoking tank. There was a sizable hole. Kurt's frozen wound didn't bleed.

"Legs of Russian soldiers walked back and forth. Somebody climbed inside the tank, but nobody looked underneath. Heavily bundled Russian soldiers came to help check. They lifted four bodies from the tank and laid them on the ground. The second tank rolled on leaving the bodies. The soldiers walked behind the tank. We waited and followed them. Our parkas were the same color, so they didn't recognize us in the mist.

"My knee was frozen stiff. Kurt supported me. We found a tool shack on the way and crawled inside and rested. My knee gradually loosened. We walked for two days until we came to the first German lines. They had pulled back. The Russian attack was successful. That had never happened before. Up until then, the Russian's resistance was minimal.

"We found our artillery unit, but everything was in an uproar. Our previous VB position was destroyed, and the replacement was dead. High-ranked staff officers had just arrived and began investigating. Our previous officers were released, but Kurt and I were put under house arrest without a hearing.

"'You did not offer resistance. That is a disgrace,' said the investigating officer. The Führer ordered punishment for anybody who left his position. The investigation focused on the VB. 'Why didn't you report the attack? Why did you leave your position?'

"We responded over and over that we had been relieved, and were five kilometers from the VB when the Russians attacked. We had no radio communication. The explanations didn't convince them. The Führer ordered, 'Heads must roll!' 'You should have gone back to your posts,' was the answer. We became victims of Hitler's purge. We were demoted and kept under arrest."

My mother had told me that my brother was demoted. She never gave an explanation and didn't talk about it. I didn't know what to say. "What a coincidence that you and I met."

"There are no coincidences," said Tony. "I am now paying Kurt back. Our lives are predestined," he pointed to the sky. "Your brother and I became friends and remain friends." Tony looked tired. "Let's get ready. Tomorrow will be our first busy day." We packed our stuff and left the tower. "They were smart not to waste your brother's experience," Tony added, "he was transferred to the artillery officers' school to help train cadets. And I was promoted to master sergeant two years ago."

The story stirred my emotions. I couldn't sleep, but I relaxed on my comfortable bed.

Very early the next morning I left my warm bed, had coffee, and raced up the circular stairway behind Tony to the bell floor. Roland and Alfons stayed downstairs. I was excited about my first live artillery shooting experience. This was different from training. Tony switched our positions. He promised to help, but would, for the most part, leave me alone.

The crisp, clear air helped my concentration. Tony watched me making the final measurement. I checked the wind and thought I was finished. But Tony made more changes. Finally, I called the first shot and waited. The first grenade whistled over the tower. The waiting was nerve racking. I didn't see the grenade, but I heard the explosion. It landed near the river, far from the spot I figured.

"Don't worry," said Tony, "Not too bad for the first shot."

The Russian camp became active. Bunkers and grenade launchers were only 200 meters from the explosion. Tony checked my corrections calmly. This time I checked carefully and wrote the adjustments in our book. I called the new order downstairs. Alfons repeated, never questioning me. I was the boss today. The second grenade roared over and fell almost on the designated spot. The Russian camp became frantic with activity. A mortar crew ran from the bunkers far ahead of their practice schedule. Infantry fire blasted the tower. A hundred bullets rang from the two bells.

"They know we are here," yelled Tony into the noise. "They know we have artillery." Deafening metallic sounds echoed. My ear drums hurt. I checked the Russian side. Tony measured. A ricocheting bullet almost hit me.

I flattened myself in our corner, and didn't dare look for awhile. Nothing bothered Tony. He worked calmly like nothing was happening. "Now all the mortars are firing," he shouted. "But only half the grenades explode. They have problems. They are crazy. They'll never hit the tower." He laughed loud.

Nothing ever phases him, I thought.

"Stay behind me!" Tony seemed concerned. "No need for both of us risking our lives for curiosity's sake." He called four new orders at once. Thirty shells roared above us and hit the Russian camp. The Russian headquarters was on fire. Tony took a long look and wrote the results down. He was satisfied.

"We are finished today. Let's go! Don't forget the map. You can finish it at the convent. We can even call our artillery from there. From our beds, if necessary." Like reptiles, we crawled from our protective corner while bullets ricocheted around us. I stuffed my precious map in my notebook, deep inside my parka pocket. I didn't want anything to happen to it. The measurements were important, and they were mine, made by me.

The wireless boxes were ready. Alfons and Roland shouldered them and carried them to our room in the convent.

"You've got to keep the equipment ready at all times!" ordered Tony.

Our principal meal, consisting of vegetables and dumplings, was set when we came into the kitchen. The nuns insisted on punctuality. The night meal was usually light, just bread and milk or coffee. We were asked to be in the kitchen two minutes before six o'clock because the nuns liked to go to bed early. Breakfast was at seven sharp. Tony adjusted our observer's schedule accordingly.

"We'll go to observe at different times and not make it a steady schedule. That confuses the Russians. Roland and Alfons stay the first three hours. After that, you can go and scout the storage buildings." We spent at least six hours every day on the bell tower floor to observe.

The next day, Roland and Alfons brought an armful of toys into the kitchen, nail clippers, toys, combs, brushes and various little things. Everything was marked Made in Japan. "Where did you get these?" We inspected every piece. The nuns showed joy, especially when they were told to safeguard these things. They giggled like little girls clutching what they liked best to their bosoms. For instance, they had never seen nail clippers before. Alfons showed them how to use them. The prescribed lunch hour was forgotten, and so was our observation schedule.

"There are a thousand things in the warehouse!" Roland waved both arms. "Sentries watch the entrances. But we went to the river side and climbed through a hole where Russian mortars had demolished the wall."

"Let's go after lunch," suggested Tony. "We've already fired our daily allotment. There is nothing else we can do this afternoon."

We walked the warehouse row immediately after lunch. First, Tony confronted a pair of sentries, both were in their sixties. They were posted at the entrance of the largest storage hall and respectfully saluted the master sergeant. Their large steel helmets hung over half of their faces. They proudly wore spotless new uniforms. Obviously, they were recently drafted.

"What are you watching?" asked Tony.

"We don't know, Sir! The warehouses are off limits. They are too exposed to the Russians. It's dangerous to go inside." They clicked heels and saluted correctly.

"We are artillery observers." Tony explained, "We need a good place to observe from and direct our artillery. This warehouse may be the place. But we have to check it first. As you know, artillery is independent and not under the jurisdiction of the infantry. Don't worry, I talked to your captain and you can report we were here and checked this warehouse." Tony knew well, these old geezers had never spoken to their captain and never would speak to him. Their suspicions were justified, so Tony walked past them before they could make a decision as to what to do.

We followed him into the dark warehouse, the size of a football field. Wide openings on the river side allowed light to filter in. We saw pallets of merchandise that reach the ceiling. I walked down a row of burlap sacks. "It looks like flour to me," Roland stuck a finger in a hole ripped by a shrapnel and tasted it. "No, it's powdered sugar!" Alfons stuck a finger in the hole and confirmed that it was sugar.

"Look, big squares of parchment paper. That tastes like salted butter." Tony called from another row. "These sacks here are salt." The warehouse was filled with food enough to feed a city for weeks. The stuff was just laying there rotting. They had had no time to distribute it. We checked all the rows.

"Smells bad. These are rotting potatoes and onions. Let's take the good onions home and leave the rest at the river side. No need to bother the guards," ordered Tony.

I love butter! I used my pocket knife and sliced a big piece off a twenty pound parchment wrapped package. I ate the piece like an ice cream cone and loaded the block on my shoulder. The others had gone through the hole. Alfons carried a bag of salt and Roland a sack of sugar. Tony gathered a bunch of firm onions in a burlap sack. We crouched down and walked along the river. The guards didn't see us.

Back in the convent kitchen, we dumped the stuff on the kitchen table. The nuns eyes were as round as cartwheels. They pressed both hands to their mouths. "Salt!" mumbled the oldest nun and hugged Alfon's gift. We learned how precious salt was, by far more precious than butter or sugar or onions.

"There is not a pinch of salt in the city. I hate to cook without salt," explained the oldest nun. We had learned in history class that Roman soldiers were paid in salt, which they traded. The word soldier relates to salt. "Why is salt so precious?"

The old nun kept hugging her salt bag like a baby. She took it away, hiding it in a closet as if it was gold. My huge block of butter didn't make an impression. The sugar was nice and was appreciated. They considered the smelling onions almost useless, but they sat down and began peeling them.

"Do you need more salt?" asked Alfons. "There are at least a thousand bags of salt. I will bring more until you run out of hiding places." The nuns covered their mouth in disbelief. "Ja, ja, ja! Bitte!" they sang those words like in a church choir.

Since there was nothing else to do, we went back to the warehouse. I counted and found there were indeed a thousand bags of salt. We carried two sacks each on our shoulders. I couldn't resist and grabbed a second square of butter. Roland took a bag of sugar. We still thought butter and sugar were more important than salt. Tony, always the most practical, filled a burlap sack with potatoes. The heavy load required frequent ducking, and it became difficult to avoid bullets from the Russian side.Luckily, the convent was not far.

We dumped everything on the kitchen table, and the nuns rolled out every word they knew in the German language. "Thank you! Thank you! Especially for the salt!" They ignored everything else.

The infantry kitchen messenger brought our military meal in metal pots. He landed his pots between sugar, butter, potatoes, and onions and, when he noticed, his eyes widened. We told him the stuff had come from the convent's storage. One nun cut a thick slice of butter off and melted the butter into the military stew; another nun sliced an onion and carefully measured salt adding it to the food. "Now, that tastes better," she concluded. The messenger sampled the concoction, and ate with us from then on.

"Our salt comes from the Adriatic Sea," explained the oldest nun. "Since the trains were cut off, we have no more salt in Croatia."

"Now, we need meat and chicken to go with the salt." I remembered a chicken farm near the river that I had seen from the tower. Tony remembered it, too. "Let's go tonight and check how many chicken are still alive. The place is exposed to sharpshooters, so we'll go when it is dark."

I sketched the chicken farm on my artillery map and figured how to get there. Shortly before midnight we walked along the river, crawling the last stretch to the chicken barn. The entrance was difficult to find. Roland broke the hatch which made a lot of noise, but the Drava River between us and the Russians was noisier. Hundreds of chickens sat quietly in rows in the darkness. We crouched inside the low building. The chickens clucked at us. "Damn, I have a goose," Roland shouted. "Let me get him. Forget the chicken. A goose counts for four chickens." We heard shots from the Russian side.

"The damn Russian have night goggles. Let's get out of here."

"No, you talked too loud," I told Roland. But I wasn't comfortable in this building and the starving chickens were becoming noisier. I grabbed the largest chicken and kept it quiet by tucking it under my parka. The bird decided my warm chest wasn't bad after all.

"That's not a goose!" mumbled Roland next to me in the darkness. He was upset. "That's an old cock. Damned, he'll take hours to cook and will be tough." We climbed the river bank and the Russian fired. Roland and I fell on the ground. But the cock began fighting. Roland climbed the embankment and rolled down the other side. I followed him. The cock quieted down and the sporadic shooting stopped.

The lights were still on in the convent kitchen. The nuns waited. I wondered if they were worried or just -wanted to know what we would bring this time. They sat at the kitchen table with great expectations. The youngest nun, by far the prettiest; grabbed Roland's large cock and quickly rung his neck. To my amazement, he was dead in three seconds. Next, my chicken suffered the same fate. Four birds were killed, gutted, and plucked in minutes and were ready for cooking.

We soldiers stood in amazement. "None of us could have done what you just did. I have never killed a chicken." We were amazed.

"We were raised on farms, and preparing chickens was one of our jobs. We'll cook them in the morning and add dumplings in the afternoon."

The cock had unusually long tail feathers. Each of us selected a long feather to mount on our cap. "In Austria, we are allowed to wear only eagle feathers," Tony told us, but he also took a cock feather.

It was nice and warm in the kitchen. Despite the hour nobody felt tired, so we sat around the large table and talked. The nuns were more talkative and carried the conversation.

"Why didn't you go to Agram, in Croatia?" asked Alfons.

"We were packed, but Mother Superior decided she needed volunteers and asks us to stay," said the oldest nun. "We are not afraid of Muslims," added the youngest nun who had more education. Alfons didn't understand what Russian soldiers had to do with Muslims, and neither did we.

"But aren't you risking your lives here? You are facing Russian soldiers, though they are still on the other side of the river."

"Mother Superior said Russians are Muslims. I am a Serb. I can talk to them. I know how Muslims think. I am not afraid. We lived with Muslims in our village."

Tony shook his head and decided to practice his skills as a future educator. "The Russians don't have a religion," he told them. "Communism is their religion." He stressed the word *communism* emphatically. The nuns didn't understand. They had never heard of communism.

"Everybody has a religion," determined the oldest nun. "The Russians have a religion. We have three religions in my village, and we had a minaret and two churches. There is nothing wrong with that. Fighting for a religion is right. A religion requires sacrifices, and it is worth dying for. The Russians fight for their religion, and we Christians have our religion. We are willing to die for Jesus, our God."

That puzzled me. How little knowledge they had about politics? They knew the bible, but they had no idea why we were here or what we fought for.

"Do you know why we Germans are here?" I asked innocently. They shook their heads and weren't very interested. There was no need to know that.

"Aren't you Austrians. Then we are neighbors. What's the difference between a German and an Austrian?" asked the oldest nun, still not very interested.

"There is no difference," said Tony. "We speak the same language." Tony pointed at Alfons and me, "They are Germans." He pointed at Roland, "And he and I were born in South Tyrol which for a short time belonged to Italy. We were always Austrians." The nuns were confused.

The oldest nun searched for an answer. "My father said when the Austrians came they took our land. My father was a Serb and my mother was a Croat. Our relatives argued all day about politics and where the borders should be. I didn't understand what they disagreed on. Thank God, my parents sent me to the convent and I enjoy being a nun. My mother told me, "Serve the Catholic religion, that's all that matters, and you will be happy forever. She was right.""

The young nun stood up and pointed at the oldest nun. "I disagree. The Croats are our enemies. Your mother was a Croat. I hate Croats, especially the military Ustasha. Your mother is an enemy. That, my uncle told me. Maybe your mother was a fine woman in your mind, but she is still a Croat and should have stayed in Croatia."

"Then why did Mother Superior take the convent to Croatia? Tell me!" asked the older nun. Now they all became angry. Alfons pacified them.

"Let me tell you why we Germans came. Do you know of King Peter of Yugoslavia." The four nuns shook their heads negatively. They had never heard of a Yugoslavian king. "Your king and his government asked the German army to come and get rid of the communists."

The young nun spoke. "We have never heard of a Yugoslavian king or the communists." Alfons was at his wits end and skipped the history lesson. It was too late for that, anyway.

"We are friends," he said, "and as long as we stay here, we'll help you, I promise that." We four agreed and nodded. Alfons extended his hand across the table. The nuns gladly took his outstretched hand and warmly clutched our hands, too. For a while we sat holding hands.

The next morning we stayed in our room and had breakfast. The battery called early. We had our equipment and were ready. I covered a thick slice of bread with an inch of my butter and topped that with an inch of powdered sugar. Careful not to inhale the light powdered sugar dust, I lifted the three inch monstrosity to my mouth. My comrades had waited for that moment to tickle my side. I blew half of the powdered sugar in their faces. Then I built the same monstrosity and blew it around again. We had plenty of everything.

After breakfast, Alfons and Roland visited the infantry sharp shooters. They admired the dangling cock feathers and wanted to know what the feathers signified. "A feather is the prize for excellence in sharp shooting," Roland lied, "and I can prove it." Roland got a rifle with a telescope and showed them how an experienced South Tyrolian deer poacher shoots. He had the reputation of being the best sharpshooter in our regiment. After his demonstration, he was also famous among the infantry soldiers. They gladly lent him rifles when he and Alfons showed up.

A few days later, Alfons and Roland came into the convent kitchen and an old man sat there warming his hands at the fireplace. "Do you have salt?" he asked them in broken German. "I pay good price."

"How much do you pay?" asked Alfons who liked that kind of trading. He became an experienced trader when he accompanied his father once a week to a cow auction.

"I pay 1,000 Kuna for a sack of salt," said the man. Alfons knew he would start with the lowest price. The man pointed at the salt sack next to the stove. Alfons had no idea, how much 1,000 Kuna was or what it would buy. Alfons pulled Roland to the furthest kitchen corner and discussed the price. They whispered, the same way he had seen it done in all the cattle trades. Five minutes later, they returned.

"Three thousand Kuna," declared Alfons firmly. One of the nuns covered her mouth in disbelief. She indicated Alfon's price was outrageous. The man was not perturbed, but shook his head negatively.

"Two thousand Kuna," he countered, doubling his first offer. "That's final." Alfons pulled Roland back to the corner. Every offer had to be discussed. That was the custom in Bavaria. Never show your satisfaction! They both whispered and came back.

"We agree," said Alfons, "but you must buy our butter, sugar, and toys."

"I only want salt," said the old man firmly. "When can I have the salt?"

"We'll have twenty sacks here this afternoon," promised Alfons. That was followed by an endless discussion in Slavic between the man and the nuns. The young nun translated.

"He comes from far," she said in German. "Nobody has salt where he lives. He wants more than twenty sacks, perhaps forty sacks, and he'll bring a friend or two and donkey carts. He asks that you tell the German soldiers to let them pass." At that very moment Tony walked into the kitchen. He had heard the last part of the conversation. Tony, as master sergeant, had many bureaucratic functions.

"Tell him not to worry, I'll write him a pass." He took one pre-printed document from his leather pouch and prepared a pass for the farmer. The man raised his hand and showed four fingers. "Four o'clock!"

Forty sacks of salt were in the kitchen after lunch. But Tony and I had to be back at the tower. We saw nothing unusual on the Russian side and returned to the convent kitchen at five minutes before four o'clock.

Two unattended donkey carts were in the courtyard, and three civilians waited in the kitchen. The exchange of salt and money went quickly. The old man handed eighty thousand Kunas to Alfons in loose packages and various denominations. Alfons trusted him and without counting left the packages of money on the kitchen table. We helped them load the salt after they took a sample from two sacks.

"We need more salt," said the old man on his way out. "How much do you have?"

"Forty sacks by tomorrow morning, ten o'clock."

They left, and we made several trips to the warehouse until we counted forty sacks of salt. The nuns had to provide an additional storeroom and helped to sort and identify the unfamiliar Kuna notes. The bills were packaged into bundles and tied together.

Tony took a bundle, what appeared to be eight thousand Kuna, and handed it to the nuns. They made signs of the cross over all bundles and accepted their share. They had never seen so much money. It was a miracle! They knelt on the kitchen floor and gave thanks to God.

"It's not a sin!" Alfons assured them. "The onions and potatoes were rotting in the warehouse. Nobody is allowed to go into the warehouse. It's a dangerous place. Salt is of no use to anybody if it sits in a dangerous place. We'll bring you the salt. You sell the salt, and everybody is happy. You deserve ten percent of that money." The nuns knew a commission was the custom in every trade. They were thankful.

Twice a day we brought salt until the new storeroom was full. Six of our desk drawers were filled with Kunas, the denomination of Croatia. We needed an additional desk and brought one from across the street. The nuns traded and deducted a quarter of the money. Nobody knew how much money there actually was. The sorted bundles were stuffed in the desk drawers, but we never counted. We weren't interested. The city had nothing to buy. We couldn't do anything with the money.

One morning, Tony received a message from the battery. We were told to stay in the tower for eight hours instead of the six we normally spent. The captain said a Russian army was advancing in our direction. They walked at night. All communications had to stay open twenty-four hours. The schedule was tight. We allowed two hours to get salt. But nothing unusual occurred on the Russian side. One day Tony approached me in private.

"I can feel in my bones that the Russians will attack, maybe even today or tomorrow."

Two hundred salt sacks were in our storage inventory. That satisfied our daily trade. We planned to get a third desk for the bundles of Kuna notes. The question of what to do with the money began to nag us.

The nuns also traded for meat, chicken, and whatever was useful. They used their own money to buy things for the convent. The meals had improved considerably. We lived like kings.

Gloomy thoughts about the advancing Russian army were pushed from our minds. Nothing could diminish the marvelous feeling of wealth and well-being. Alfons skillfully arranged his transmitter earphones upside down in a large porcelain wash basin so we could listen to soft dance music from Vienna before we fell asleep. The porcelain basin neatly amplified the sound. We had a nice fire in the fireplace, and we were well fed.

One night, at almost midnight, the door swung open. The captain stormed into the room wearing battle fatigues, "The Russians are attacking. They already crossed the river. Get to the tower at once! We need artillery," he shouted. Two sergeants behind him also wore steel helmets and full battle gear.

"They're coming on platoon boats." The captain ran out of the room as quickly as he had come.

We jumped from our warm beds. I stuck my feet in the legs of my trousers and while contemplating what to do next, I felt Tony's hand on my shoulder.

"Wait!" he said calmly. "We'll stay here. Alfons, get the battery! It's too late to go to the tower. To get across a 200 meter river takes time." Alfons established contact with the battery quickly. Now Tony took over.

"Alarm! Four cannons, fire six rounds each, target, Assault I. The Russians are on the River Sava." The cannons were positioned every night before we signed off. Assault I was the target. That was the place where the Russians were most likely to attack from. "Give me the captain, quick!" In less than thirty seconds the captain was on the line. It was decided to blast all four cannons at once on target Assault I.

I spread my artillery map on the desk while they talked, and had already heard the first muffled sounds of four rounds of grenades roaring over our building. I waited anxiously for the detonations which sounded way off and in the distance.

"I hope they hit the target." I almost prayed. The shots had to be correct. We practiced every day. But it didn't sound right.

"We've got to check from the tower. The explosions sounded like they were far off!" I shouted. Tony ignored me.

"Captain! I need 100 more rounds, the same target, Assault I. As much as you can give me, change cannon 2 and cannon 4 and shoot six rounds. Then, 100 rounds on target Assault II, to be safe, and keep cannon 1 and 3 on Assault I. Blast them! We are going to the tower. I'll call back. Sign off." Tony's voice was calm and confident as ever.

Assault II was considered the secondary potential launching site. Alfons and Roland stormed ahead of us already up the stairway. We heard our heavy machine guns firing. Luckily, the fire came from our side. That meant the Russians had not landed. Our own grenades roared over our heads and exploded in bunches at the river. Tony laughed behind me.

"Don't worry! There is no other place they can attack from. We targeted them correctly." I stayed near Tony. We crawled like snakes in the courtyard toward the tower. Mortar shells exploded everywhere around us. The light from the sporadic explosions made the tower look ghostly. We passed Alfons and Roland who had the heavy metal communication boxes. Shooting on both sides accelerated. That sent chills down my spine. I was glad to know Tony was on my side. We didn't go in the tower.

"It's too dark and late," he whispered. Alfons and Roland set their equipment up and established contact with the battery.

"Continue shooting! The same targets!" shouted Tony turning to me. "I'll go up," he said. "You stay here! Only one of us needs to be upstairs, and that is me." Infantry fire increased. A real battle was in progress.

"Listen to the machine guns" whispered Tony. "The fire is coming from the launching side, which tells me they couldn't take off and are still on the other side."

The shadows of two men appeared running from the riverside. I sure hope they are not Russians, I thought, and cocked my rifle in that direction. I recognized them. It was the captain and a lieutenant. Both were breathless and fell next to us on the ground.

"Glad we found you," coughed the captain. He grinned broadly, "Keep the artillery on the same targets! You hit the spot, exactly where they launched the boats. Your grenades smacked them. A dozen platoon boats are loose in the river and are sinking. Congratulations!"

Tony told Alfons. "Tell the captain: Boats are sinking. Change Assault I to spread 100 meters north and add twelve rounds. Cannon 2 fire 100 meters east. Cannon 1 and 3, 100 meters south. Tell them, all targets, bull's-eye! The Russians are not coming! I'll go up the tower and call back."

The infantry officers applauded and congratulated themselves. Foolishly, the young lieutenant got up and performed a wild dance. At that moment a rocket exploded meters from him. He was hit. "Damn!" The young lieutenant held his arm.

Tony jumped to check. "Roland take the lieutenant to the convent," he ordered. "He is bleeding badly. And tell the nuns to make bandages. We must stop the bleeding. Shrapnel cut his artery. I'll go upstairs, but you guys wait." In spite of his order, I went up the circular stairway with Tony. He didn't object. We ran faster than ever. Bullets hailed from the bells. But we were used to them, and routinely spread my map on the floor in our corner.

"Don't use that damn flashlight! For heaven's sake! You should have that map memorized by now." Tony was unusually sharp and called downstairs changing directions. I could barely hear Alfons repeating. Our artillery shells kept exploding on the other side and illuminated the ground. I saw flickers of explosions and many soldiers dragging stuff from the water. Boats floated helplessly away laying upside down.

"That victory belongs to the artillery," said Tony proudly. "You can wait a lifetime for shooting like this." He saw no need to stay longer.

"Call thirty rounds, the same targets, and stop. The assault is over! Tell the guys Congratulations! Keep the same position and the same targets."

Alfons repeated and called back. "The captain wants to talk to you." We ran downstairs. Tony listened for a long time but didn't answer.

"Yes Sir," was all he said and hung up. "Let's go home and find out what happened to the lieutenant."

"What did the captain say?" I was too curious to hold back.

"He wanted to make sure the assault was over. He heard the Russian had brought boats by night. He still has plenty of shells just in case. He had all the answers, as usual. He'll be coming tomorrow to inspect the sight."

Tony smiled. "I know him well. He is just sorry that he wasn't here and wasn't the VB. He always wants to be in the middle of things. The Russians won't attack at least not now for a while, until they have artillery and armored vehicles. We taught them a lesson. The Russian officers don't understand German light artillery. That was a teaser. I call that a stand-still, but not a victory. They don't know that light artillery hit them. The heavy artillery would have blasted them away. Once the Russians get their artillery, you can kiss the city of Osijek goodbye. I wonder if they know we have no means to attack them." After a while he added, "We should get out of here. This city is lost."

The shooting stopped. We ran safely across the courtyard and to our basement. We found a big commotion. The lieutenant laid unconscious on the kitchen table. Two Red Cross people worked over him. The nuns wiped blood off and looked concerned. Ripped bandages and paper covered the floor. The lieutenant was hit by more shrapnel then we initially thought, and not only in his arm. The city commander trailed by a swarm of staff officers came running downstairs. We saluted. He checked the wounded lieutenant and asked for Tony. He had no helmet and appeared uncomfortable in battle gear.

"Here you are," he pumped Tony's hand. "Take the lieutenant to the hospital quickly, or he'll bleed to death. I wanted to be first to congratulate you. I just finished talking to your captain," he shook my hand, too.

"You were brilliant. You both saved our city. I heard, how you prepared the artillery map," he told me. "I want to thank you, and later you can explain how you determined their launching site. They were defeated in fifteen minutes." He shook Alfons' and Roland's hands too. "Next week we'll have our own artillery."

"I wonder why you are not an officer," he asked Tony on his way out.

The next day, earlier than we expected, the captain came ducking his way through ferocious small arms fire and mortar explosions. He laid flat on the ground before entering the building and saw two civilians under a donkey cart waiting and hiding.

"What an inferno!" he remarked and smiled when he finally came downstairs. "Was it always like that? Let's go to the tower!" The captain enjoyed war and its action. Tony and I were on the tower early in the morning and checked the damage on the other side. A few boats still floated in the river. Destroyed vehicles were scattered on the river bank. The sharp metallic ring of bullets hitting the bells surprised the captain while we were still on the stairs.

He was visibly impressed. He didn't expect that much noise. But nothing ever scared him. I slowly opened the trap door. The captain was ready to climb up, but I held him back. The noise almost drowned my voice.

"Sorry, Sir. You'll have to follow me. It's dangerous in there. And I know my way." He looked puzzled, but followed my instructions. The noise was stronger than ever before, almost unbearable. We couldn't talk. We passed the bells. Tony came up last and occupied his corner spot behind the telescope. "They sure act crazy over there," observed the captain. "Was it always like this?" He asked the second time. Neither of us answered.

It was never like this before. My field glasses showed soldiers running and acting as if they expected a German counter attack. I scanned the familiar territory. On the hill, near their headquarters, I noticed something new. Soldiers had just pulled an anti-tank cannon into position. They turned the barrel in our direction. There wouldn't be much time before they would fire the first shot.

"An anti-tank cannon is ready to shoot, straight at our tower," I yelled. The captain was not familiar with the territory and searched for the cannon's location on my map. "They didn't have a cannon last night." Tony didn't even wait. He packed the telescope. "You are right. They are aiming at the tower. Let's get out of here, quick!" We had one minute.

He grabbed the telescope and crawled like a snake to the trap door. The captain followed. I was last through the door and raced down the circular staircase. Halfway down Tony shouted, "Pack your stuff, guys! Quick! Get out of here!"

The captain grabbed a heavy transmitter box and jumped out the door. An enormous explosion hit the tower and air pressure made us fly through the door. Stones and dust pressed behind us. A bell came rumbling down the staircase and stuck in the narrow well. A second explosion followed. Watching from the courtyard we saw the top of the ancient tower crumble. I was amazed at the quick destruction.

"That tower is history! I've seen enough," declared the captain as he dusted himself off. The Russians fired a third shot, followed by a fourth and fifth in rapid succession. The tower was now half of its former size. Stones and dust blew down the sides. Captain Kroener, dirty and dusty, stood smiling in the courtyard. He looked like those formidable German warriors they showed in magazines who always grinned and seemed amused by the adventure of the war. He showed no fear.

"You don't have to look for another observation spot. We are leaving," the captain told Tony. He then elaborated, "The First Mountain Division ordered me today to join them in Hungary. We'll leave in three days. I told the city commander, 'General Kuebler wants us at Lake Balaton in Hungary!' The city commander asked me to wait until his heavy artillery gets here. He is a nice old man. I agreed, but we'll stay three more days. Frankly, I don't believe they will ever get the heavy artillery. We'll get our cannons and wagons ready and load as much supplies as we can get. In three days we'll move out. I plan to go along the Hungarian border, west, in the direction of Zagreb. Before Zagreb, we'll turn north and cross the Hungarian border. We go to Lake Balaton's western shores. Pack your money and come to the battery in three days."

"Yes Sir!" Tony smiled. He was as dusty and dirty as the captain. The picture of these two brave men engraved itself in my mind. Both were fearless, the product of a brutal war. They liked danger. I wondered how they would ever live without it.

How did the captain hear about our money? Nothing escapes him, and rumors travel fast. Why aren't we going the short way north and along the Danube River? Is he still worried about the SS military police? Actually, I was glad to leave Osijek in spite of our fine quarters and the comfort of the convent.

After the captain left, Tony explained, "We'll stay in Yugoslavia for awhile because the Russians can't take Osijek without artillery. They have only one cannon and aren't ready to cross the river. They can't advance. You can see that now."

"How can we spend our money? How much time do we have left in Yugoslavia?"

"Three days here and three more days on the road."

Back in our room, we emptied our desk drawers and stacked the bundles of money on the table. To count the many Kuna notes would take too much time. We split the bundles without sorting them into four parts. Each stuffed his part into a knapsack. And what was left, we gave to the nuns.

"How much do we have?"

"Probably enough to buy the convent," estimated Roland.

The nuns prepared a beautiful farewell dinner for us. They wondered why we left so many bags of salt, the butter, the sugar and the toys. "Keep everything," we said.

After the dinner, the head nun brought a beautiful silver box inlaid with semi-precious stones. Ceremoniously, she placed the silver box on the table and opened the cover. Solemnly, she handed each of us a picture of Jesus Christ with an inscription in Slavic. The nuns folded their hands and prayed. And we folded our hands and prayed silently with them.

I tried to remember how many months, or even years, it had been since I had prayed. The last time must have been when I attended a Protestant service in school. This silent prayer with the nuns and my comrades was more meaningful than any service I had ever attended.

I wish you the very best, I thought and repeated the words in my mind. I felt the intensity when these seemingly insignificant words passed through my mind repeated over and over. A happy feeling sent chills down my spine. These were my real friends. At this quiet moment, border disputes, nationality, and up-bringing were disregarded. The four Serb nuns wiped tears from their eyes and embraced each of us before we left.

Chapter 9

Christmas Surprises
Croatia

It was December 16, 1944 when we left Osijek. "How much money do you guys have?" Hugo inquired with a hint of jealousy. But we always shared what we had. We walked at the head of the long column. Everybody seemed to know about our salt money.

"I don't know. I have no idea. You can help spend it," I answered. The generosity surprised them. They began discussing how they would spend my money. Alfons and Roland had blabbered about the salt trade. But, even with all that money, we couldn't buy anything. All the businesses were boarded up. Here and there an inn was open. Whenever Tony would call for a break, a bunch of my new friends would gather.

"Are you going? Let's spend your money," so we went to an inn. I would hand the innkeeper a bundle of Kuna notes and say, "Everybody is invited. If you need more, let me know." That became the routine. He would take the notes, count, and his eyes would widen.

"How much did you give him?" asked my fine friends.

"I don't know! I didn't count it. How much does a *slivovitz* cost?"

None of us knew. We relied on the integrity of the innkeeper, besides, we didn't care. Everybody considered my money as their money. They were concerned, though, that I might be cheated, and drank as much as they could.

"Bring something to eat!" I ordered the innkeeper. My main goal was to get rid of the money. He hustled into the kitchen and brought bread and plates of dumplings with cooked vegetables and a little meat on the side.

"Sorry that's all I have," he apologized. "That doesn't matter. How much do you need?" He counted. But I gave him more. He handed me my notes back.

"You gave me too much." I was almost disappointed when he returned my money.

"How is slivovitz made?" asked my friends.

"Made from plums. We also have *rakija*. That is cheaper, made from sour plums. Here, everybody orders the best, and that is slivovitz!" I gave him five more bills. "Invite the locals and use this money as long as it lasts!" He stared in disbelief. Though the circle of my friends grew larger and we stopped in every village, in at least one functioning inn it seemed I would still have Kunas left when we get to Hungary. Slowly but surely I tired of the slivovitz. It became repulsive. I did not know how to get rid of my money. Having it was no longer fun. I didn't want to disappoint my friends. But money was becoming a real burden.

Tony finally came to my rescue. He took me aside. "The captain is complaining. You guys get drunk in every inn on the road. You've got to stop that! He doesn't want that. I told Roland and Alfons, too."

"Tony, I must thank you. I am tired of slivovitz. But what can we do with our money?"

"The captain discussed that, too. We'll find cows and pigs and buy them on the road. We'll add them to our food supply. You guys stay out of the inns!"

In the next village, we went to a large farmhouse which had a sizable stable. The farmer was in the cow stable and carried two buckets of milk on a hanger over his shoulders. He screamed wildly when he saw the four of us. "Please! No!" He thought we would confiscate his livestock. But Alfons tapped his shoulder and explained in the same way he had talked to the nuns in Osijek.

"We want to buy cows and pigs." The emphasis was on the word *buy*. "We'll pay." He showed him a bundle of money. "How much does a cow cost?"

The farmer didn't believe him. He thought Alfons would trick him. "No! No!" He cried and called for his wife. She came running, and both blabbered in Slavic. The lady was tall and more resolute. She was an energetic woman and grabbed Alfons' money. She peeled a few dozen notes off.

"That is for one cow." She spoke broken German and waved the bills in his face. She didn't know that Alfons was an experienced cow trader, but he didn't argue with her. He handed her two additional notes.

"These two notes are for the best cow." The wife understood. She turned to her husband and both nodded in agreement. The final price was now established. The farmer couldn't believe what his wife just did. The price must have been triple the normal price.

"How many cows do you want?" Now he spoke German well.

"As many cows as you want to sell," said Alfons. The farmer raised his hand, "Five." He pointed five fingers in the air. We took the required Kuna notes from our knapsacks. Tony counted and evenly pooled the money.

"How much is a pig?" he asked. The farmer, now encouraged scratched his head and took a bundle of notes from Tony's hand. He peeled off six bills.

"That much. But I have only two pigs," he admitted.

"Do you have friends we can buy cows and pigs from?" Tony addressed himself to the farmer's wife who seemed to be more fluent in German.

"Wait! Ten minutes!" She waved at her oldest daughter, sending her away.

Tony ordered Roland to get the captain. He needed to know how many cows and pigs we should buy. Minutes later, the teenage daughter returned with two farmers strolling behind her, hesitant but not wanting to miss out on a lucrative trade. Six other neighbors arrived five minutes later. The lady decided to conduct the trade business inside the house and waved for everybody to follow. When we were assembled, she became the agent and explained the trade conditions first in Slavic. A long discussion followed. The wife became impatient and shouted at the men. Tony interrupted, "Tell them the price stands." The discussion continued in Slavic. The wife argued furiously.

"The price is right," she confirmed to us in German. "They want to know if you want to see the animals?"

Tony said. "No!" And that surprised the farmers. They shook their heads in disbelief. Alfons took Tony aside, "That's a big mistake." The resolute farm-lady turned to the six farmers, scolded them, and then turned to Tony. "I'll check the animals. You don't need to worry. I won't allow them to bring their sick cows. They have twelve cows, and six pigs, and also have chicken and geese." She suggested a price for a chicken and a goose. Tony accepted the price and took money from our knapsacks.

"We'll buy the twelve cows, six pigs, thirty chicken and five geese! Let's figure the total. Tell them to bring the animals, and we'll count the money. All the chickens and geese must be slaughtered." Tony brought up a new condition.

We still didn't know how to count the money and spread the bundles on the table. The farm lady was our agent and counted the amount she needed. She sorted the bills and properly paid each farmer. I still had half of my Kuna notes.

A herd of cows and pigs were driven by small boys into the farm's yard. They were followed by flocks of chicken and geese. Our captain arrived and began to inspect them.

"The pigs must be slaughtered, too!" The captain set a new condition. "Pigs walk too slow. Tony, appoint some men who know how to drive the cows. I hope somebody in the kitchen crew knows how to slaughter the big animals. If they don't, they'll have to learn."

We paid more for the slaughter of the pigs, and one farmer argued for still more because we wanted them split and tied on the side of our four cannons. The trade was now completed, and half the village was assembled to help with packing and tying. We paid additional money to everybody who worked. The farmer's wife called a meeting. Slivovitz in glass jars came from across the street. Water glasses were filled with it and passed until everybody had one, including the boys. We toasted and shook hands.

Alfons pulled me aside. "I think, the smart woman got more than triple the price."

"Who cares? We made a bunch of people happy and got rid of that stupid money."

In the next village, two days later, we bought more animals. But this time, we knew the price and didn't have to haggle. The trade went quickly. I suspected the people waited for us. They had heard about the trade and the excellent price. But the animals moved slowly. The cows had no desire to compete with the speedier mules. We noticed anxious faces in every village waiting to make a trade.

Ludbreg, near the Hungarian border, was the final stop. "We'll take a three day rest," announced the captain in the market place. It was two days before Christmas. "We'll have special Christmas rations on Christmas Eve."

"Do we have mail?" somebody asked.

"I am afraid not. All the mail goes to Lake Balaton. We are still far south. We'll all have to wait until we get there. The Russians are now a hundred kilometers east and are moving north. I figure we'll be safe here. But sentries must be posted day and night."

It was the first time I didn't have even a letter on Christmas.

I volunteered for guard duty. I figured that way I'd escape guard duty on Christmas. Tony pointed to the church tower. "You know the church towers. I hope this one also has a circular stairway," he laughed, "there won't be much to see."

He was right. The two hours were very boring, and I missed Osijek.

The flat fields were covered by the wintry frost. The streets were quiet. No one worked, and only a few people went to church. I was tired from too much slivovitz. The alcohol still cursed through my veins. To kill time, I began to wonder what my mother might be doing. We always had the Christmas tree decorated by this time. Cookies, stored in tin cans, were in hiding places but they were not safe. My brothers and I watched my mother and knew where she hid them. Every year she promised to change the hiding places and often even forgot where she hid cookies in the first place. I became homesick.

How do Croats celebrate Christmas? Will they be upset about us soldiers being in their village? Are the Croats really our Allies? I looked down at the snow covered red roofs. Are these people friendly? "Croats were considered to be very independent. But the Ustasha militia was an Ally." Tony warned us, "These villagers care for themselves. And Tito is a Croat."

After the dull, two-hour watch, I went to the battery kitchen, tired and hungry. Why was the kitchen two kilometers from center of town? The cook knew me. Everybody knew me since I had money. He smiled and handed me three packs of cigarettes, five chocolate bars, and a loaf of sweet bread he had baked himself. The dinner was chicken stew. "How many cows are left?" He pointed to one hand. "Only five?"

"We'll buy more after Christmas, and more chicken. I like your chicken stew." For that compliment I was awarded a second loaf of Christmas bread.

"How much money do you guys still have?" I was, in his opinion, a hero. "Who knows. We never counted the money." I was proud to be considered a hero, even if it was just for money. "I can't believe that you never counted the money. Isn't it fun to have it?" He was like my friends who wanted to know how rich I was. Money was a new experience. Since I had money, I had gained recognition. But everybody's envy wasn't fun.

I left the kitchen and searched for my new quarters. The observer's quarters were identified by a blue chalk sign and a cross on the head beam of a door. Two men rode ahead into town, counted the houses and marked them. Each group had its own color. On a side street, close to the center of town, were four houses marked with blue chalk and the cross. I selected the house furthest away. The door was wide open and a joyful voice shouted in German.

"Wie geht s Kamerad?" (How are you comrade?)

A large man, about forty, stooped his head at the door frame and heartily pumped my hand. "I speak German and need practice. Where are your friends?" He inspected me carefully. Maybe I wasn't what he expected? I was too young. His house wasn't bad. Tony, Hugo, and Fritz were in another house. I didn't mind being alone. I had had too much slivovitz, was tired, and didn't want to talk. The lady of the house came from the kitchen to greet me. She was short, stout and had a friendly face. Before shaking hands, she reached down her long dark blue gown and wiped her right hand.

"She doesn't speak German," warned her husband and laughed with a roar. "You and I can talk about women as long as we want, they don't understand German. Meet my daughter Ana and my two youngest." We shook hands. They made me feel like I a relative who had come visiting. Twenty year old Ana was very pretty. She blushed when I inspected her, perhaps, a little too long. She wore a white scarf over her head like her mother did and also wore a long dark gown that reached her ankles.

The man pulled me inside. *"Willkommen!* My name is Alex." His heavy hand laid on my shoulder until we were in the living room. He gave me a friendly push and made me sit in the only comfortable upholstered chair. The house was small but looked neat.

"Ana speaks a little German, not much. My wife doesn't understand at all. Ana married a Ustasha soldier. Hey Ana, speak German!" he ordered. Ana blushed and refused. A little later she said a few simple sentences. Alex roared with laughter as he translated. I indicated that I understood every word. Alex enjoyed teasing his pretty daughter. He thought he was showing affection. But it was annoying. Ana angrily ended the conversation, when he joked about her harsh German pronunciation, and began arguing in Slavic. He translated that too, every word, and that annoyed her even more. The smaller children stood and watched in amazement. So much excitement had not happened before.

The living room had a large fire place, which was used for cooking. There were two other rooms, a master bedroom with an enormous bed from wall to wall. The other room was small and also had a bed. "You can sleep here. Ana sleeps in our bed," Alex ordered, in spite of my strenuous objection that I didn't want to take anybody's bed. Alex insisted. "My family sleeps in the large bed. We have room for Ana and the small children. They sleep at our feet."

Alex took me to the outhouse, thirty meters from the house, behind the dung hill and showed me his freshly painted hay barn next to the stable.

"German farms are larger, I know that. Because I was there." He insisted on telling me his life story when we were back in the warm living room. Alex was one of six children, and there was no place for him on his father's farm. Therefore, Alex learned the carpenter's trade. After the apprenticeship he went to Austria as a journeyman. There was not enough work there either. "But I learned German and earned more money in one year than I ever had before. I sent money home and went to Holland and had to learn another language. In Belgium I learned a third language. They took advantage of me until I understood the languages. Languages are very important. After a couple of years, I got tired of learning languages, and I was homesick. I went home. Money isn't that important. It's better to be home and have less money."

Alex waited for me to show my approval of his decision. I nodded. It was also my first Christmas away from home. The year before, I had furlough and spent Christmas at home with my mother.

"I had money when I came home," Alex told me. "You can marry anybody when you have money. There was still no carpenter work. I bought this farm from my wife's uncle, married, and became a farmer. I am not rich; but I am happy. I have seen the world and for that they respect me." Alex clapped his large chest. "Everybody in this village asks my advice. I've been in the world."

I thought of my Kuna bills, and wondered why these bundles in my knapsack didn't make me happy? I may have even more than Alex. Perhaps, I could give him my money as a Christmas present. That would make me happy. But I doubted if he would accept it. Alex was too proud to take money for nothing. Kuna will be worthless in Hungary. "Don't trust Croats!" warned Tony. I don't even know Alex. I decided not to think about money anymore.

Alex jumped up apologizing profusely. He had an appointment and forgot. "We make schnapps two days before Christmas. I have an ancient recipe. My schnapps tastes really good. But we still need to improve it." He stormed from the house and left me alone in the kitchen. It was suddenly quiet.

The two women sat at the open fire and talked in Slavic. I listened for a while and sensed I understood them. When I was a little boy, I listened to the grownups. I didn't really understand them but somehow sensed what they were talking about. The same thing happened here. The two small children danced around and stared at me like I was a new house animal. Their mother noticed and sent them outside. She motioned for me to follow her into the master bedroom. She had a jar of cookies hidden behind a curtain, just like my mother did at home. They were mixed cookies stored in a tin can. Most were yellow, some were round and looked like the soft butter cookies my mother baked. I tried one. It was made from pork fat, not from butter. It tasted strange. My hostess watched anxiously for my reaction. I didn't like the taste, but smacked my lips pretending to enjoy it. She took a handful from the can and brought them to the fireplace. We ate and conversed in sign language.

Ana and her mother spoke Slavic and laughed. But I understood more than they thought. Ana's German was quite good without Alex interfering. I asked them to repeat twenty Slavic words, then I began mixing Slavic with German. They laughed and teased me. I didn't mind. We talked for hours. Suddenly, Hugo stood behind me. He had come to check on what I was up to.

"Why didn't you come to our house?" he didn't know Ana could understand. Ana grabbed my arm to oppose my leaving them. Hugo smiled. "I understand. Bring extra containers tonight. We'll get fruits, nuts, and chocolates after our regular food," he laughed and left. My silly conversation with the two women was too much for him. I asked for two plates to take to the kitchen tonight.

"No!" They shook her heads. "Why not." I tried my Slavic.

Alex came back at that moment and inquired what we talked about.

"No way! You are not going to your army kitchen," he yelled in German. "You are my guest in this house. You eat with us." That was it! I was hungry and looked forward to the special ration on Christmas. But Alex wouldn't have it. He made me help him and his friends set a barrel of rakija on the kitchen table and taste the newly distilled rakija schnapps. Alex and his five friends were already tipsy. The distilling had taken its toll. I was introduced to them with a sweeping gesture and a long speech, partially in German, but mostly in Slavic.

Alex searched for his equipment to tap the barrel and after that, poured the rakija into a china wash basin. Water glasses were dunked into the bowl and filled.

"Zivio, drug Tito!" Alex lifted his glass and roared. His friends laughed and bent forward. "Zivio, drug Tito!" the toast was repeated. They clicked glasses with me. When I joined the chorus, they laughed even more.

"What does 'Zivio, drug Tito' mean?" I asked Alex in German.

"That means, 'Down with Tito!'" He looked me in the eyes and placed his heavy hand assuringly on my shoulder. Everybody laughed again. Should I believe him? I suspected the toast meant the opposite. But I didn't care. We repeated the toast a dozen times, and they laughed more each time. Who cared? I was hungry and drunk.

"Absolutely not!" Alex said, grabbing my army tin pots and hid them in the master bedroom. That was the end of my special Christmas ration, the German cookies made from butter, not from pork fat, and the variety of nuts and chocolates. I stayed and kept toasting with Alex and his friends.

I vaguely remembered when I fell into Ana's bed, still fully clothed and asleep as soon as my head hit a cushion. Six water glasses filled with clear white rakija proved too much for my empty stomach. The next morning, I opened my eyes and recognized Alex standing near my bed with a full glass of rakija. I thought I was still dreaming. Life crept back into my brain, my eye-lids flickered and Alex roared once more, "Zivio, drug Tito!" We clicked glasses cheerfully; but I pressed my lips tight and didn't take a sip. Alex didn't notice. My head spun, and it wasn't even breakfast time.

Thank God for breakfast. It consisted of ham, eggs, and rich white bread. It was excellent. Alex drank rakija instead of coffee. I refused. "Not during breakfast." After breakfast I went to the open water well, stripped to the waist, and stuck my head deep into the ice-cold water. I swore not to drink today, not one drop of rakija. I had no duties, but seriously considered asking Tony to assign me to sentry duty. I needed an escape from Alex and his friends. I felt refreshed from the ice-cold water, "Please no rakija, today." I told Alex.

"What else can we do if you won't celebrate? Can you play cards?"

Anything but rakija, I agreed. He brought a deck of cards. We played a simple kids game, two pairs scored, and he who finished first, won. The game was boring. While we played I became hungry, but nobody prepared lunch. How could I escape, find my pots, and get to the army kitchen? It was impossible.

"On Christmas Eve, we fast," explained Alex, like it was a matter of fact. "Do you want schnapps? Don't you fast in Germany on Christmas Eve?"

"No more rakija! Please!" I looked for something to eat. Alex followed my eyes.

"No! You can't go to your kitchen. I won't allow it." Only a pot of water boiled on the fireplace. There would be no food in this house. But I knew where the Christmas cookies were in the master bedroom. I didn't dare take them without permission. Alex poured me half a glass. We continued the boring game.

Don't they eat at all on Christmas? Was that their custom? I became angry. Christmas Eve was more important than Christmas day at home. On Christmas Eve we had a festive meal late in the afternoon. Only family participated. Fresh poached trout or carp was served with fine breads, cheeses, herring salad, and pickled red beets as side dishes and all sorts of cookies for dessert. My mouth watered from thinking of the good food. Alex intuitively knew what I thought.

"Don't worry, Magda and Ana will prepare a good meal tonight. We eat after midnight. There will be plenty. We'll eat well into the morning." He clicked my glass. "Ana's husband might come, on furlough! He doesn't like the war. We hope the Russians don't show up. We have enough fuss between ourselves, the Muslims and Serbs. We don't need the Asian-Russians adding to our problem. Most Russians don't know knifes or forks or what they are for. They eat with their hands, and when they use an outhouse, they never use paper to wipe themselves. They have no culture or manners, no Christmas, or anything." Alex waved his huge hand in disgust. He won the last hand.

The rakija made me tired. I was in no mood to discuss politics or religion. Does Alex like Germans? I wasn't sure. But he liked me. That I was sure of. "Alex, do you mind if I take a nap?" I had to get away from the alcohol.

"Sure! I wake you at midnight."

Half asleep, I heard people moving around. Straw was carried into the house. Were they hiding their Christmas presents? The children spread straw a foot high on the floor next to my bed and giggled.

"Greetings! One hour before Christmas!" Alex brought me a glass of rakija. "Christ was born in a barn and slept on straw. We also must sleep on straw on Christmas like Jesus, Mary, and Joseph. That is our custom." Ana dumped an armful of straw next to me, the dust made me cough. She laughed. Everybody was excited. Magda cooked at the fireplace. I felt much better.

Lots of pots were on the fire. Ana set the table in a festive style. Alex and I sat next to each other on a bench. Everybody watched the clock on the wall. Exactly at midnight, they shouted like we do at New Years. The women brought the pots and lifted the lids. A fabulous smell saturated the air. The feast began with roasted chicken, then mutton, pork, and slices of lard. Trays of brown and white bread were placed at the end of the table. Cabbage, dumplings, and relishes were in the center. The fine dust of straw made me sneeze. We were ankle deep in it. I had never had hay fever on Christmas Eve.

We feasted and, while Alex wasn't looking, I thinned my rakija with water. The hidden Christmas cookies were placed on the table and greeted with enthusiasm. The feast took several hours. One by one, the children first, slid from the bench and fell on the straw. They were instantly asleep. Alex and Magda knelt on the straw and said a long prayer. They were last to collapse and stretched themselves side by side on the floor. The huge bed stood empty.

I sat for a while contemplating the peaceful scene. They gave no presents and nothing needed to be unwrapped like we did in our house on Christmas Eve. I wondered if they were too poor to exchange presents. But they were happy. I learned later that presents were given on January 6, Three King's Day.

The enormous family bed stood empty. I considered that to be a waste, so I carefully walked over the sleeping bodies and stretched myself on the huge, comfortable bed, twisting and turning in all directions, enjoying the unexpected luxury. I didn't disturb anybody. I slept like a log. The big bed was my Christmas present.

The next morning, nobody woke me. The women and children were in church. Alex checked the rakija barrel. "Not enough rakija," he declared simply. "We've got to get more. My friends come this afternoon and we play cards." I shuddered, oh no, not that kids game again! Alex read my mind. "No! This time, we play for money. Do you have Kuna? If you don't, I'll give you some."

"I have Kuna. We are paid in Kuna." I told Alex and looked for my knapsack full of Kuna, which was still under Ana's bed. I could make Alex a nice

Christmas present. I would lose in the card game, so he could get my Kuna. My Kuna would be worthless in Hungary in a few days.

"We play Black Jack, or what's called Seventeen and Four," explained Alex. I knew the game. I lost all my money playing it when I joined the 6th Battery. Then, it took my new comrades only two hours to win my money.

There were six of us who played. Alex explained the rules. The dealer position kept alternating. We began, and no matter how bad I played, I won. I played recklessly. Alex screamed and scolded me. I didn't want to win. I made obvious mistakes. Alex scolded me again. But I still won. I just couldn't lose. They applauded my unusual luck, and shook their heads. They even stopped drinking. I noticed the friendly mood changed when I kept winning. I took much of their money. There were no more toasts of "Zivio, drug Tito!"

A few wrinkled Kuna notes were still stuffed under the rakija glasses, but I was in possession of most of their money and embarrassed. I stopped, put my cards down and asked Alex to switch games to Poker, because I was never good at poker. I hoped I would lose a bit easier. But my luck continued, and their faces became more sour. I threw my cards down and stopped.

"Alex, I want to invite you to the inn. It's Christmas, I keep winning and I want to spend that money I won. You tell them!" Alex translated. Their faces lit up. They agreed. We left the cards on the table and went to the inn. Only one inn was open on Christmas. Men had to go somewhere while the women prepared the food. The sweet smell of tobacco swayed in the large, sparsely decorated inn filled with men sitting on benches.

Alex suggested in German, "Slivovitz! Nothing but the best."

Alex didn't know how experienced I was in Croatian bars. A bald innkeeper greeted Alex and ignored me. I pulled a large bundle of Kuna notes from my knapsack. His eyes opened wide and the picture changed. I said in Slavic, "Two slivovitz for each person." The words sprang easily from my lips, partially, because I'd listened to Slavic all day and had said the same sentence many times before. Everybody was surprised. Soon I was the center of attention.

Alex, half-drunk, put his arm around me and demonstrated that we were friends. He introduced me in various languages. His speech became longer. The men at the banquet tables loved Alex and his showing off, though their interest gradually dissipated. That changed when the slivovitz arrived and my friends shouted, "Zivio, drug Tito!"

The room was momentarily silent. Everybody looked and waited for my reaction. Alex clicked my glass repeating the toast. We laughed. Alex shouted in German into the room, "That means: down with Tito!"

Now everybody laughed and clicked glasses and downed slivovitz. I ordered two more rounds and gave the innkeeper a bundle of Kunas. He stuffed them quickly under his long white apron.

"Slivovitz for everybody!" I yelled in Slavic making a circle with my arm which meant the entire room. A roar of approval went up. The men raised their glasses and shouted, "Zivio, drug Tito!" when the slivovitz came. Alex became concerned when I ordered the third round and then a fourth. "Do you have enough money?"

I wasn't quite sure, so I went to check with the innkeeper. Alex followed me. The innkeeper pulled the notes from under his apron. He peeled a few off and gave me a bundle back. I pushed the bundle toward him and ordered, "Use it!"

Alex noticed the amount of money. His eyes widened.

"These bastards drink too much," he yelled in German. "They are going to spend your money," he took the bundle of Kuna and pushed it into my pocket. But I refused. Alex was a big man and was drunk. I figured he could become violent, but I gambled and slapped the bundle into the innkeepers hand.

"That money stays! I want you to use it if it takes all night. Alex, tell him!" Alex was perplexed. We were both drunk. He didn't expect me to oppose him and hesitated. Then he put his arm around and roared, "You are my friend, I'll do whatever you want." He motioned the innkeeper and said softly, "Spend his money! Let's go home!" Everybody watched with intense interest.

Alex was my host and my protector. He laid his arm around me and, waving back and forth, we left the inn arm in arm, crossed the street in a wide circle hollering German marching songs. "Zivio, drug Tito!" I heard the toast inside. The fifth round was served.

"Do you know what that actually means? It means, 'Hail Tito!' But who cares." That was fine with me, too, I told Alex. He was my friend and that was more important.

The next morning, we bought more cows, pigs and chickens and paid the triple price. There was one bundle of Kunas left. I didn't need my knapsack anymore and handed it to Alex. "Here is a Christmas present, Alex! Thanks for everything!" The last bundle of Kunas was inside, but Alex didn't know.

Chapter 10

Ambush

Balaton Lake, Hungary

When we arrived at the First Mountain Division, a line of cows trotted behind the artillery column. We looked like a band of warriors from the middle ages. The pigs tied to the cannons and chickens in boxes were admired by all. At Varazdin we had crossed the border to Hungary.

My father had sung about the Hungarian roses in Varazdin. I saw no roses in the dreary town of Varazdin, south of Lake Balaton.

"The Russians gave us the devil at Belgrade. Now they broke through and are here," announced the captain. "We'll show them our muscle this time. SS military police inquired about us, but our division staff sent them in the wrong direction. We'll stay on the main road."

Yells of approval greeted us. It was good to be with these guys. The cows and pigs caused enormous excitement. It was amazing. They greeted us like long lost friends.

"You are safe. Don't worry about the SS."

We roasted chicken and invited others. Captain Kroener pumped an infantry officer for news.

"How is Eisele?" was his first question.

"He is fine. You should hear about Captain Poessinger, his friend."

Much earlier, Poessinger had become famous when his unit went on furlough after fighting two years in Russia. Poessinger had driven the train non-stop from Russia's Black Sea to Vienna by simply taking over the train engine and directing the train not to stop until Vienna. Trains were diverted and had to wait on side-tracks until Poessinger's crazy train passed by. They had driven into Vienna's station with soldiers on the train's roof shooting the glass out of the station roof. Splinters fell over the tracks. All trains between Odessa and Vienna were delayed. Poessinger was a legend since he single-handedly took the largest Maginot defense fortress in France and took a thousand soldiers prisoner.

"What did he do this time?"

"He was on furlough and Gauleiter Wagner invited him to attend a speech in Munich. He sat in the front row. Captain Poessinger didn't like it when the Gauleiter said, 'While our armed forces seem to crumble, we at home continue the fight and will win the final victory. We will be the country's last defense.' Poessinger got up and yelled, 'Disgusting!' He climbed the platform and belted the Gauleiter in the face. Nobody stopped him."

"Nobody stops Poessinger," confirmed somebody.

"The guards were scared. Poessinger stormed to the station while the Gauleiter laid on the ground. He boarded the next train and came here. They searched for Poessinger in Munich and even called here to arrest him. We told them Poessinger was on furlough as he stood near the telephone."

"What else is new at home? We haven't had mail in months."

"No good news comes from home. Munich is destroyed. Gauleiter Wagner is still in a coma. He had a nervous breakdown and hides his embarrassment in a hospital."

"I hope Poessinger stays here," said Lieutenant Stoll.

"You are not kidding! Nobody wants to go on furlough anymore. All the cities are destroyed. This isn't a war between soldiers anymore. It's a slaughter of civilians at home. Since they can't beat us in an honest battle, they destroy our cities, kill innocent women and children and demoralize us on the front lines. They couldn't beat us otherwise." We were speechless. The infantry officer pulled a newspaper from his pocket.

"Read this! I received it yesterday. 'Hamburg, December 23, 1944. The asphalt melted from the fire, people on the street were either dead or stuck in hot asphalt. They struggled, their hands stretching asking for help while their feet were stuck. They knelt on hands and knees until they died. Desperate to be pulled out, they screamed as long as they could. Nobody helped, as helpless as they were.'"

He folded the paper and put it away. "That was my wife. Nobody saved her."

"That's terrible. We've got to stop it," said Lieutenant Stoll. "That can't go on. We have to finish this war." They were all motivated to fight again.

They drove us to the artillery observer station, an abandoned two story farm house. The house was almost entirely covered by a huge chestnut tree. I was glad that, for once, we didn't have to walk. Infantry soldiers dug trenches everywhere on the way.

Tony marked positions on a new artillery map while Joseph, Roland, and Alfons unloaded equipment. Captain Kroener seemed unusually nervous today.

"Stoll, take the advance observer position and go up that hill, four miles from here." He pointed at a spot on the map. "I don't like the report I received from reconnaissance. Our air force stinks. They have eighteen year old pilots flying without proper training. They don't see anything. Remember Osijek? Nobody saw the Russians advancing with tanks and artillery until they suddenly rowed across the river at night. Don't they know Russians move at night?" The two officers studied the map and I watched their pencils wandering over the landscape.

"What do you think? Where will they come from this time?" Kroener pointed at a prominent road point. "From there," answered Stoll. "That's the road. They'll move heavy equipment here, and where the road forks on that hill is a good spot for an observer. I'll take Roland and Joseph along." Lieutenant Stoll prepared to leave.

"Alfons, use the infantry office downstairs as our reception room! Yes, they will come here, I will guarantee it." Kroener marked the hill with a red pencil. "The Hungarians are on the left of us. That is a weak spot. They'll target that area."

Stoll and the wireless operators left. Every four hours they called back and reported seeing nothing. Lieutenant Stoll joked for a half hour with Captain Kroener. There were no Russians. Captain Kroener told him to call every four hours regardless of whether there was anything to report.

The next morning we all waited for the call. It was long overdue. The captain paced the room. He took his field glasses and searched the slope. I saw infantry soldiers calmly digging trenches in the open field. Behind them was a forest. I remembered our VB group. Three men had disappeared in that direction last night. Captain Kroener didn't joke as usual. He seemed even more nervous than the day before. Everything was quiet.

"Alfons, call Stoll again! I want to talk to him," Kroener called downstairs.

"There is still no word, Captain. Something might be wrong with their equipment," answered Alfons from downstairs.

Captain Kroener saw me. "I want you to go and check. You know where the VB is, and tell Lieutenant Stoll to call." He pulled me to the map and pointed at the red circle. "For Christ's sake, Joseph or Roland, one of them at least, should be able to fix that damn equipment!" I knew the location from yesterday's conversation.

"Take the map with you and come right back." That meant I had to walk at least five or six hours, maybe more. I grabbed my rifle, took more ammunition from the shelf and a large piece of bread. I went straight to the hill and passed the working infantry men who ignored me. I came to the forest and heard somebody yelling, "Russians!"

I turned pale and checked to see who had yelled. That must have been my imagination. Nobody shouted. Behind me the soldiers worked calmly. When I reached the forest, I stopped and listened again. I had a strange feeling. Anxiety took hold, and I imagined all kinds of calls of danger. I walked carefully and watched every step, especially avoiding the dry branches. At the same time I looked for a potential hiding place. There were many where I could disappear in a hurry. My nervousness caused me to sweat. I always hated being alone in a forest. By now our infantry was out of sight behind me. Don't worry, there is nothing, I mumbled calming myself.

After walking an hour, I sat down to check the map. I should be pretty close to the VB station. When I unfolded the map, I distinctly heard something saying, "Be careful!" Was this the suicide mission, I had waited for? I tried to joke to myself. But I wondered if Russians had surprised Lieutenant Stoll. The captain sent me here because of the VB's malfunctioning equipment. Nonsense! They reported nothing unusual. Nobody surprised these guys. They were the most experienced soldiers in the world. I will find them. I continued walking uphill.

There, that's them! Why are they coming back? I saw soldiers coming downhill.

I stopped. These soldiers wore brown uniforms. They were Russians. Now about 100 meters from me, and not just three, but a hole bunch with more following behind. Russians were coming downhill pushing branches from their faces. They hadn't seen me, yet. I dropped quickly behind the nearest large rotting tree trunk. They came toward me. How many? Who knows! I shuffled loose soil from the side of the trunk and dug a shallow hole. Already they were only seventy meters away.

There was still time to break branches and cover myself. I laid still and waited. I heard foot steps and sticks breaking under boots. I stopped breathing and dug my face deep into the hole, still wondering how much of me stuck out. Can they see me? Let them walk around the tree trunk, please! They may even step on me. Nobody talked. I was too afraid to make changes. They were already too close, but I felt I should look. The urge to look made me put my face even deeper into the ground. My heart raced. Did they pass? I waited for what seemed like hours before I dared to look. The backs of brown uniformed men walked twenty meters past, going downhill. Each had a rifle under his arm. Soldiers on my left also walked down hill in a long line combing the forest. Nobody came behind them. Cold sweat covered my entire body.

My first thought was, they found the VB. But I would have heard shots and Joseph's machine gun would have blasted. No, they couldn't have! I counted more than 100 of them, not enough to attack our infantry. That was a patrol on a scouting mission. Perhaps more were on the way? I allowed two more minutes to calm myself down and waited. Nobody came. I had to find the VB and warn them. When I started planning my anxiety vanished. I thought the danger had passed. But I was wrong.

Carelessly, I walked uphill in an upright position, thanking my sixth sense for warning me. I had felt the Russians, like Joseph, before I had even seen them. But I was behind a long line of Russian infantry soldiers. That was not comfortable. And on my way back, I had to pass them again. I was on top of the hill. I laid down and began to crawl and look for a sign of the VB station. It didn't take long. I saw the grey canvass with mortar craters all around it. I crawled inside and discovered three dirt-covered bodies stretched in various directions. The canvas covered them, but they didn't move. A thick lump formed in my throat. A shudder went down my spine. There were the two wireless boxes which covered Joseph, and Roland sat crouched in an embryo-like position behind. The third body was Lieutenant Stoll's, covered by a cloth. I crawled first in his direction and saw at once that he was dead.

"Glad you came!" I heard a faint voice and quickly turned, "Glad to see you," groaned Joseph. He moved the two metal boxes off his body and could even sit up. I put an extra canvas over Lieutenant's Stoll's face.

"What happened?" I asked, and tears came into my eyes. "Glad to see you, too. Are you alive?" It was a stupid question, but I didn't care.

"They shot their mortars this morning," Joseph said barely audible. He sat now and straightened his boxes. His right arm stuck in a loose blood-soaked bandage. The arm was seemingly useless. He checked a box with his left hand. "I have a hard time with my arm," he told me. "Look out and check the front! The whole Russian army is setting up camp, only a few meters away from us." He groaned when he leaned back. "They came silently last night. Stoll was on watch. He saw them. I tried to make contact, but then the first mortar shell hit." He paused, "They were lucky to hit us with their first shot. I couldn't make contact. Roland was hurt, but at least he is still alive." Roland opened his eyes. I felt like hugging him. I told them what I saw.

"A Russian infantry patrol passed by me about a kilometer away. They didn't see me."

"They missed us, too! Lieutenant Stoll was killed by the first mortar shot. I covered him, and then I was hit, too. There wasn't anything I could do. They shot fifty mortar rounds. I crawled under my boxes using them as my cover. The radio is slightly damaged, but I think we can fix it, if only I had a good arm."

"I'll help you," groaned Roland, who crawled on his elbows then laid on his side. "My leg is busted. Hurts terribly! Afraid the leg is broken. Push a box over here. I have two hands, I can work." Roland's face showed the pain. He was bloody and caked with dirt. "Can you do something with my leg?" he pointed at their first aid box.

I was glad I'd had first aid training in France. I ripped Roland's trousers and saw a deep open wound which needed covering. I found a short stick and pressed it on his leg before I started to bandage him. Roland held the knot to prevent further bleeding. He held back his screams several times when I tried to straighten his leg. Joseph pushed another small stick in his mouth. I gave him pain killers and poured water from a bottle in his mouth. Carefully, I bandaged the leg. Roland guzzled the water like his life depended on it. In the meantime, Joseph worked on his box. "You'll fix that one!" he told Roland. "You are the better mechanic." And with that, he pushed the second box to Roland. Then he turned to me.

"Check the Russians and see what they are up to." I'd almost forgotten the Russians. "Hope they are not setting a tent on top of us." Joseph's joke showed he had gotten his second wind of energy. "Their patrol won't come back for a while. Roland, we've got to hurry. Fix that radio."

I crawled and laid to the side of Lieutenant Stoll's body. I had to push him aside to get to the edge of the hole. Stoll's dirt-covered field glasses laid next to him. I cleaned them to check the immediate vicinity.

"Holy smokes!" I almost shouted, but refrained myself to a whisper. "Do you guys know what we have out there?" A thousand soldiers set up tents on a plain field, only meters away where the slope ended. We were at the edge of a huge Russian camp. On a nearby road came an endless column of vehicles and brought more soldiers. They brought cannons, wagons, and supplies. Many brown uniformed soldiers walked behind wagons on the road. The column stretched to the horizon. Tanks rolled in the field. It was the Russian army and we were almost inside their camp.

Shuttering and scared, I wanted to tell my friends. I couldn't open my mouth. But they knew already and weren't interested. They worked feverishly on the radio repair.

"Can you fix these boxes? Do we have a chance?" I asked anxiously, "I've got to report back to the captain. If you can't fix the wireless, I must go." Joseph winced.

"Just stay where you are, next to the poor lieutenant, God rest his soul, and watch the Russians! We don't want to walk into the patrol, and they shouldn't walk into our hole. I don't know if we can repair the damn equipment. Our cannons could make a dent in that damn Russian camp. That's our best chance. Artillery is our best and only weapon. I don't think we can get out of here without being seen. I agree, we should leave before the patrol comes back. You decide if we should go back! That's my suggestion.

"Didn't you learn how to shoot artillery in your fancy cadet school? Once we fix the equipment, you do the shooting. You have the lieutenant's measurements, and you can use his numbers. He had everything figured out. Artillery is our best chance. We'll knock them down, and when that's done, we'll go home. Hurry Roland!"

There was pain in his face. That worried me. Neither were able to go anywhere. But they worked feverishly. The boxes were open, and strings of wires hung out. Roland was almost inside his box working with the wires. He broke off some and connected others. Joseph's head was stuck in the other box. His right arm hung uselessly at his side.

"Roland hold that wire right here! I got it," he mumbled from inside.

I cleaned the dirt from the lieutenant's map. All the significant points were marked along the road. I found his measurements relating to the marks. The road forked here.

I guessed the first Russians had arrived very late. They shot fifty mortar shells to secure the near forest, and they didn't even know how successful they were. The next morning, they sent the patrol. That was the picture. The patrol went into the forest in a single line and later spread out and passed the VB position. The way I saw them in the forest they spread far on all sides. Here these Russians felt pretty safe and secure. They didn't suspect anybody was watching them. I could even hear them talking. On the road stood an officer shouting directions to approaching vehicles. He told them where to turn. Hardly any soldiers wore jackets. They braved the cold without concern. The mortars which killed Lieutenant Stoll stood before me unmanned.

"I got it!" Roland called softly from behind. Joseph's head came from inside the other box. I told them they were geniuses.

"We'll stay. I'll wait until you fix the equipment. Then we'll call the captain. If the equipment doesn't work I must leave alone and report to the captain. I can't take you back by myself, but I promise I'll come back with help."

I should leave before the Russian patrol returns, I told myself. That gives me an hour. My guys can't walk. I had to help them both. Roland, with a broken leg, couldn't walk five kilometers. Joseph had lost too much blood. I needed help to get them and the heavy equipment to our camp. I desperately hoped they would fix the wireless and I could then direct the artillery to save us all. That was our best chance, like Joseph said.

Hurrah, for German engineering! They made stuff simple, so repairs were easy, even in difficult situations. Joseph tried to make contact. I felt confident about my shooting ability. I had gained a lot of experience in Osijek with Tony's help. The targets were laid out, the figures and measurements were made and in my hand. I couldn't miss. But the shells would be close. That didn't scare me. At least not yet.

"Did you make contact?" I asked them.

"In a minute. I hear sounds, the lines are open."

"Can the Russians pick us up?" That possibility suddenly occurred to me.

"They could if they paid attention. But I doubt that."

I crawled back to get closer to the equipment. I could only whisper. The Russians were close. Now the boxes were close. Joseph and Roland laid behind them.

"Sixth battery! Can you hear me?" Joseph called in a low voice. There was no answer. "Damned shit!"

The Russian bivouac expanded by the minute. Tents were set up on our slope. I saw a truck turning and soldiers jumped off, walking in our direction, much too close for comfort.

"The line's open. I can hear them." Joseph kept his voice down. I sensed excitement. "Call the captain, fast!" He almost yelled. But the pause was too long. I straightened my map and laid Lieutenant Stoll's papers next to me. I was ready. Joseph handed me the receiver. "Captain can you hear me?" I heard faint voices. And then I could hear him very clear.

"I hear you, Stoll. What happened?"

I explained, as calmly as I could where I was and what happened to Lieu-tenant Stoll. Then I waited. I couldn't wait much longer and began describing the Russian camp. I stopped and listened. There was silence. The line seemed dead.

"Captain, can you hear me?" Did he hear what I said?

"Yes, I heard you." The captain was there all along. He now broke the silence. "How are the other two, and how are you?" he asked calmly. His voice was loud, clear and sharp. I explained. He was not satisfied and asked more details.

"What can you see. Explain the Russian camp and where they build it!" I sensed he was mad about his best friend's death and wanted revenge.

I described the Russian camp calmly and added approximate distances and numbers of soldiers and vehicles. "I can even hear them talking," I said. "Captain, a large Russian patrol passed me in the forest on the way. They are coming your way, maybe 100 or more infantry soldiers."

"How long ago was that?"

About forty minutes ago." I wasn't quite sure about the time anymore.

"I gather the patrol will come soon. We'll get ready for them. We'll give them a nice welcome. I hope I can see their faces. Can you bring the two wounded back?" He paused, "On second thought, wait, we must dispose of the Russian patrol first."

"Captain, I can shoot artillery. I have Lieutenant's Stoll's measurements, the map and all his figures." There was silence. Then he gave his final decision.

"Yes, of course you can shoot. I saw what you did in Osijek. Tell me once more exactly what you see!" I started from the left, described the growing build-up, their thirty tanks and field artillery. About eight cannons took position with mortars on the side. I explained the road and what went on. The hot point being the fork. I recounted vehicles, with what had just arrived. I recounted the tanks because they moved around. "Captain, that's not everything. More is coming on the road. I can only see about two kilometers and more may be behind the hori-zon. That's not the end of the column. More is yet to come." There was silence. "Captain did you hear me?"

"Yes I did. I want you to be honest. Think! You are inside of a Russian camp. Your position will be made a target. Can you figure targets further outside effectively?" There was silence again. "I just changed my mind. I order you to leave."

I completely ignored the order and answered eagerly, "Yes! Sir! No Sir! The two guys can't walk. Of course, I can hit targets further outside."

"You are in a very precarious position. You are dead if one shot misfires. Everyone of you will be dead. There is no room for error. I think you should come back." When he paused, I knew he'd let me stay and shoot.

"From what you described, it looks like we're dealing with a Russian division, maybe more. Time is important. Our division cannot defend against a fully equipped Russian division. We may surprise them with our artillery and hurt them while they set up. That will at least delay them. And that may give you a chance to get away. We'll start. I'll give you two shots. Remember, your life is on the line one way or the other. You may also run into the Russian patrol." There was silence again.

Joseph pulled closer. He untied the lieutenant's leather pouch from his body." Tell him you have the tools, and you can shoot! We'll help you!"

"Captain, the first two shots must hit the crossroad, that's where the road forks. And after that, we'll move our shots south along the road before hitting the camp." I sounded confident.

"OK, I'll give you two shots. Crossroad first, with our second cannon."

I was sure Lieutenant Stoll had targeted correctly, my command went through clearly. Lieutenant Stoll was known for accuracy. I almost hoped the shots needed corrections, so I could prove myself. I began figuring the next targets up the road and the camp. That was our own position. These shots better be accurate! I measured ever so carefully and moved them a shade more south. Then, we waited for the first two shells.

The captain reported, "They are on the way." I heard a roar above close to our heads and watched the explosions side-by-side, exactly in the center of the road where it forked.

"Absolutely, no correction necessary!" I told the captain. That is Lieutenant's Stoll's revenge, he measured perfectly. And from now on it will be my revenge. As Lieutenant Stoll laid next to me, I felt I did the shooting for him.

"Bull's eye, Captain!" Four more shells exploded. "We hit the center of the fork and lots of equipment is flying around." The captain's response was, "OK. All four cannons, each six rounds! Give me the next targets! Start figuring!"

"I already did. Here is target NR-2, Captain." I passed on the measurement.

"That will land on your head," said the captain.

"I pulled 200 meters south, Captain."

"OK. Keep reporting!"

The first shot at the camp was crucial. Any stray shell off the mark and we would be dead. I figured the surprise was over. The Russians would look for the observer. It worked. The first four shots landed in the camp's center and caused frantic activity. Each following explosion added to the confusion. Dozens of wagons turned and the road became blocked. The four cannons continued firing. Russian soldiers ran into the field, luckily, in the opposite direction from us. I told the captain to correct 100 meters to the north. New explosions hit. They were devastating. I let them continue.

Joseph looked over my shoulder and pointed at the map. "Pull east and use only two cannons. Keep the two remaining cannons on target NR-2. Spread the fire to both sides of the road."

He was right. I measured and passed the new commands and explained what happened. The next shelling was very effective. Two tanks were now out of commission; rotating on only one carrier band. The crew left the vehicles. Many of their wagons toppled and were destroyed. Dead and wounded soldiers covered the field. I reported the results, and noticed my voice was high from excitement. The captain seemed to notice and was equally excited. Most importantly, he believed me. We were destroying a Russian Division. Explosion after explosion hit. Minutes became hours.

"We must work fast, before they find you. They will be coming for you." the captain called. He reversed himself, "Hold your horses. Don't give more targets, not yet. We must shell the road." Up to now, I hadn't counted the explosions. The result was enormous devastation.

"Celery." He used my nickname, which meant he was really excited. "The entire regiment will give us sixteen of their heavy cannons. Here is Commander Wirth on the line. I'll help you direct. We'll go further north and further back and blanket the field. The much bigger shells will be killers. You haven't seen them yet. Stay on the line and talk to the colonel!"

"Yes Sir," I whispered to inform Joseph and Roland about the changes. They smiled, but their grins worried me. I could see their pain. It was awful. Much happened in minutes. I wasn't sure how much time elapsed.

Colonel Wirth came on the line. I briefly described the scene. He passed the receiver to Captain Kroener who took over. I was thankful for all the experienced help I could get. Thirty big shells whistled over my head and fell very close. They exploded with a tremendous roar. They were devastating.

"Those are the big ones," Joseph and Roland jubilated. Further explosions came and were enormous, bigger than I had ever seen. They were more destructive than the Russian shells that hit us near Belgrade. When the dust settled, I saw the Russian tanks laid turned around, toppled, and clumps of soil still fell on them. The Russian soldiers were trying to escape now. I reported what I saw.

"Are you guys all right? How many more tanks are there? I want to hit them before they come and get you." I measured. Most tanks circled near the crossroad. They were now within target NR-1, I informed him. A minute later twenty-four shells roared over and exploded in succession on and near the tanks. It seemed, we could not miss today. The explosions also toppled tents.

"Did we hit them?" the captain sounded anxious. I sympathized with him, he couldn't see, and he had to rely on me. "Bull's eye," was all I could say. I didn't know, how better to describe the scene. I imagined his smile.

"Colonel Wirth is on the line. He wants to talk to you. Describe what you see the way you just explained it to me. Here is Colonel Wirth." A deep voice was on the line.

"Colonel Wirth here. Give me your name, quickly, and your rank!"

"Gunner Sellier, Sir." My first words caused silence. Obviously, he was not informed that I had no rank, and I directed his entire regiment.

"Are you sure you are trained to do the job?" he asked. "Never mind," he added quickly, "tell me what you see."

I gathered my thoughts and described the theater. I started with target number one, and described the tremendous overall destruction. "Colonel, I suggest, we target both sides of the road. Then, we should move 200 meters east, gradually. You should use your heavy artillery only on the road, and concentrate the light field artillery on target NR-2, the tent camp, and everything else closer to the crossroad. Spread your fire one kilometer north and use my position to measure from. There isn't much room between me and the Russians; therefore, all the shots must be accurate. So far, everything is on target, Sir!"

"Will do!" said the colonel. Joseph smiled. He liked how I ordered the colonel. "Don't forget you are their eyes. They depend on you. Keep ordering the way you do. You sound like a veteran officer. They like that." Roland turned and awkwardly showed his approval. I had learned artillery talk from Tony in Osijek.

Shell after shell roared over and exploded almost immediately. We became covered by dirt. A lump of soil hit me. I ducked. I only stuck my head out when it seemed safe. When I made my reports, I tried not to get hit. A 7.5 cm shell bounced off a tank. It came close to us. The shell stunned the tank, made him stop and turn in another direction.

Radio communication began to fade. "Please not now!"

"Sellier! Can you hear me!" I hardly heard. "General Kuebler will give six heavy Howitzers to assist from ten kilometers back. They now have your position. The combined artillery operation will be coordinated by Major Brendel from now on. He's regiment staff and will be your contact man. Stay calm and make your reports brief. Don't hesitate to make suggestions. You are doing fine. I am proud of you. The artillery works like a Swiss watch, like it did years ago."

Shell after shell exploded. The Russian camp was in shambles. I had no idea how long the bombardment lasted. Minutes? Hours? Soldiers ran on the slope, Joseph reached for his machine gun. I was scared.

"I won't use it," he assured me, "as long as they run by. But they won't get to the forest either." And they didn't. Shrapnel mowed them down. Soldiers who weren't killed stayed on the ground. The road was clogged from tumbled equipment and wagons.

"This is Major Brendel, 79th Regiment. I am your contact from now on, Sellier. I have your measurements and the targets. Give me a brief description. Time is important!"

I made my report to him. "Heavy artillery and six howitzers will target the road. We'll target east." They'll start one kilometer from the crossroad. If that's too far, pull them closer, but not further than you reasonably should. I'll synchronize the heavy cannons. Target NR-1 is the identification. I need your comments. Don't bring the howitzer closer than 500 meters. You hear me? I want no hero stuff! One stray shell and you are dead. And we need you. Give me all tank positions! And the artillery! Find them!"

"Yes Sir!" I saw tanks criss crossing the field. I measured and gave him the closer artillery positions. My measuring took less than 30 seconds. I had everything under control and gave major Brendel directions. Joseph looked over my shoulder.

"You are doing fine, not bad at all."

The heaviest artillery shells sounded like a fleet of airplanes flying in. They exploded and lifted tons of rocks and dirt. Most importantly, they were accurate. The Russians ran from the road and into the field. Why did they stay on the road so long?

Major Brendel took my report calmly. "Now, we'll go after the tanks, and get the artillery once more and the rest of the equipment. These are the primary targets. We don't chase enemy soldiers. How close can you pull the 'Heavy' in? A thousand meters? Agreed, affirmative!"

The new barrage of shells first scared me, but slowly I became used to them. They exploded further away and sounded like thunder following lightening.

"Major! Nine T-34 tanks are rolling east. They are taking off and are trying to fool us. Now they are turning south and are going into the field." Major Brendel adjusted. He shot brilliantly.

"Good! We'll get them. We must consider the wind. I'll change 300 meters south. Has the wind picked up?"

I heard Roland groan. Was he unconscious? He looked it. He had continually lost blood and looked like a ghost. Joseph dripped water on his mouth and urged me to concentrate.

"Keep going! I'll take care of him!" The water worked a miracle. Roland sat up and began working again.

"Don't give up on me, baby!" Joseph cussed the equipment. He had problems.

"Major can you hear me?"

"Barely. Out!" Brendel's voice faded. I couldn't do anything but wait and watch.

Sixteen cannons of our regiment's artillery blasted into the Russian camp. A few explosions came dangerously close. I needed to make changes immediately, but couldn't. Dirt and debris fell on me.

"Major, can you hear me?"

"Yes, I can, again loud and clear! What happened?"

"Wireless went out, we fixed it. You hit the tanks, three got away going east."

"Good! I'll pull after them. How far can you see? Explain!"

It took a minute to describe. All the new explosions added to the destruction. Littered wagons covered the road, laying on top of each other and blocking the escape. The Russian camp looked like a disturbed beehive. Soldiers ruthlessly pushed each other before falling.

"Good!" was the major's comment when I told him.

"Light artillery fire is getting too close. Pull east 200 meters," I ordered.

"Will do! The Russian patrol you mentioned came and engaged our infantry. They did no harm. They were decimated and are on their way back.

I want you to pull out. Good luck! And be careful. You did a good job, by the way. I'll continue the mop-up. Sign off!" His departure was abrupt and surprised me. He was right. We could now escape and nobody would notice.

"We are leaving!" I told Joseph and Roland and took a last look at the awesome destruction. I thought of Belgrade. The Russians did the same to us.

"War is insane. It should be outlawed! Let all the leaders duel each other!"

By now, Lieutenant Stoll's body was completely covered with dirt. I placed a few more rocks on the canvass before we left. Joseph grimaced from pain shouldering the metal boxes. He avoided the use of his wounded arm. I helped and strapped the boxes on his shoulder. He insisted on carrying his machine gun. "If we get stuck we'll need the radio and my machine gun."

Roland needed a new bandage and a firm stick on his busted leg. He rested his left arm over my neck, when we got up. He hobbled on one leg and insisted on helping. We couldn't crawl. That was impossible. We took our chances and walked. Explosion after explosion hit the Russians. That kept them busy. They didn't notice when we walked away.

I encouraged them. "We have only four or five kilometers and always downhill." Roland groaned with every step. He used his good leg as much as he could, but finally hung only over my shoulder. We made slow progress. Where was the Russian patrol? I began to worry but didn't mention it. They'll walk back in a single file, I figured. And they would walk in a hurry since they heard the artillery explosions.

Joseph worried me. He looked pale from too much loss of blood. And he carried too much, the two heavy metal boxes and his '42 model machine gun. Roland hung on my shoulder. I saw no way to hide quickly with the two in such bad condition.

"Watch for the Russian patrol," Roland mumbled on my back. He read my mind. He scared me. I had to stop and Roland slipped from my shoulder and landed heavily on his back. Joseph sat down unconcerned. He looked exhausted, and didn't even take his metal boxes off. We had walked about 45 minutes. What could I do? Neither could walk anymore. I would stay and would make Joseph call for help. Where was the Russian patrol? The artillery explosions sounded far off, and there were fewer bursts.

"I guess the light artillery stopped," I spoke loud to keep them awake. They noticed, and they listened. "Don't worry about the Russian patrol," said Joseph. "They are not coming. I can't feel them. They took a different route. We don't have to hurry."

My anxiety vanished. I always trusted Joseph. His sixth sense was better than anybody's. "I'll take the boxes, and you carry the '42 and help Roland, if you can," I said. I was anxious to get home quickly. I took the two metal boxes from his shoulder and avoided hurting his arm. I hoisted them on my shoulder. Joseph pushed Roland on the boxes. The total weight I now carried was enormous. I struggled to keep my balance when I straightened my knees. I had to take care of Roland, my friend. We walked slowly for two more kilometers. Roland needed urgent help and so did Joseph. Joseph walked behind and helped to keep Roland on my back. I hardly bent my knees as we moved slowly.

Thank God, Roland was conscious. Sometimes, he would dangle his good leg down and try to take a load off me. His weight became too much. I couldn't hold him anymore and had to unload him. He slipped off. His eyes were closed.

"Is he dead?" I asked Joseph. He checked. "No, he isn't dead, he just sleeps. Let's rest, and this time we'll rest for twenty minutes. You need a rest as well. And after that I'll take Roland on my good shoulder."

We both knew that was impossible. Joseph's condition wasn't much better than Roland's. His right arm bled. Thankfully the Russian patrol must have passed us. I had less to worry about. After a fifteen minute rest, I strapped the boxes over my shoulder, Joseph hoisted Roland on top. The combined huge load made me walk like a robot. I concentrated on not stumbling and avoiding rocks and branches.

My blood pressure increased. My head was light, and suddenly I felt I had to drop Roland. I was too weak and couldn't stand longer. Black was before my eyes. I dropped to my knees and felt my heart flutter. My heart beat faintly, too rapidly. Blackness took hold. Suddenly, I felt my heart romping, like it wanted to cleanse all my arteries in a few hard strokes. The heavy beat was irregular. After a few hard romping strokes, the beat was back to normal.

I opened my eyes. Above me, the tree tops swayed. I knew I was back in this world. Roland, beside me, stared with his eyes wide open and looked scared.

"What happened to you?" Joseph knelt next to me.

"I think I had a heart attack," I said weakly.

"I noticed you walked strangely. Something went wrong. Anyway, I am glad you are back and all right. We couldn't have made it without you. You'll get a medal for this. And if they don't give you a medal, I'll give you mine."

"And mine, too," added Roland.

"We are not home yet." Joseph sounded like the old Sarge. "We'll rest a minimum of fifteen minutes, and this time I mean fifteen minutes, not five."

He leaned his machine gun on his leg. "Don't worry about the Russians, what's left of them. They are running. I have never seen anything like that in six years of war. You spotted those shots perfectly, just like you were an experienced officer."

"You could have done that too, Joseph! The measurements were done by Stoll."

"I'll be honest. I can't measure my belt. I can only transmit. One learns shooting in a school under proper training. There is a difference. If you hadn't shown up, Roland and I would have tried to go home. But I am not so sure we could have made it." Joseph talked in his heavy guttural Tyrolean dialect and sounded tired. "I haven't eaten in two days. That makes me tired. That was what you were thinking of, right?" He read my mind. I needed the fifteen minutes badly. And they became twenty minutes.

We got up and dragged on. I was sure the farm house was near and only about one kilometer away. I saw the end of the forest, and there it was, our farm house. I felt safe. But I also wanted to rest again. It was too late. Infantry soldiers climbed from their fox holes. The sight pushed adrenaline into my blood stream. Joseph and I hobbled, and Roland hung from my shoulder.

German soldiers surrounded us and waved excitedly. They took Roland off just in time. I was at the end of my strength. I barely managed to set him on his good leg. He kept holding on to my shoulder like he had a cramp. He wouldn't let go. Two soldiers hoisted Roland on their shoulders like he weighed nothing. More soldiers came and grabbed the wireless boxes from my shoulder. They carried them to the farm house. Some argued and wanted to carry me and Joseph, too. But we refused.

"Are you 'Celery?'" grinned a young soldier. He knew my nickname. "That's a funny name."

"It's not a funny name. It's my nickname." I was proud that he knew me.

"How was it?" he asked repeatedly.

The farm house was alive. Hugo ran down the steps with Fritz behind him. Roland laid outside on a bench. Captain Kroener bent over him.

"Are you all right?" I heard Tony's voice behind me. Joseph's arm bled badly. Tony grabbed his machine gun, and this time Joseph did not resist. The captain came and hugged both of us, Joseph and me. "Welcome home!" That was all he could say. He didn't mention Lieutenant Stoll.

"I want to eat," Joseph said and sat next to Roland on the bench. Somebody changed his bloody bandage. Roland was laid on a stretcher. He was unconscious when they carried him away. I also felt hungry and realized the slice of bread was still in my pocket.

"Come inside!" ordered Captain Kroener. "We have Hungarian *gulyas* soup and Croatian *raznici*."

"What is that?" asked Joseph. I didn't know. Kroener was an international gourmet; his family owned a Café-Restaurant in Garmisch, Bavaria. "Raznici is a dish of sweet onions, pork, and veal on a skewer, very slowly grilled."

We went upstairs. Deliberately, I ate slowly, remembering when I ate the first food too fast after walking days in the swamp. The captain brought glasses of red Hungarian wine and filled them to the rim.

"The wine is from Lake Balaton," he said. "But, don't drink too much! Major Brendel and Colonel Berger are on their way. You must report to them," he pointed at me. "Joseph, I want you to go to the hospital and take care of your arm! You hear me?" Joseph nodded. He looked very pale.

I was nervous about reporting to high ranking officers. It scared me. I saw the pictures of destruction in my mind. What else can I tell them.

"Do I have to report?"

"You deserve a rest. But we can't lose time. We have to know if the Russians still are capable of attacking. That is important," urged the captain. I nodded. Captain Kroener took my map and spread it on the table. He poured me more wine. "I hope that will revive you. Don't fall asleep! We need you." The wine helped. It didn't even make me drowsy. I began to concentrate. The captain pointed at the map and the marked spots and asked what happened there.

Colonel Wirth and Major Brendel ran upstairs at that moment but stayed in the background, so as not to interrupt the captain. When they came forward, they greeted us and shook hands. The captain introduced me, quite formally. I noticed how dirty I was. Major Brendel treated me like an old friend. He wore the German Cross in Gold, the second highest bravery medal. I thought he was too young to be a major. His face appeared hard and uncompromising.

"I enjoyed our conversation this afternoon," he laughed.

Colonel Berger wore the Iron Cross from the First World War. He was much older. "Tell us what the Russian camp looks like! By the way, I appreciate what you did." He shook my hand for the second time.

"Yes, you did a great job!" added Major Brendel seriously.

"Describe what the theater looked like when you left! How much is left? Do you believe the Russians can regroup?" asked the colonel.

"No Sir, they won't be able to, not for a week, Sir!" I said firmly, and everybody laughed. Their laughter showed pride. "Major Brendel, you destroyed all their escape routes. The 'Heavy' did the destruction as far as I could see, about five kilometer to the horizon. The Russians are completely disorganized. I don't think many escaped."

"Good!" said Major Brendel. "Fair enough!" added Colonel Berger.

"Tomorrow morning we'll meet the general here. He will decide the next steps. You are to come along and make the on site report. We'll evaluate the information from air reconnaissance before we leave. Infantry has already sent patrols." The colonel smiled, "I would like you to sit next to the general tomorrow, Gunner Sellier."

"I doubt that you will be gunner much longer," he added.

Colonel Berger could have been my father. He shook my hand warmly for the third time. I saluted. Surprisingly, Major Brendel saluted back sharply without hesitation. That showed respect. "It was a pleasure having worked with you, Sellier," he barked. "I recommended you for the artillery officers' school as soon as possible. Colonel Wirth, I am sure, will approve." They shook everybody else's hands and ran downstairs.

Captain Kroener barked, "Go! Get some sleep!" He imitated Major Brendel. "Wash up and get ready for tomorrow. I want to inspect you before six o'clock," and added warmly, "I am proud of you. Especially, that you brought Joseph and Roland back."

The next morning, washed and ready, I saluted the captain minutes before six o'clock while he shaved bare-chested before a broken mirror in the kitchen.

"This blade isn't worth a damn," he cussed. "Let me see you! It's not every day you will sit with a general. Put another shine on your belt! That won't hurt! Aren't you lucky? You don't need to shave.

"Joseph is in the hospital. His arm was infected. He lost a lot of blood. Frankly, I am more worried about him than Roland whose leg is in a cast and is doing fine. He'll be on furlough soon. I thought you would want to know that."

Two old Hungarian farm women prepared breakfast. We sat down and ate together. "From now on, I want you to take care of our supplies and to tell these ladies what to cook! That's a good assignment for a medical student. Don't you think?"

Several cars pulled up at the farm house. The general stepped out and greeted everybody amiably. He shook hands with many but to save time, skipped a few.

"Congratulations on an excellent job," he rested a hand on my shoulder. "I want you and Colonel Wirth to ride in my car and sit next to me."

The officers made a circle.

"The report from air observation is the Russians are regrouping about ten kilometers east. Their units were vastly diminished. It looks like units from Budapest may join them. That tells me they still plan to attack in this area. Rebuilding will take weeks. I am trying to get tanks and re-enforcement for the artillery.

"Everybody who participated yesterday is to be congratulated. But, let's not be fooled, gentlemen, we were surprised. And we can't allow that to happen again! Reconnaissance failed! The troop movement was not reported. If it hadn't been for an alert VB, the Russians would have broken through and would be here today."

We went to the cars and the general accompanied me and showed me the seat in the back next to him. Colonel Wirth took the front seat next to the driver. Four cars drove behind us for five kilometers into the forest that I knew so well. I didn't say a word while Colonel Wirth and the general chatted.

"When we get there I want you to explain the battle field," said the general. "I would also like to see the camp, and where the mortar and artillery positions were. I'd like to know everything you can remember." The general glanced at me and noticed my face was pale. Actually, I was in shock at seeing the field and the many dead corpses. I had to close my eyes. I couldn't identify anything from where we were. Everything looked different from the moving car. The destruction was horrible. An eerie quietness spread over the field. That was the only thing that was different.

"General, may I suggest that we go to my observer position. We can see the entire field from there." The smell of powder and smoke and fire began to nauseate me.

"A good suggestion!" The general walked next to me up the slope.

For the first time, I noticed the ring of small craters from mortar explosions below our location. These were the mortars that killed Lieutenant Stoll. The officers assembled at the observer hole. Everybody could tell a body was under a canvas covered by much dirt and rocks.

A driver brought a shovel, and Captain Kroener began to dig out a mortar crater. He furiously dug into the crater to extend its depth. I wanted to help him, but he refused. It was a last honor for his friend and he wanted to do it alone. Nobody spoke until he finished. One dead body became more tragic than the thousands of others on the field. The general helped bring the canvas and place the body into the hole. We stood at attention. The general spoke a few words in honor of Lieutenant Stoll. He was a fine soldier, he said, who gave his life to save thousand of German comrades.

I turned to the thousands of dead Russians laying on the field. Tears dropped from my cheeks. I felt I should apologize to somebody. But I didn't know to whom. My nerves were frazzled, and the smell was nauseating me more and more. What a waste!

I heard the general talking to me. He wanted to learn as much as possible about the theater and especially the time sequence. An officer took notes.

Soon he had heard enough. He stood next to me. "I want you to be my guest for lunch in one week. Colonel Wirth suggested that you should attend the artillery officers course. The artillery school has moved from Lueneburg to Rokycany near Prague, in Czechoslovakia. I will call the school commander to get the exact date. You deserve to become an officer. You displayed great skill. We need officers like you. I am proud of you."

Every officer shook my hand. "Congratulations." One added, "Thank you." The general asked Captain Kroener to sit with him on the way back. I took a back seat in the third car.

Ten days later on a Thursday morning, Tony inspected me. To my surprise, he was also in full uniform. He made me shine my boots and belt once more.

"The captain asked me to check you," he said apologetically. "I am going with you to the the general. We'll stop at Colonel Wirth's house first and pick him up."

We had breakfast with the captain who handed me a yellow envelope and laughed at the look of shock on my face. "That is not the yellow envelope you brought me in Bosnia when you arrived from training. Be glad! That envelope was lost a long time ago."

He sipped Hungarian wine. "I guess my scolding had the desired good effect," he smiled. A jeep came, loaned from the infantry. A driver waited down-stairs.

The division headquarters was eight kilometers back in a small village. We drove by soft rolling hills reflecting the winter season. I thought it must be pretty here in the summer in peace time. The colonel's house was in a circle of hedge roses without blossoms. "Come right in!" he shouted from inside, "I need to sharpen up, too, because I don't have lunch with the general every day. We can walk to his house."

The jeep and the driver stayed. The general's quarters was a small castle, seemingly an upper class Hungarian family estate. Tall trees lined the driveway and led to the curved entry. An orderly showed us into a small, cozily decorated living room. The general sat in a fine upholstered chair. He got up and shook hands. I was surprised that Tony stayed. The general greeted him first.

"I am glad you came. I can now send four officer-cadets to the artillery officers' school. We need officers. Colonel Wirth told me that you agreed to become an officer." That was a big surprise for me. Tony acted uncommitted and remained at attention, but gradually relaxed. I remembered how firm he was about not becoming an officer.

"I appreciate the consideration, General. I gladly accept the promotion. The 6th Battery needs officers. But they also need an experienced master sergeant. I have some recommendations." I was surprised and glad at the same time. Who could be more qualified than Tony? Tony, Hugo, Fritz, and I could travel together to Rokycany and attend the artillery officers' school. I loved the thought.

"Very good!" The general smiled. He didn't expect to be turned down.

"We shall officiate the promotion of Gunner Sellier before lunch, and then we'll celebrate during lunch with an exquisite Hungarian wine while we discuss further details." He waved to a young lieutenant who brought a box on a tray and a package.

I stood at attention before the general. He unpacked.

"As of today, you are promoted officer-cadet." I didn't know if the general knew it was the second time. "Lieutenant, please help me to put the cadet stripes on and the shoulder straps. You will leave in two weeks and attend the artillery officers' school in Rokycany." When the general opened the box, he looked solemn like an officiating priest.

"With permission of the Führer Adolf Hitler, it is my pleasure to award you with the German Cross in Gold. As you know, the German Cross in Gold is the second highest medal given for bravery and the highest a combat soldier can receive. It is usually presented by the Führer himself, but that was not possible at this time. A letter from him is on its way.

"I commend you for being alert and taking unexpected command as an officer. You directed our artillery fire under the most difficult circumstances, thereby preventing a surprise assault by a Russian division. That saved thousands of lives. You showed exceptional courage by directing our artillery precariously on your own location. And you were not afraid to endanger your life. You deserve this medal.

"In addition, I award you with the Iron Cross first and second class, because you unselfishly brought two wounded comrades home with their equipment. You showed the courage and quality of a very fine soldier. Congratulations!" The lieutenant helped the general fasten the medals. First, the German Cross in Gold was pinned on my right uniform pocket and the Iron Cross on the left pocket. I was very proud. At lunch I sat next to the general.

"I meant to ask about your father. He and my brother were dear friends and often went hunting together. My brother Joseph and your father fought in the First World War as lieutenants. My brother lost half of his face in France, you may know. A grenade scrapped his face, but luckily didn't explode." I thought back to when General Joseph Kuebler came, he looked very scary because of his distorted face. I wanted to run away. But in time I got used to him.

"My Dad is home. He now helps by recruiting *Volkssturm* soldiers to repair destroyed railroad tracks after each night's bombing."

"I know, these men are in their sixties and maybe seventies. They have a tough job. The bombing of our cities gets worse. I lost my own home, and my dear daughter burned to death." The general shook his head. "In a modern war, civilians are worse off."

[Four months later, General Kuebler surrendered the First Mountain Division to American troops in Austria. He successfully avoided surrendering to Russian troops. A communist Yugoslav war tribunal requested him to appear in Yugoslavia. He was hung in Belgrade in 1945, accused of alleged war crimes.]

Balaton Lake, the Following Week

"I insist you call me master sergeant." Tony laughed. "At least until Jakob takes my job." Everybody admired my medal. The German Cross in Gold had a large black swastika on a gold background and was framed like a star.

"Hitler designed that medal himself," Hugo showed off his extensive knowledge which was only half factual. We sat upstairs at a table with a washbasin filled with Hungarian wine, the ladies called it *keknyelue*. We celebrated my promotion and our departure to the artillery officers' school.

Captain Kroener had me coordinate our supplies with the Hungarian farmer's mother and daughter. Communication was difficult. I decided which meals to cook, but it took ten minutes to communicate to them. I unpacked new supplies and talked in a Bavarian dialect which sounded to me to be similar to the Hungarian language. They seemed to understand me. "*Does da*" (this here). I pointed at a staple to be prepared for today's meal, "You cook and you eat with us." But it appeared my dialect was not so similar to Hungarian.

"*Toell toett. Ja Ja*," they nodded and pushed me from the kitchen. At noon we had some delicious stuffed cabbage, but it was not what I showed them. Everybody enjoyed the stuffed cabbage. I said nothing, but after lunch I went to the kitchen and pointed at the staple I had showed them that morning. "*Does da*" (this here). Please cook that tomorrow." I spoke Bavarian. They clapped their hands, "*Ja, Ja, toell toett*," they understood. The next day came the same stuffed cabbage.

"Have them fry a chicken tomorrow, instead of cooking the same stuffed cabbage," suggested Tony. He even brought two stray chickens, he found in an abandoned farm. I gave the chickens to the ladies. "*Cook Does da*." I used Bavarian dialect.

"*Toell toett?*" They laughed, bewildered. Our meal was stuffed cabbage, but this time with chicken.

"When are you changing the menu?" asked Captain Kroener. I explained my difficulties with them. "*Does da*, you said? No wonder, *toell toett* is Hungarian and means a dish; it is stuffed cabbage in any form. No wonder. That sounds like *does-da*.

"You don't need a cookbook. You tell them three times *does da* and point at something, that means stuffed cabbage to them in Hungary. Why don't you let them cook what they like and don't interfere anymore." Our meals became much more interesting; but were always heavily spiced with pepper. That forced us to increase the consumption of Balaton wine. We were allowed to use two huge barrels in the basement. Wine with a meal was a custom in Hungary. It still didn't dilute the spicy food.

The Russians came back a week later as predicted and built trenches in the snow opposite us. This time we watched them. And obviously, they were not ready to attack. They waited for supplies.

Captain Kroener ordered me, "You go three kilometers north and set up a secondary observer position. I have a feeling they will attack there." He showed me a place on the map. "Watch for the sharp shooters! They lay outside the trenches and aim at your head. You must crawl all the way!" The trench began behind our farm house. I crawled three kilometers to the point. A bearded top sergeant was in charge. He made room on his bunker and had me sleep on a board next to him.

"My name is Paul. Be careful! I lost two men in the last two days. All head shots. Those Russians are deadly. Don't show them any part of you." He handed me a wooden stick which had a mirror attached. "Watch out! They aim at mirrors too." We sat in the trench. I held the mirror up and made a sketch of the other side. Paul sat next to me.

"When you see a heap of dirt moving, it's a Russian who's laid outside motionless for hours. I can't understand how they can stand the cold that long. Their gray-white parkas are perfect camouflage. You'll see them only when they crawl like lizards back into their trench. Then it's too late. The Russians are supposedly a Moscow elite unit, specially trained for the winter. They have their best unit here. Which tells me they'll sure attack this spot like hell."

My stick bounced in my hand and splinters rained on my shoulder.

"I told you! That was a guy standing next to the tree," Paul pointed at my developing sketch. "I can't see him anymore, he just left. They give them a cup of sunflower oil to drink before they go on watch, and then they drink a pint of vodka. That keeps them warm. Our own sharp shooters, as good as they are, can't be in the snow like these Russians."

I selected four targets, measured and called the numbers to the captain.

"You'll get three rounds, no more. And check the measurements once more. We don't have much ammunition. I want you to stay three days."

Sergeant Paul was disappointed. "If you guys have no more shells that means they will ration our bullets, too. What do they expect? Without artillery, we are finished. We can't hold them just with rifles." Paul was a six year veteran. We sat at night in the bunker with a kerosene lamp and talked. Paul was convinced that we would still win the war, maybe not quickly, but eventually.

"What school did you go to? I haven't seen an artillery guy with the German Cross in Gold before. What religion do you follow?" I wasn't Catholic and that amazed infantry men. Most of these hardened men were once farmers who had learned trades in a town. They were all Catholics.

"I think I won't attend church every Sunday anymore. The priest in my village is stupid. I can't believe what he tells us every Sunday. He says everybody who isn't Catholic will burn in hell." Paul did most of the talking.

"To be honest, I haven't gone to church since the beginning of the war and I haven't missed a thing. I read philosophers like Kant instead, and I learn more from him than the priest." I wondered why city-folks joked about supposedly narrow-minded farmers. They were equally intelligent.

"Do you remember the Muslim professor who spoke German and his daughter played German songs on the piano? She went to a Muslim monastery. That man was more educated than any priest in my neighborhood, and he was a Muslim," Paul said as he turned the kerosene lamp's light down. "His house was a palace. He had his private minaret in a beautiful rose garden. We talked during the evenings and I learned more about the Balkans than I could have read. His message to us was, 'Keep the communist out! Your religion and mine will fail if the communists stay. Every man should believe in a God and God's love. The communist took God out of their lives. You Catholics are religious, I can see because you respect me for what I believe. A soldiers mission is to defend his religion.'"

I didn't understand what he meant by that.

"Let me explain! During the Middle Ages came crusaders through the Balkans with a mission to drive Muslims from Jerusalem. I believe war between religions is wrong! We should respect each other. Men should fight paganism. We Muslims live among Catholics and Orthodox Christians. The godless religion of communism, we must fight together. Joseph Tito is a Croat, but a communist first. He doesn't fight for Yugoslavia. He fights for communism. We Muslims must resist him. Germans and Italians need our help. But don't allow the Italians to govern the Balkans. They are poor administrators, as is evident in poor Albania." Paul scratched his head, "I'll never forget that honest Muslim.

"The man was right. The Russians should not win the war. Asians overran our land before, and we drove them back. We have to do it again. Let's get some sleep!" I sensed Paul was unusually nervous when he wiped his assault rifle for the third time.

"Is something wrong?"

"Yes, something is wrong. I am not superstitious, but I feel the Russians are coming tonight, because every time I touch my gun my skin itches." He looked worried. I leaned back on our wide bed board and took my shoes off. Paul sat next to me but he didn't lay down. I had learned never to disregard a veteran's sixth sense and to watch for the signs, even if it's only an itch.

"Paul, can you lend me an assault rifle?" Paul was happy to give me a machine gun. "That lock needs repair, but when I used it last it worked." He laid down, but kept his shoes and jacket on. His assault rifle was next to him. A candle burned on the table. I also became nervous and couldn't sleep.

I must have dosed off. I awakened to somebody yelling, "The Russians are coming!" In seconds, Paul was on his feet and out the bunker door. He fired his assault rifle until his magazine was spent. I jumped next to him and gave him my magazine. My shoelaces weren't yet tied. I pointed my borrowed machine gun left into the unknown darkness. There could have been friends or enemies. I discovered my jammed lock. Paul had already disappeared in the darkness, and his soldiers followed behind. I didn't dare shoot. I only saw moving shadows, and a barrage of rifle fire met them. I fidgeted with my lock, switched the safety back and forth and was afraid I would hit Paul or his men. Suddenly Paul was next to me and grabbed my machine gun. He knocked the lock against the wall and fired. Why didn't that gun work for me?

"Here, take it! I am out of bullets!" He handed me the gun. "It fires now." He left to check the other side. I heard shots not far and in the darkness couldn't figure if they came from friend or enemy. I didn't dare fire. Everything was quiet seconds later, and suddenly Paul was next to me again.

"Listen everybody," he shouted and used his full voice, "we shot six Russians. Their bodies are in the trench. More Russians are outside in the snow. Fan out and get them! Sharp shooters don't work at night. You are safe. That stupid bunch tried to surprise us. It didn't work." A few seconds later I heard shooting in the field.

"That was close. But this time we got them all," somebody yelled from the field. Artillery was useless. There was no room for it. I felt useless and shivered from anxiety. I still held the malfunctioning machine gun and was secretly glad not to be an infantry soldier. Paul yelled, "It's over! We've got them."

My respect for the infantry grew immensely. Somebody reported there were fourteen dead Russians in the field, only thirty meters from the trench.

"Why didn't they jump into the trench?" Paul shook his head in disbelief. "They yelled like green recruits when they weren't even close. Those can't be their best soldiers."

I reported the assault the next morning. The captain knew about it. "They must be desperate to send a patrol on a suicide mission. That is stupid. Come back here!" he ordered. "We can't help the infantry, and the Russians won't attack for a couple of days."

There was more wild exchange of infantry fire in the morning. I crawled back in the trench and kept my head near the ground the entire two kilometers. The Russians shot fiercely, disgusted that their assault didn't work. And our infantry shot rapid bursts, equally angry, at the Russians for considering them stupid. I heard mortars and their shells exploding in the branches of the chestnut tree over the roof. Splinters trickled harmlessly through the foliage.

The Hungarian women seemed happy when I came back. That they worried, pleased me enormously. Somehow they sensed I was in danger. This time I understood them. I accepted the fact that the Hungarian language was not like my Bavarian dialect and was very difficult. I learned to focus on their talk. The older lady took me to the basement and to my surprise showed me to a huge pig in a cage, friendly and curiously sniffing. I couldn't believe that nobody saw the animal before. "How did you manage to feed the pig?"

"It's yours," she motioned. "We can't feed it. You keep it."

I informed the captain. But he was not pleased.

"It's too dangerous to slaughter a screaming pig only 300 meters from Russian sharpshooters. Tell her to keep it."

"But our food supply is getting low, Captain," warned Tony. "These women don't have food for the pig either. They can't keep the animal. We might as well help and eat the fat pig together. We shouldn't let it starve to death." The captain agreed.

"Who can slaughter a pig?" Nobody volunteered, because nobody knew how.

"I'll do it," offered Alfons. Tony poked me. "He doesn't know how. He couldn't kill his chicken in Osijek. The nuns had to finally do it." But Alfons, seeing everyone was doubtful, became determined. He found a knife in the kitchen and a hammer. We took the pig's cage to the back of the house.

"That hammer will make the pig unconscious, and I can slaughter him" Alfons explained, but didn't convince anybody. There was a problem. The cage was too low and narrow. When he crawled inside we could see immediately that there was no room for both the pig and Alfons. And especially not enough room for the pig's execution.

"You must kill him inside the cage. Don't let the pig get outside," ordered Tony. "The Russians can hear him scream." When Alfons crawled inside, the pig realized his life was in danger and backed off. Alfons lifted the hammer and hit the pig behind the neck on a thick layer of fat. That stunned the animal. He was sure this guy was no good and pushed Alfons to the ground. The pig, screaming fiercely, ran over Alfons and out of the cage. Once outside, it acted like an unbroken mustang and screamed and criss-crossed wildly around the farm's backyard. The frightening noise was exactly what the captain wanted to avoid.

The Russians ceased their fire and listened. They seemed to discuss what the noise was all about. Even only 300 meters away, they couldn't figure out what was going on. Captain Kroener was forced to take matters in hand. He walked stoically to the rampaging pig with his loaded pistol in his right hand. He shot once and hit the pig between the eyes. The pig was dead and fell, twitching its legs. The silence lasted at least five minutes, then the Russians started firing again.

The two farm women shook their heads in disbelief. In their opinion a man was supposed to know how to slaughter a pig properly. How can the German army win this war? The women took over. Hot water was prepared. We dragged the pig to them, and they scrubbed the skin and began a professional butchering. Ten minutes later, the pig was cut into pieces and preparation for the evening's dinner began. We ate pig stew simmered in sour cabbage and feasted on pork for three days. We raised our glasses and toasted the women, *Szekely Gulyas*. The women scolded, *Szekely Gulyas* is not a toast. It was the dish they had prepared. We shouted *Szekely Gulyas* often and with enthusiasm. So they didn't dare change the recipe.

Four days later, Tony, Hugo, Fritz, and I left Hungary in a truck. And after many stops along the way, we arrived in Rokycany in Czechoslovakia.

Chapter 11

Artillery Officers School
Rokycany, Czechoslovakia

Friday April 20. That was the Führer Adolf Hitler's birthday. "We'll celebrate at five o'clock sharp in the barracks auditorium. Dignitaries from the city will also attend. Colonel Rauch will give an address. Everybody must attend!" The announcement was made over the barrack loudspeaker.

April 20 was a regular workday. And even in Rokycany a few red swastika flags hung from windows. The grey apartment buildings looked otherwise dreary. Hugo and I watched two soldiers who were counting the flags.

"Do they really believe Czechs love Hitler and celebrate his birthday?" We wondered. "If they get a paid holiday they may not care," I guessed. "The swastika flags are hung by Nazi officials. No matter how much they pester the Czech population, they wouldn't spend money on a flag."

We had time between two lectures, so we smoked a cigarette at the army barracks gate. The buildings were solid, built decades ago with thick stone that had turned black. They once belonged to the Austrian-Hungarian Empire, but were recently renamed *Nibelungen Kaserne* for more of a teutonic sound.

"I notice when we run into air raid cellars we all become Allies underground. Why do you suppose they bomb Czech cities? That seems stupid. Now the Czechs hate the Allies. Two thousand civilians were killed in Pilsen last week, and the British were declared enemies. Maybe they liked the Austrians better fifty years ago. In the air raid shelter a family didn't mind telling me how they hate the Allies, with a passion."

Hugo took the last suck from his cigarette and burned his fingertips. "I don't think they mind us. We help them when their houses burn. A Czech asked me how he could volunteer for our anti-air unit. 'I want to shoot an airplane down,' he said. I told him to go to the office and get a uniform. He works for us now."

"Do you think Hitler will make a speech today on his birthday?"

"No! He never does. He is too modest. I wonder if they'll celebrate his birthday in Munich? I doubt it. The allies drop bombs by day now. But somebody will count the flags."

"After the speeches, let's go to the Soldatenheim. They have special food and won't ration the beer on Hitler's birthday. The barracks food makes me sick."

Hugo, Fritz, Tony, and I lived in the same room. Barracks food was really bad so it was the main topic of conversation. The black coffee was herbs with a few coffee beans. For the first few days, the meals were high class; but then the standard slipped. Complaining was useless, because the officers ate the same meals and complained, too.

Because of Hitler's birthday, the afternoon's lecture was canceled. I was glad.

"That was not the real reason. The school commander is meeting with his staff." Hugo, as usual, had all the latest information.

"Meeting about what?"

"About the school's future. I heard from two officers that we are separated from Bavaria. That's why we don't get mail. An infantry officer from Prague saw Russian tanks in the hills of Silesia, only eighty kilometers from here. Do you honestly believe we'll finish the course?"

"It's time Hitler brings out his super-secret weapons, or the war is over," said Tony. Almost everybody still believed in the super-secret weapons.

"Hugo! Please don't spread false rumors! Stop that nonsense," warned Fritz.

"Listen! One officer came from the Danube," Hugo showed his annoyance. "They actually saw American tanks driving in the direction of Passau. There is no doubt we are cut off. Why don't we get mail?" Hugo was notorious for worrying.

"Let's listen to the 4:00 P.M. news. Maybe they'll tell us something more." The loudspeaker played German march music, interrupted by news reports every two hours. The office adjusted the sound to a higher volume for the news.

"Four P.M. news. German units repulsed a Russian attack at the Oder River. They completely eliminated a Russian beach head. A hundred Russian tanks were destroyed at the Spree River. German defenses shortened the line to stay effective."

"Ha, ha, ha!" A cynical laugh came from somebody's bed. "They always shorten the line. It means they are back at the Spree River. Defeated somewhere, they call shortening defense lines more effective."

"What do you expect?" Fritz sounded annoyed, "When they shorten a defense line, it makes sense. The defense is effective, and that is exactly what they should do." The broadcast continued. "Field Marshall Schoerner repulsed a Russian attack in Silesia. His troops pushed the Russians back into Poland. Schoerner prepares his counterattack."

"That's the real news, not rumors," Fritz pointed at Hugo. "Your infantry officer saw the tanks when they escaped from Schoerner."

"Sounds good, but now aren't you spreading rumors yourself? That sounds too optimistic to me," remarked Tony. He hadn't talked much lately.

"The tanks at the Danube River were American tanks and not Russian," Hugo responded to Tony's remark. "That means Schoerner is cut off. We are in Schoerner's territory and will eventually join his army. Schoerner has never been defeated. He is the best. They cannot defeat him. He overtook the Greek Metaxas line with only one regiment from our division. He occupied Greece in a couple of days. Nobody defeats Schoerner as long as he still has bullets left."

Twelve cadets lived in our room. We took a poll. Who thought Germany would win the war? Most believed we would win. I thought because we were close to becoming officers, we couldn't think any other way. But the possibility of defeat crept in our conversation. Openly admitting Germany could lose took guts. Nobody wanted to be the first to make that statement. He would be called a traitor. Defeat was impossible.

I didn't know what to believe anymore. Did the broadcast tell the truth?

We walked to the auditorium, Building C, shortly before 5:00 P.M. The theater-style auditorium could easily accommodate 230 cadets. We shined our boots, because it was Hitler's birthday, but more importantly because we intended to visit the Soldatenheim after the speeches—considered a waste of time since they were always the same.

A bunch of officers stood on the stage but ignored us when we strolled in. I noticed they had anxious faces. Obviously, they were in a serious discussion.

Military flags alternated with red and white Nazi flags decorated the stage. Two large loudspeakers flanked a podium in the center. Behind the podium were lines of brown, rusted metal chairs. Those of us who were in the auditorium sat on comfortable upholstered chairs. Hugo sat next to me; he whispered: "I tell you, they'll close the school. Wait and see!"

"For Christ's sake, Hugo, our course doesn't finish until July."

"That doesn't matter! We'll defend Prague. I guarantee it! American tanks were sighted between Eger and Pilsen, only sixty kilometers away." Hugo's information was seldom accurate, so I took it lightly.

Nevertheless, his opinion and the stressed faces of the officers worried me. The loudspeakers were tested. Not everybody had arrived. Three high ranking brown-shirt officials came in by a side door, followed by four black uniformed SS officers. They walked on stage and raised their arms. One could easily detect the officers' reluctance to raise their arms to welcome the government bureaucrats.

Colonel Rauch went to the podium. But before he spoke, they played the two national anthems which sounded harshly metallic through the ancient loudspeakers. Colonel Rauch waited. We stretched our right arms shoulder high standing at attention and sang both German anthems—the *Horst Wessel Lied*, added in 1933. My right arm became stiff from holding it up for so long. I wondered how an old lady managed to hold her arm up through those two long anthems. Luckily, I was in excellent physical shape. I'd just turned twenty, which was another reason to celebrate at the Soldatenheim.

When Colonel Rauch began, we sat down. In the first ten minutes he recited the same boring Hitler accomplishments we had heard many times before. But he added something new, "The Führer surprised us when he showed his military genius. At first our generals were reluctant to accept him as military leader, but gradually they learned to appreciate his natural military skills."

Colonel Rauch raised his voice. "In spite of many military successes, we have difficult times. I am convinced, though, that Germany will endure to the final victory. Soon, we will see new and powerful weapons with immense power with which the enemy cannot compete. I never doubted the ultimate victory. New weapons will brush our enemies from German soil." At this time we rose and applauded with dignity. My comrades smiled with stern faces in approval of that part of Colonel Rauch's speech. However, nobody expected what came next.

"Our Führer, Adolf Hitler, asked me to promote all you cadets to officers on his birthday. You are lieutenants of the German artillery as of today."

The announcement caused stunned silence. The good news came too suddenly. Eventually, the unexpected news sunk in, and then shouts, yells and whistles started. The noise exploded into a tumultuous roar. We jumped from our seats, clapped, and embraced each other, totally disregarding the traditional German discipline. The colonel allowed the riot to last five minutes. He waved and asked us to sit down.

"Of course, you realize that your promotion is premature. Some of you may be called to active duty to help our defense. The course will still finish in July, but all of you will be promoted today, on this special day."

We were too excited to realize what he had just said. Shouts went up, "As of today we are lieutenants!" The excitement drowned out the speeches. The Nazi officials and SS administrators spoke, even though our loud whispers annoyed them. Their speeches were anti climactic and mostly ignored. Exhilarated, we left the auditorium.

"I told you the school wouldn't close," I scolded Hugo. He was too excited to argue. "You were wrong," I insisted, but he just laughed.

We were so excited, we decided to skip the Soldatenheim.

On Monday morning, we received our new uniforms with lieutenant insignias and appropriate shoulder flaps. Hugo wore his officer's cap. While we dressed in our new uniforms the loudspeaker droned. "Attention please!" Fifty names were called. "The names just called must report to the office, pack, and leave for Silesia." There was no further explanation.

"Did you listen carefully? Our names were not called."

"See, I was right." Hugo poked my ribs. "They will go into combat as lieutenants. When we dug the trenches at the outskirts it wasn't just exercise. We'll stay here and defend Rokycany. Do you remember the infantry officer who showed us the anti tank missile launchers? That lecture had nothing to do with artillery officer's training. I told you guys, we'll fight here when the time comes."

Every new officer brought his own pistol. My pistol was a birthday present from my uncle, Alex Mauser. He even had it engraved at the factory in Oberndorf. I showed them the special Mauser pistol.

"Don't tell me that Mauser is your uncle?" Tony was impressed. "The Mauser lock is the best rifle lock in the world, invented in 1898. Will you inherit the Mauser fortune?"

"No way! Uncle Alex is poor. The government took his factory. He never was rich or a good business man. The fact that he doesn't like Hitler didn't help. He never kept his mouth shut. They took his factory and gave him an office with his name on the door."

That afternoon an orderly brought a message for Fritz and me. "You gentlemen are requested to report to the commander's office."

Tony's face turned sad. "That means you guys are going. We won't see each other for a while." He put his arm around me. "I wish you luck!" He tried not to be emotional.

"We don't know why they called us. Don't speculate!" In my heart I knew Tony was right. Fritz and I would get orders to leave. We dressed in our new uniforms and went to the commanders office.

The sergeant was unusually polite. I wasn't used to that kind of treatment. He escorted us to the colonel's office. We saluted raising the right arm. The colonel ignored it. He waved us to a side table which had a map.

"I have selected you two for a very important task. You are both from Bavaria and that is important. You must deliver two packages of documents to Army Headquarters." He pointed at the map. "We are encircled, but you should be able to get through. The documents are very important." He laid his hand on two bulky envelopes, "The thicker package contains requisitions to go to army provision headquarters in Traunstein, Bavaria. The smaller envelope is more important and must be delivered to Army Headquarters as soon as possible."

Colonel Rauch appeared distraught. His collar was open, his face looked flushed. "I don't know where Army Headquarters is. The location is classified. My guess is somewhere in the vicinity of Berchtesgaden," he pointed to the map. "I suggest you go in that direction and inquire at every city commander's office. I'll give you special credentials, which when shown, they are obliged to help you find it. Army provision headquarters is your secondary destination in Traunstein. I selected you because you have excellent records, and you are from Bavaria. You must get there! Those documents are very important. I rely on you." I was flattered. Never in my wildest dreams did I expect to go to Army Headquarters. That felt like a promotion by itself.

"It won't be easy," said Colonel Rauch, pondering the map.

"Looks like we are cut off. I might as well tell you, that American tanks were seen at the Danube River driving toward Linz. A few tanks might go into the mountains and others might be in the hills. You must cross several enemy lines. The trains from Prague to Pilsen are still running. You should take the train to Pilsen, cross the mountains, and find a way to get across the Danube. Quite frankly, I don't know where you can cross."

That problem didn't concern me. The thought of going to Army Headquarters excited me. And headquarters was in Bavaria, close to home.

I pictured Army Headquarters like I had seen it in the weekly newsreel. Generals standing before an enormous map moving their divisions from one place to another. They pushed pointers on the oak table that saved Hitler's life in 1943 when Count Klaus von Stauffenberg's attempt to assassinate Hitler failed because of the weight of the table. I will be standing near it to present these important documents.

"Your identification papers have diagonal red stripes," continued Colonel Rauch. "That means utmost importance! You show the identification to anybody and they must help you. Even a general must give you transportation and, if necessary, give you his own car. It's that important. I repeat, you must get to Berchtesgaden! Every city commander will help you."

Who would be in charge? I imagined it would be Fritz. He was older and more mature. Colonel Rauch read my mind.

"You are equally ranked. Neither of you is in charge," he said simply. "You both must stay together. If you become separated or one is killed, I want this package to get to Army Headquarters first." He pointed at me, "You take this package. The order of priority is Army Headquarters first, then army provision in Traunstein, though both packages are important. Guard them with your lives!" I felt he put the fate of the artillery school and its provisions in our hands.

"Any questions?" Fritz didn't answer. I thought this was as good a time as any to ask for a furlough.

"After we deliver the documents, Colonel, will we get a furlough or a few days off?" When I spoke, I felt embarrassed. Wasn't there anything more important to ask for? Fritz's stern face showed disapproval.

Colonel Rauch wasn't annoyed, or at least not like I expected. He even smiled. We had taken a big load off his shoulders. "Of course, you deserve a furlough after delivering these documents." He called the sergeant. "Issue furlough papers for one week and keep the dates open!"

"Yes, Sir!" Keep the dates open? I never heard of such a thing. Can we determine the dates ourselves? That was impossible. It made me wonder if the colonel knew we wouldn't come back?

How far is Berchtesgaden? How long will it take to get there? American tanks have crossed the Danube and are driving toward Munich. They will be in Munich when we get to the Danube. Colonel Rauch figured that. A second question crossed my mind. If Czechoslovakia is cut off, how can we return? I decided not to ask.

Colonel Rauch shook our hands and bade us farewell. I was very excited about the important assignment and getting close to home. I was excited about getting out of Czechoslovakia, leaving the school, and being promoted to lieutenant. An enormously happy feeling was growing inside.

When we got back to our barracks room we told our speechless friends. Hugo was envious. "Why wasn't I selected? I live in Berchtesgaden."

"Will you come back?" they asked.

"Of course, we'll come back." But I wasn't so sure.

Somebody in the office had said that Russian units were eighty kilometers to the east. That meant we wouldn't be back. I refused to think further than that. I would decide when the time came.

We Edelweiss Pirates of the First Mountain Division spent our last evening together. Neither of us said much. Tony searched his worn, observer's leather pouch and looked for the official forms he always carried as master sergeant. "They may come handy. These stamped forms are blank. You can fill in your destination, the date, and whatever you want. I always kept blank forms, just in case. It's a master sergeant's privilege."

Tony shook my hand. I felt the vibration, and tears welled in my eyes.

"Come and visit me in Innsbruck anytime, I mean it," he was also full of emotion. Tony had saved my life and become my best friend and teacher. Hugo tapped my shoulder, "Would you please take a letter to my mom in Berchtesgaden? You know her address. She hasn't heard from me in months and would be thrilled."

"Of course, I'll take your letter. I'll be glad to."

Hugo wrote his letter in a hurry. I stuck the letter in my pouch with the important documents and swore that his letter would be delivered before any other document.

I fulfilled that oath on the day fate showed me my future life's profession.

Chapter 12

Dangerous Assignment
Bohemia to Berchtesgaden

It was Wednesday, April 25. We left early for the railroad station. The trains from Prague to Pilzen were overcrowded but surprisingly punctual from Prague. Bohemia's Pilzen was famous for the beautiful old buildings of German heritage and its tart light beer. Many buildings were now destroyed. Civilians crowded the train and carried bundles and suitcases packed in a hurry. I wondered where these people were going.

"Escape from the Russians. There is nowhere else to go but west," said an old woman. I wondered why they didn't stay? What would the Russians do to her?

"End Station!" called the announcer from the train's platform in Pilzen. Air raid sirens hollered their typical up and down whining in the confusion.

"Air raid shelters are across the station," yelled the railroad announcer. Everybody hurried across the street carrying their bundles and suitcases and quickly scurried down the steps of the air raid bunker. The benches were filled with sleeping people. Most seemed to live there. A uniformed guard saluted Fritz and me, reminding me that we were officers.

"What do you know about the air raid?" I asked.

"They bombed Nuremberg and now they fly over Weiden to bomb that city for the third time this week." We checked the map. "Weiden is sixty kilometers from Pilzen. "Why bomb Weiden?"

The old guard tried to be helpful. "Because of trains going from Weiden to Linz and Vienna. That's a good place to drop their last bombs on the way home. They bombed Pilzen on their way home."

"We are wasting time." I decided, "Let's not go into the bunker. We should use our fancy identification, get help and go to Linz before the Americans get there." We shouldered our packs and went back to the railroad station. There, we looked for the military office. Everything seemed deserted.

"You should be in the air raid shelter!" ordered a seventy-year-old soldier who wore a black belt over his civilian jacket to indicate he was officially in the military.

"Where is the officer in charge here?" asked Fritz.

"I'll show you." He led us to a basement filled with office supplies. Between these cases and paper boxes sat men and women working. A rotund captain seemed to be the station's military commander. He sat among them.

"We need help, Captain." Fritz addressed him, "We must get to Army Head-quarters and we need transportation. We can't wait until the air raid is over." I pushed the special identification under his nose. The extremely important letter impressed him. The elderly captain studied the writing calmly and said nothing. When he got up, he waved us to follow.

"I want to get away from this turmoil myself," he said outside. "You won't believe what goes on in the station. Soldiers and refugees come from everywhere. Nobody knows where to go." Whispering, he added, "I wish I could get away before it's too late. I know of a convoy going to Zwiesel. I'll take you there. The turmoil gets on my nerves, and it gets worse every day."

A short distance from the railroad station we saw soldiers loading a truck behind a storage building. The captain in charge smiled and shook hands with the station commander. He ignored us. The two seemed to be friends.

"I am overloaded," he explained, "I can't take anybody. We're going to the air raid shelter when we finish loading," That was an excuse to get rid of us. He had no intention of doing that. I pulled our identification papers out and pointed at the red stripe. "I am sorry! You have to take us. You have no choice." That was the first test to see if our documents were really regarded as important. He also noticed my medals and pulled back. "Why aren't you in a shelter?" I asked to scare him. He was outside illegally.

He glanced at the railroad commander as if to ask, why did you bring me these people? But he said, "O.K. I'll let you sit on the front wheel cover. I have no more room on the truck. The fenders are wide and you can sit on them. I have wood fuel, not gasoline. We'll stop at intervals of twenty minutes, and you can help to load the burners with wood. We can't go fast. That's all I can do."

Fritz climbed on the left fender, and I took the right. "Thank you, Sir." Every twenty minutes we loaded wood into the blasting burner on the side of the truck. The destruction of Pilzen was vast. The truck drove around heaps of rubble in empty streets. By now the airplanes had passed. I felt safe and didn't worry about bombs. We came to the outskirts of Pilzen, but the truck had to climb a steep road into a forest.

"Can't you go faster?" Fritz asked the captain every time he stopped.

"No! I told you before!" We had driven three hours at walking speed when Nepomuk, the next town, finally appeared in the distance. Upon checking the map we found we were only twenty kilometers from Pilzen. "Riding this truck it will take two days to get to Zwiesel," I informed Fritz.

"Sorry, I am not going to Zwiesel," answered the captain who overheard me." I'll follow the road south and cross the mountains as soon as I can with this truck." We checked the map again and decided to find better transportation. Nepomuk was large and would have a military office. We found the town commander's office in the unusually peaceful market place. He was not helpful and sat lethargically in a comfortable armchair reading a book. Our identification papers didn't impress him either. He hardly looked at them.

"There is no way for you to get out of this town. We have no more gasoline. You may ask about the two SS trucks across the street. They took my last fuel to go across the mountains."

The very young SS soldiers were loading an almost new truck. We talked to their officer. Fritz raised his right arm first and saluted him. The SS officer stopped working and stared at Fritz suspiciously. "Heil Hitler!" Fritz said softly. The captain grinned and responded by lifting his right hand to the rim of his cap, saluting in the former army style. "I am nobody's fool," he said. "I look at your faces and can tell you don't like to salute our way. I am not sure if I still like to salute that way anymore." He asked pointing at me, "What's up?" I was flustered and didn't know how to react. Why did he point at me? He seemed like a likable fellow, in spite being with the SS, and he was a front line officer. Fritz showed him our red striped identification papers.

"Do you recognize that? We have urgent messages for Army Headquarters in Berchtesgaden." The SS captain didn't react with urgency. He smiled and shook hands.

"Glad to help out. I plan to go directly to Zwiesel across the mountains. You can join me. We leave now. One of you can sit in my cabin." Then pointed at me again, "Perhaps you would want to sit with my soldiers in the back of the truck." Why didn't he like me? Did he consider me too young to be an officer? He had noticed Fritz's gold rimmed Hitler Youth emblem, and that, qualified him to sit in the cabin. I climbed in the back while the SS soldiers checked me out. They weren't much younger than I was, perhaps sixteen or seventeen. They may have wondered why a guy who didn't need to shave was a lieutenant. They didn't see my combat medals under my winter coat and wondered how respectful they should be. I said nothing, enjoying their distress.

The truck rolled on and drove quickly into the forest. It swerved at every curve so that we bounced off each other. I only saw what was behind us as it flew by. After an hour, the truck pulled into a small town and stopped. Water was replaced. This was the crest of the mountain. From there on, the road went steadily downhill into the Danube Valley. Not far from the village we stopped again and waited for a farmer standing in the middle of the road. He was waving while holding a bicycle at his side. He looked like he wanted to hitch a ride. Our car engine drowned out his words. The driver turned the engine off. I heard the farmer shouting, "Go back! American tanks are on this road, very close. Can't you hear them?"

We listened and clearly heard the deep rumbling sound typical for approaching heavy vehicles. They were already close, perhaps around the next turn. The driver started the engine and began turning the truck on the narrow road. He needed four tries. I expected the tanks to show at the next bend. What could I do? I had still time to jump out and hide in the trees. I knew Fritz would follow. I was ready to jump and put the documents for Army Headquarters under my arm. The truck made its last turn and sped off. I sat back quite nervous, but saw no American tanks. We all breathed easier. The farmer's bicycle was on the truck. He sat bewildered between us. I grabbed his hand and thanked him. The gesture calmed him down. He smiled.

We drove the short distance to the village at full speed and raced along the main street. White bedsheets streamed suddenly from many windows, the result of a secret command.

"They are surrendering," yelled one young soldier and waved his rifle toward the anxious female faces behind half-drawn curtains. The young SS soldiers looked annoyed. That worried me. A white bedsheet was a sign of surrender and considered treason by them. Would they shoot? I laughed, stood up, and purposely waved at them hiding behind the curtains. I pretended they made a joke with the white flags. The young soldiers became distracted watching me. They joined my laughing. "Did you think we are Americans? You came out with your bedsheets too early!" The women, realizing it, pulled their bedsheets back, waved, and laughed sheepishly. They had made a mistake, and they knew it. The young SS soldiers still waved and laughed, but most important, they did not shoot. But no harm was done. If they had shot, I was ready to pull rank and would have taken the guns away.

Our savior, the old farmer, left the truck and the young soldiers helped him lower his bicycle. He smiled when I thanked him again and quickly disappeared into a nearby house. The much slower American tanks would not come for awhile. These people were not in danger. But why did they show white flags? They were scared and sick of the war. But they wouldn't come out and welcome tanks. When we sped away, three scared chickens scattered across the street. They were the only living creatures on the street.

The SS captain had decided to go to Strakonice, forty kilometers south. He had heard of German units building a defense around that town. His information proved to be correct. In a field near Strakonice stood heavy caliber cannons pointing the large barrels in our direction. The cannons could easily demolish tanks. But there were no soldiers around to service the cannons. Strakonice was a beehive. Most people were stranded refugees or German soldiers. Everybody was in a hurry, but without purpose. I saw no organized fighting unit. The SS officer stopped, parked his trucks at the market place, and we discussed the situation. The captain now wanted to go to Passau. He thought his unit was there. But Passau was too far north. We thanked him and left to find the town's military office.

The people in the marketplace seemed concerned only with getting some food or to a safer place. The city commander looked distraught. "Yes, you can cross the Danube," he assured us. Our urgent identification worked magic again. He told a young lieutenant to take us to a truck which was leaving to go to Linz. The truck driver simply refused us. "I can't get to Linz with a quarter tank of gasoline, a load of ammunition for my unit and you." I stuck the urgent identification under his nose and made sure he noticed my hand was on my pistol holster. That changed his attitude.

"We'll go as far as we can. Make room!" We climbed into the truck cab and he drove off. After a few kilometers, he turned left on a narrow road. I wondered if we would see the American tanks here.

"It's safe on back roads. Americans never drive back roads," assured the driver. Most houses were boarded up and deserted. The truck's gasoline gauge showed more than a quarter tank of gasoline. "We'll make it to Obermoldau, high in the mountains," Fritz said, after checking the map.

"If they have no gasoline, we'll be stuck." The map showed there was a gas station in Obermoldau. When we got there we found the station was also the town mayor's office. "Sorry, we have no more gasoline." That was the standard answer at every gas station. People waited in line. "Why do we have ration cards when there isn't food?"

The town mayor in Obermoldau was a civilian wearing a German uniform jacket to make him look official. "Nobody comes here one way or the other. You can see there is no traffic in either direction," he told us. Our fancy identification immediately lost value.

I had an idea. "Get us two bicycles!" I asked the town commander. I figured a bicycle was just as good under the circumstances. The town mayor knew our papers were important. He felt obliged. The road from the high mountains must go downhill. And on bicycles we could hear tanks before they could see us and have time to hide in the bushes. The forest had plenty of places to hide.

The portly town mayor scratched his bald head. "Bicycles?" Fritz liked my suggestion. Before the man said no, Fritz touched the mayor's arm and pointed at his oversized uniform jacket.

"Look! You are the highest German representative here in Obermoldau. You have full authority over all armed forces. You know the importance of our orders and that we must take these documents to Army Headquarters." Fritz waved his thick yellow envelopes before his face. "If a general must help, then you can get us two bicycles." Fritz's speech had the desired effect. The town mayor felt honored to be called the representative of all the armed forces in Obermoldau. He waved at an old man on a porch. He had been watching but doing nothing. They both whispered. The old man left and soon returned with two ancient bicycles. His face was bitter. He leaned the bicycles against the house. I thought he probably had taken them from a relative. They were surely the oldest bicycles in town and had only half-full tires.

"Yes, the tires are a little worn, but some air will help that situation. That will get you down to the valley." The town mayor was pleased. I decided not to argue and pumped air into the tires. By now it was late afternoon.

We hopped on the old bicycles and struggled against the rusty mechanism. I peddled fiercely uphill, then, luckily, the road went downhill. From there on I enjoyed the ride. My bike went fast, and even faster when the road was steep. I felt I was ten years old and remembered that I never used my brakes. There was not a soul on the road, the curves were wide, air blew in my face, and I just let go. Fritz and I raced each other, but soon he was far behind.

When the forest ended, I stopped, and waited for Fritz. I enjoyed the peaceful sight of the Danube Valley. Finally Fritz came. From our hill, we admired the famous river which we hadn't seen beyond the trees. We saw the red roofs of a village further down.

Fritz sighed. "That ride was fun! I never rode downhill that fast. You looked like an ape on a broken bike. That bike is too small for you," he laughed, "and you are supposedly a distinguished lieutenant on an important mission. I could not keep up with you."

"Maybe you are getting old." Fritz didn't like my joke.

"I am not washed up," he was annoyed. I decided to not tease him anymore. I discovered a sign on the road saying Rohrbach. Fritz checked the map and found Rohrbach. The town was not far from the river. He leaned back exhausted from the ride. We rested. Neither of us was ready to leave.

"This must be Germany by now." Actually, it was Austria. "What do you think is going on in Rokycany?" I wondered. I suddenly began to worry about my friends.

"I am glad we left." Fritz was depressed and searched for an answer. "To be honest, I thought about our friends just now. I would like to join them and wouldn't mind fighting with them just to get it over with," he said. "After seeing the result of the bombings and the disorganization. It makes me shudder. I know our comrades will fight, and they will not give up. They will die defending Rokycany. A man like Tony never gives up. I can't imagine him as a prisoner. They won't lay their guns down." I noticed Fritz wiping a tear from his eye.

"Are we losing the war?" he asked. "Tell me! Give me an honest answer!"

Fritz expected straightforward answers. But I didn't want to talk about it. I actually lost hope when our division was destroyed in Yugoslavia, but I never told anybody. I knew then that the war was over, but I didn't want to admit it. I hesitated. "We have fine army units which fight fiercely. Perhaps Hitler will bring out the powerful weapons. When they come, we'll win." My words didn't even convince me. I needed more time to think. "I know I am not going to die, at least not yet. I'll stay alive," I told Fritz.

He smiled. "I like you, even though you often act like a spoiled brat. But when you must perform you are the best! I can understand why Colonel Rauch selected you for this job. He knows you are reckless. He judged you by your 'don't care' attitude, the typical attitude of a spoiled brat. I could see that again when you rode your broken-down bike downhill. You didn't use your brakes, not even once. You rode like an irresponsible kid who doesn't give a damn. That's why he selected you. You are reckless and irresponsible. He figured with that reckless attitude you would make it to Army Headquarters. Colonel Rauch reads people well. He knows that you have the sixth sense."

I didn't think Fritz's opinion of me was flattering. I was a little perplexed. What does he know about me and my sixth sense? I don't even know anything about it.

"Why did he select you for the job? Tell me!" I countered.

"He knows I am loyal, and I serve the Reich. I would sacrifice my life for a mission like that. My records show I was a Party official, and he assumes I will be loyal to the cause. I am older and more mature. He thought we made a good team. And you know," Fritz put his arm on mine, "I think he was right."

"I won't let you die," I told him spontaneously. The thought came to me and was meant to be a joke. But it didn't come out that way. "I mean, you shouldn't die for a cause. I won't allow you to die for that." I became serious about it. "There is no cause worth dying for." I remembered when my friend Volkmar von Richthofen had said the exact words in school one day. Volkmar upset me at the time. But now I realized how right Volkmar was. We all had changed a lot since then. "I would give my life to save a friend. That I would do." I felt I was a soldier in the business of dying for each other, but not for a cause. Fritz stared without answering.

"Let's go!" He ended our conversation abruptly.

The tires were now completely flat. We fastened our bags on the bicycles and pushed them, avoiding holes in the road, until we came to the peaceful village of Rohrbach. No military, neither ours nor Allied forces, were in sight.

"Let's stay overnight here? What do you think?" I suggested.

We saw three people raking weeds in a field. I called in my best Bavarian dialect. They didn't look up. Two were women. The man was middle-aged and completely ignored us. I leaned my bike on a tree and went into the field. The women wore typical farm skirts down to the ankle and a babushka, which covered the face to the eyebrows. They must be mother and daughter, I thought. The husky young man continued chopping weeds. But the women smiled.

"We thought you were American soldiers," said the older woman in my dialect. I enjoyed hearing my language. It gave me the sense we were home. "American troops are on their way, they said in the village."

I stared, maybe a bit too long, at the pretty younger woman. She noticed and blushed. She was very pretty, and would be even more so if she took her babushka off. She was about eighteen. I hadn't seen a pretty German girl in ages. "We don't wear American uniforms," I pointed at my German lapels. I purposely addressed the younger woman. But she kept her eyes down and pretended to inspect the weeds.

"I wouldn't know one uniform from the other," she said softly. Her voice was exactly what I hoped for. Her eyes still focused on the tips of her heavy boots. Suddenly, the middle-aged man stood next to her. I noticed his faded brown uniform jacket was that of a Polish prisoner of war. Polish war prisoners worked on German farms replacing male workers in the army.

"Andreas," he introduced himself without offering a handshake.

The younger woman became more talkative since Andreas showed up.

"See him. He has a Polish uniform jacket, and that is the same style as yours. Just the color is different."

"It's not true," said the older woman. "We know German uniforms. My husband wears a German uniform and so does my son Hans, Maria's brother. They are in Russia." She sobbed a little when she said that. "I wish I knew where they are?" She wiped a few tears off her cheek. "If Andreas weren't here, I wouldn't know what to do! He runs our farm. I couldn't do without him." Andreas looked embarrassed. Obviously, he understood German well.

"You want to stay overnight with us?" he asked in decent German with only a trace of an accent. "You are welcome!" The tone of authority surprised me. I nodded. Of course we wanted to stay here. We walked to the farm house pushing the old bicycles along. I was curious about Andreas. He showed even more authority inside the house and opened the cupboard above the kitchen table bringing a bottle of homemade prune brandy. He found three glasses and set them on the table. "I made that brandy," he said with pride and poured three glasses full. We toasted while the women busied themselves in the kitchen.

I tried to get a proper perspective on the situation. We were German officers on a life and death mission, toasting with a Polish prisoner of war who acted like he owned everything. The owner and his son fought in far away Russia. American units were coming. Why didn't he tell me, "Go to hell." He could just wait for the American forces and then go home.

"I am glad you are here," said Andreas politely after the next toast and poured the glasses full again. The prune brandy tasted like the slivovitz we had had in Yugoslavia.

"What happens when the Americans come? Prost!" I said, testing his honesty.

"Nothing will happen! Prost! I'll stay here. This is my family. I won't leave." Maria brought a steaming bowl of soup with dumplings swimming on top.

"The bread crumbs are toasted in butter. Pour them over the dumplings!" She enjoyed that we ate heartily and liked her cooking. We were very hungry.

"Were you a farmer in Poland before the war?" asked Fritz.

"No. I worked with farmers. I sold them farm goods. I wasn't a farmer but I learned how to run a farm. I became a real farmer here and like it."

"My husband asked Andreas to stay and become his partner," the older women explained. For simplicity sake, I called her Mother, which was the custom in Austria and in Bavaria. She liked that. "We need Andreas! Our son Hans doesn't want the farm. He was a salesman for a paint contractor. He doesn't like farming."

"Do you mind my asking, Andreas, how you came to this farm? Aren't you under some kind of a control as prisoner of war?"

"Sure, I'll tell you. I became a prisoner on the fifth day in September, 1939, without ever hearing a shot. We were in prison camps, and I was bored. They wanted volunteers who could work on farms, so I raised my hand. They bussed us to farms. We worked all day, and in the evening they bussed us back. One day, they told me to stay on this farm. I was told to report once a week to the office in town. Most fellow prisoners worked in factories and made grenades. I was just lucky."

"He hasn't reported to the office in a year," Mother laughed. "Everybody in Rohrbach knows Andreas. He helps many people. They call him when they need him."

"Six years is a long time," said Andreas. "My mother died, my father was dead when I was five. My brother is a cheat. He took everything that belonged to me. I don't want to see him anymore. What is there in Poland for me?" he grinned a bitter smile. "If I can have Maria, I'll stay forever," he said with a boisterous laugh and for the first time was embarrassed.

"Maybe I am too old for her." He turned to Maria whose face turned red.

"You are not too old for me. Don't always say that," Maria blushed and showed she didn't mind him at all. Mother kept herself busy and smiled. She offered no opinion.

Thursday, April 26, 1945

We slept in a huge, family-size bed upstairs in one of many empty rooms. Our cover was a huge warm pillow stuffed with goose feathers. We had finished the bottle of prune brandy the night before with Maria sitting next to Andreas, her arm under his. We talked till midnight about the war and worried how it might end. The most important concern for Andreas was, what would happen to 'his' farm and 'his' family.

"I will never fight as long as I live," he told us firmly. "War makes no sense."

Maria fixed scrambled eggs the next morning as soon as we came downstairs. "We only have scrambled eggs on Sundays," she said. But we were special guests. She cut thick slices off the grey home-made bread in the center of the table. We dunked the bread in a bowl of hot milk mixed with Ersatz Kaffee. That gave it some flavor. The coffee was awful. Mother was in the stable milking cows.

"Andreas, do you know where to cross the Danube?" asked Fritz.

"Go to Linz. There are many bridges. The bridges here are destroyed. They still stand in Linz, but they put demolition devices underneath."

"Mama has a friend who drives to Linz every day," said Maria. "He trades winter potatoes and farm goods. I'll ask him if he can take you along." After she finished breakfast, she left to look for the man. Fifteen minutes later, an ancient truck loaded with potatoes came sputtering up. An old man climbed slowly from the cab. He was severely crippled and had to bend his head sideways.

"Sure, I'll take you. I am glad to have someone help me unload my potatoes. I haven't seen healthy fellows like you in years," he chuckled and chewed on an empty pipe.

"Can you use our bicycles?" I pointed in direction of the old bicycles.

"Sure! I'll make a new car from them." We all laughed, but he didn't. He insisted that we take his statement seriously. His truck was a composition of many parts.

We departed from Andreas and Maria, our new friends, with a touch of sadness. Andreas shook our hands firmly. "Good luck! And come back anytime. You can help me with the farm." We looked puzzled. "I am not a prisoner of war anymore. I'll stay here."

The bench cushions in the truck cabin were ripped. I slid to the center and tried to arrange my feet between a maze of cables and wires. I couldn't stretch my feet. They would have been on top of the running engine. The old man laughed about my concern.

"This truck runs well. You'll see! I am a hobby truck mechanic. If the engine stops, I'll take parts from the left side and put them on the right side. That gets the engine going, it hasn't failed so far." The ancient vehicle sputtered at a speed of five kilometers per hour. We made frequent stops and helped with the unloading of potatoes. The people were not even surprised at artillery lieutenants delivering potatoes. They had seen everything.

They talked about the weather. I noticed no money was exchanged. They trusted each other and had a barter system. The old man liked to get auto parts for potatoes. After each transaction, we continued with a lengthy conversation which delayed the trip considerably. We learned this year's harvest was bad and Americans and Russians had advanced from both sides. That was of interest to us. These people were a good source of information. "The radio said we will win the war, and it will be over soon," said an old man. He was optimistic.

"But my cousin heard Russians are on the other side of Linz, and my neighbor already saw American tanks on the other side of the Danube," cautioned the lady from next door.

"No, I believe what the radio said," insisted the old man waving a finger, "and not what your cousin heard from a neighbor, who heard it from another neighbor. That is BS."

We could see the Danube River for the first time behind the willow trees. The river, lovingly described by composer Strauss as 'the blue' Danube, was not very blue, but dirty and brown. I wondered where Strauss was when he composed his famous waltz? It certainly wasn't here. His music was written a long time before these wars. I remembered the Danube in Yugoslavia wasn't blue either.

"Don't go to Linz," suggested a woman. "Why go that far when you can cross the Danube in Ottenheim. We use the ferry boat." That made sense. We decided to leave the old man and his slow truck and look for the ferry boat. All the conversation was interesting but took too long. It was now late afternoon. We walked toward the river and saw the Danube made a bend. The river was wide. There were no bridges. "It's too late. We can't cross the river today. Let's stay overnight in a farm house."

We saw a light near the river and walked down. We found a large farm house. The light above the entrance indicated someone was there. I knocked on the door. There was no answer. I tried again and found the door was open. We went in the hallway and knocked at the door to the left. Somebody turned the light off. Fritz knocked again. I used my Bavarian dialect, "We are travelers. We have come a long way. We would like your permission to rest for a while." The approach worked. Southern farmers were known for their courtesy and hospitality. Never turn a stranger down. The house was now completely dark. But the door opened a bit, and the face of a scared old woman appeared in the frame. She held firmly to the door knob and kept only a small space open.

"I am alone here," she blurted, "I am scared. My husband is not here. He is with the Volkssturm."

"Can we sit down for a while?" I asked politely. Reluctantly the door opened all the way, and she turned the light on. The tiny frail woman walked back to her kitchen table where she had been mending heavy stockings. She pointed to the bench. We sat down without saying a word. She stared, inspecting us. After a while she seemed satisfied. She changed completely.

"I am so glad you came," she blurted out joyfully, now fully at ease. "I am afraid when I am alone. I hear the wind whistle from the river and that scares me. My house is too big. I can hear the ghosts upstairs. My husband says, 'You are nuts.'" She just kept blabbering away, non-stop. "He, my husband, is a cripple. A horse stepped on his foot and crushed the bone. He is more than sixty and can't walk straight. They still drafted him. How can they use him? He was always exempt from service, every year. Not anymore. They told him to go and fight! He has never used a gun in his life. I went with him to the draft board and carried his bags. I told the soldier I have to stay with him, because he can't carry any heavy loads. Don't let him lay on a cold floor, he has arthritis, and he can't shoot, he is nearsighted. "'Yes,' the sergeant said and pushed me out. They had old men and fifteen-year-old kids in this Volkssturm. What are they going to do? They'll kill them. All of them. None of them knows how to fight." She turned around and stared.

"I'll fix you something to eat. I have blood sausages today. The butcher slaughtered and had blood left over. I can't eat all the sausages. The blood won't be good tomorrow." She went to the storeroom. From there we heard her.

"I saw you coming when you walked along the fence. Two men in uniform. I thought, my God, they are Russians. That's the end of me! They'll take me to Siberia. It was too late, and I couldn't lock the door. But I am glad you came, and now you are here." She was back, peeked into a pot on the open fire and ladled boiled blood sausages and several dumplings from the pot. We ate, and it occurred to me, that neither of us had said a word. The old woman spilled her anxieties and fears on us. They came from the heart, stored for weeks. She would only pause to catch her breath. We used the moment to cheer her up and calm her down. She continued talking and never listened. "Go upstairs. Take a room. All the doors are open. They are the men's rooms. My girls are gone. I have no work for them." She interrupted herself, "I am afraid to go upstairs myself. I sleep on the bench in the kitchen next to the stove. It's warmer here. Good night!"

We went upstairs into the first room which had two beds. Before I closed the door, I heard her crying downstairs. "If Alfons dies, if he doesn't come home what will I do? Me, an old woman, with a big farm. Why wouldn't they let me go and fight with him? I would rather die."

Friday, April 27

The next morning our hostess seemed very cheerful. "How did you sleep?" she smiled and greeted us. "You should have slept longer. Why don't you stay? You can stay as long as you want." She sat where she had slept, next to the stove. Now she seemed rested and everything was set for breakfast.

"Unfortunately, we can't stay," I told her, "I am sorry. Do you know where the bridge is across the Danube?"

"Don't go! No bridge is safe. They will be blown up. Alfons told me. He and the Volkssturm guard them," she scratched her head, "but a family, one kilometer up the river has a ferry boat business. They can take you across and they are easy to find." She placed two more fried sausages on my plate. Sausages, homemade bread, jam and butter was our breakfast. The Ersatz Kaffee tasted bad. While we ate silently, she stared. "When will the war be over? Will we win?"

"Of course, we'll win," said Fritz. But she wasn't interested.

"Why don't you stay?" she urged for the second time. "Alfons wouldn't mind. He would like it. They'll blow the bridge into pieces sometime today, they told me yesterday." That was alarming. We thanked her and walked upstream. The Danube was in a thick fog.

We saw a small ferryboat just pulling off a dock. But a thirteen-year-old boy on the rudder saw us coming. He shouted forward to his father, who stopped rowing and waited for us. The boat had a steel wire guide which led the boat across to the other side. Six freezing German soldiers huddled on two benches in the boat. The cold moist air bothered them. We jumped in and squeezed ourselves between the soldiers. The old man rowed carefully and watched the current. The boy in the back steered and shouted his instructions like a professional. The cold fog was good protection.

We couldn't see the other side. That made me nervous. The infantry soldiers were quiet. "Where did you come from?" I broke the silence asking the guy next to me.

"From south," he answered simply. Answering only two words was rude, I thought; but then he added, "We came from Vienna and were told, 'Go to Ottenheim, not Linz. The bridge in Ottenheim is safe.' We were on patrol, but got lost and found this ferry. 'All bridges will be blasted, anytime,' they said," he pointed downstream into the grey mist. "We listened to a radio broadcast from Munich this morning. They identified themselves as the Free State of Bavaria. That was strange," he added.

Perplexed, I poked Fritz, "When they said 'Free State of Bavaria,' does that mean Bavaria is autonomous?"

"I am sure. That's what it sounded like to me." He had no further explanation. But then he remembered more information.

"They reported Hermann Goering, the commander of the air force, resigned. They didn't say where or if he was arrested."

"That is preposterous and not possible!" shouted Fritz on my other side.

The fog lifted, and we could see parts of the other side. I strained my eyes and saw military vehicles parked on top of the river bank, still too far away to identify. Were they Americans? The thought scared me. We came closer, and I could tell they were German trucks. A man holding two goats waited peacefully on the landing dock, ready to take the ferry back. Everything seemed normal to him. I wanted to hear more about the news from Munich. But it was too late. We landed, and Fritz hurried from the boat up the river bank and toward the trucks. "Hurry! The trucks are our last chance," he called back. He walked toward a major, who was conducting a meeting with his officers and stood between them.

Fritz rudely interrupted the meeting, "Excuse us, Sir! We need transportation. Can we rely on you? These are my papers. We must take extremely important documents to Army Headquarters in Berchtesgaden."

The major did not look pleased. He checked the identification papers carefully and tried to find flaws. He turned the paper over and over. "And if I said no?" he asked calmly. That upset me, I stepped forward.

"Then I'll shoot you," I said calmly and took my Mauser pistol from the holster. "I hope you are smart enough to obey extremely important orders." I wasn't sure at all if I would shoot him and desperately hoped he would make the right decision. He stood surrounded by battle hardened comrades. Shooting him would be my instant death. They wouldn't let me get away with that. The major frowned, and lifted a hand to warn me. Then he saw my German Cross in Gold.

"Calm down." He turned to his officers, "Take these two officers to my truck. They can sit in my cab; and make room for the other soldiers who just arrived." The lieutenant wasn't pleased, he saluted casually in the traditional way, laying two fingers on his cap. But he obeyed.

The trucks were ready to leave. The major took the driver's seat. We drove over deep furrows caused by flooding. I sat in the middle, next to the major. There were no signs. I wasn't sure if we were on a road. The major leaned forward to talk to Fritz. He showed his disapproval of my behavior by ignoring me.

"I am out of fuel and food. We must get to Wels for our supplies, about thirty kilometers more. If we are lucky, we'll make it." The bumpy field road turned into an asphalt road with holes. The major glanced at me. "You are very straightforward. Therefore, you can help me get supplies, if you don't mind. I may need someone with your aggressiveness. We'll show them your urgent identification papers in the town's military office and, if we are lucky, we'll get the stuff. But for heaven's sake, let me do the talking! Agreed?"

"Agreed. No problem," I said, relieved, and we shook hands.

The soldiers in the back of the truck banged urgently on the cab window. Low flying American airplanes swooped down behind us. The major stopped. We had enough time to jump from the cab. Seconds later bullets rained into the field, lifting dirt. They tried to spray the convoy but aimed too far right. The two airplanes ascended and flew in a wide circle. The planes would obviously return. Fritz and I tried to find better cover in a trench. The major did not follow. He took a machine gun and climbed on top of the truck. Seconds later, he fired several volleys at the airplanes when they swooped down. He stood and shot, never stopping, until the planes ascended and flew away. This time their bullets missed the mark completely and sprayed harmlessly into the field.

The major's fire must have irritated them. The attack lasted only seconds. We watched the airplanes fly away in a straight line. Thank God! The major came down and also watched them leave. He was excited. "I think I hit one plane," he shouted. "I hope it goes down." I saw no smoke, the sure sign when an airplane was hit. I admired him, standing fully exposed on the truck, firing away. The trucks had not been damaged. A few bullets had made holes in the canvas during the first attack. But the engines weren't hit.

We drove another twenty minutes and were stopped by a roadblock. Two trucks stood sideways and were on fire. Soldiers worked frantically to extinguish the flames. The major pulled up asking if they needed help.

"No. We'll leave the trucks and move on. Thanks!" We drove by the burning vehicles into the field. There was a traffic jam at the outskirts of Wels. We were stuck. Military police tried to restore order, but the conditions remained chaotic. Most vehicles drove west blocking each other. We moved slowly into town—go, stop, go, stop.

The major suddenly made a turn off the main street and stopped in the driveway of a large farm. His trucks followed and parked side by side. I wondered why American planes didn't attack this town packed with military vehicles? Wels was unprotected and would have been a huge target. Air attacks here, now, would result in an enormous disaster. For reasons, unknown, they preferred chasing individual trucks on lone side roads.

"Let's go to the city office." The major waved to me, and we both went to the town center. A long line of people waited at the city commander's office near the marketplace. Two sergeants controlled the entrance asking everybody to stay in line. The major pushed passed and whispered to me. "Give me your identification papers!"

We walked inside and stopped at a door signed, City Commander. Without knocking we went inside and extended his hand jovially to a surprised captain. The captain's strained expression changed to annoyance as he shuffled papers on a large desk. He thought we were playing games with him. "Who said you could come into my office?" he shouted.

"I need urgent help, Captain. Please pay attention! At least this once! We have no time to play games." The major showed him the document with my identification and immediately pulled the document back. "You will notice this document has the red stripe of extreme urgency. Our orders are classified. We must be at Army Headquarters as soon as possible and need gasoline for six trucks and appropriate supplies for thirty soldiers."

"Let me see that again!" said the captain. He was no fool. He inspected the striped document carefully. I lay my army book next to him. "You may want to have my photograph for identification?" I said. The town commander inspected my army book and my picture. He was satisfied.

"Tell me what you need, Major?" he asked abruptly. The major poked my ribs and without hesitating, recited from memory a huge number of supplies, adding things that were not needed, but could be used for barter. The town commander didn't question anything. He scribbled the request on a requisition pad and called a soldier.

"Write that on a formal requisition. I'll sign it later. And help the major get his stuff." We left quickly with a smile. On the way out the major called back over his shoulder, "Thanks." The supplies were stored in various locations for security reason. It took hours to get the stuff together. When we had everything, a fine meal was prepared.

During the meal the major told his story, often hesitating. I was surprised how much had happened to him and his small unit. "We were finally defeated by the Russians in Budapest. My soldiers were dead. The wounded probably became prisoners. The thirty-five men you see here are what is left of my battalion. We went on retreat and got to Vienna, always begging for supplies. Supplies become more important when you are losing. We did much the same as we did here. In Vienna we checked with the city commander. But he assigned us to the defense of the city. I saw fourteen-year-old kid soldiers shivering in the trenches. They eagerly waited for the enemy, shivering more from anxiety than from the cold. I talked to them. They weren't afraid. As a matter of fact, they couldn't wait for the enemy to come and shot their new rifles for no good reason whatsoever. I was told they had two weeks training. We all had goose bumps seeing how eager they were to lay down their lives. Vienna's defense consisted of these youngsters and a few old World War I veterans." The major paused and continued eating.

"Every soldier learns about fear sooner or later. Something tells him there is danger, and he knows when it is for real. Soldiers can feel that. I never did as a civilian. Usually, I reacted too fast and for the wrong reasons. I followed my reasoning and my imagination. As a veteran, I learned to use all my senses. A soldier knows danger even if he can't see it. We feel danger. Instinct becomes the defense and makes us react. And usually, when instinct calls, we react correctly. I have no idea how many times instinct saved my life. When I saw these youngsters in Vienna, I knew we had no chance. The youngsters were very vulnerable and might die. Besides, the conditions in Vienna were chaotic. Every six hours, like clockwork, Allied bombers attacked. I never saw chaos like that in all six years of war. I searched my soul and came to a decision.

"My responsibility now was to care for my soldiers. They trusted me. There was no more purpose in this war. I decided to bring these guys home. I will not let them down. Budapest was hell. The war had finished for us there. Now Vienna would be slaughtered. I gave orders to leave Vienna, and we never saw the enemy. But I also paid a price. Since I gave that order, I have lost my pride as a professional career officer. I became a deserter." The major, now full of emotion, leaned back and left his food. Fritz turned away, frowned, and shook his head. The major didn't notice.

"The war should have ended long before that," he continued. "Too many people who couldn't defend themselves were slaughtered. I knew before our defeat in Budapest that the war was over. I still ordered my guys into the trenches to fight. They followed my orders because they trusted me, and most of them died," he said sadly. "I knew in Vienna that these fourteen year old, spirited boys would be slaughtered. And that became too much. There was nothing I could do. These kids didn't know that they had no chance. Not to be able to do anything bothered the hell out of me!"

The major sounded like he was making a confession. But I understood. I remembered Osijek's defense. That was almost the same situation. We had four light artillery cannons and that was the city's defense against a huge Russian army. They promised supplies that never came. Captain Kroener pulled us out. But he didn't give up. When do you make that decision? I sat quietly and thought about what I considered to be very important. Fritz and I would also have to make a decision, and soon. Fritz sat with his back toward me. I wondered what he thought. I sensed he didn't like the major's story.

Fritz was brought up in the old school which taught that a proud German soldier never leaves his defense line or retreats before he sees the enemy. Fritz was loyal. I couldn't fault him for that. He worked for the government and had helped to manifest the Nazi ideologies. I respected Fritz for his idealism. He only wanted the best for the German people. It may be wrong to continue fighting, but Fritz would not change. He always stated his belief with sincerity and conviction. Most of us agreed on his points. We agreed that Europe was better off unified. Germany, in the center of Europe should become the leader. England was powerful because of her colonial possessions, but England had less resources. As an island at the edge of Europe, she was a secondary power. England would not be able to unite Europe. A united Europe might be a threat to her.

France, on the other hand, almost unified Europe under Napoleon, who was a brilliant military leader and statesman. German history classes taught us that Napoleon's administration improved the condition in Germany and in the fragmented states he occupied. Napoleon became too egomaniacal and was defeated. He disregarded the severity of the Russian winter. Hitler knew well what

Napoleon's mistakes were. He, too, invaded Russia in late summer, and with arrogance made Napoleon's deadly mistakes.

Hitler convinced the German people that Europe should be united. But German tanks became stuck in ice not far from Moscow. The German defeat began there because of Hitler's arrogance and blunder.

What would happen now? We might become communists and live under Stalin's rules. That was hard to imagine. What would happen if Germany won the war militarily? Was Europe ready for Hitler's leadership? We soldiers were the first to see fragmentation in individual national pride. Nobody manages inbred nationalism unless he uses brute force. We would have disaster and pockets of civil wars forever. I tried to find a solution. Maybe it's best to lose the war. The thought stayed in my mind. I really didn't care anymore. I was used to watching out for myself. Living under communist rules might be possible.

The major poked me. "Do you remember that you threatened me this morning?" I was still embarrassed. He grinned. Why did he bring up the incident? I liked and respected him. "When you said you would shoot me, I got mad and was ready to arrest both of you. Yes, that would have been treason. In a flash I realized, I should use tolerance and not behave like I had years ago. You didn't look like you would shoot a German officer. Why did you say that? You must have known my soldiers would kill you and float you upside down in the Danube River. I permitted the insult and swallowed my pride. Perhaps I know the war is over. That saved your life. But it also became a lesson for me. I had sworn not to kill anymore, especially not a German soldier. Thanks for helping me get the supplies. We can live in comfort for another week, and by then we'll be closer to home." I didn't answer. The major was a model officer. He cared for his men before anything else. I almost wished I could become part of his group.

We left Wels and followed a winding narrow road. The major believed that road was safer than the Autobahn. The air attack of this morning still stuck in our bones.

My beloved Alps hid in the clouds. As we drove higher, a steady drizzle turned into snow flakes. "My guys don't like becoming ice cycles." The major saw his freezing soldiers in the back of the cab with little protection. He decided to stop at St. Leon and stay overnight in the first barn he could find. It was almost dark when we came to St. Leon. We drove into the rain soaked driveway of a farm courtyard. The trucks slid and spun before they stopped.

Fritz had been quiet during the whole trip. I wondered what he thought. The soldiers began unloading. I crossed the street and checked Hotel Gasthof Simmerl. I heard Fritz behind me but he never said a word.

"I prefer the beds in a hotel over sleeping in a windy barn on wet hay. Do you agree?" Fritz answered, "I agree," but barely opened his mouth.

Most small mountain hotels were owned by families and had no reception desks. I didn't expect one. There was nobody around. The place seemed deserted. The owners often sat in the dining room. I checked, but it was empty. From the kitchen I heard someone moving pots and saw a corpulent woman busily chopping onions. She didn't look up when she saw us.

"We need two beds for tonight. Can you help us?" Our fancy identification wouldn't mean much to her. But, at least she knew we weren't thieves. She wiped her hands on her apron and, without saying a word, walked to a keyboard with twenty keys. She took the first key, walked clumsily ahead of us upstairs and opened the first room on the left without speaking. The room was very nice, light and spacious. The furniture was luxurious. Two chests were hand carved and color- fully painted. Two decorated china basins with water pitchers stood on the chests. Towels hung from the sides. Most importantly, the beds were very comfortable and covered with high feather pillows. Everything was clean.

"I bring you hot water," she said without mentioning a price or registering. We were the only guests.

"She was cooking something." I told Fritz. "Let's see what it is." I went downstairs. Fritz worried me. The lady put two plates of stew on the kitchen table with forks, knifes, and spoons.

"That's all I have," she told me. "The dining room's closed. You can eat here."

"Thank you! That will be plenty." Fritz came, and when we sat down he opened his mouth for the first time. "Do you have a radio?" he asked.

"No radio," she shook her head, "broken, a long time ago. Nobody fixes radios here in this town."

"Does anybody have a working radio? They might know what's going on."

"Nobody is interested. The war is over, anyway," she said. "I'll bring you a glass of home made beer. You can stay in the kitchen. It's warmer here. Hot water will be in your room shortly. I'll take the water up before I go to bed. But you must turn the lights off!" We sat peacefully in the large hotel kitchen.

"What did you think of the major?" I asked Fritz. He needed to talk.

"I don't know what to think," Fritz shook his head. He looked discouraged. I wondered if he could finally admit that the war was over. I still didn't want to say it, not yet anyway. Everybody else, even the hotel lady and the major, said the war had ended.

Fritz rested his head in his left hand and suddenly blurted out what bothered him. "He shouldn't have done that! He knows better. He is a deserter. It was shameful to leave Vienna's defense." Fritz stared. "Tell me! Why did we all swear an oath? Doesn't our oath mean something. An oath is holy and can never be broken. We are still alive, and we can fight. The war is not over."

For the first time I felt older than Fritz. Now I had to deal with his outburst prudently. "Be realistic, Fritz! There are two options left, in my opinion: one, Hitler has powerful weapons and will use them. Then we will win the war. Or, two, if he doesn't have the weapons he should give up and stop the slaughter." My face flushed. I sounded emphatic and that even surprised me. These were new ideas for me.

Fritz stared. He looked puzzled. "Nobody would have dared to suggest that three month ago." I noticed he smiled. Encouraged by his smile, I continued. "Maybe Hitler has the powerful weapons, but he can't use them because they are not ready. Then he still must give up. He is crazy otherwise. He doesn't give a damn about us soldiers who fought. To be honest, I don't think Hitler has the weapons. He doesn't mean a thing to me anymore. And my oath is no longer valid." I banged my fist on the table and the dishes bounced. For the first time, I had openly cussed Hitler, and I did it in front of Fritz, a loyal Party member. But I was mad and didn't care.

"I intend to keep one promise," I told Fritz. "I will finish this mission. But my oath to Hitler doesn't exist anymore. It's gone! You and I depend on each other. We are friends and we are comrades, though we may have different opinions. But I consider you more important than Hitler. When our mission ends, I'll go home. You can depend on that. And I'll get there. We'll both get there!"

Fritz shook his head and smiled. "Soldiers fight for ideals, and for dreams. Wasn't that always true? Gross Deutschland was a dream for us and was worth fighting for." He rested his head on his hand. "Europe was going to be united and would extend to the Ural mountains. Germany needed agricultural space." I noticed he used Hitler's rhetoric. "Germany is too crowded, we need space. We are an industrial nation. But to have the rest of Europe would help. We can teach Europe. We have superior schools. Germany could have become the empire of Charlemagne. It is a pity!" he sighed and wiped away a tear.

"I swore my oath and so did millions of other Germans." I said nothing. Fritz began to sob. Then, just as suddenly, he stopped.

"To be honest with you, I lost confidence, too." he said quietly. "If Hitler doesn't stop the slaughter now, I don't know what to do." I knew how hard it was for him to come to this point and wondered how many millions of disappointed Hitler followers there were by now.

"Yes, it's just you and me. And that is what counts from now on." Fritz offered me his hand across the table, "Let's not pretend anymore. There will be no more miracles. We'll drink our beer and go to bed!" He talked calmly. He had adjusted and I was glad. From then on it was just Fritz and me that counted.

Saturday, April 28

I slept late the next morning. The hotel bed was too comfortable and warm. I felt Fritz standing next to me. He was fully dressed and his shoes were wet. This was the day we would get to Army Headquarters. My imagination went wild.

"The weather is worse today." Fritz informed me, "Our friend, the major, already left. We better get going." He pretended not to care about the major. "He didn't like me. The major didn't like that we went to the hotel. He was a possessive ass expecting us to become obedient members of his team. I never thought he would go to Berchtesgaden. That was too far out of the way for him."

I dressed quickly and went downstairs to the kitchen. Our breakfast was already on the table. We ate, and afterwards Fritz asked for the bill. "I wish you luck," said the lady simply. "I don't need your money. You need more luck than I do." We thanked her and took our bags outside and sat them near the curb. The weather was bad. Military vehicles sped by, both ways, up and down. Armored trucks splashed the rain puddles. More traffic went toward Berchtesgaden. I wondered where they all came from and if they fought the Russians or the Americans, but I kept my thoughts to myself. No more emotional talk. I'd had enough the night before.

A jeep stopped at the hotel entrance. A young lieutenant hurried inside. A few minutes later he returned. I could have told him to go to the kitchen. "I can't find anybody. I just wanted something to eat," he told us. The lady closed the whole operation after we left.

"Can you take us to Berchtesgaden?" I asked.

"Sure, hop in, that's where I am going." We didn't need our fancy documents. "My engine needs cooling. From here, the road will be steep."

Fritz seemed to be in a good mood. He reminisced about Berchtesgaden and the valleys he hiked when he was with the Hitler Youth Corps. As he described the beauty of Lake Königssee, the Watzmann, and the entire area, he became more excited. I thought he exaggerated. I didn't know Berchtesgaden. But Hugo had told me it was a beautiful place.

"Did you meet Hitler since he had his mountain retreat?"

"I saw him often in Berlin, but not as a minor Hitler Youth official."

"Why did you leave that high government position in Berlin? You have never told me."

"I might as well tell you now. I never approved of corruption. I became tired of fighting against the power of money. I made my reports, but they laughed. They classified me as an outsider and asked me to quit. The highest ranked were the worst. They took money, precious art, and whatever pleased them. They had exorbitant expense accounts, frequented the finest restaurants and some even had private brothels. The party of socialism was not as modest as it proclaimed. Most lived a feudal style. And the worst was, nothing was being done about it.

"Hitler himself lived reasonably modestly. He closed his eyes to it. Goering became the richest man in Germany. Hess, the most intellectual of Hitler's friends, was snubbed. They laughed when Hitler allowed him to fly to England and negotiate a peace settlement. Hess was called an idiot. I still believe Hitler wanted Hess to succeed. He often said he didn't want war with England. France was the archenemy and Germany's competitor in Europe. Hitler never liked Himmler. Himmler formed the SS, but Hitler strengthened the SA and appointed Bormann as his personal assistant to check on the SS and Himmler. Hitler seldom invited Himmler into his private circle of friends. He didn't trust him. Bormann controlled the SA and the SS at the same time. Their meetings lasted past midnight. These lengthy meetings were cruel. At least they gave everybody an excuse to sleep in. The offices were empty in the morning. Everybody did what they pleased. The strange thing was, Hitler left them alone as long as they showed loyalty to him. That was enough. He joked and amused himself with their antics.

"Speer was his closest friend. Speer was a brilliant architect and a good organizer. Hitler and Speer had much in common. They spent many weekends together. Architecture was Hitler's hobby, too. Speer became Hitler's personal architect and later also directed the entire defense industry. That gave him power. He never took advantage like the others. Hitler's weakness was his uncompromising loyalty to his old friends. I didn't know to whom to complain. They told me to quit. And when I'd had enough, I took their advice and volunteered for the front line. I felt better where the action was. You know the rest of my story."

I didn't know what went on in Berlin and neither did anybody else. The papers never told about the self-serving bunch in Berlin. A few jokes were made, but they weren't taken seriously. The bunch in Berlin took advantage and busily took care of themselves.

The clouds lifted and it stopped raining. Sways of fragmented fog drifted in the valley and Berchtesgaden laid before us. We finally saw the Alps. The narrow cobblestone streets were clogged with military vehicles. Berchtesgaden was a military bastion. Heavy artillery tried to squeeze through narrow streets. A Tiger, Germany's heaviest tank, was apparently unable to move and was left parked in a school yard. The town got ready for it's last defense. I wondered who was in charge.

"Isn't that ridiculous to maneuver heavy artillery and tanks in a town. Why don't they stay outside," Fritz complained. The chaos was obvious.

For a long time we were stuck next to three trucks loaded with young German soldiers—none seemed more than fifteen years old, but all were in immaculate new uniforms. Their faces were full of excitement and pride. They were ready to fight. In high pitched voices they sang marching songs, a SS soldier directing them. At the end of a song, they swung the rifle above their heads and shouted enthusiastically, *"Sieg Heil!"* (Hail victory!). I couldn't help but become intoxicated by their spirit. I felt uplifted and sad at the same time. Deep down in my heart I knew this last defense was useless. But I felt the urge to join them. Wouldn't it be fun to raise hell once more, one last time? And die with a smile? I shouldn't let the fifteen-year-old spirited kids go it alone. Tears welled into my eyes.

Reality took over quickly. The trucks moved, and their singing vanished. I looked at Fritz, he also had tears in his eyes.

"I'd like to go with them," he was dead serious and lifted himself up to go. "I wouldn't mind getting killed," he said. I had to think of something quickly to change his mind. He might just do that. "Don't forget, we have a job! We are not finished yet." He immediately sat down. "Yes! I forgot. You are right." Duty and discipline always came first with him.

"After we deliver the documents, I suggest we take our furlough." That sounded like a joke. We both knew it was impossible. Fritz broke into a hysterical laugh which relaxed both of us. He grabbed my arm.

"You are priceless! You had said before that you would save my life. I suppose you just did. This was the day." I knew, he would be fine now, and he would not sacrifice his life for the cause, at least not as long as I was around.

Cemetery Seeon near the Kirch Seeon cloister, now under protection and regarded as a monument, is where Claus and Fritz were kept by the Americans

Cloister at Kirch Seeon near Lake Chiemsee where Claus and Fritz became prisoners

View of Berchtesgaden with the famous [mount] Watzmann rising steeply in the background

This type of farm house is typical high in the mountains of Upper Bavaria

Typical of the mountain homes Fritz and Claus were invited to stay in. It is common in mountain villages for these large, remote farms to have their own chapel—often dedicated to a lost beloved one

This typical Bohemian farm house is similar to Alois' home near Traunstein. Note the compost pile in the front yard, between the house and the road

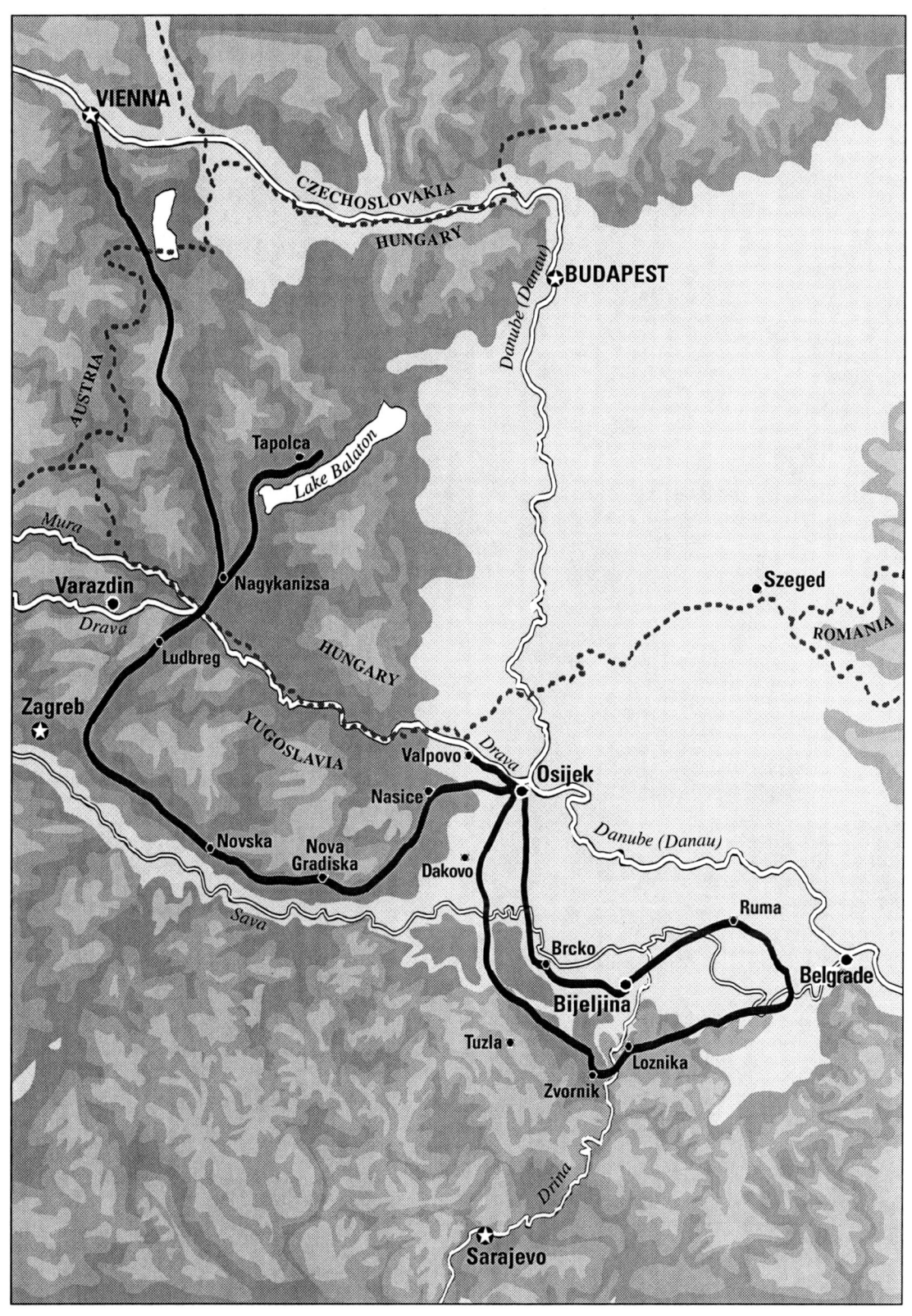

Map of Claus' journeys as a soldier with the 79th Mountain Artillery in eastern Europe

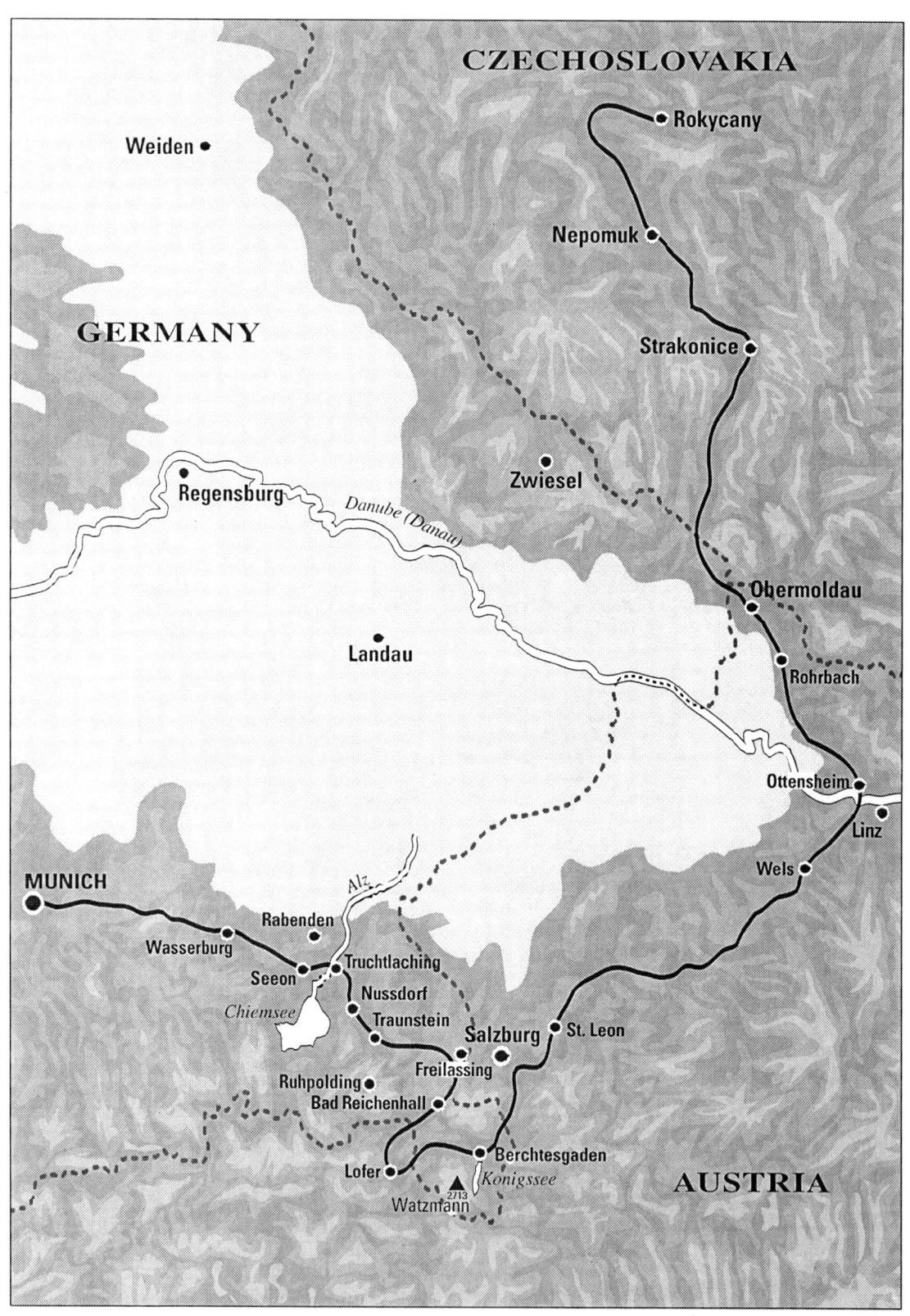

Claus' journey from Officer's Training School in Rokycany to Berchtesgaden and home

Their first encounter with Americans was at this bridge over the Alz River at Truchtlaching

This peasant bread which stays moist for over a week
was our principal nourishment during our journey home

Citizens coming and going in the streets of Munich, May 1945

Munich, May 1945. Translation: For this Hitler needed 12 years

Haus (Hotel) Geiger on the outskirts of Berchtesgaden

Fifty-four years later in 1999, Hugo Geiger and Claus reminisce at
Hugo's home in Berchtesgaden

Chapter 13

Army Headquarters
Lofer, Austria

O ur driver was untouched by the confusion in town. He knew where Army Headquarters was. There was no need to look for the city commander. He promised to take us there. He circled slower vehicles smartly and sped serpentlike uphill toward a park. In the park I saw a luxury hotel facing Mount Watzmann. The driveway had a sign, Haus Geiger. That was Hugo's hotel, our most important destination; but it couldn't be Army Headquarters.

"Are you sure this is Army Headquarters?" I sounded like I was scolding the lieutenant, "The sign read, Haus Geiger." The lieutenant became confused.

Two air force soldiers came from the entrance in blue air force uniforms. He apologized. "You are right, it is Air Force Headquarters. I am sorry." A group of high ranking air force officers left the hotel and walked to their cars.

"Never mind! Don't worry," Fritz grinned and nodded affirmatively. "We are in the right place." The lieutenant didn't understand. He now had doubts about our intentions. He left us and drove off quickly.

"He probably thinks we are spies. He never checked us. He just drove us here."

The guards at the hotel entrance checked our identification. We actually wanted to go to Army Headquarters, we explained. Our documents had the proper classification. They were used to that and showed us into the elegant hotel lobby. "Please inquire at the desk!"

"I can see Hugo waltzing around in here in his latest Alpine-style costume, kissing the ladies hands and acting like a big shot. What a beautiful place this is."

The hotel's atmosphere reflected a dignified elegance, yet still maintained the typical rustic Bavarian style which was expected from a famous Bavarian resort. I forgave Hugo for bragging about his hotel. It was beautiful.

The almost empty lobby was peaceful. Five air force generals sat in comfortable chairs and talked. The silence, compared to the chaotic hustle in town, seemed strange. An elegant dining room was behind the lobby and through it's picture window were the majestic Watzmann Mountains rising above the park. My grandfather referred to 'Haus Geiger' as the ultimate first class hotel. He was right. He often stayed here.

"I am glad we came." Hugo's letter burned in my pocket, "Let's find Frau Geiger." Air force military personnel behind the desk were helpful. They would call Frau Geiger and asked us to wait in the lobby. In the meantime, I admired the antique furniture of the Hapsburg period, the tall Viennese china vases, and rows of armored knights along the wall.

Finally, Frau Geiger came. She was a small, middle-aged, and attractive lady dressed in Bavarian costume. But why did she hesitate when she saw us? I looked down and noticed my dirty boots. Our uniforms were not clean. It dawned on me that we must look like front-line officers. In her mind we had bad news, a typical army letter, '... sorry to notify you that your husband (or son) has given his life for the fatherland ....' Letters like that were always delivered by officers.

I jumped and greeted her enthusiastically. "Don't worry, Hugo is fine, I have a letter from him." She came and embraced me like a son and turned to Fritz and embraced him too. Her face was now full of joy.

"Where is this idiot's letter?" she laughed with tears in her eyes. I pulled the letter from my bag.

"I haven't heard from him in months, nor anything from my husband. Let me read the letter first, then I'll take you upstairs, so you can take a nice bath. I am so glad you came!"

She read the letter. Whatever Hugo wrote on that last evening in Rokycany wasn't important. Hugo wasn't a philosopher. He just wrote that he was fine. But it didn't matter, Frau Geiger had tears in her eyes. He was fine, that was all she needed to know. We could tell her more.

"How is he? You tell me everything during lunch, after you've had a bath!"

A broad curved stairway led up. "These are my private rooms. The air force took all my room keys. I am not allowed to touch them. Security measure, they say." She disliked the lack of trust.

The first room was my room. It was immaculate, clean, and luxurious, I could see the massive, snow covered Watzmann. While I admired the mountain, Frau Geiger was on her knees in the bathroom starting the hot water for my bath.

"You need a new shirt and underwear. I'll give you Hugo's. He wouldn't mind." Fritz was in the adjoining room where she also started the water for him. "While you are in the tub, I'll lay the fresh clothes on a chair outside."

I peeled off the smelling blue-grey flannel shirt I had worn for three months. In Yugoslavia the shirt was soaked in a lice repellent made by an American pharmaceutical firm. Since I had worn that shirt I had had no more lice. A nice Muslim man had traded the repellent for coffee. He didn't need lice repellent because he was used to the lice. The repellent came in a parachute along with other supplies for Serb partisans. United States research knowledge about lice made my life in Yugoslavia much more tolerable. German research lagged behind. I wondered if Frau Geiger had noticed the bad odor.

I laid comfortably in the bathtub and watched it fill to the rim with hot water that was gradually turning brown. I wondered if I should tell Frau Geiger that Hugo and I had squashed hundreds of lice every night before we went to sleep. She knew her son well. She even called him an idiot, probably because she loved him.

After the bath, I put on Hugo's civilian shirt and noticed a problem. We were not to wear civilian shirts under the uniform, and Hugo's light blue checkered collar, stuck out. Fritz had the same problem. He wore a red checkered shirt and his collar showed. We both felt new-born after the bath and walked with confidence into the luxurious dining room downstairs. At the entrance, we saluted smartly, "Heil Hitler."

Mrs. Geiger sat at a the best window table with a magnificent view. As we walked the rows of white clothed tables, I couldn't help wondering where Field Marshall Hermann Goering usually sat. But then I remembered he had just resigned or Hitler had him arrested. I asked Frau Geiger if she had heard any news about Goering.

"He never came here," she explained, "Most commanders stayed in Berlin. But now tell me about Hugo and yourselves! How long have you known each other?"

"A long time. Since Hugo left home." I dragged the conversation out because the meal was fabulous. I began the story when Hugo and I first met in Garmisch's railroad station before we were even in uniform. I left out the fact that Hugo bragged. I was telling her about our training in France, when a clear consommé with tiny liver dumplings floating in the broth was served. Fritz added, we were all good friends, but we split up after the initial training when we were sent to the front line. The soup plates were removed. The waitress brought a silver platter and served slices of roasted sirloin of beef, Russian style. Small peas, carrots and potato croquettes were presented on a smaller silver platter.

I did not tell her about my jail time in France and advanced the story to when Hugo and I saw each other in Yugoslavia. In the meantime, the waitress poured a beautiful, Auslese, Schloss Johannesburg wine into crystal cut glasses.

I talked about the devastating battle at Belgrade, but I was careful not to tell too much. That took time. A second bottle of the same wine came. I told how Hugo escaped and that he crawled into the battlefield at night and bypassed a Russian camp. I left out that he later fell in love with a beautiful Serb girl and almost became a farmer.

When the dessert came, we had several choices. I selected a black forest cherry cake, and told Frau Geiger that I hadn't experienced a meal like this in many years. Frau Geiger leaned forward. "We eat like this here, because it is Air Force Headquarters," she looked around as she whispered. "I manage the supplies. Believe me, no other hotel has food like this—at Army Headquarters in Lofer, maybe.

"Lofer is not far, maybe two hours, and on the Austrian side. It's located in the hotel Zum Brau. Somebody will drive you there, they told me. The owner is a good friend of mine. I'll call her and ask her to take good care of you."

I told Frau Geiger that my grandfather often stayed in this hotel and added spontaneously, "Hugo is really lucky to work and live in a splendid hotel like this. That must be fun. I envy him." She smiled and looked a little sad. "Who knows when he will come home, if he ever comes?" I didn't answer.

"Hotel work is not easy. One is tied to the job, day and night and on holidays. Then we work even harder. What profession are you thinking of after the war?"

My standard answer was, "I will study medicine." But I hesitated this time. Since I had arrived at this hotel, a new idea had begun to formulate. "I'll probably go into the hotel business," I said without the slightest idea what that entailed. Why not? Studying medicine was now impossible. It would take eight years. Munich was destroyed and the university was closed. Nobody could study. Medicine made no sense. I should do something else, I thought and said, "Perhaps I should go into the hotel business by starting as a cook."

The statement sprang boldly from my lips. "Since we ate this fabulous meal, the hotel profession appeals to me. A cook can go into the world and work on ships and live anywhere. Who knows?" Frau Geiger and Fritz looked astonished. Fritz especially. He knew I wanted to study medicine and eventually would become a doctor. He considered my sudden change of mind a sign of my immaturity. He was used to that. In my army book, my profession was listed as medical student.

Frau Geiger answered thoughtfully. "Your idea makes sense." She surprised me. "We all have to change. To leave the country makes sense as well, and cooks are needed everywhere. You will, at least, have food every day. That is essential to survive. In my case and in Hugo's, we can't leave. We have this hotel. That is a burden. Sometimes I wish we didn't have the hotel. But I cannot change and just go away. I still have hopes we'll win the war. But if we don't, we will all be poor, worse than before Hitler. Who knows what the future brings? Cooks always eat. I remember when we had nothing to eat. If those times come back, I'll close my hotel and only prepare a soup which will be served from the kitchen. I thought about that already."

I was much more optimistic. New thoughts sprouted in my brain, "One day, I would like to own a hotel like this. Times will change, and in life everything goes up and down. Bad times turn into good times. Hugo can help me and give me advice. I think I should first learn the kitchen, and later learn management."

"What a great idea." Frau Geiger was excited, she lifted her wine glass and made a toast. "Hugo would love it and so would I. What will you do, Fritz?"

"I'll find work in a bank in Munich. I must stay in Munich and take care of my disabled mother."

"How is she getting along without your help?"

"An old friend lives with her and helps out. I receive money from the government and can afford quite comfortable quarters. But without that money, we cannot exist. That worries me." Fritz had never told me that.

"Is your Dad still alive?" asked Frau Geiger.

"He emigrated to the United States. As far as I know he is alive, but he doesn't help. I left school early to support my mother. And luckily, I made high ranks in the Hitler Youth. Before that I worked in a bank in Munich which offered me publicity work to get more business." Fritz blushed. "I know I can do the work in a bank, and I am not used to telling my personal story. Sorry I bothered you." Frau Geiger touched Fritz's arm. "You are not bothering me. It won't be easy for you after the war," she added thoughtfully. "You are Hugo's friends. You went out of your way to bring me his letter. I love and respect you, Fritz. You are not like your father. My home will always be open for you." Fritz squeezed her hand. I'd never seen him that emotional. He had changed a lot. Breaking with the past was not easy for him. It was easier for me. If I am poor, so what! I would become a cook. It was a good idea. But most importantly, I was free and made my own choices. I was confident everything would turn out fine.

An orderly came, clicked his heels and stood at attention next to the table. "I am ready to take you gentlemen to Lofer, if and when you are ready."

"Please, wait fifteen more minutes! We'll meet you at the entrance," said Frau Geiger who had planned to call her friend in Lofer.

The road to Lofer went steadily downhill. Not one car came by. At a bridge, half way down, I noticed the emblem of Tyrol, a fierce looking bald eagle. We were in Austria. Tony would be proud to see us here. I imagined my comrades of the First Mountain Division. I wondered how they were and if they were still in Hungary? Many were from Tyrol. Joseph was now a master sergeant. I was confident he and Roland would get home. They always did.

I felt we were close to Army Headquarters and became nervous. Soon I would see many army generals. Would they even talk to us lieutenants? How would they react? What should I say? How should I address them? I had no idea what was in the yellow package. My imagination carried me away. Headquarters is most important. I had never in my life witnessed how life and death decisions are made. I would see generals ordering millions of soldiers from one place to another. I bring them information that will enable them to make those decisions. Later, I can tell my grandchildren I was there on April 28, 1945, when the German Army Headquarters, having my information, turned the war victorious. That day the final battle began and World War II ended.

Deep in thought, I heard Fritz asking the driver, "Are we already in Lofer?"

"Yes Sir! This is Lofer, and here is the Hotel Gasthaus Zum Brau."

"Thank you, Sergeant!"

My impression of Hotel Gasthaus Zum Brau was negative. A grey wall, four stories high with small inset windows looked like a prison. No guards were posted. Three late model German jeeps parked unattended before the massive wooden entrance door.

The building was formerly the town's brewery. The age was indicated by the massive stone floor laid centuries ago, and the arched ceiling was like a church's. Wrought iron chandeliers hung from the high ceiling, providing only dim light. The candle shaped bulbs hadn't been dusted in years. Oriental rugs were spread over the massive stones and gave the armored knights along the walls a ghost-like dignity. The rugs must have been brought back by knights from the orient long ago. Woven tapestries adorned the walls. Carved antique wooden chests and chairs stood between them. The lobby was closed off at the end by a massive oak wall with a door in it. Loud voices and laughter came from behind the door. That must be the headquarters assembly room, I thought.

To our right, at the main entrance, sat a major on duty in a small reception room. We saluted respectfully, "Heil Hitler!" much sharper than usual, because this was Army Headquarters. But I wasn't sure if it really was our headquarters.

The major removed his legs from the top of his desk but didn't stop reading his magazine. His jacket hung loose over his chair. Casually he answered "Heil Hitler!" and leaned further back to look up. We both stood at attention. Reluctantly, he got up and also raised his arm. Fritz, speaking for both of us, stated our names, ranks, and where we came from.

"We have messages from the commander of the artillery officers' school in Rokycany, Czechoslovakia. May I ask where we can leave them? And we'd like to get confirmation."

The major pushed his magazine aside, put his coat on and barely buttoned it. He circled his desk and silently shook hands. Ceremoniously, I handed him the crumpled yellow envelope with the life and death information. He glanced at the package but, without acknowledging the importance, flipped it over his shoulder. The precious package we had guarded with our lives landed in the corner on the floor in a heap of scattered papers and envelopes.

"I assume you want to stay overnight?" He leaned over the registration book and scrutinized the last page. I followed his pencil down a row of names of high ranked officers and generals.

"There is a bed in room 37," he handed me a key and said to Fritz, "and in room 36, Colonel von Einsalm has a bed. Here is your key. Are you hungry? The officers are just finishing their dinner in the assembly room, behind the oak wall down the hall. You can join them when you are ready!" He made a jovial gesture.

What was going on? I stayed stiff at attention because that major never said, at ease. Finally, he cleared things up.

"I guess you didn't know that the Army Headquarters was dissolved today."

My mouth slowly opened. I turned to Fritz who was pale. We stared at each other. "Dissolved?" I asked still not believing. "Do you mean the war is over?"

"No! I didn't say that. I said this headquarters is no longer in existence, as of today. As far as I know the war continues." The major was slightly embarrassed.

I clicked my heels. So did Fritz. Bewildered we turned and went upstairs. It was obvious the major would not tell us more.

"Did you see, how our important document ended up in the corner of the room on the floor? They told us to sacrifice our lives for that?" I became bitter. "He just flipped the package over his shoulder. And we faithfully protected that garbage. What a joke!"

"I still can't believe it. They closed the headquarters. And the war is still not over." Fritz shook his head. "I'll meet you in five minutes outside the assembly hall."

"Does anybody believe the war is not over? They must be crazy," I said loudly standing on the wide stairway. I didn't care if anybody heard me.

I knocked on the door of room 37. There was no answer. I walked in. Nobody was there. Clothes laid scattered over the room and even on my bed. I made room for myself. Did these generals direct the war during the last six years? What a sorry sight.

I met Fritz downstairs. We hesitated before going inside. I finally opened the heavy oak door. The room was filled with sways of thick cigar smoke. Old corpulent men, in shirt sleeves sat side-by-side at banquet tables in the smoke. Uniform jackets were casually flipped over their chairs. They were having a good time telling jokes. I checked for ranks, but couldn't distinguish them since they didn't wear jackets. Their trousers had red stripes on the sides telling me they were generals.

We saluted sharply, "Heil Hitler," at the entrance. Nobody noticed or responded.

The laughter and shoulder slapping annoyed me. They acted like nothing had happened. I remembered the faces of this morning, the just-recruited fifteen-year-old soldiers. They expressed so much enthusiasm in their singing and with a trust in their leadership. These men were their leaders and would guide them to victory. They were ready to give their lives. Luckily, they didn't know these leaders were eating and drinking and had not the slightest enthusiasm for battle.

I brushed the image off and looked for a quiet place to sit and eat.

Empty brown Rhine wine bottles laid scattered over the tables. A few still dripped. Neither of us wanted to bother with the generals. Two unused china settings at the end of a table each had a full bottle of wine in front of it. Three officers sat at the other end of the table. We ignored them, and they ignored us. Because a few hours ago we were still ready to sacrifice our lives to come here, I thought they were not our equals.

Sunday, April 29

I woke and saw my room mate, Colonel Pflueger, was up and ready to go. He wore a stylish light grey uniform and high, thin, black leather boots. The iron cross was pinned on his jacket along with other medals.

"I didn't want to wake you." He was friendly and introduced himself. Then he pointed at the German Cross in Gold on my jacket. "You got this medal while you served in the artillery? That must have been quite a battle. Glad to meet you. Where are you heading?"

"To Army Provision Headquarters in Traunstein and then back to Rokycany, in Czechoslovakia." It didn't seem right to tell him that I was going on furlough.

Pflueger's orderly came and grabbed his bags. "I wish you luck," the colonel saluted formally, raising his hand the old-fashioned way to the rim of his cap. I didn't respond because I was sitting on the edge of my bed in my underwear and felt saluting was not proper. He quickly left. I should have asked where he was going, and why Army Headquarters was dissolved. It was too late for that now, and I had many more questions.

The loud voices on the street aroused my curiosity. I went to the window and saw rows of jeeps lined up on the street. Orderlies packed and arranged luggage into the vehicles. The officers were in full uniform and chatted with each other next to the cars. The mood seemed depressed. They shook hands repeatedly until the first car rolled off, a second followed, then a third, and soon they were all gone. The street was empty and quiet. Fritz and I were the only ones left in the hotel. I washed and dressed quickly and went to Fritz's room. There was nothing but two unmade beds. Fritz must have been downstairs. I went to the empty lobby, but something made me go to the reception room. There were papers scattered all over the floor. Our yellow envelope was still unopened in the same place on the floor, right where the major had flipped it the night before.

Should I open the package and see how important the document actually was? I didn't, but gave the envelope a friendly kick to make sure it knew I came to check. "I hope you realize you are at Army Headquarters where you are supposed to be." I made the sign of the cross over my envelope and pushed a heap of papers on top of it.

I found Fritz in the empty assembly room sitting by himself at the same table we had the night before. A rotund waitress in a black dress and a white lace collar poured coffee. "Fresh rolls will be here in two minutes." Jam and butter was already set. Fritz didn't hear my cheerful "Hi!" He didn't even seem to notice when I sat down. I anticipated a difficult conversation.

"There is no hope. They left. Everybody went in different directions."

"They probably went home," I quipped. Fritz looked up. Quite frankly, I didn't feel depressed, only annoyed. Fritz wasn't the only one who once was loyal to Hitler. Three of my best friends had believed in Hitler, and they were dead. Dieter, my best friend in school, always wore his Hitler Youth uniform proudly. Three months earlier I had heard from my mother that a Russian tank rolled over him, but not before he shot his last anti-tank shell.

My second best friend, Klaus, walked into a forest in Russia and was met by an ambush. He was left dead deep inside Russia. Klaus disliked Hitler. His older brother married a Jew and joined the SS to protect her. He also died in Russia. She was left alone.

My third-best friend, Texas, who was from Argentina, joined the air force. After forty-eight kills as a fighter pilot, he was shot down over the Atlantic. Texas never saw his homeland or his parents again. After his death, he was awarded the Knights Cross. We were called the four musketeers in school and always stuck together. Now I was the only one left. I had reasons to be depressed, also.

"How is the coffee?" I asked and hoped Fritz would say something. He said the war was lost, which was the turning point for him.

"What do you think we should do?" I asked more urgently. Our next decision was important. I had made up my mind not to go back or fight anymore. Fritz looked up. "We'll go to Traunstein, and deliver the last document," he said simply.

"And after that?" I pressed.

"We'll take the furlough and go to Munich," he smiled.

"And after the furlough are we going back to Rokycany?" I had to make sure. It sounded innocent.

Fritz laughed bitterly, "Stop joking! There will be no more trains to Rokycany. And I am not walking back." Ironically our heavy-duty soul searching occurred in the halls of the former German Army Headquarters. "Do you think Hitler knows his generals jumped ship? What are we going to tell Hitler if he calls? I'll pick up the phone. Here is Hitler on the line. 'Yes, Sir Mein

Führer Hitler. No, Sir, Mein Führer! Everybody at your headquarters has gone. It's over, Sir! You should go, too!'" Fritz laughed.

I knew Fritz. Once he made up his mind, he wouldn't go back. But he sounded bitter, maybe even suicidal.

"Let's pack our things and leave!" Fritz got up and packed two fresh rolls in his paper napkin. We didn't know, how important food would become. I remembered the excellent map they had in the reception room. I took the map from the wall and studied the roads from Lofer. We first had to cross the border to get to Reichenhall. Traunstein was about fifty kilometers from there, but we had to walk all the way. It might take two days. How far off were the American troops? They would know at Army Headquarters. I may indeed call Hitler. I showed Fritz the map.

"Where do you suppose the German defense is?" I tried to figure it out on our map.

"I have no idea!" Fritz was not in the least interested.

"We are lucky to have our high priority identification. It will be our protection. Let's go!"

Chapter 14

Provisions Headquarters

Traunstein, Germany

The streets of Lofer were deserted. I had no regrets as we left the former German headquarters. I felt strangely exhilarated. I felt free! For the first time I felt I could go anywhere I wanted to. No officer could tell me to do this or that. There was no authority. Since the generals were gone, I felt independent.

Now it was just Fritz and me. We were free!

On the other side of the street rolled a heavy-duty cart pulled by one ox. The farmer on top had winter potatoes. He covered his face with a wide rimmed hat and pretended not to see anybody. There was no time for conversation today.

Three kilometers outside of Lofer, we passed three unarmed German soldiers. They walked with difficulty, very slowly. "Where are you going?" I asked.

"Home!" was the answer. The one with a thick bandage on his foot talked. He limped between the others who supported him.

"Where is home?"

"Berlin," he said. "And I go to Bonn," answered the one next to him. I stopped.

"You are 1,000 kilometer from home, and you are limping. How do you think you'll get there?"

"You are wrong. It's more like 1,200 kilometers! We were released and told to go home. What else can we do? We are going home. I don't care how far it is. Do we have a choice?"

"There is a big battle around Berlin. Aren't you scared? Bonn was already taken by the Allies. How do you think you'll get there? You can hardly walk."

"Here are my papers," said the one with the bad foot as he pulled a document from his pocket.

"It says, 'Released from the hospital,' and the doctor said, 'Do the best you can!' We need the beds for the next bunch of wounded soldiers that comes in.' I am going home. What else? At least I can limp. I have a bed at home, I hope." He laughed cynically and walked on.

Five kilometers further downhill, a semi truck stopped behind us. A milk face young SS officer called from the window. "Identification, please!"

"Why?" I said defiantly. I never got used to the arrogant manners of SS clowns. But Fritz pulled the identification document from his pocket. He didn't like SS officers any better than I did. He held the paper under the officer's nose.

"I am glad you showed up. Now you can take us to Traunstein!" said Fritz calmly. It sounded more like an order. Fritz forced a smile. The SS officer studied the identification. Satisfied, he handed them back.

"Sorry, I can't take you. I have no room. My orders are to bring these soldiers to a defense position and to control the road. My soldiers must relieve others who are waiting."

Fritz opened up his upper uniform pocket and pulled a notebook. I smiled, I knew what was coming.

"What is your name, please? State your rank and your unit number!"

The young officer's superior attitude changed. Before he could answer, Fritz shouted from the top of his lungs: "Did you ever read military regulations? Aren't your SS regulations the same? Remember page 43? It says you are supposed to help any officer who has this most important mission under any circumstances. Read up, man! Did I understand correctly? You did refuse to take us? I want you to step off this vehicle and show me your military book!"

The young SS officer stepped from the car and saluted sharply, "Heil Hitler!" Fritz responded less sharply. The young faces in the back looked on curiously.

"Make room in the back for the officers!" shouted the SS officer.

"No." I opened my coat and let them see my German Cross and my swastika medal. "We'll sit in the cab. You drive! We must get to Traunstein today."

I pushed my bag into the cabin, and Fritz took his time writing the SS lieutenant's name in his notebook. We settled comfortably in the cabin. We drove down into the valley of Reichenhall. The young SS officer babbled incessantly, trying to impress us.

"We set road blocks and check on soldiers who are wandering around. Some of these bastards seem to think the war is already over."

"What are you going to do with them?"

"We take them prisoners. They will be investigated for treason and court martialed. You agree, these soldiers are traitors. They refuse to fight. I am convinced some would even cross the enemy line and give themselves up." Luckily, he missed the three soldiers we had seen before who were going home to Berlin and Bonn. I was glad. We came to the first houses in Reichenhall and the traffic became heavy.

"You can let us off at the city commander's office," I told him. Fritz read my mind. We wanted to get away from this guy. He agreed silently.

"Drop us off here!"

"Yes Sir," smiled the SS officer. He was also glad to get rid of us.

We stepped from the car. I shook hands with the soldiers in the back and felt sorry for them. I wanted to tell them the war is over and not believe this milk-faced guy. Unfortunately he was their only source of information and they believed what he said. One wanted to inspect my swastika medal. He had never seen one. "I want one, too," he told me.

Fritz, in a gesture of friendship shredded the paper on which he wrote the SS officers name. "I won't report you this time," he said, and deliberately forgot to shake hands. Without our document we would have been defenseless. This guy could have easily arrested us. And then what?

"Let's take our time! If we don't get to Traunstein today, we'll be there tomorrow." Fritz agreed. Reichenhall's famous hotels were now converted into hospitals. The former famous resort looked sad. Reichenhall was now a Red Cross city. According to the Geneva convention, the city could not be bombed. The large Red Cross signs on the roofs and the sides of building signified its exempt status. Indeed, there was no destruction.

"If the SS defends this city, then what happens?"

"They'll drop bombs. What else? That's part of war. Can you blame them?"

We walked into the entrance lobby of a hotel and directly into the dining room, which was converted into a Cafeteria. Nobody was there. Fritz took a tray and handed me one. I had never been in a cafeteria other than in the army mess hall. The ample selection of food made it different. I took plenty. The old lady behind the counter didn't complain. A man in an open white coat entered in a hurry. He was surprised to see us.

"I thought all soldiers had left. Why are you here?"

"We came to eat, but we didn't see anybody. Are you a doctor?"

"I am an assistant doctor, in charge of two large hotel hospitals. They released all the wounded soldiers yesterday, and nobody consulted me. A doctor's opinion doesn't count here anymore. Were you two just released?" he didn't give us the time to answer. "Six month ago we were six doctors and each had an assistant. Now I decide who is released and who is not. I lost my jurisdiction. Nobody communicates anymore, and it seems everybody is in charge. I also have no more supplies." He added in a whispered tone, "I hope the war ends. Eat as much as you want! The kitchen doesn't know how many patients we have in the hotel. Nobody told them that there are none."

We ate and packed additional food in our bags. We walked north after leaving the hotel and saw only a few Red Cross vehicles parked on the street. Reichenhall had hardly any traffic but the picture changed near the Autobahn. There chaos reigned! Groups of army trucks caked with dirt stood stranded all over. Soldiers with sullen faces sat in the field and waited. There were endless rows of vehicles on the Autobahn in both directions. Where were they going and for what? The deserted trucks were either out of gas or close to it.

We witnessed an argument between a driver and a dozen soldiers. The driver waved to us, he needed our help. "Can you officers please explain to them that I can't go to Berchtesgaden. I must go to Salzburg. The sergeant tells me I must follow his orders because he out-ranks me. Would you please tell him!" Fritz produced our identification document so that everybody could see the important color markings.

"You will go to Freilassing and then to Salzburg, and you will take us!"

That pleased the driver. Freilassing was on the way to Salzburg. The sergeant and his men pulled back. We climbed into the cabin. After we drove a few kilometers we got stuck in a traffic jam. Military police waved vehicles around into the open field, but it didn't create much movement. If Allied airplanes had attacked they would have plenty of targets.

The once formidable German military machine was a dying corpse, struggling, but barely alive. It was sad to see thousands of well-intentioned soldiers going nowhere. Nobody knew that their military headquarters was dissolved. They kept going. I felt the urge to get away from it all.

"Let's walk from here," I suggested. "We have time. Let's find a farm and stay overnight and rest. What's going on now makes no sense to me anymore."

After checking the map, we discovered we were almost in Freilassing. The chaotic traffic on the Autobahn was in contrast to the beautiful Alps looking down on us peacefully. I discovered a small farm that looked like a scene out of Humperdink's opera *Hansel and Gretel*. The brown shingled building had a balcony around the second floor and geraniums in spacious boxes were red against the deep brown walls. We had to cross a wobbly, wooden bridge. I saw trout struggling up a stream. At the house we discovered the main door was wide open. I knocked on a few windows. There was no answer.

"Somebody is here. Why did they leave the door wide open? Let's check the barn!" As we approached the barn door slowly closed. "They are frightened! I don't blame them." I called, "Don't be afraid, we are passing by and would like to sleep in your barn." No answer. "We'll help you with repairs around the house."

The barn door opened a crack, and a young woman's frightened face appeared, ready to shut the door again and set the bolts from the inside. Before she could, I stated our names and ranks, "Two lieutenants from Czechoslovakia," and made a formal introduction.

The unusual introduction worked. The door opened. Three small children pushed the door wide open still holding tightly to the long skirt of an older girl. I greeted the smallest girl and extended my hand asking her name. She wiped her nose with the back of her hand. Her big blue eyes expressed trust, but before she answered, she checked with her older sister.

"We have never seen lieutenants before in our whole lives," the older sister said and blushed. Her fear was gone. Four young girls began inspecting our officer straps.

"Are you coming from the war? I am Barbara," the older girl introduced herself, "and these are my sisters. The tallest is just a cousin who lives with us. Her father is in the war and so is my father. Our mother died four month ago. But I am in charge," she blushed after making the firm statement. "Sometimes, I wonder if I am doing a good job? I am only fifteen."

"Can we sleep in your barn, Barbara? We'll cut firewood and help with the repairs. We want to help." The four girls were excited, the smallest reached for my hand. Barbara took a posture of authority toward the girls.

"All of you, come to the house. I just finished baking bread." In a procession we walked to the house.

"And I helped make cookies," added the twelve-year-old cousin.

"Nobody comes here, ever. Only my aunt, once a week comes to help. I wish my father was back. Everybody in town talks about the war. When will it be over?"

We didn't answer. Inside the sparsely decorated living room were a few simple pieces of furniture. Everything was immaculately clean, and the worn wooden floor still showed moisture from a recent scrubbing. Fresh garden flowers sat colorfully arranged in a glass on the dining table.

"You are doing a fine job, Barbara. Your father would be proud of you. How can we help?" Barbara took me to a large kitchen storeroom. Apples and winter potatoes aerated in the darkened room in an open chest. "We'll make dumplings and apple sauce, and you can peel. We'll all work together." She blushed, "Officers don't peel anything. I forgot."

"And I can knit," yelled the second youngest and brought the beginning of a shawl.

"Don't worry! We peeled plenty of potatoes as recruits in boot camp." We sat at the kitchen table. Everybody peeled and prepared the evening meal. Barbara did the most and also did most of the talking. "When do you think the war will be over? Are we winning?"

Fritz laid his knife aside and said calmly. "We don't know. We know it will be over soon and your father and uncle will be home. Everything will be all right."

"I hope so! I don't even care if we don't win the war." Barbara held her hand before her mouth indicating she shouldn't have said that. But we smiled. "The neighbor lady told us American tanks are on the Autobahn and will be here soon. She has a radio. She also said there are black Negro soldiers from Africa with the troops. And she is afraid of them. And so am I."

The twelve-year-old cousin squealed, "African Negroes eat people. Don't they?"

"No! They won't eat you." I had to squelch that nonsense. "Why do you think that? They are American soldiers with black skins, but their ancestors came from Africa."

"But, a magazine shows how black people boil a man. And my dad said they'll eat him after they finish dancing. I am afraid," insisted the young cousin.

I had seen a magazine like that some time ago. Dark-skinned cannibals killed a missionary in my magazine. I told the girls those people in the magazines may not even live in Africa. I remembered the Olympic games in Berlin, in 1936, when many American Negroes participated. In one event, the broad jump, a German student by the name of Lutz Long, competed against Jesse

Owens, an American Negro. Lutz Long jumped as far as Jesse Owens but lost in the final jump. They had the most exciting competition in track and field. The spectators never sat down. The newsreel showed Lutz Long and Jesse Owens walking off the field with their arms across their shoulders. They became best friends.

"I knew a nice black man," I told them, "who wore a splendid uniform and greeted people at the entrance of the yearly circus. He was a Negro and talked just like us and was very friendly. He gave us boys candies."

Barbara got up and pulled an old magazine from a shelf. "Are you sure?" I checked the date of the magazine. It was sixteen years old. "My cousin found the magazine in the attic. Look at the pictures! Don't they scare you?" In the centerfold danced an African tribe, they were tall skinny black people, hopping and wearing terrifying masks and waving long spears with feathers attached to threaten others. The girls became more scared when they carefully inspected the pictures except the smallest girl who held her hands over her eyes.

"I showed the pictures to the priest." Barbara looked up. "That's true!" He said, 'They kill missionaries.' Everybody who was in church is now afraid."

"The black skinned soldiers you talked about are not Africans. They are Americans born in America, and they went to school there. They have priests and churches. They are not like those people in the magazine. Those are primitive tribes who are hundreds of years behind the times."

Barbara believed me. "That takes a load off me! We talked about it, and decided we should hide in the barn when we see a soldier come."

The ten-year-old cousin was still not satisfied. "You said you saw only one black person in your life. How can you judge them?"

"It's true, I don't know people with black skin. But that doesn't matter. What counts is where a person lives and how he behaves. They won't harm you."

"There is one more thing," Fritz intercepted, "You should know that in war certain rules prevail. They are called the Geneva Convention. Those rules are accepted and followed by everybody, friend and enemy. For example: prisoners cannot be tortured, is one rule; unarmed girls will not be harmed is another. Reichenhall cannot be bombed because the city is a hospital city and unarmed wounded soldiers live there."

"That's true, Reichenhall was not bombed," Barbara recalled.

After we ate, we did various chores that were too heavy for Barbara, like splitting firewood. We even found time to wash in the cold creek.

Monday, April 30

"Will you take us to your neighbor who has the radio?" I inquired while we ate breakfast. We had to know where, approximately, the war zone was. Barbara avoided the question.

"Tomorrow is May 1! On that day we always have a church procession, and a May tree is hoisted in the center of the marketplace. But not this year. The priest announced after mass, yesterday, there won't be any celebrating. I was so looking forward to dancing and wearing my new Bavarian costume. I am now fifteen, and for the first time, I would be allowed to dance with the grown-ups. That darn war! Why do you want to know about the war?"

"We can't stay here, Barbara!" That was actually what concerned her. "We have a military mission, and we must go to Traunstein."

Fritz looked up. "Yes, we have a mission," he ladled hot milk from his bowl and dunked homemade rye bread into the milk to soften the crust. He did not sound very convincing. Fritz and my thoughts were synchronized. He was glad that I had made the statement.

He once labeled me as being reckless. Now he assumed I might want to stay, get civilian clothes and not finish our last mission as promised. The package from Czechoslovakia contained requisitions for the artillery school. But they wouldn't be filled. We were sure of that. Our mission was over. I was tempted to stay. I stayed awake the night before and carefully considered our choices. First, there was fifteen-year-old Barbara and the girls. They needed help and protection. That seemed more important than our useless mission. Barbara had civilian clothes from her father. We could pretend to be farmers, stay and provide for the girls until her father and uncle came back. I did not want to discuss that in front of Barbara.

"Let's go to Traunstein," I said and got up. "We have made a promise."

Fritz said nothing. He also got up and packed. While packing, I made a new promise, just to myself. After we finished the business in Traunstein, I would definitely go home. That will be my last mission. Fritz looked up, smiled and nodded. "I agree," he answered, reading my mind.

Tears were in Barbara's eyes. "I know you can't stay. I understand. I am sorry. I'll take you to the neighbor. You can listen to her radio news." The four girls went along. After we crossed the creek, we passed a lush apple orchard. At the end was another house like Barbara's. An old farmlady greeted us outside.

"I saw you coming. I know what you want. I don't listen to the radio anymore. All day long they play march music, and there are bits of news in between, but it's always the same, 'We are winning the war,'" she said. "In town they are talking about American tanks on the Autobahn. I don't know who to believe anymore?" She pulled me aside.

"I help Barbara and the girls. I promised her father before he went back into the war a long time ago. I hope he is all right. We haven't heard from him in months." She added, for everybody to hear, "I have fresh milk. Drink and listen to the news!" The news broadcast came from Rosenheim, a station near Munich. Every hour on the hour was the same old story: "German forces are holding. The defense was shortened. Adolf Hitler took command in Berlin, et cetera . . . ." The girls found cookies in the storage room.

"I don't know what to believe anymore," the old lady said for the second time. Neither did we. But we didn't want to start a discussion that would startle the girls.

A tall, skinny old man, about eighty, joined us. "I heard you want to go to Traunstein," he said. "The girl told me," he pointed at the cousin. "I can take you. I have gasoline and drive stuff to Traunstein. I trade. Army Provision Headquarters is in the barracks outside of town. Maybe they will trade for my apples," he chuckled. "They won't need what they have much longer."

The old man's truck looked surprisingly new. We parted from the girls and the old lady. He drove on a dirt road between fields. "Where did you get this truck?" I asked.

"In a trade. You can get anything and everything today, even military vehicles."

"You wouldn't want to be caught in a military truck? Would you?"

The old man chuckled. "Everything has changed. I am not dumb. I take you along because you are officers, and you can deal better with the sentries. I hope you have good identification."

We drove into town on empty streets. Traunstein seemed deserted. We stopped at the town commander's office and suddenly heard a shot. Somebody inside yelled. "American tanks are in town . . . !" We ran inside.

The town commander's body laid slumped forward over his rifle. The nozzle was still in his mouth. "Why did he shoot himself?" I mumbled. The old housekeeper had the answer.

"He was a professional officer, from the First World War. He never understood why they lost that war. And now they are losing the second war. That was too much for him!" The housekeeper was now in tears. "Why did I tell him what my neighbor said?" Her neighbor and friends came and took care of the major. We helped them to dig a grave in her backyard.

Outside of Traunstein, the main gate of the barracks complex was closed. A sentry sat forlorn in a guard house and smoked. Bored, he threw his cigarette on the floor without extinguishing it. When he saw us, he saluted clumsily. Fritz ignored the cigarette. "Where is your officer? Is the Army Provision Headquarters open?"

"Nobody is here." The elderly soldier adjusted his belt, which had slipped from hours of useless sitting. The cigarette butt still burned and smoke ascended in a straight line. I stepped on the butt.

"Open the gate!" I told him, "We'll find the officer ourselves." Our old man started the engine and drove through the gate.

"You won't find anybody. I told you!" yelled the guard from behind. We saw five buildings, all loaded with stuff and unprotected. The corpulent soldier followed us. "Next time, just push the gate open. I'll keep it unlocked." He acted friendly but lethargic. "They closed the office last Sunday. Everybody left. Me and four others stayed. We guard these buildings, but that doesn't make much sense to me. This is my last day."

I noticed every door was open and saw a few civilians rummaging inside. They saw us and quickly hurried out a back door and through a hole in the fence. We found rows of blankets, tents, knapsacks, shoes, and clothing. Everything was neatly stacked and well organized.

"Is all this unprotected? There is enough stuff for an army." The old farmer's eyes became larger than wagon wheels. "I am sure glad I brought you."

"Load up! Take what you want! Why not? Take a few blankets to the girls!"

"I sure will! You tell me how much I can take." He still wasn't sure.

While we quickly inspected the buildings, we found more civilians inside. That meant that Allied troops were not yet in town. "I suggest, we each pack two knapsacks with stuff we can use later for barter." I asked the old man, "What do farmers need most?"

"Blankets and boots." He helped us select the proper stuff. "Farmers need anything. But they like pots and pans and kitchen stuff most."

"We can't overload, because we must walk to Munich," I warned. We packed and unpacked and considered the weight of two knapsacks. Our farmer friend loaded his truck. Grateful, he said thanks and good-bye.

"I'll come back tomorrow. That's for sure. I'll also bring a few friends."

"Don't forget to take things to the girls!"

"I will, I will! Don't worry!"

We packed four knapsacks systematically. We discussed walking fifteen kilometers per day. That would get us to Munich in about two weeks. Some stuff would be traded and lessen the weight. We considered ourselves lucky to find the stuff.

At the open gate the guard didn't even bother to look. Instinctively, I turned south on the empty street. I didn't know why, because Munich was to the west. Something told me to go south, and as usual I followed my intuition. Fritz didn't ask or complain. He told me once, "you have instinct," and he trusted me. We had no destination and lots of time. I felt very good about that. Seeing American tanks wouldn't bother me. We could disappear somewhere quickly.

"Let's go and check the traffic on the Autobahn. Perhaps we'll see American trucks rolling there." The Autobahn was the best place to find out what was going on. The German defense line must be close. We planned to avoid both.

"From now on let me worry about the SS," suggested Fritz. "I can handle them. You keep the identification and more importantly, keep your mouth shut." Fritz produced his Hitler Youth medal that could now be of value.

At the Autobahn bridge I bounced my heavy load off my shoulders, stopped and wrote in my pocket calendar: "30 April 1945, we completed our mission!" I yelled as loud as I could across the empty Autobahn, "I am free, at last! This is an important day!" The Alps stood before me with an eternal majestic silence. "These mountains never worry about war or peace. They are wise. They are always beautiful. And after seeing the nonsense humans are capable of, they can't be bothered. Humans climb around on them, they destroy, they rebuild. And the mountains watch. They've watched humans for thousands of years and nothing has ever changed." Fritz leaned across the Autobahn railing and looked worried.

"I've never seen the Autobahn like this, this empty. Where are the Allied forces?" A man limped across the overpass. He came from the other side and waved. "Don't just stand there! American tanks are on the Autobahn. Can't you hear them?" We three stood and listened. I remembered the noise of tanks on the narrow mountain road in Czechoslovakia. They were very close. But here I heard nothing.

"Where did you see them?"

"I didn't see them. But the radio announced them. They must be very near." The old man whispered, not to be overheard. We stared at the empty Autobahn.

"If neither of us can hear them, then they are very far," I concluded and shouldered my two knapsacks and began to walk across. Fritz followed.

"Another one of those damn rumors," he said. But the man had scared us. We walked directly into the forest and felt safer. Everything had to be taken seriously from now on. Perhaps Allied tanks would come in a few minutes, or in an hour, or eight hours.

"Let's find a radio," I suggested. "I saw a red roof on the hill behind us. There must be people, and it isn't far. Let's go!" Fritz shouldered his knapsacks. Neither knapsack fitted him. He juggled them around as he trekked uphill. The farm house was not as close as I thought, but it was well hidden by fruit trees. It appeared to be safe.

The front door was open, like it had been at the girls' farm. Nobody answered our calls here either. "They must all be scared, by now." We walked inside. The entire house was one room, a combined kitchen and living room. Water boiled in a pot on an open fireplace. Somebody must be around! I didn't want to intrude and went back outside.

We relaxed under an apple tree. A stout, middle-aged woman with two children holding her apron approached very hesitantly from the barn. She pushed the children from her apron when she saw us and covered her mouth.

"I thought you were American soldiers when we saw you coming up the hill." She talked very fast. A huge man appeared behind her. He was about seven foot tall and held a pitch fork in one hand for protection.

"Are you Germans?" He stepped close and inspected us. Obviously, he couldn't see well, but he wore no glasses or shoes. His clothes were ragged. His inspection took some time. "You scared us. I heard you. I knew right away you were Germans. Come in. My name is Alois." The man bent his head under the door frame and walked into the kitchen.

"I don't like the Prussian soldiers. There were too many last week. They talk fast. And the wife and I can't understand them. Now American soldiers are coming. If they speak fast and I can't understand them, I won't like them either. At least I can understand you." His wife stirred the wood in the open fireplace back to a full flame.

"Nobody comes visiting us," she said. "But, during the last three weeks, it has been awful. Our house was a beehive. The soldiers were hungry. We don't have enough to feed them all. We'll give milk only to the Bavarians. The Prussians and the Americans don't get milk. We just pretend we don't understand them, you know," she smiled, embarrassed because hospitality was always to be adhered to religiously.

"We don't like foreigners," said Alois waving his huge arm. "I am afraid of guns." His rotund wife sat down. The large table took most of the room in the kitchen.

"I remember my school teacher once said that every soldier plunders and steals. Do you think the Americans are any different? Will they steal our things? The next door neighbor said, they would." I used my strongest Bavarian dialect to show we could be trusted. My two knapsacks leaned against the wall. The two children attacked them immediately and pulled things from the side pockets. Their parents didn't interfere. To keep some order I gave each child an aluminum knife and a fork. They weren't interested and scattered my other stuff on the floor. I handed the older girl the fork again. She acted amused. Her younger brother asked his mother what the fork was for.

"You eat with that," she explained. "But we don't. We only use spoons here. I have one pot, and everybody helps himself from that pot with a spoon. We are poor. I can't afford dishes and knives and forks like the city folks. I learned cooking on a fireplace and Alois likes it that way. Because you are Bavarians, I will let you stay for dinner. I cooked dried prunes and potato dumplings. You can eat with us."

We thanked her. The water boiled, and the dumplings floated on top. When they surfaced, she dumped the water and placed the big pot on the table. Steaming hot plums were ladled over the dumplings and melted butter poured on top. Each of us received a metal spoon. Without a plate, we all fished dumplings from the pot with the spoon. Since I had never eaten that way, I watched my host. He held his dumpling on the spoon and bit pieces off until it was gone. Then, he fished a prune with the spoon, added juice and butter, and if he still had room added a second plum. There was plenty of food.

Eating that way took time. Plenty was spilled on the table. The spills were occasionally wiped off with the hand or a sleeve. The kids slopped the juicy stuff and dropped their dumpling on the table. They retrieved them by hand and stuffed the remains in their mouth, whichever worked best for them. Not much was said during the meal. Eating was a serious matter.

"Do you have a radio?" I asked Alois when he finished his fourth dumpling.

"I never had one. I don't need a radio."

"How did you know that American soldiers are on their way?"

"A neighbor told me. She has a radio. She hears the news every day because she needs to know. She teaches school."

"Can you take us to her? We need to know what's going on?"

Alois pointed at his bare feet soaking in a bucket of hot water under the table. "I don't go anywhere after dinner, and for sure never after dark because I don't wear shoes. I must go barefoot all day and at night I have to soak my feet." I noticed the skin of his feet was thick and callous.

"He only wore shoes twice in his life," the wife added busily, "the first time was when we got married, and the other time was to his father's funeral. My cousin is a shoemaker. He made him a pair. Nobody carries his size."

While she talked, I remembered a pile of enormous size boots in one of the storage rooms in Traunstein. I mentioned it to our giant host and he became immediately excited. He jumped up and spilled the hot water from his bucket under the table. He wanted to go to Traunstein right away and acted like a little boy on the day before Christmas.

"Do you think those boots you saw will fit me?" he yelled.

I had no intention of going to Traunstein. It was dark outside. American tanks might be there already. Alois grabbed my shoulder and asked the same question over and over.

"Do you think those shoes fit me?" Facing American troops didn't bother him. Shoes were more important. I was in a dilemma. Alois was my host and I didn't want to argue with him. Fritz solved the problem.

"The barracks have no electricity," he explained to Alois, "You can't see anything now. Why don't you two go in the morning by daylight? Alois, you can also get more things, as much as you want. Take your wagon and get yourself two or three pairs of shoes! The stuff goes to waste, and that is a shame. I had planned to go to Ruhpolding tomorrow to visit an aunt. I haven't seen her in years."

I didn't like Fritz's idea. We were not to split up, and now he was going to Ruhpolding alone? The commander in Rokycany told us explicitly to stay together! But Fritz was determined. And Alois was so happy, he agreed. Therefore, I gave in. It was a relief not to argue further.

"You can stay in my house as long as you want," Alois announced, "shoes or no shoes," he thanked Fritz for his brilliant suggestion. "I'll show you to the barn. We'll find a good place where you can sleep in dry hay. Tomorrow, you'll chop me some firewood after we get back from Traunstein. I want logs stapled along the house for insulation."

"How about the news? When are we going to hear the news?"

"Not tonight. We must sleep. I can't afford kerosene. I never go out at night."

He had already forgotten that, minutes ago, he was ready to leave for Traunstein.

Tuesday, May 1

Fritz woke me by sunrise. I watched him stuffing our identification into his pocket. "I'll take them, I'll be back by late afternoon. You won't need this identification. But don't take chances and don't get caught by the Americans!"

"All right. And you watch out for SS patrols. I don't like them, not even on the defense line. They have bad manners. And don't let them arrest you! Always have the identification ready!"

The night before, Alois gave me his jacket to wear in Traunstein. He promised to let me visit the neighbor lady and listen to the news first. If American troops were in Traunstein, we would stay home. Americans might let me pass. In Alois' civilian jacket, I looked like a farmer. But it didn't make sense to take chances. They might be at the barracks now.

That Fritz was going to Ruhpolding worried me. What would he do if the SS didn't accept his identification? I should have gone with him. He had already left. It was too late to stop him. The children ran in and out of the stable. They ran off to have fun. I suspected Alois sent them. He was anxiously waiting to go.

"I already waited an hour," he grumbled when we met. He made final adjustments to his mule. His wife brought a bowl of hot milk and a slice of bread for me. Alois' jacket was much too large. I rolled the sleeves several times but it still looked like a coat. Alois wore another jacket and clean trousers. He looked much better.

"This is my city outfit." It didn't bother him that my jacket didn't fit. "Three times a year, I go to the city. And that is too much. I have somebody else buy my stuff and pay him a commission." We pulled away and turned left at the bottom of the hill.

"Aren't we going to the neighbor's to listen to the news first?" I asked, but Alois didn't respond. That made me nervous.

"No, we'll do that on the way back," he mumbled. His decision was final. "The lady is never home in the morning," he lied.

When we got to the Autobahn, we saw no traffic. Traunstein was deserted. Alois talked only to his mule, often whipping him. It didn't help.

The barrack gate was wide open and there was no guard in sight. Hundreds of civilians rummaged in every building loading up as much as they could. They all had hand pulled carriages. There was not much left but I saw the huge army boots were still there. They were too large for anybody. Alois tried a pair. He smiled. They fit perfectly. He giggled like a little kid and looked for a second pair.

"Don't forget socks!" I told him. Alois liked the idea. He never wore socks. "Let's get more." We filled his large cart with blankets, tent material, parkas, and dozens of socks. I was surprised that he also took cooking utensils, forks and knives. The mule observed us loading with suspicion.

"He always does that," Alois said. I wondered why he didn't wear the new shoes?

"They have to last for the rest of my life. I will wear them on Sundays."

I heard Allied airplanes behind us. There were no more air alarm sirens. The planes swooped down spraying bullets on the asphalt. Alois kept smiling. He didn't care. I became concerned when more planes swooped down. Luckily, they didn't shoot.

"They patrol the Autobahn," I told Alois, hollering into the noise. I realized Alois had never experienced the noise of airplanes or danger like that. He didn't know one airplane from another, nor that the bullets could kill him. The only weapon Alois knew was his pitchfork. However, the mule sensed the danger. Now, for the first time, he ran. We crossed the overpass and the mule hustled desperately uphill until we came to Alois' house. The children ran outside and greeted us.

I was surprised to see Fritz sitting under a tree. Something must have gone wrong in Ruhpolding. I didn't expect him back that early. Fritz tossed his Luger pistol from one hand to the other and didn't even notice us. He was deep in thought. We jumped from the cart. I sensed Fritz was roaring mad.

"What happened? I didn't expect you back so early?"

"I almost used this gun today," he said and finally looked up. He was pale. "Maybe I should have shot the bastards?"

"Shoot whom? What happened?"

Chapter 15

The Wounded
Near Ruhpolding

Fritz's face became flushed when I asked him what had happened. I urged him to talk, but he was not ready. Gradually, he started, but often halted between sentences.

"I came to a check point on the road, not far from Ruhpolding. Young SS soldiers stood there, the same characters we met at Reichenhall. They checked the road south, toward Ruhpolding, but never looked in my direction where I thought the Americans would come from. Perhaps, the American troops were in Ruhpolding, I thought, and the SS defends against them here at this point. But I saw unarmed German soldiers coming from Ruhpolding, just like we saw them between Lofer and Reichenhall. Some could hardly walk. They looked exactly like the ones who were released from hospitals and were obviously going home. They were probably told to go home, their beds were needed.

"The SS soldiers stepped in front of them. I was immediately alarmed, so I went into the forest to watch from there. Something was wrong. The SS officer took the papers from every soldier but didn't even bother to read them. He shredded the papers and stepped on the pieces. The young SS soldiers had a sign they waited for. Each grabbed one of the wounded soldiers." Fritz had to stop.

"Then, I witnessed the most horrible scene I have ever experienced in my life. They tied the German soldiers up, put their hands behind their backs and attached pre-printed signs on their chests: I am a coward, I don't want to fight!" Fritz paused again.

"After they had pinned the signs on the soldier's chests, they put ropes around their necks, threw the ropes up a tree, and hoisted each soldier up, one-by-one. They hung wounded German soldiers! Can you believe that? They all struggled desperately, and some screamed. I will never forget that! I saw innocent German soldiers trying to free themselves, wiggling their feet in the air and struggling. The young SS bastards took their time, pulling the ropes up slowly. That gave the bastards time to cuss and yell, 'Cowards!' Eventually, the yelling and whimpering faded. The fifteen-year-olds still yelled, 'Cowards,' even after the old soldiers were dead."

Fritz's face was now snow white. "I was mad—I never have been as mad before. I can't tell you how mad I was. I pulled my pistol and walked with my identification in one hand and my pistol in the other in their direction. If they wouldn't read my identification, I could at least shoot a few. I walked like I was in a fog and intended to shoot six bullets. Six guys would be dead before they could hang me! But, something stopped me.

I stood in the middle of the road with my gun in my hand and suddenly realized: this is the height of madness. Germans killing Germans. That brought no satisfaction for me. That realization brought me back to reality. Killing young misguided Germans. I could not be part of that. And I walked back into the forest." Fritz's hand shook. I knew Fritz was no coward. I had seen him in action. I should have been there.

"Did they see you?" I asked anxiously.

"They never bothered to look in my direction. These idiots! If Americans came, it wouldn't have concerned them. They were told to kill defenseless German soldiers. They still cussed and shouted at the dangling bodies until jeeps with replacement soldiers came. They greeted them with loud yelling and hollering, to demonstrate they felt like heroes. The replacement youngsters congratulated the first bunch and inspected the dead hanging soldiers. None of them was old enough for real combat."

I sat next to Fritz. My blood pressure was way up. I wished again that I could have been with him. The two of us would have shot twelve of these bastards and strangled the rest. But I said nothing. Fritz had more to tell.

"I felt very ashamed hiding in the forest. I held my loaded gun and for a while seriously considered using the gun on myself. I looked at my Hitler Youth swastika emblem and for the first time, I was ashamed of it. I had worn that emblem proudly. But I had nothing in common with these youngsters who wore the same emblem. Killing them would never have given me satisfaction.

They didn't deserve to die believing they were heroes. For me, patriotic duty died a slow death. I sat and cried, I don't know how long. When I couldn't stand the horrible scene anymore, I walked away deeply ashamed."

Fritz buried his face in his hands. "Can you tell me what has become of us? Did the war make us beasts and murderers? Why do Germans kill Germans? What happened?"

He stared at me with a glazed look. I had nothing appropriate to say. I kept my mouth shut. I knew if I had been there, I would have used my gun. I would have shot six of the young bastards without blinking an eye. But Fritz didn't. Why didn't he shoot them? Because he was older and wiser, and ultimately, he used his head. I admired Fritz and was glad I wasn't there with him. We both would have been dead.

"It takes guts to walk away from a situation like that," I said.

Alois just listened. He didn't say a word. Perhaps, he didn't understand. He was lucky. He had never worried about government affairs or discussed politics or war. He was exempt from the service because of his extremely poor eyesight. He may not even know the difference between the SS and the regular army troops or why the two entities existed. But he knew something unusual had happened this day.

"Do you want to hear the news?" he interrupted the silence. "I promised."

Fritz needed time to recover. We waited a while and then walked with Alois to the forest. We came to a farm, and the lady with the radio greeted us from the second floor balcony behind empty geraniums boxes. She was middle-aged, tall, blonde, and well dressed. Alois told us on the way that her husband recently died. She went daily to the local elementary school as a volunteer. That made him think she was a teacher. Actually, she was a retired professor from Munich's university and had owned the farm as a retreat. Now it was her residence to escape from the daily bombing of Munich.

"Frau Professor Brendel," she introduced herself formally. "I am sure you want to hear the news? The people here listen only to music. Nobody is interested in the news. They don't care about the war or what happens elsewhere anymore. I don't blame them. The news is not good."

She turned the radio on. We heard classical music. Bruckner's 7th Symphony played majestically. "Why don't they play march music today, as usual?"

"Listen! Here's the news. Something special must have happened today."

The announcer began. "We interrupt the program to bring a special report from our affiliated station in Hamburg."

"Why Hamburg?" We were all surprised.

"This is the German Headquarters of Admiral Doenitz in Flensburg," the announcer began. "Our Führer Adolf Hitler is dead." A long pause followed.

"He fought the Bolshevik invasion and died defending the Operational Headquarters in the Reich's Chancellery in Berlin. He died surrounded by loyal friends. The night before, our Führer married his loyal companion, Eva Braun, in a simple ceremony." We were all stunned. At least we thought Hitler would die in battle.

"We read now our Führer Adolf Hitler's last testament." We heard the shuffling of paper. It was usual for Hitler's speeches to begin with a recital of his accomplishments. We had heard them a hundred times. The announcer read the testament.

"The Führer wishes the German people to remember him . . . ." He began reciting Hitler's accomplishments. We waited for the second part. The second part usually brought new and bold decisions, for which all Germans waited. He stated that Hitler said, "Germany became the greatest nation on earth under my leadership. I cancelled the shameful dictate of Versailles, and Europe became Gross Deutschland. We were at the threshold of victory; however, the German people betrayed me, the German army refused to fight—officers and soldiers alike betrayed me. They refused to go into the final battle. The German people, therefore, did not deserve the victory."

I leaned back. Did I hear right? Hitler's testament rambled on.

"What did he say? We German soldiers betrayed him? We betrayed Hitler?" I turned to Fritz. I couldn't believe he had said that. Yes, that was the essence of Hitler's last testament. I was raging mad.

"He dared say that? When twelve million Germans have died. That is his testament? Did you hear that arrogant lunatic bastard? He said we Germans betrayed him, him! Now I understand why so many said he was crazy! There is no doubt in my mind anymore. We laid our lives on the line for that lunatic. He made us swear an oath to him, to that crazy idiot, to him personally."

Fritz seemed equally perplexed. Tears were in his eyes. Fritz had already experienced too much this afternoon. I was sure there was not much loyalty left for Hitler. I cussed and called Hitler the worst names I could think of. I had never cussed him before. But now I wished his ghost would show up, so I could throw the tea kettle and anything else I could get a hold of in his face. I was roaring mad. Fritz turned away.

"I always wondered if the man wasn't crazy," he mumbled.

"That testament confirms it. He was completely crazy." I told everybody.

Alois sat like a statue. The lady of the house was pale and stone faced.

"Yes, Hitler was an arrogant, evil man," she confirmed. "He was hiding his evil character behind a modest appearance. People liked him, because he seemed modest. They couldn't see the devil in the man.

"He displayed intelligence and leadership. Driven by ruthless egomaniacal urges, he deceived the German people. We all liked the idea of Gross Deutschland. That was talked about for centuries. It was a dream. Germany is Europe's stronghold. Hitler's pursuit of an existing dream made him powerful. He guarded his personal power and paid any price. In the meantime, you soldiers laid your lives on the line.

"Hitler was a manipulator. He purposely spawned prejudice and hatred among ethnic groups to gain political approval from stronger groups he needed. Hitler condemned Jews and gypsies and made them convenient pawns. He knew the clergy would approve. The churches had preached against Jews for centuries for their own selfish reasons. Most people believe Jews killed Jesus, the son of God. And most people believe the priests before believing anybody else.

"Hitler developed clever slogans to excite the German's national pride. He brought back forgotten Germanic Gods and symbols. He was a master politician and manipulator. A few may still believe in his legacy. But history will judge him otherwise. In France, they still believe that Napoleon Bonaparte was a great leader. Napoleon and Hitler, they were both egomaniacs who destroyed themselves."

I was amazed at how she talked. No one had explained Hitler to me like that. She was right. Hitler's myth faded. We were free of him.

It would be hard for Fritz. He had wasted his life on a madman. Sadly, many of my friends were still fighting for the man, defending a lost cause. I wanted to tell them, even now. To shed an oath sworn to a lunatic was easy, but leaving my friends was not.

Six years of enormous suffering and useless fighting gradually sunk in. Why did we fight, even though we already knew that the war was useless? An official end to the war was not yet declared. A German soldier doesn't leave his comrades. I could not betray my friends while they still fought. We had never had good information. Radio and newspapers had told us only what they were told and we accepted it. Germany had become prosperous like never before, so nobody questioned anything.

Any war is insane. I was now convinced.

Fritz turned and calmly asked, "Why did millions die? That madman claims we betrayed him! I was close to him and never noticed he was mad. That question will live with me for the rest of my life."

Wednesday, May 2

I couldn't sleep. Too much had happened in one day. Thank God, Hitler was dead. SS kids killed helpless wounded German soldiers, I could never forget nor forgive how they hung them from trees. Fritz and I could have been among them. That tore my nerves. And hearing Hitler's testament was the last straw. If there was ever a sense of loyalty to the Third Reich, it was gone.

I watched the millions of stars in the sky. The barn door was wide open. Why do they flicker? Stars don't care about a mess on earth. Europe lays destroyed, and Germany. Everybody can breathe easier. The rest of the world doesn't mind. Why should they? There will be millions of explanations for this decade. But how long is a decade in God's time? Experts will distort what happened. They'll teach at universities and will be considered experts because they write books. I wonder if anybody will actually learn from this experience? Only God has the answer. He watches man's foolishness. And fighting continues on his planet earth. Is that what God has in mind?

American soldiers will be here today or tomorrow and take the bunch of young, crazy SS soldiers prisoner after they had thrown their guns away. What will the Americans think about the German soldiers hanging from the trees? They'll wonder who hung them. They are Nazis, of course! That serves them right! A few less to fight against! That's what they'll think. But what made the SS soldiers so cruel? Lives don't mean much in a brutal war. But that was not true either. Front line soldiers respect everybody's life. I knew the hung soldiers would always haunt me.

The moonlight left a cold shine on my cross with the swastika. I had killed thousands of Russians and got that medal. The thought made me shudder. I couldn't be proud of that!

Fritz slept quietly in the hay. He once believed in Hitler and Great Germany. How many soldiers received bravery medals for that dream? Bravery medals make you vain. Medals were awarded at sports events, as well, to stimulate competition. Do bravery medals stimulate killing? I couldn't believe that. The black swastika emblem was the symbol of hate. I would hide that medal in a drawer in my basement and never show it to anyone. However, I was proud of the Iron Cross. I saved two friends and brought them home to safety. I deserved that medal.

Those few years of the war for Gross Deutschland will be remembered by history. Soldiers on both sides are not very different from each other. Most don't know the cause of their fight, but they fight to protect each other. The SS youngsters in uniform still bothered me immensely. Why were they so cruel and at only fifteen years old?

Fritz woke up. "What are you doing sitting up all night?"

"I've been thinking a lot lately. Tell me, would you fight a war if the cause were different?"

"Never! I will not fight for any reason. I've learned that a human life is important. We lost sight of that. I will not be tricked into killing anymore."

I thought about that. All religions preach respect for your fellow man. That was Jesus' principal gospel, simple and true. "I wished I had paid more attention to Jesus Christ and respected my fellow man. It sounds simple but is hard to follow in war. We had Hitler and forgot to listen to Jesus. Our national pride was more important."

Fritz nodded. "That's true. I never stopped believing in God, and I still have faith in God. He will help us to get home." I felt that way, too.

Chapter 16

Free at Last

Nussdorf near the Alz River

Alois came back barefoot from working in the field. He sat down in the kitchen and tried on his new boots. Then proudly he set about moistening them with a sponge. "This is cow's urine. It makes them softer."

"Why don't you wear your boots during the day? You now have two pairs." I told him for the fourth time."

"No!" he answered brusquely. "They must last me forever."

He looked up and suddenly declared. "You should stay! I talked to Mary. You can use our room upstairs. I have two sets of clothes. You can each have one and help me on the farm. I thank you for the shoes." This was the first time he showed emotion in the form of appreciation.

"Thanks, but we must move on to Munich. I want the American troops to see real German soldiers in real uniforms and not just SS bastards."

Alois nodded, he understood. "Mary, pack food to last two days," he called, "they've got to go." We rearranged the knapsacks and added the smoked pork filets Mary brought from her chimney. She handed us two loafs of bread and lots of bacon.

"Come back, and stay as long as you want," I heard Alois call from the house as we walked between apple trees on our way downhill.

The weight of our four knapsacks slowed our progress. There was still no traffic on the Autobahn. We left Traunstein, slowly walking north on a field path, while the Alps at our backs watched us. I whistled a mountain song I learned from a woodworker who skillfully added a yodel to the song that sounded like the echo from his valley.

Fritz was surprised. "How many mountain songs do you know?"

"About a dozen." That surprised him even more.

"I barely know that many. I taught Alpine songs in the Hitler Youth," he said. "We harmonized and practiced singing canons. Singing was my hobby. Let's sing together, first the songs we both know. I'll sing and you yodel." We sat in the field and began. Fritz hummed. I can remember melodies, but not words, and I can harmonize. Fritz used his full voice. I was amazed how beautiful his tenor was. I sang harmony and added a yodel at the end. Fritz grabbed my arm. "You can really yodel. That is beautiful. We'll go on a stage and make a living."

"Let's practice and find every song we both know." We felt more inspired with the mountains watching us and sang for two hours from the bottom of our hearts. Every song was a source of joy. "Let's practice that every day. We have all the time in the world. And maybe we'll end up singing in a Munich beer hall."

"You are a dreamer. Nobody has money. People worry about more important things. But our singing sounds good." While we walked, we hummed and harmonized. The singing relaxed us. I hardly felt the weight of my knapsacks. I had never felt free like that before.

Fritz wanted to stop too often. I found it annoying. But we both placed our pistols into our pockets to be ready for eventual SS check points.

It was already late afternoon when I saw a beautiful massive Bavarian farmhouse majestically standing on a hill. The house faced the mountains. "Let's go up and stay there overnight! We are in no hurry. They may be able to tell us where the American troops are. I am ready for a glass of milk," I suggested. We walked a steep path uphill and noticed two shabby looking people leaning against each other on a bench with their heads stuck together. They looked old, but were only teenage girls in German work force uniforms. Obviously, they were exhausted and in trouble. We greeted them but they didn't respond.

"Do you belong to that farm?" My question was stupid. One of the girls sat up. Her face had streaks from tears running down her dirty cheeks. She was about eighteen, but looked considerably older.

"The lady of the farm threw us out. She ordered us to leave," she sobbed, "but we can't walk, and there is no place to go." She used the high pitched Prussian accent. I knew that was a problem. Bavarians disliked the Prussians and treated them accordingly. The other girl also sat up. Her hair was stringy and unkempt and her face was even dirtier. She was a little older than her companion.

"We are hungry and wet. And we don't know what to do anymore. Last night we slept here in the field and we almost froze to death. The lady gave us milk but told us to go away. She shut the door. What can we do?"

I looked down the steep hill to imagine where they had slept on frozen soil. It was apparent they needed more than food. They needed real help or they would die. One girl put an arm around the other girl and stammered, "We are from Silesia. The Russians occupied Silesia. We can't go home, and we don't want to. We are afraid of the Russians. They raped the girls in our work force camp. I am very scared."

That was enough for me. "I'll get you some milk from the farm lady. We'll help you. We have food." I cut a piece from my bread and placed it in her dirty, frozen hand. They held the bread for a long time before they began nibbling the dry crust. The second girl seemed stronger. She spoke slowly, "We were in Hungary, assigned to a work force. We helped the farmers. Russian troops came suddenly, but we got away." The other girl took over. "We stayed on a truck for days, but yesterday, they ran out of gasoline and let us off." She pointed in the direction Traunstein. "One soldier said, 'The Americans are here,' and everybody scattered. We walked into the field until we came to this farm. The lady was so rude. She closed the door. And we asked only for water and to wash our faces. We left and slept in the field."

Fritz sliced a few pieces from the smoked pork filet. The rude farm lady upset me. How could she leave these girls in their misery in the cold field and refuse to give them water? I got ready for a stern conversation. I knocked on the door to be polite, but didn't expect an answer. I walked inside with the intention to use very strong Bavarian vocabulary.

"I have nothing!" I heard. The voice came from the a dark corner at the window. A woman sat on a bench and had listened all along to our conversation. She looked distraught.

"I gave everything I had to soldiers." I didn't believe her. But I didn't question or scold her. I greeted her in my best Bavarian dialect. Most Bavarian farmers were religious and hospitable. Hospitality was a virtue. Not helping strangers was considered a sin. They were expected to be courteous and ask for nothing in return. Older women were usually addressed as mother, as it shows respect for her age and dignity.

"How are you, Mother?" I began quickly "I don't need food, I'd like to sit down and rest." She would never disallow a stranger to rest. And, by now she should offer me bread and water. But this old lady shouted. "What's the matter with these girls? They are filthy and dirty. Can't they take care of themselves. They should go home." She gestured toward the window and moved a chair for me to sit down. She had overheard our conversation. I judged from the tone of her voice she was bothered and embarrassed. I used a different approach, warm and determined.

"They cannot go home because Russian soldiers occupy their homes. Their mother and father may not be alive." I had the lady's full attention. She stared at me.

"They can't go home?" she repeated sadly lifting an apron to her mouth.

Above the fireplace on the mantle, I saw a picture of young German soldier. "Who is he?" I asked and held the picture in my hand. She started to cry.

"That's my Joseph. I don't know where he is or where my husband is. They drafted him even at his age." The tears flowed. "If only I knew where they are?"

"I hope Joseph isn't hungry." I inspected the picture once more, "How old is Joseph? As old as I am?" That worked magic.

"Bring the girls in the house!" she blurted and rushed to the door. "I want to help them." She waved for them from the door. Fritz came along. "*Gruess Gott.*" He used the solemn form of greeting. From then on, the old lady talked incessantly. The ice was broken. She explained how she couldn't be careful enough living alone. She didn't trust anyone. The girls understood half of what she said because she spoke in a heavy Bavarian dialect. She disappeared and kept talking while rummaging in her storage room. When she returned she poured milk for everybody.

"I'll fix you something to eat." She told me, "You look like my Joseph. I hope he isn't hungry. Let's go upstairs. I'll fix the beds. All my beds are empty. I don't have men around anymore. You can wash up," she told the girls and waddled upstairs ahead of them.

"I wonder if the Russians were the same ones we had to face in Hungary," I asked Fritz when they were all upstairs.

"I don't think so. The girls stayed further north and helped the German Hungarians." The lady of the house came back downstairs and heard us talking about the Russians.

"I want to know about Americans. What are they like? They will come soon. I am scared. Why do they force girls that young into the army?" She didn't wait for an answer, "I heard what the girls said. Yes, I should have brought them inside."

Fritz appeased her by laying a hand on her shoulder. "The girls were in a work force, not in the army. All young women had to join a work force."

Mother didn't listen. "The whole week was bad," she lamented. "The Prussian soldiers came, and everybody wanted food. I couldn't feed them even if I wanted to. And I didn't understand them. Go away, I said, I can't understand you. That was wrong."

She kept talking and brought food from the storeroom. She chopped vegetables and onions and still talked. She called upstairs from the stairway asking the girls to come down. There was no answer. I went upstairs and found them laying on their beds, sound asleep.

"Let them sleep, Mother, they need it." She finally quieted down.

Two hours later the girls came downstairs remarkably rejuvenated. They introduced themselves, "Heidi and Ilse. Thank you," said Heidi without addressing anyone in particular. I watched how slowly and deliberately they ate. They were smart. Obviously, they hadn't eaten a decent meal in weeks. After Ilse finished she got up and hugged the old lady. "We said bad things about you, and I want to apologize. I am sorry," she said in her Prussian accent. By now it didn't matter anymore. Mother blushed.

"I am so glad you came." Tears were in her eyes. Hugging and kissing was not a Bavarian custom. But mother showed her appreciation. She turned to me.

"I promise I'll take care of them." After a while she told me again, "You look like my Joseph. You are like him." Both girls hugged her. The three hugged and cried for a while. The girls ate more, but I urged them to tell us what happened in Hungary. That wasn't easy for them. Heidi began. She said, there were about 200 girls, all eighteen, and all came from Silesia. They came in freight trains to Hungary and stayed in an ancient castle not far from the Austrian border. The castle walls were made out of brick, they were very thick and overgrown with ivy. The castle was their home for months. During the day they worked individually in nearby farms. They had fun, they said, and kept a good relationship with the farmers. Many spoke German.

A unit of German soldiers who had retreated from the Russians came. The officers were adamant that the girls should leave right away. They offered to help them with the evacuation and to bring them across the river and to Austria. But the girl's leader behaved stubbornly. She refused because she had no orders to leave.

Heidi and Ilse turned pale and hesitated to tell us more. They looked at each other, and warned that the next part of their story would be horrible. After the German unit left, the Russians came. A convoy with Asian Russians drove into the castle. Heidi and Ilse worked two kilometers away for a farmer. The farmer had told them, "I don't trust them. Stay in my turnip bin!" He hid the girls and went back to the castle to check.

The farmer was in Siberia during the First World War as a prisoner of war. He still spoke some Russian, but he didn't trust them. Two hundred Russian soldiers quietly checked all the buildings. The farmer came to the castle, and suddenly heard a few shots of sporadic infantry fire. They came from on the second floor, and somebody shouted, "Hide! They will rape you!"

The work force leader on the second floor had a few girls with her and ordered them to resist. The girls had rifles. But this group was no match for Russian Mongolians. They stormed up the stairs and dragged the girls downstairs. Other soldiers in the courtyard made five groups of girls. Nobody knew for what. That started it. The girls objected and began to resist. Two Russians grabbed a girl, dragged her inside, and systematically raped her.

The other soldiers ripped the girls uniforms off and dragged them by their hair into a lineup. Almost naked, they paraded them around in a circle. The rest of the Russians hollered and applauded. They shot their rifles. Each grabbed a girl and raped her. Heidi was now pale and sick. She stopped. "We heard them screaming all night, even from our hiding place in the turnip cellar."

Mother went down on her knees. "Oh, Holy Mary, please save their souls! I have never heard anything like that." Neither had we. I always believed the Russian soldiers were like us. We fought fair and never behaved like animals.

"What happened next?" Fritz, though horrified, wanted to know everything.

"Because the turnip bin was far from the house, the farmer came hourly to check on us. He told us more horror stories. He saw naked girls running across the field and neighbors picking them up. He decided to take us across the river to the border that night. His wife packed food for us. We had no moon to walk by and the castle was in total darkness. We heard girls crying from the pain of repeatedly being raped. It sounded like whimpering. We were at the river before dawn. Thank God, we were now in Austria. The German officer who had told us to leave before was still there.

"Yes, we can hear the screams, even from here." He was very upset and so were his soldiers. "I have 100 men. We'll go back and take the castle, but no prisoners this time. By now, the Russians are exhausted. I guarantee they will be dead. Let's go!"

The Hungarian farmer helped to find a truck for us. That truck brought us here. Don't ask what we saw on the way. I kept my eyes closed all the way."

Ilse confirmed that statement, and the old lady hugged her.

"Tomorrow, I'll find Joseph's school atlas. I want to know where you were, and where Silesia is, and where your parents live. You can stay here as long as you want and can help me. I am glad I have company." Mother was in shock from the girls' story. "Tomorrow I'll get you some clothes. You'll look like civilians. I am sure the Americans will treat us better than the Russians."

"And you," she pointed at us, "you men can take the other rooms upstairs. I have eight empty rooms, but you leave the girls alone! You hear me?"

She didn't really mean that seriously. But she waved a finger jokingly.

"You can stay here, too," she added as an after thought. "I have men's clothing, and I need help. Good night!" She went to a small room next to the kitchen. Before she disappeared, she pointed at me. "You sure look like my Joseph."

Thursday, May 3

"Mother, you teach Heidi and Ilse the Bavarian dialect," I told her during breakfast. "When we come back, I want to understand them." Joseph's school atlas was on the table. The girls showed her where Silesia was. But the Prussian dialect was a problem.

"I didn't know Germany was so big!" mother reflected at the lecture. "The Russians don't need Silesia. They can leave that to the Poles."

"They will probably keep Poland and Silesia for themselves," Fritz said seriously. "I am sure Stalin keeps everything he conquers. He has had Poland since 1939."

"Perhaps the Allies will convince Stalin to set up a king." A new idea sprang up. "Like they did in 1919. The British have a bunch of princes with nothing to do. They may have a hard time with their friend Stalin." But Ilse was not interested in political fantasies. "I want to know when and how I'll get home?" "Me, too." Heidi agreed. "And I don't care who governs."

We packed up and bade them good-bye. "Come back any time," mother squeezed my hand. I was sad to leave. The three women at the door waved their arms linked and draped over each other. The fate of war had made new friendships. Two Prussian girls and a Bavarian woman would have been unthinkable ten years before.

We went back on the same path, leaving the silhouette of the Alps at our backs. There were German soldiers now walking in the same direction, west. Many had rifles, but others didn't.

I looked for places to hide in case Allied convoys showed up. American troops must be close, by now. We walked for two hours and then decided to rest. I spread out the large military map. While everything appeared peaceful, I somehow felt uncomfortable, as if we were in the eye of a hurricane.

"Where do you think they'll come from? They can't all drive on the Autobahn. They'll come on a road like this. Let's bypass Lake Chiemsee." I wished I could see the first Americans. Then it would be easier to make decisions. The spring sun felt warm. We began humming a song and practiced for an hour.

"What else do we need? We have water, food and, most importantly, we are free." I talked to myself. "I'll leave the country." Fritz looked puzzled.

"How are you going to do that?"

Ever since our stay at the beautiful Hotel Geiger, I've often thought about that fabulous meal. "I want to own a hotel like that." I announced firmly, "I'll become a cook and leave the country. As a cook I can go on a ship. They need cooks. Frau Geiger told us. I can work without even speaking the language. One day, I might own a hotel like Haus Geiger."

"You are full of weird fantasies, as usual." Fritz shook his head.

"Why not? I am free. I can do what I want. I see plenty of opportunities."

"Why don't you go to America, the land of never-ending opportunities?" Fritz laughed. But I was serious.

"Not a bad idea. As soon as I see the first Americans, I'll ask them." I joked, "Maybe their army will hire me and take me along as a cook. I'll go across the ocean with them."

"Do you even know how to boil water?" Fritz became thoughtful. "I can't get used to the idea of becoming a prisoner, at least not yet. I'll stay in Munich for the rest of my life. I'll find a job." Fritz was firm. He believed that was what he would do.

"I don't want to become a prisoner either, but if I am a cook, I can eat every day." That concluded the talk of my still nebulous plans.

The next town we saw was Nussdorf. We checked the name on the map. A farmer came out of the first house. "All German soldiers, don't worry," he said. "The town is full, we have a fully equipped light field artillery unit." We walked into town and watched them unloading. Fritz asked somebody. "Where did you come from?"

"Normandy, France. That's where we started out. We are an independent unit, but I believe this is the end. Where did you guys come from?"

"From near Prague, a town called Rokycany," Fritz told him.

"Sounds like East meets West here in Nussdorf. The last time we took a position was two days ago, west of here at the Inn River. We never fired a shot. It's over now. The captain called a meeting within the next hour. Sounds like we will disband and go home. Where are you going to go?"

"Home, to Munich. Good luck!" "Good luck to you, too."

We decided to stay and find a place at the end of the village. It might be the final day before we see Allied troops. We wanted to sleep peacefully one more night. A small house at the far end of town and away from the road looked like what we wanted. The owners, an older couple, acted like they had expected us.

"We have a sergeant from the artillery here. Three can easily sleep in our house. If more come, they'll have to sleep in the barn," said the old man. The sergeant's name was Albert. We only introduced ourselves by first names. The old couple sat on a bench next to the oven and never moved. And they never said a word, just listened. Two hours later it occurred to me to ask them for a radio.

"We don't have a radio. But we know where the American troops are," said the old man, "Six kilometers from here, in Truchtlaching, at the River Alz."

"Holy smokes! Are they that close?" Sergeant Albert became excited. "Who told you? How do you know?"

"A neighbor came from Truchtlaching this afternoon. He said, the Americans are looking for German soldiers and taking them prisoner."

"What else did he say?" We were anxious, but the story developed slowly.

"The neighbor said nothing happened. Nobody shot anybody. The German soldiers piled their guns in the center of the marketplace. The Americans brought a table and a few chairs from the city hall, lined the Germans up and checked their army books. They returned the army books after they stamped them. That was all."

"That sounds too simple." Fritz wondered, "Stamping the army book means they declassified the soldiers, but were they free to go home?"

The old man scratched his head. "Everybody has asked me the same question. My neighbor didn't know. The soldiers gave them their belts and guns. I almost forgot, they also took their shoulder straps off."

"Without a belt and shoulder straps the soldiers were declassified. Every American would recognize them as disarmed German soldiers."

That made sense. Our host remained silent. He had no other information. The Allies would be here by tomorrow morning. We were sure of that.

Friday, May 4

I tossed all night on my hard bed and became quite nervous. Fritz sat on his bed and watched me. He never undressed. It was still dark outside.

"Today is the day. For the first time, we'll see American soldiers."

"Nothing we can do about that. Feels like the executioner is coming."

"What shall we do? Shall we stay here and wait, or . . ." asked Fritz.

"I'd hate to become a prisoner. I was just beginning to enjoy my new freedom. I don't want to give that up. We won't even have time to practice our singing."

The old couple sat on the same bench in the kitchen and ladled hot milk from a bowl. They nodded gravely when they saw us. The woman got up and fixed us breakfast. "I am not surprised you couldn't sleep," said the old man while the woman fried bacon and broke four eggs over it.

"You have to eat," she said, speaking for the first time since the day before. "What will happen? Besides, I don't want the Americans to get my eggs. Do you think they will take the farm away from us?" She was worried and definitely not ready for a quick answer.

"What would they do with your farm?" I answered with a question. "They don't need your farm. They need you to work, so they can collect taxes from what you sell."

"You mean everything will stay like it is?" The old man seemed relieved. "I won't mind the Americans if they let us stay."

Albert came from a small adjoining room next to the kitchen. He wore a civilian shirt and not his uniform jacket. "I found this shirt. Can I buy it? I'll stay. You tell the Americans I will work for you! Will you do that?" The old man smiled and nodded. "My fiancee lives only fifteen kilometers from here. I'll go and marry her next Sunday and start my life as a civilian." He laid a five mark coin on the table.

The old man carefully fingered the coin. I thought it was too much for a used shirt. But the old man took the money. We could see the road to Truchtlaching from Albert's room. We waited, watching the road.

"If you don't want to become prisoners," the old man said, "you can go down a path and get across the Alz River on a small foot bridge. Hardly anybody uses that bridge. It's made for only foot traffic." He meticulously explained the location to us and how to get there. The farmer's wife packed us bread and smoked dried beef.

Chapter 17

The Americans Arrive
Seeon near Lake Chiemsee

"Here they come." I heard Albert shouting from his room. We rushed into his room and saw a large cloud of dust still in the distance. It indicated either that many cars were on the road or that the wind blew a lot harder.

But, finally, we saw American jeeps only half a kilometer from the house. Soldiers sat in their cars in light brown uniforms. Each held a rifle leisurely while contemplating the scenery. They weren't worried about unfriendly shots firing at them.

"Let's go!" I pulled on Fritz's arm. "It's now or never!" We shouldered our knapsacks, shook hands with the old couple, and left by a back door. Before us was an open field and sixty meters to the forest. Will they see us? The column of American jeeps was down the road. I guessed they wouldn't care much about us.

The two knapsacks swayed on my back as we ran to the forest. I dropped them as soon as I could. The first American convoy passed 100 meters from the road. "They look to me like they are going on a picnic. No patrols! No securing the immediate area." The light armored vehicles advanced leisurely into the town of Nussdorf. "I wonder if the entire war was like that for them? That's almost an insult."

"They know nobody shoots anymore. Why should they worry?"

"But still, the officer in charge is irresponsible," I insisted. "There could be pockets of resistance. Remember the arsenal of weapons we saw in Berchtesgaden. They could be here and counter them. A '42 model machine gun could mow them down with one spray. It's irresponsible to take risks. They don't show respect." That's what bothered me.

"Why should they? The war is over." Fritz was right.

We walked on the edge of the forest, almost in the open. I counted them. Twenty jeeps, a long column of heavy trucks, and more were still coming. The first jeeps disappeared in a cloud of dust. We realized that in the excitement we'd missed the path to the foot bridge across the Alz River.

"Let's go to Truchtlaching and meet them. We are going to have to do it sooner or later."

The forest ended. We saw a massive stone bridge with traffic going both ways. A few soldiers guarded the bridge. On our side were two young Americans engaged in a conversation with four former prisoners of war, perhaps liberated Poles. One American gave them cigarettes. They lit cigarettes and smoked but the conversation seemed strained. Neither understood the other. We had two choices. We could wade in freezing deep water across the rapid flowing Alz River or walk across on the bridge. Of course, the American guards would stop us and investigate. It was no longer avoidable. I chose the comfortable way. "Let's go!" I walked onto the bridge, and Fritz followed without objecting. The first two guards paid no attention. Their conversation became more animated. They continued smoking their cigarettes.

We passed.

"Can you believe that? They didn't say a word." We walked twenty more meters. I heard a shout from behind: "Hey you! Do you have pistols?"

"No." I answered without turning, quickly dropping my knapsack to hide my pistol holster. We walked on. "They must have seen our pistols." I whispered and lowered the knapsack even more. "The man in Nussdorf said they'll take the belts and shoulder straps. Let's take them off. But it's too late now." I looked back and noticed the guards still conversed without concern about us. They probably thought the guards on the other side would check us. We walked in the direction of the next guards who looked friendly. They leaned back with one foot against the stone wall and chatted. They nodded as we passed them.

"Whoa! That was easy. They assumed the other guards checked us." Fritz poked me. We walked briskly. After a curve we rushed into the forest and out of sight.

"Looks like they don't bother anymore. They let us go home. But we need the stamp in our army book. Let's bury the pistols and get rid of the belts and shoulder straps. They have no more room in their prison camps. What do you think?"

"They don't need prison camps. There is no more resistance. Sending the German soldiers home saves them lot of trouble."

"But the war isn't over yet. At least, not officially. I can't believe that."

The forest looked like a battle zone. Abandoned army vehicles were everywhere. Cases of supplies laid around. I even found a library truck filled with books. A trailer with canned goods was more important, though. Another truck had gas masks and blankets. It was like an army provision center. Everything was going to waste. For our pistols, we needed heavy-duty oil paper, which we found in a rifle box. A gas mask container became the coffin for our pistols. Fritz dug a hole with an army spade and I marked the location. When the pistols were buried, I checked the library truck. Fritz added the location of our pistols to my sketch. We intended to return and retrieve them when it was safe. In the library truck, I found a thick science book.

"What do you want with a science book? You told me you never liked science."

"But this book describes science in a way I can understand."

"Pack some of the canned goods instead. In school you paid no attention. Admit it. You dreamt about other things. Remember? Now that you are older and more mature, science is more interesting, but pack some more useful things." I didn't listen and squeezed the thick book into my bag thus adding two more pounds.

Without a gun I felt naked and unarmed. I was not yet ready to surrender. We laid our belts over the pistols' burial ground making a cross.

"Should we rip our shoulder straps and insignias off?"

I said, "No," spontaneously. I intended to keep my medals. Fritz agreed.

We walked toward Seeon, a town near Lake Chiemsee. American jeeps passed us from both directions. Soldiers smiled, obviously relishing their victory. Many showed us the V-sign. The rifles were laid behind them.

Why should we hide? Undisturbed, so far, we walked into the town of Seeon which seemed like an American infantry camp. I still couldn't believe nobody checked us. Every house was occupied by American soldiers who ignored us as they unpacked.

But at the end of town things changed. There was a roadblock ahead. Our leisurely walk ended. A half-dozen American soldiers blocked the road at its narrowest point by the town's cemetery. We continued walking, since it was too late to avoid them.

We were greeted by pointed rifles and told to drop our bags. The young faces under steel helmets looked stern. I heard actual English for the first time. I wondered why I didn't understand, then remembered. Even though I had a year of English in school, it was not a mandatory language, so I skipped all the classes, convinced that I hated foreign languages.

On both sides of the road sat American off-duty soldiers wearing casual outfits. They watched the inspection. We were the spectacle of the day. Everybody wore watches from their wrists to their elbows on both arms. They were trophies of the war.

I wondered what one person could do with twenty wrist watches? Perhaps America didn't have good wrist watches. The leisurely atmosphere indicated the war had ended long ago for them, but a few more trophies were still obtainable. For that reason they sat at every check point. One off-duty soldier came up to me and began fingering my German Cross. He stared at the swastika emblem. But the soldier on duty pushed him away and took my medals. He tried to hide them, but it was too late. Everybody had seen the swastika medal. They rushed up. None of them had ever seen a German Cross in Gold before, and everybody wanted it. The large swastika was the perfect souvenir. My iron cross didn't interest them. They had many of those, and the price was low.

The soldier in charge smiled. He knew he had something valuable. And, because he was on duty, he had first right. He allowed the others to inspect the swastika medal before a bargaining began. I didn't quite understand the process, but judging from the heat of the argument, I figured the price increased rapidly. I hoped the price would continue to move up, and they would continue to argue.

The final price must have been exorbitant. A nineteen-year-old soldier won. He took my former medal, showed it off, then traded it for other medals and a wad of money. Toyingly, he looked at me with appreciation.

I had no idea what he finally paid for it. Thousands of Russian soldiers died before I was awarded that medal. The Russians were in the wrong place, and I was in the right place. I was a lucky hero. What will this young soldier say at home about how he got my medal?

Fritz, next to me, suddenly shouted in broken English. "I wish to see your officer!"

The on-duty soldier had grabbed Fritz's gold pocket watch, but Fritz pulled back furiously. He held on to the gold chain. It was his grandfather's pocket watch. Fritz repeated the demand to see an officer during the struggle, and, surprisingly, he recaptured his pocket watch. The soldier let go.

"He had never seen a pocket watch like this one," Fritz said to me. His face was still flushed. I used the distraction to cut the straps off my wrist watch and slipped it into the fold of my uniform jacket. My soldier didn't notice, but he was smart. He saw the leather straps on the ground. He knew. Without hurrying, he confiscated my Swiss pocket knife first, then searched for the watch in the pockets of my uniform. It took a while, but he found the strapless LeCoultre watch in the fold of the pocket. However, a watch without a wrist band seemed worthless to him. The watch could not be displayed. He started to give me the naked watch back. I extended my hand, but he changed his mind. The watch joined my Swiss army knife in his pocket.

We were told to divide the content of our knapsacks into two piles, food in one pile and blankets, kitchen utensils, and military supplies in the other. I was allowed to keep a pair of socks and a shirt, but no underwear. While I stuffed the socks back in, I tried to add a metal spoon, a fork, and an aluminum knife from the other pile. But my soldier put his foot on the three kitchen utensils and sternly motioned me to put them back.

"Why?" I used my only word of English, and pronounced it perfectly.

He explained, "That is a weapon," pointing to the aluminum knife.

"That knife can't even cut scrambled eggs," I tried to say, but was unsuccessful. He took my army book, found nothing unusual in it, then handed it back. There was one more check. He made me roll my shirt sleeves up. All SS soldiers had their blood type tattooed under their armpit, but army soldiers did not. He saw no tattoo and was satisfied. He finished with Fritz and me and motioned for us to go to the cemetery.

Behind us a young man waited his turn to be searched. He was wearing a civilian outfit, a white shirt and black trousers. He also had a new bicycle and protested fluently in English. "Why are civilians searched?" he asked. He had a leather-bound notebook clamped on the bicycle stand.

"I am passing through," he claimed.

The soldier, impressed with the man's fluency in English, slowed his search. He might have let him pass, but his comrade was leafing through the leather notebook, not very interested, until he found some photographs. Suddenly, he shouted with alarm. He found a picture of an SS officer who looked like the civilian. Both soldiers ripped the man's white shirt off and lifted his arm. There was the SS blood-type tattoo. The civilian insisted in fluent English that the man in the photo was his twin brother. It was useless. The soldiers roughed him up and pushed him to the ground. They held a rifle on his neck. He was ordered to follow us into the cemetery.

"Why did you bring the photo? You didn't have anything else." I asked him innocently.

"I told the truth! That is my twin brother. Besides, it's none of your business." He passed us and walked ahead, wanting nothing to do with me. I was glad.

"The arrogant bastard! I wonder if they will ever stop acting superior?" Fritz's face was still flushed from the struggle for his pocket watch. "I hate SS guys," he said, "ever since I saw them hanging innocent German soldiers!"

Shivering German soldiers sat on grey gravestones scattered along the wall. I noticed the wall was only a meter and a half high, thus not impossible to climb. Most soldiers were without coats and some didn't even have jackets. Fritz and I shared our blanket. We unfolded it and spread it over a wet gravestone. The cold ground was worse than the cold air. The fine drizzle turned into snowflakes. Fritz and I huddled together to warm ourselves.

"They are infantry soldiers. Infantry never likes to deal with prisoners. I don't blame them. They'll take us to a camp. Somebody else will take care of prisoners."

I was hungry and wished they had left us our food. A large carton was dropped over the wall and caused quite a commotion. Soldiers ripped open the box but found only pipe tobacco, not food.

"Are they kidding, giving us tobacco?" Some began chewing the tobacco.

Saturday, May 5

We sat overnight without food, freezing in the cemetery. New prisoners came. Behind them was an American officer who ordered the soldiers to spread out along the wall. They pointed their rifles and were ready to use them. The officer yelled in English, but his voice didn't carry. None of the freezing German soldiers wanted to understand.

"I'll go and see what's going on," I said and went to the gate.

The American officer was glad to see somebody come. He looked like a nice guy. "Are you an officer? Do you speak English?" I shrugged and answered in German.

"Who speaks English here?" I shouted over the heads of the German soldiers. "We need an interpreter?" A captain got up and introduced himself. He spoke English fairly well. The American and German captains shook hands and spoke English. The German captain shouted, "Listen everybody!" He repeated it until he got everyone's attention.

"We'll go to another village and stay overnight. Walking is better than sitting in the cold rain. Perhaps there is food. Officers, please line up at the head of the column!"

Fritz and I walked together past the gate. A dozen jeeps waited and drove up and down the marching column. The pile of food, bread, bacon, and everything we had, now soaked by rain, laid beside the road. The soldiers stayed in their jeeps. We should have stayed in the forest, but it was too late.

I counted approximately 200 prisoners. We walked in rows of three. Halfway through town, we turned right in the direction of Lake Chiemsee. We stopped at a farm with two hay barns. The English-speaking German captain ordered us to form a circle and consulted with his American counterpart.

"We'll sleep in the barns," he announced. "No smoking, please! And I'd like you to form two groups!" Everybody roared. "Smoking, what? They took everything and gave us pipe tobacco, but forgot to give us matches. Tell him to give us food!"

I helped to divide the group. Some German prisoners had already gone into the barn. I heard a sharp whistle. It came from the corner of the building. The American soldiers heard it, too, and watched. I went to the corner and saw three older women with baskets. They waved from behind the building. "For you! There is more to come."

I thought it best to talk to the German captain. He and a few prisoners came. In the meantime the American soldiers watched unconcerned. They never left their jeeps. Six more women came and joined the first group. They brought more baskets and milk. "We forgot the cups," one scolded the others.

An American soldier stepped from his jeep and walked slowly toward the group, without saying a word, posted himself five meters from the women. A companion soldier joined him. A third American brought a stack of paper cups from his jeep. The women cut bread and spread lard and sprinkled salt on top.

"We don't have much, but we are glad to help," the oldest jabbered at the American soldiers. They kept stoically five meters away. The word, *food*, spread like wildfire. Groups of German prisoners came running. The first received bread and milk. Fritz and I began to control repeaters. There was barely enough. The American soldiers watched and pretended not to notice the frenzied feeding.

One of the soldiers said, "Thank you," addressing the oldest women when they packed up.

Sunday, May 6

Again, Fritz and I shared our blanket. The night was unbearably cold. We huddled and wished our clothes were dry. The barn roof was covered by a thin layer of ice. The yard was frozen. The English-speaking German captain slept next to us. Before we went to sleep, he explained what the American captain told him.

"Trucks will take us to a concentration camp in Dachau. Too many German prisoners are here and elsewhere. They are not prepared to take care of everybody."

Dachau was fifteen kilometers from Freising, where I was born. I had never seen the concentration camp, but I had heard about it. I thought it was a jail. The newspaper wrote that new concentration camps would replace outdated city jails. Prisoners would build their own buildings and roads. They would make ammunition and assemble cannons. That would be better than having them sit in jail cells. They closed the city prison in Freising and transferred criminals to Dachau.

"Is there room in Dachau for us with all those prisoners?"

"I wondered, too. But the American captain said they found only starved political prisoners in Dachau and released them. The camp is now empty."

Fritz frowned. "There weren't that many political prisoners. I can't believe that! The Jews received passports and, as far as I know, left the country years ago. Jews who didn't leave the country had to wear the yellow star, and could stay home. They weren't put into prisons. Concentration camps were for rehabilitation and were glamorized in Berlin. Prisoners were to learn trades to become productive. They build their own barracks and everything else that was needed. Concentration camps were away from the cities and supposedly, were a healthier environment. I hope they didn't let the gangsters and murderers go. That would be a disaster!"

Neither newspapers nor radio mentioned concentration camps. Nobody was interested, anyway. Everybody worried about the war.

The barn awoke. All the German prisoners got up. I heard the same grumbling about not getting food or coffee. We officers were first to go outside. It was cold. The sky was gray. The American guards huddled frozen under their covers in the jeeps. The American captain came this time with a lieutenant who spoke some German. He asked him to inform us that the lieutenant was now in charge of prisoners.

"We'll return to the cemetery. But you will spend this afternoon in a camp." He didn't mention which camp, and he wasn't very concerned about the lack of food. He simply avoided the subject. We formed into a marching column. The German captain translated the orders like he had done the day before. The American lieutenant didn't interfere. I tried to find the young SS officer we had encountered, but he was no longer there.

We covered our heads with blankets for protection against the freezing drizzle. The jeeps drove on the sides of the column. From a house came a woman who quickly passed slices of bread to a few. The soldiers in the jeeps didn't bother her.

More prisoners were in the cemetery. Now it was overcrowded.

Fritz and I elected to sit on a new gravestone, but the stone felt as cold as the others. Whoever was recently buried was better off than we were. Everybody talked about food and the abominable weather. Some looked forward to getting to Dachau, because Dachau would be better than freezing in a cemetery.

At midday, the sun broke through. I savored its warmth, as sparse as it was. "From now on, I shall only worship the almighty sun," I told Fritz. "Nothing is more important than the healing rays from above. That will be my religion."

Fritz said I was nuts. "Sun worship isn't new. That's the oldest religion on earth. Why would you want to stray from a simple religion everybody understands to a very complicated one?" I didn't know.

The gate opened. Twenty American soldiers lined along the wall with their rifles ready. They motioned for us to get up. We formed a column and again left the cemetery. We walked to the farm where we had spent the night. A hundred American soldiers waited. There the young American lieutenant asked the English-speaking German to split the prisoners into smaller groups and have them sit along the hay barn.

Fritz and I, as officers, stayed back and waited. We had hoped to be by ourselves. Nobody objected when we sat under a tree near the house. There were six soldiers guarding us. There were lots of soldiers with nothing to do. The six of them chatted among themselves and ignored us. It became warmer. I remembered three days before, when Fritz and I sat in the sun and practiced mountain songs.

"Do you remember the song that went like "... the sun rises, and ..." I couldn't remember the lyrics, as usual. Fritz began the song. He remembered. I followed and harmonized with his singing.

"Sounds good. Let's try again." Fritz used his deep full tenor voice and sang somewhat tempered, so as not to disturb the guards' conversation. The soldiers stopped talking and listened. We began again, and this time used our full voices. Spontaneously, I added a yodel. The six American soldiers clapped and moved closer. "More!" they gesticulated.

Our repertoire consisted of about two dozen songs, and many had yodels. Those were my favorites. I tuned my voice and searched for a yodel. Every time I yodeled, chills rolled down my spine. We sounded nearly professional, and when I yodeled, the soldiers clapped. More soldiers came, sat down, and urged us to continue. We had joked when we talked about being entertainers, but here we were performing before an international audience who seemed to appreciate our singing and yodeling.

We noticed that more off-duty soldiers without helmets or rifles joined the group. One sat next to me and began accompanying my singing in German. His pronunciation was very good.

"Where did you learn German?" I asked.

"In Minnesota. We sang these songs when I was little," he spoke flawless German. I had heard about Minnesota. My American Indian books described it, and I knew some Germans immigrants went there.

"We don't speak German anymore. That changed during the war," he explained.

Others wanted to learn the German lyrics. Fritz had a chance to show off his experiences as a Hitler Youth music instructor. He became the teacher. Groups prepared for canon singing. Three groups learned the German words. The American translated.

"Let's not use words, let's just hum the melody. We'll start from the left, that will be the first group to begin when I give the sign. The second group will follow, then the third when I give the sign again."

Several initial failures occurred but that was to be expected. The groups began again. After a while the singing became quite good. More soldiers arrived. They were asked to wait before they could participate. Everybody wanted to learn my yodeling.

Fritz and I sang some songs by ourselves. A few soldiers left to get something to eat. "Can you get us something to eat?" I asked my German American soldier friend who sat next to me. "We haven't eaten in three days." He looked surprised, then got up and consulted with his sergeant in the background. He came back and said in German, "We'll get you something to eat, but not here. You must go with me to the farm house. We are not allowed to bring food outside." That didn't matter to me.

"Follow me!" he told me in English. Fritz and I went with him into the kitchen. The entire group of singing American soldiers came along.

Dozens of kettles of food sat on a stove. Plates were filled. The sergeant personally fixed us two plates. We wolfed the food down while still standing.

"If you want more, you have to sing more," he said and laughed. His words were translated. He ladled second helpings on our plates.

"No problem." We wolfed that down, too. Lumps of orange colored dehydrated sweet potatoes stuck in my throat. I had never eaten them before. The German-American soldier observed my grimacing.

"Army food is lousy, I hate sweet potatoes," he told me.

"Our food was worse," I said. He laughed and translated my sentence. Everybody laughed. After the third helping we began to sing again. A soldier wearing a helmet interrupted.

"The trucks arrived and the first convoy with half the prisoners has departed." He sounded like he was glad. The others ignored him. We began song number ten.

"Fritz, let's practice group singing again." I wanted a distraction to delay our departure. I wasn't anxious to get to Dachau. Fritz organized three groups. Singing inside the house improved the sound quality considerably.

"Teach us the German words," my friend asked. Two young soldiers also spoke German. They recited the lyrics together among themselves. That made it boring for the others.

"I have an idea." I told the three in German. "Let's take a break. And if you let us go home, we'll come back tomorrow and practice some more." I meant it as a joke. But they took me seriously and looked surprised. I asked my German-American friend to talk to the sergeant.

The sergeant listened. Fritz hummed a sweet new melody, I watched the sergeant's reaction intensely.

He smiled and got up, "You are nice guys. We'll let you go! But you must leave by the stable."

Extremely nervous, pretending to be casual, I asked him calmly, "Our knapsacks are under the tree. Can somebody bring them to the stable?"

"They'll be at the stable exit. Don't get caught! Good luck!" The three German-speaking soldiers took us to the stable. We passed two rows of cows before we came to the other end. The helmeted American soldier was there and handed us our knapsacks.

"Thanks!" I said in my very best English. "Good luck!" he answered.

Thank God it was very dark outside. A few remaining German prisoners still sat on the other side of the barn, but they could not see us. Casually, we walked into the next corn field. Wilted corn stacks protected us from sight. We ran uphill and into the next forest.

"You sure had a lot of nerve asking them to let us go," laughed Fritz while we ran.

"Did you want to go to Dachau?" I coughed my answer.

Fritz shook his head. No, he didn't want to go either. We wanted to get home to Munich!

Going Home

Good-bye to the Mountains

In a forest meadow, we found a log cabin mysteriously illuminated by moonlight streaming between trees. Without the moonlight, we would have missed the building completely. There wasn't much hay inside. But at least we had a roof over our heads. The cabin was used to feed hungry deer during the long cold winters. This winter, though, nobody had the time or hay to feed them. We scratched a little wet hay into a corner and spread the blanket on top.

The air was freezing cold. I remembered a method of relaxation taught by the Indian philosopher Rabindranath Tagore. I used his method successfully on several occasions and brought his book to boot camp, but later lost it.

Close your eyes! Relax all your muscles from the bottom up. Concentrate, and relax every muscle in your body. Start with your toes, envision your muscles in your feet and move up. Focus on your leg muscles. Relax. Relax your thighs and feel the warmth going through your body. Take a deep breath. Relax. Focus on your fingers one by one. Slowly relax the muscles of your fingers and relax moving up your arms, up to your shoulder. Relax the muscles of your face and the muscles under your hair. Relax. And always take a deep breath. Amazingly,

Tagore's method worked. I relaxed and drifted to sleep.

Monday, May 7

When I woke up the next morning, my skin felt sticky and uncomfortable. I definitely needed to wash, and I was thirsty. Last night I saw a pond in the meadow. The shallow water was easy to find. Insects were flying and dancing above it. I heard the humming and listened to the sounds of nature. Never before had I paid much attention to these sounds. Today I enjoyed them and the surrounding quiet immensely.

It was good to be alone in nature, away from the war. All would be fine.

The ice-cold water felt like punishment, but later became refreshing. My skin opened and began to breath. I stood naked and splashed and scrubbed vigorously. I had no soap. I looked up, saw the swaying trees and felt reborn, ready for a new life. I moistened my mouth with water, but was careful not to swallow.

Back in the cabin, I saw Fritz had company. A young farmer sat on the floor. His left leg was crippled, and his crutches lay at his side. I sat next to him.

"Sepp," he introduced himself. Sepp was short for Joseph. "Also, First Mountain Division," he said, "Glad to see you Edelweiss guys still wearing the uniform." Sepp shared warm Ersatz Kaffee from a thermos with us.

"I came to check my forest. Lots of soldiers are around," he explained. "I was shot by snipers in Yugoslavia last year. My knee joint is still stiff," he pointed to his leg. "The town is full of Americans. They are heading for the mountains."

"Do you think they'll meet resistance?" asked Fritz. He had told Sepp about us. "Could be! There are still desperate soldiers in those valleys."

"What soldiers?" I asked. "We saw only young SS and Volkssturm."

"Not them. There is a battalion of tough fighting French Vichy soldiers. They hold out. They can't go home, and it looks like they'll fight to the bitter end." Many foreigners wore German uniforms. Muslims in Bosnia, even Russian Cossacks on horses. "There is a division of 12,000 Russians holed up at the Danube," Sepp explained. "They were Russian prisoners, but volunteered to fight Bolsheviks, mostly Ukrainians. They'll fight because they can't go home either. Stalin will kill them."

"Can you help us to get to Munich?" I showed him our map.

"Stay in this forest. It belongs to me. Then go west and avoid the open field! The Americans are not anxious to take prisoners. They don't know what to do with them. They won't take you unless you walk into them. At the Inn

River they posted check points. Those are the only ones I know of. I don't know what else to tell you."

"Do you know where prisoner of war camps are?"

"One is in Bad Aibling, but is not well organized. They may even use the concentration camp at Dachau. You don't want to go there?"

"No! I won't go to Dachau."

"I wish I could help you guys! Good luck!" Sepp put his crutches under his arms and moved surprisingly quickly down the road. He turned, remembering something. "I heard a radio report. They'll sign an armistice tomorrow. That may end this stupid war."

We came to the edge of the huge forest and needed a rest. It was dusk. Not far, partially hidden by apple trees, we could see a typical Bavarian farmhouse. Carefully, we crawled between the trees and ran to the hay barn. I opened the squeaky heavy door, just enough to sneak in.

"Did you see the farmer?" Fritz's voice was near me in the dark." I saw him leaving the cow stable. A bunch of American jeeps are in front."

"Nobody will find us in the hay," I said. "The Americans know the war is over. They won't bother with us anymore. They didn't even post guards."

We climbed the wooden ladder to the second floor. From there, we waddled in the soft hay to the farthest end. I found a small knothole, the only source of light and looked out. Fritz fell in the hay and was immediately asleep. I heard water dripping from the leaky roof. I was too hungry to sleep. My twenty-year-old constitution demanded food. I wondered how he could sleep without food?

Fritz was at least seven years older and had four years of war under his belt. His experience showed. He was used to not eating.

I thought back to how I had imagined a soldier's life. It would be glamorous, and showing off bravery medals would be exciting. But they were gone. That didn't bother me anymore. Why did I ever think medals were important?

The barn door squeaked and I saw a light flickering. Someone was below.

"Hey, where are you?" I heard a faint voice with a Bavarian accent.

"Here!" I answered immediately regretting it. I hid deep in the hay.

Someone climbed the ladder. The dark figure was a thin, old man holding a lantern. I stood up. The lantern's rays found me. Without saying a word, the old man came wobbling through the hay in my direction. He held the lantern ten inches from my face and inspected me carefully. Fritz woke and pushed the hay off. Now the lantern illuminated his face.

"I like it," giggled the old man and shook his head. That was the end of his investigation. I noticed he carried a basket. He took out a checkered cloth and spread it on the hay. He placed the lamp carefully in the middle. Silently, he began to unpack.

"Mountain troops, I see," he said, briefly looking up at the Edelweiss flower embroidered on my sleeve. Warmth flickered in his eyes.

"This food comes from the American soldiers in my kitchen," he chuckled and pointed at the basket." I've never seen stuff like this. Egg powder, they mix with water. The yellow powder makes scrambled eggs. They showed the wife how to do it. It works, I guarantee. Have you seen egg powder before?" He sat down slowly, while he balanced the lantern.

"And this stuff here they call Spam. Looks like ham." The fried meat slices made my mouth water. We inspected them together.

"Brought my own bread. Their bread is awful!" He waved his left arm in disgust. "You can roll their bread and get rubber balls."

"Fourteen American soldiers are in my kitchen, all young fellows, nice guys." A broad grin covered his wrinkled face. "I like it," he said. "You are here, and they are there," he pointed at his house.

More came from the basket. "Chocolate and candies! One speaks German, I can hardly understand him. I think he said, 'we can't use it all,' and gave me that stuff."

I put Spam on the farmer's bread, covered it with a heap of scrambled eggs, and wolfed it down. It tasted good. The farmer watched silently. We feasted.

"I know how it is," he moved closer and whispered. "I was in the infantry in the First World War. The French caught me in 1915. Three lousy years I spent as a prisoner behind barbed wire in France. They fed us a watery soup with turnips and boiled potatoes once a day. I was always hungry. We talked all day about running away, but we never did. I am glad you came!" Again I saw a friendly flicker in his eyes. Fritz looked up. He stopped eating and reached for the old man's hand.

"Thanks!" he said. "I am glad you know how it is. We'll get home. As long as we have food. That's all we need."

Casually, the old man said, "The radio announced that the armistice will be tomorrow at noon."

He lifted himself clumsily, his voice trembled, "I lost two sons in this war. They were mountain troopers like you, and now they are buried somewhere in Russia," he turned away, "still don't know what for," he said with a sob and shook his head in disgust. Abruptly, he grabbed the empty basket and lantern, and wobbled back to the ladder.

"Hope you get home all right!" he called from the ladder, and then from downstairs. "Don't smoke in my barn! You hear me?" The barn door squeaked shut. I packed the bread in the red checkered cloth.

Tuesday, May 8

At the first light of morning filtering in through the knot-hole, I pushed the thick layer of hay off and crawled from my hiding place. I counted eight American jeeps out front. Nobody guarded them.

It was freezing cold without a blanket. But the hay kept me warm. Only my crumpled uniform jacket protected me. The moist underwear I wore since Berchtesgaden felt like cold, wet sheets glued to my skin. Fritz got up. We waddled through the hay, down the ladder and discovered a small side door. We pried the door open and snuck out. The apple orchard covered us. We ran to the dense forest and felt safe. Years of war had taught us direction. We walked west.

Through the foliage I could see a green field. We waited as long as we could before leaving the safety of the forest. There was the breathtaking silhouette of the majestic Alps once again. But now they were far away. Why do they never change, I wondered. Were the Alps the reason I volunteered to the First Mountain Division? That was almost three years ago. I loved these mountains!

Fritz grabbed my arm. "Hold still! I heard something." But it was nothing, only the wind rustling leaves.

"Let's get rid of these uniforms," Fritz said, "we are not safe in German uniforms behind American lines." He began unbuttoning his jacket. "Those scarecrows over there might help." Fritz pointed at two scarecrows standing lonely in the field.

I walked to the smaller one and lifted off the moist jacket. My arms made it barely through the wet, swollen material. The sleeves ended below my elbows. Two large holes in the elbow disappeared under my armpits. But the jacket fit around the shoulders.

"It will air out in a couple of days," Fritz said. "We'll walk home looking like stinky scarecrows and nobody will bother us."

I wondered if Fritz knew just how awful he looked. A large crumpled hat covered his face to his nose. A dirty black jacket hung from his shoulders to his knees. I was used to seeing Fritz in his lieutenant's uniform. He always looked handsome and distinguished. Now he looked like a live scarecrow. My sides hurt from laughing.

"Don't laugh! You don't look much better." Fritz danced around having fun. I draped my uniform jacket over the scarecrow's wooden skeleton, made a few adjustments and deliberately turned the uniformed scarecrow southward.

"I'd like you to watch the mountains," I told him. "I was once a proud mountain soldier, and I want you to continue to do your job well! Watching out for birds is now your job. Today is Armistice Day. There is no more war, and I don't need a uniform." I had given my uniform a last order.

"Do you feel sentimental about the uniforms?" asked Fritz next to me.

"Not really. Just sad and bitter."

"I wonder what happened to our comrades? Did they fight the last battle in Czechoslovakia? Officers and former cadets don't give up easily."

We sat down for a while and admired the mountains clouded in a white morning mist. I thought of my friends. Most were twenty years old, like I was. There was never enough time to bury them.

Now, it was only Fritz and me, walking home—to Munich.

Epilogue
Munich

A week later in May 1945, I arrived at my parents house and found nobody there. The house had a deep crack on one side caused by the air pressure of an exploding bomb. The bomb had destroyed the house across the street.

A neighbor gave me our house key. I was hungry.

After I changed into civilian clothes, I went to the nearest store. I found it closed. All the stores were closed and boarded up. I walked through the streets filled with rubble until I came to the center of Munich. I saw only a few civilians. The facades of houses still standing marked the edges of the streets. There were no street cars. Surprisingly, the large railroad functioned, and so did the Hotel Excelsior across from the station. American jeeps were lined up in front of the hotel. Officers with bags rushed in and out.

At the hotel's side entrance, marked Personnel and Deliveries Only, I saw a well-dressed lady conversing with an American sergeant. She saw me and looked astonished. There weren't many young German men my age around at the time.

"May I help you?" she asked in German. My answer, "I am looking for a job," surprised her.

"Can you cook?"

"I've peeled many potatoes in my life," I said spontaneously. I saw men and women in white coats in the kitchen. Without answering, she waved me inside. The American sergeant followed. He had a notepad and settled at the kitchen table.

"Here is a new cook," announced the lady to eight older men. In time I learned they were all famous chefs of Munich's destroyed hotels. Now they worked together on an equal basis.

The American sergeant didn't speak German. He motioned me to write my name, birthday and birthplace on his work pad and, after calculating, he told me, "You'll be paid 110 marks, according to age. A jeep will take you home and pick you up in the morning. There is no other transportation."

⸺ ⸺

I had a job. I began learning English and systematically learned the cook's trade from Munich's finest chefs. In 1953 I was hired as a chef-trainee by the Hotel Statler Company in New York. Later they allowed me to advance into a hotel management training program. Eventually, I became a proud U.S. citizen. But, that's another story.

Printed in the United States
206058BV00002B/7/A